T0320803

Development, Distribution, and Markets

Development, Distribution, and Markets

Edited by
Kaushik Basu
Maitreesh Ghatak
Kenneth Kletzer
Sudipto Mundle
Eric Verhoogen

OXFORD
UNIVERSITY PRESS

OXFORD
UNIVERSITY PRESS

Oxford University Press is a department of the University of Oxford.
It furthers the University's objective of excellence in research, scholarship,
and education by publishing worldwide. Oxford is a registered trademark of
Oxford University Press in the UK and in certain other countries.

Published in India by
Oxford University Press
22 Workspace, 2nd Floor, 1/22 Asaf Ali Road, New Delhi 110 002, India

ISBN-13 (print edition): 978-0-19-013005-3
ISBN-10 (print edition): 0-19-013005-9

ISBN-13 (eBook): 978-0-19-099334-4
ISBN-10 (eBook): 0-19-099334-0

Typeset in Adobe Jenson Pro 10.5/13
by The Graphics Solution, New Delhi 110 092
Printed in India at Rakmo Press Pvt. Ltd.

Contents

Part B: Labour, Land, and Financial Markets

Part C: Political Regimes and Economic Development

Introduction

KAUSHIK BASU, MAITREESH GHATAK, KENNETH
KLETZER, SUDIPTO MUNDLE, ERIC VERHOOGEN

As a discipline of inquiry, development economics has had a fascinating trajectory, all the way from 1776—the publication year of Adam Smith's *Wealth of Nations*—to contemporary times, as we grapple to sustain economic growth and cope with the unravelling of the global political order. At the very beginning, there was little to distinguish between economics and development economics. With the western world still very poor, the overwhelming concern of economics, as exemplified by the work of Smith and the early writers, was development and the economic advancement of nations. This changed towards the end of the nineteenth century, when attention shifted to the micro-foundations of economics, and with the pioneering work of Leon Walras, Vilfredo Pareto, Stanley

Jevons, and several others, we saw the birth of general equilibrium theory, the modelling of market oligopoly and perfect competition. This marked the birth of neoclassical economics and interest in development waned.

Starting from the end of World War I, and certainly from the middle of the twentieth century, nations, peoples, and vast lands under imperial control became aware of their own identity and potential, and broke loose from the yoke of colonial control to become independent sovereigns, with their own agenda for planning, development, and growth. With that, development economics emerged once again, this time as a distinct but prominent sub-discipline of economics. There was a flurry of research in development, with prominent contributions from Arthur Lewis, Albert Hirschman, Ragnar Nurkse, Paul Rosenstein-Rodan, and others. New ideas, such as those of dual economies and poverty traps, the vital role of rural–urban migration, balanced growth and the vicious circle of poverty were born. As we grappled to understand the poverty traps in which several of the newly independent nations were caught, development economists reached out to neighbouring subjects, such as politics, anthropology, and sociology.

As we work on putting this book together, it is 100 years since the publication of John Maynard Keynes's angry book *The Economic Consequences of Peace* (1919). It was his realization of how rational policymaking can get thwarted and distorted by political interests that provoked this book. The effort to integrate economics with political science since then has progressed, but still too slowly. Likewise, for other neighbouring disciplines in which economics is embedded, such as sociology and anthropology, the level of interaction of these disciplines with mainstream economics has remained woefully inadequate.

Perhaps because of having one foot on the treacherous ground of 'primitive' cultures and poor feudal societies, development economics turned out to be an exception. It had a disciplinary and an ideological catholicity not easily found in other areas of economics. In the research done in development, we thus see reflections of not just the general equilibrium of the late nineteenth century but also the 'Cambridge School', going back to Alfred Marshall, Arthur Cecil Pigou, and also Joan Robinson, who adopted a partial equilibrium approach, which was not as overarching as Walras' general equilibrium but, for that very reason, was more capable of getting into the weeds and being more focused on important aspects of markets and human welfare.

One off-shoot of this was the early research on labour and credit markets in developing countries, for instance, done by Amartya Sen and Amit Bhaduri, that drew on this Cambridge heritage. Interestingly, some of the later research on interlinkage in credit and labour markets in developing economies which used elements of both the Cambridge School and more traditional neoclassical economics—we are referring here to the work of economists like Pranab Bardhan, Avishay Braverman, and Joseph Stiglitz—became an inherent part of the methodology of understanding and analysing development and economic backwardness. We also saw in development economics infusions of ideas from the works of anthropologists, like Raymond Firth, Bronislaw Malinowski, and Clifford Geertz.

This heady brew gave rise, by the middle of the twentieth century, to what we today describe as 'modern development economics'. Modern development economics, bolstered by the rise in formal econometric research and the availability of data from developing nations over the last few decades, is what we teach today in colleges and universities under the label of development economics. With the rise in prominence of multilateral international organizations such as the World Bank, the United Nations Development Programme, the International Labour Organization, and the International Monetary Fund, and also the blossoming of research centers in developing nations, development economics is now also an integral part of policymaking.

One economist whose contributions are almost co-terminus with the emergence of modern development economics from the mid-twentieth century and whose writings played a big role in the formalization of the subject and also its outreach to neighbouring disciplines is Pranab Bardhan. Bardhan wrote in one of his early books *Land, Labor and Rural Poverty: Essays in Development Economics* (Columbia University Press, 1984),

> Over the years I have taught several courses at Delhi, Cambridge (Massachusetts) and Berkeley. But I always have a nagging sense of unease at the amorphousness of the material I am supposed to cover. ... There is a pervasive atmosphere of 'anything goes' and the students cannot be blamed for considering the subject as one of the soft options.

He then went on to explain how his aim was to change this, to bring rigour, economic theory and econometrics to bear on the concerns of development and the puzzles of land and labor markets in poor nations. This book and, more generally, Bardhan's large body of work played a significant role in development economics coming into its own as an important and rigorous discipline. The essays collected in the current volume have all been inspired by aspects of Bardhan's work.

Bardhan's early research was on modelling economic growth with machine obsolescence, on growth in the classic dual-economy model of development *à la* Arthur Lewis, and, some years later, on endogenous growth theory. He also did prominent work on the relation between international trade and development, the analysis of inequality and poverty, learning and growth and the role of technology transfer, the analysis of agrarian economies, share tenancy, interlinkage in agrarian markets, and the problem of rural indebtedness.

In terms of method, we see the same broad interest and engagement. Over the years, Bardhan engaged in theoretical modelling and analysis, the building of mathematical models, and running large-scale regressions with secondary data from developing countries. He also went out into the field, and engaged in hands-on data collection, akin to what several anthropologists have done and few economists do. This kind of research (which he did with Ashok Rudra), which echoed some early anthropological research, such as the important work by Frederick Bailey, provided an empirical counterpart to the theoretical literature that emerged on interlinked markets with important papers by Joseph Stiglitz, David Newbery, Avishay Braverman, Jean-Philippe Platteau, and others. Interestingly enough, there was also effort to draw in ideas from 'feudal practices' in *advanced economies*, such as the research on slavery in America that one finds in the book *One Kind of Freedom*, by Roger Ransom and Richard Sutch, which raises a host of questions on power, exploitation, and interlinkage, though from a different perspective.

This literature distinguished itself from a lot of mainstream economics by its openness to our neighbouring subjects, such as anthropology, sociology, and politics, and the willingness to trespass disciplinary boundaries, to use an expression made famous by Albert Hirschman. Even in terms of methodology, development economics became one field of economics in which there was use of formal statistics, and also 'thick descriptions', made popular by anthropologists. This is also a discipline that has a lot of interface with politics and political economy, as is visible in the chapters that follow. This happened both because political scientists reached out to economists, eager to use some of our formal methods and because in economics, and especially in development economics, there was an obvious interface with politics and political institutions.

There is no surprise that Pranab Bardhan was one of the longest running chief editors of the world's most important development economics journal, the *Journal of Development Economics*. Bardhan was its chief editor from 1985 to 2003. Through his research and editorial work he has had a deep influence on the shaping of our thinking in economics and economic policymaking, from the fine-tuning of trade policy, through policy interventions in the agricultural sector, to strategies for corruption control.

Development economics has today reached a maturity it did not have even a few decades ago. We hope that this book will reflect this maturity, the catholicity of methods used by development economists, and the broad range of interests we find within the broad area of development. The book features chapters on a multiplicity of subjects, organized under three broad clusters: (a) the mitigation of poverty; (b) the nature of markets in developing countries, in particular the market for land, labour and credit; and (c) the political economy of development. In what follows, we briefly discuss each of these chapters.

Anti-poverty Policies

The first section includes five chapters that grapple with thorny questions of how to design anti-poverty policies and under what conditions we can expect them to be successful. Key challenges for designing redistributive policies include the leakage of spending to corruption and inefficiencies in targeting recipients or managing programs. Four of the chapters concentrate on programs and policies for India, and the fifth covers international experience with cash transfer programmes. India is a natural focus for these discussions, for a number of reasons. India has a long history of trying to combat poverty, with notable successes and failures. As a newly independent nation, trying to develop and maintain a political system that is democratic and progressive, India has been an iconic case study of development from the time of its independence in 1947. Because of its pioneering use of sampling methods for collecting representative data, it has been an economy that is extensively studied by economists and statisticians around the world. And while Pranab Bardhan himself worked on problems of developing economies in many parts of the world, his special focus has always been India.

Dilip Mookherjee considers the underlying causes for the relatively low proportion of expenditures on poverty-reduction programmes reaching the poor in India. Despite substantial spending on a wide variety of such programmes, the average rate of benefit pass-through is persistently low and varies greatly across regions of the country. Mookherjee gives an overview of spending leakages in anti-poverty programmes in India and identifies two leading causes: the capture of benefits by local elites and political clientelism (the manipulation of local spending to ensure the political support of pivotal constituencies). Both create biases towards providing private benefits, such as farm subsidies, jobs, or housing, rather than public goods, such as infrastructure, schools, health clinics, or sanitation. Decentralization of policy implementation and delivery has arguably exacerbated these biases. Mookherjee discusses the challenges of designing a social-welfare system in India that avoids these dangers and is able to transfer a greater share of resources directly to the poor. He points out that when criteria-based transfers are made directly to households, they become politically neutral, and significant reductions in poverty and improved health and education outcomes result. Conditional cash transfers are one approach, proven to be workable in Latin America, and universal basic income, as advocated by Bardhan and others, is another approach, still controversial but worthy of consideration.

Martin Ravallion analyses in more detail one of India's flagship anti-poverty programmes, the National Rural Employment Guarantee Scheme, arguably the largest income-support scheme in the world. Reviewing the evidence on the impact of the programme, he highlights the rationing of employment by local authorities, generating high rates of unmet demand for employment, especially in poorer states. Ravallion identifies two explanations for such rationing. One is decentralization, which can improve the allocation of public funding but also imposes costs of implementation on local governments. Another is corruption. Ravallion presents a model that illustrates how partial efforts to combat corruption can decrease employment and exacerbate rationing in workfare programmes. This model is consistent with evidence that rationing reduces the gains from employment guarantees but does not undermine the targeting of the guarantees to the poor.

Bruce Wydick reviews the evidence on the effectiveness of cash transfer policies and analyses theoretically when one would expect a basic minimum income to have sustainable long-term effects on individuals' productivity and income. Conditional cash transfer (CCT) or unconditional cash transfer (UCT) programmes have demonstrated significant positive short-term effects on consumption, educational attainment, and health outcomes in Latin America and elsewhere in developing countries. But the evidence on long-term impacts of cash transfers is mixed. Lasting effects on incomes, consumption, and investment tend to be stronger where employment opportunities are better and educational attainment higher, and greater for CCTs than UCTs. Wydick considers how behavioural extensions of a basic household model—to include, in particular, aspirations in decision-making, constraints on cognitive capacity and executive control, and/or time preferences that are endogenous to consumption and self-control—might help explain the long-term effectiveness of cash transfer programmes. He concludes that programmes targeting people with higher aspirations are more likely to have long-term impacts.

Abhijit Banerjee and Esther Duflo focus on a different aspect of anti-poverty policy, broadly defined: the provision of healthcare. On paper, India's healthcare system seems a model for delivering universal health services in a large, poor country. But using a detailed survey of the healthcare experiences and outcomes of the poor in Udaipur district, they show that in practice both public and private healthcare services are of distressingly low quality. For example, public healthcare centers are more often closed than open, while private providers are always open but offer inappropriate, inadequate, or dangerous care. Do these failures reflect problems of supply, demand, or both? Banerjee and Duflo report on a series of randomized experiments seeking to identify policy levers. The experiments include programmes that monitored attendance by nurses at rural public health clinics, trained private practitioners, and offered nutritional supplements to children with vaccinations. The results have been somewhat disappointing overall, underlining the difficulties of improving healthcare quality in settings in which the poor themselves may have difficulty distinguishing high- from low-quality care. Banerjee and Duflo offer some possibilities for improved regulation and training of private doctors, but conclude that improving attendance at rural public health centres is a challenge.

In any discussion of anti-poverty programmes, there naturally arises the question of how interventions are going to be paid for. Parikshit Ghosh and Debraj Ray make a provocative proposal: a sovereign fund for India, along the lines of shared-ownership funds in Alaska and Norway. Both of those funds are based on sales from oil reserves. Ghosh and Ray propose a fund based on the returns to private capital held by publicly traded Indian firms. The appeal of the proposal is that India's sovereign wealth fund would be started with lump-sum transfers in the amount of 10–20 per cent of outstanding corporate shares. The earnings of the fund would be distributed as universal basic income (UBI) or through alternative means-tested programmes. The proposed lump-sum initial transfer of stock would circumvent two problems. One is that consumption in the present does not need to be foregone to build savings to finance future consumption in a poor economy. The second is that it is a non-distorting tax on capital, although future taxation of new corporate issues would be distortionary. Ghosh and Ray address several core issues concerning management, incentives, and corporate control in their chapter. This proposal is sure to be controversial, but the challenge of overcoming poverty may well require this sort of ambitious thinking.

Land, Labour, and Financial Markets

An important stream of Pranab Bardhan's work in development economics has used the tools of game theory and contract theory, along with insights from the literature on transactions costs and property rights, to understand rural agrarian institutions. Bardhan's work in this area applies core theoretical insights to policy discussions surrounding poverty measurement, income inequality, rural unemployment, and comparing alternative growth strategies in terms of their impact on poverty and inequality. The essays in the second section of the volume explore several of these issues. An underlying theme is that poverty-reduction efforts are likely to have limited impact if they are not grounded in a clear conceptual understanding of market processes, and how inequality interacts with these to create heterogeneous outcomes.

Starting at an aggregate level, Bhaskar Dutta makes the important point that while it is clear that growth and income distribution are inherently linked, standard measures of growth ignore income distribution. This makes it difficult to answer questions such as: how would one compare the economic performance of India and China in the recent past? Since the fruits of growth are not equally distributed and different countries may have different levels of commitments to pro-poor policies, a simple comparison of growth rates will be misleading. The essay proposes a novel approach to evaluating the growth performance of countries and regions. They key feature is to take inequality into account explicitly. For example, it proposes assigning higher welfare gains to an economy with more pro-poor growth, conditional on a given change in average income per capita.

Focusing on labour markets, Nancy Chau and Ravi Kanbur explore the theoretical relationship between labour-saving technical change and wage inequality. They show that the relationship depends crucially on the degree of monopsony power of employers. This form of employer power can interact with new technologies in subtle and surprising ways. In their model, as employer power increases, wage inequality first increases and then decreases. A similar pattern is shown to exist between labour-saving technological change and wage inequality. When employer power is low, labour-saving technical change can increase both total output and wage inequality, highlighting interesting interactions in the relationship between the objectives of efficiency and equity.

Maitreesh Ghatak explores the relationships between property rights, especially over land, and the incentives that producers face to make productive investments. There is increasing evidence that property rights matter for individuals' investment decisions. At the same time, Ghatak argues, there are many complexities that require more research. Given the challenges of finding suitable empirical settings where the effect of changes in property rights can be causally established, one promising direction is to combine theory with empirical work to carry out quantitative analysis of alternative hypothetical policies, paying particular attention to heterogeneity of effects of changes in property rights on different individuals and production units. Ghatak emphasizes the importance of studying the relationship between formal and informal property rights, the issue of how large-scale property-rights reforms affect not just individual behaviour but also aggregate outcomes, and the issue of how complementary reforms (for example, in training) can enhance the impact of property-rights reforms.

The final chapter in this section by Nirvikar Singh reviews recent research on financial inclusion in a number of areas, including banking, microcredit and microfinance, payment technologies, and agricultural insurance, in the context of developing countries, with special reference to India. The review of existing evidence provides grounds for optimism that new savings and insurance products, facilitated by digital technologies, will help to improve financial inclusion. In line with one of the common themes of this section, the chapter emphasizes the need to pay careful attention to institutional details for such attempts at financial inclusion to succeed.

Political Economy

The book closes with three chapters that trespass the boundaries of economics and enter the territory of politics, to engage urgent concerns of the day that are the basis of much dispute and debate. These include how the importance of caste designation in policy in India arose, progressive autocracies in Islamic countries, and the political economy of China's Belt and Road Initiative. Pranab Bardhan has written extensively on political economy, democracy, and development, and each of these chapters bears a strong connection to his writing.

Rohini Somanathan reviews the history of the conceptualization of caste in the Indian constitution and discusses why caste remains so salient as a political cleavage. Disadvantage in India is primarily defined in terms of caste. The official categories for caste are intended to represent the ordering of social privilege and economic advantage. The designations, however, were compiled under British rule and adopted as given at independence. Somanathan explains how the aggregation of social ordering by caste from the village to the nation misrepresents the ordering of social advantage when social structure and inequality vary widely across villages, districts, and regions. The chapter concludes by discussing why a hierarchy based on ritual status rather than on income, land ownership, or local power persists in public policy today.

Jean-Philippe Plateau considers the question of whether democratic or autocratic governance is more conducive to economic development. History can be used to make a case for both. Japan after the Meiji restoration is well-known as a case of successful transformation from a traditional economy to an industrial one under autocracy. Platteau assesses the experience of 'enlightened autocracy' in the Islamic world, in particular in Turkey under Mustapha Kemal (Atatürk) and in Tunisia under Habib Bourguiba. The chapter examines why these modernizers were ultimately unable to pursue successful strategies of state-led industrialization. Platteau considers this question in the context of relations between religion and politics in each case. In pursuing progressive reforms, autocrats faced reactions from clerics and from elites. The chapter argues that miscalculations by each of these leaders produced the political crises that ended their progressive regimes.

Gerard Roland analyses the motivations for China's ambitious Belt and Road Initiative (BRI). The chapter first reviews the political and economic strategies of the Chinese Communist Party (CCP) over its seventy years in power. Roland explains that preservation of the CCP's power has driven past economic reform and motivates China's current international strategy. The legitimacy of the CCP seems to depend on continuing to deliver income growth. The BRI is expected to provide greater access to natural resource supplies and help maintain high export growth. Roland argues that the BRI is not China's attempt to dominate the world. Domestic economic objectives drive the project. Roland discusses several weaknesses and problems facing China in undertaking the project, but concludes that the BRI itself is a good investment for the world being made at China's expense.

Together, the twelve essays in this volume are a testament to the breadth and policy relevance of development economics today, which, in turn, was influenced greatly by the research and writings of Pranab Bardhan.

Part A

Anti-Poverty Policies

1   Anti-Poverty Programmes in India

Past, Present, and Future[*]

DILIP MOOKHERJEE

In the seventy years since Independence, anti-poverty schemes have until recently been dominated by centrally sponsored schemes, designed and subsidized by the Central government and implemented by state and local governments. The number and variety of these schemes have been staggering. There were approximately 360 such schemes in the late 1990s (though somewhat consolidated and shrunk to 66 by 2013) spanning employment guarantees, food, fuel, housing, maternal and child health, education, pensions, insurance, lamps, power, livestock, sanitation,

* Prepared for a volume of essays in honour of Pranab Bardhan. An earlier version of this chapter was presented at the South Asia workshop at New York University in February 2017; I am grateful to participants for their feedback.

loans and financial services, livelihood programmes, storage, training, digital services, and various forms of infrastructure. The schemes were poorly coordinated, created by the Planning Commission and different departments of successive central governments, and supplemented further by additional programmes of state governments. Besides these anti-poverty schemes, other government policies have been motivated at least in part by the need to provide support to the poor, such as procurement of foodgrains, fertilizer subsidies, low-interest loans, and subsequent waivers of these loans.

The large range and variety of these programmes makes it very difficult to gauge their overall incidence or cost-effectiveness. Studies of specific programmes indicate that they have been poorly targeted, in a manner facilitating massive leakages owing to corruption and inefficiency. While the basis of Rajiv Gandhi's frequently quoted remark—that only 15 paise of every rupee spent on welfare programmes actually reaches the poor—is unknown, it is fairly close to the percolation of the public distribution system (PDS) of foodgrains estimated by Jha and Ramaswami (2012). Using NSS data from 2005–6, they found that only 30 per cent of those below the poverty line received PDS foodgrains, while 70 per cent of PDS recipients were above the poverty line. A total of 43 per cent was lost owing to diversion of supplies to the black market, and 28 per cent due to excess cost of government supply (compared with market-based supply). As a result, only 10 per cent of the total cost of the programme ended up as income supplements to the poor.

Alternatively, consider farm policies ostensibly motivated to benefit poor farmers. Public procurement of foodgrains provide income benefits to farmers in proportion to the amounts they produce and sell, which tend to be larger for farmers owning more land. Procurement also restricts supplies to the open market, keeping market prices high, increasing the cost of food purchased by landless households (the vast majority of whom are not covered by the PDS). So, the programme is essentially regressive. Loan waivers similarly benefit only the minority of farmers able to borrow from state-owned financial institutions. Data from the 2011 India Human Development Survey show that the majority of rural households do not have access to loans from banks, and rely on informal loans at higher cost: only 22 per cent of rural households obtained loans from banks, and 10 per cent from microfinance institutions or self-help groups, while 19 per cent borrowed from moneylenders and 29 per cent from family and friends. Moreover, bank loan access was biased in favour of households owning more land: only 11 per cent of landless households obtained bank loans, in contrast to 26 per cent of those owning between 1 and 2.5 acres of agricultural land, 34 per cent for those owning between 5 and 10 acres, 37 per cent for those with 10–20 acres and 38 per cent of those with more than 20 acres. In light of this, the impacts estimated by Kanz (2012) of the 2008 loan waiver programme (ADWDRS) are not surprising. Despite providing waivers amounting to four times average monthly household consumption levels, and costing 1.6 per cent of GDP, there was no discernible impact on consumption or productive investments of recipients. Had the beneficiaries been truly poor and distressed, one would expect the waivers to at least increase their consumption.

Compounding these failures are shockingly low levels of service quality in public health and educational institutions. Chaudhary et al. (2006) report absenteeism rates of 25 per cent among government schoolteachers and 40 per cent in government health clinics, which are higher in India than five other developing countries included in the study.

1.1 Reform Efforts: Panchayati Raj and NREGA

Has the Indian government attempted any reforms to reduce these leakages and targeting failures? Indeed, the past three decades have witnessed a number of such efforts, such as *panchayati raj* or decentralization of benefit delivery to elected local governments, combined with reservation of mayoral *pradhan* posts as well as council seats for members of scheduled castes and scheduled tribes (SC/STs) and women. This was part of a worldwide trend towards decentralization as an effort to improve efficiency and accountability in service delivery compared to previous bureaucracy-based delivery systems (see for example, the 2004 World Development Report of the World Bank, or Bardhan and Mookherjee 2007 for case studies from various developing countries). Bureaucrats were viewed as 'outsiders' with little understanding and stake in local communities, appointed by distant central or state governments incapable of monitoring their performance. The hope was that local democracy would shift decision rights over implementation to members of local communities who were better informed about local needs, and more accountable to residents. The extent to which these expectations have been met are mixed at best (Government of India Expert Committee Report 2013). In some states such as Kerala, the *panchayati raj* reforms seem to have been quite successful (Heller, Harilal, and Chaudhuri 2007), but less so in many other states (Chaudhuri 2007). In part, this was due to a highly uneven pattern of devolution of the three F's (funds, functions, and functionaries) across different states by state governments which were vested the authority by the 73rd Constitutional Amendment to select the extent and range of devolution to panchayats.

The country-wide adoption of NREGA over the past decade represents a significant effort by the Indian government to augment the responsibilities and funds devolved to local governments. The implementation of this programme has also been imperfect and heterogeneous across states, in terms of utilization rates, payment delays, leakages and bribes, and extent to which it has been demand-driven (Ministry of Rural Development 2012, Afridi, Iversen, and Sharan 2017, Niehaus and Sukhtankar 2013, Sukhtankar 2016). Programme leakages in Andhra Pradesh (measured by gap between wage payments disbursed by local government officials and reported wages received by households) were to the tune of 30 per cent, that is, non-negligible and of a similar order of magnitude as black market diversions of PDS food supplies (Muralidharan, Niehaus, and Sukhtankar 2016). However, it seems to have achieved some success in targeting to the poor (Sukhtankar 2016), widening the range of benefits to other poor households not participating in the programme by raising rural and urban wages (Imbert and Papp 2015, 2018), and inducing significant drops in poverty rates for SC/ST households in the slack season (Klonner and Oldiges 2019). Effects on local infrastructure have been controversial, owing partly to the absence of any reliable quantitative estimates.

Reservations of local government positions for SC/ST candidates appear to have improved targeting towards SC/ST households (Chattopadhyay and Duflo 2003, 2004, Besley, Pande, and Rao 2012, Bardhan, Mookherjee and Parra-Torrado 2010). Reservations for women candidates succeeded in shifting the composition of local government expenditures towards programmes favoured by women in some states (Chattopadhyay and Duflo 2003) but not in others (Rajaraman and Gupta 2010). But the latter also seem to have resulted in a decline in pro-poor targeting (Bardhan, Mookherjee and Parra-Torrado 2010), a rise in bribes paid by households to secure NREGA employment (Afridi, Iversen, and Sharan 2017) and lowered delivery of school services and roads (Gajwani and Zhang 2008), possibly owing to lack of experience of new women leaders. Hence the evidence concerning the effectiveness of gender-based reservations is rather mixed.

1.2 Underlying Problems: Elite Capture and Clientelism

What are the underlying causes of the low percolation of benefits to the poor, despite the substantial expenditures of these various programmes? And why is there so much variation in their effectiveness across different parts of the country?

One problem highlighted by many scholars is *local elite capture*, which varies with inequality in land, caste, and literacy. Anderson, Francois, and Kotwal (2015) show that take-up of anti-poor programmes and engagement of local villagers with *panchayat* leaders in three Maharashtra districts was systematically and significantly lower in villages with a higher share of land owned by the dominant Maratha caste. The same Maratha-dominated villages also exhibited higher cross-caste consumption insurance, social capital, and local cooperation, suggesting higher levels of dependence of the poor on help provided by wealthy landowners. In similar vein, Pandey (2010) provides evidence that government schools in UP villages with pre-Independence landlord-based land revenue systems were less functional (in terms of participation of local residents in village education committee), more corrupt (measured by embezzlement of school funds and teacher absenteeism), and had worse school outcomes (measured by student attendance and test scores). The motivation for landed elites to restrict access of poor households to government provided education is suggested by Kochar (2008). Using all-India NCAER household and farm survey data, she shows that one year of extra schooling of the poor reduced profits of landowners by 15 per cent (by lowering the supply of unskilled agricultural workers, thereby raising their wages). Consistent with this interpretation, she shows that the number of teachers assigned to government primary schools was significantly smaller in districts where farm profits were more sensitive to agricultural wages.

Political clientelism and vote-buying represents another significant problem in the functioning of democracies, particularly at the local level. Benefits are distributed by incumbent governments in a manner designed to manipulate and increase their re-election prospects, rather than genuine needs of the poor. While this is an inherent characteristic of all democracies, clientelism is distinguished from more standard forms of pork-barrel politics by conditioning delivery of benefits at a very high level of disaggregation, for example, different households within a village based on perceived political support extended by these households to local incumbents. As argued in Bardhan et al. (2009, 2015) and Bardhan and Mookherjee (2012, 2018), this induces a political bias in favour of private benefits (employment, subsidies, housing) rather than local public goods (infrastructure, law and order, local schools, health clinics, sanitation, and public health)—essentially because no one in the local area can be denied access to the benefits of these public goods. Even within private benefits, it induces a bias in favour of recurring short-term benefits such as employment, loans, subsidies, emergency help rather than one-time benefits of a more durable nature (identification/entitlement documents, land titles, tenant registration or housing).

Some argue that a virtue of clientelism (particularly compared to elite capture) is that it tends to direct benefits towards the poor, so it is progressive in its incidence (for example, Holland 2016). However, benefits are often directed to narrow 'swing' constituencies among the poor, resulting in horizontal inequity (see Ruud 1999) for ethnographic accounts in West Bengal villages). Clientelism can also motivate manipulation of inter-village programme budgets to increase re-election prospects of incumbent parties controlling higher tiers of local and state governments, depending on the nature of political competition and alignment of control between upper and lower tiers. The scope for such manipulation arises from the discretionary nature of fund transfers from district- or block-level panchayats to gram panchayats in most states, rather than defined by transparent need-based formulae. A party controlling an upper tier would be motivated to reallocate budgets in favour of lower tier governments that are controlled by the same party and facing increased competition. Evidence consistent with such manipulations is shown by Bardhan et al. (2015) and Dey and Sen (2016) in the context of West Bengal and Mukhopadhyay and Gupta (2016) in the context of Rajasthan. Such politically motivated reallocations may or may not improve targeting to poorer constituencies, depending on how political competition varies with poverty. If poorer areas are characterized by less competition, the result will be enhanced anti-poor bias in inter-village allocations—that is, panchayats in poorer regions receive smaller spending entitlements, the phenomenon that the 2017 Economic Survey referred to as 'misallocation' of government expenditures.

Clientelism may also create a wider set of political incentives that undermine long-term development. Since it thrives on provision of short-term private benefits to a subset of the poor, clientelism perpetuates their dependence of the latter on their patrons, and in turn the grip of the latter on political power. Providing benefits of a more long-term nature could reduce this dependence, thereby threatening political survival of incumbents. This is vividly illustrated by the experience of the PRI in Mexico in the late 1990s when (led by a technocratic president) it provided secure land titles to the poor, and subsequently lost political power in most rural areas (de Jainvry et al. 2014, Dower and Pfutze 2015). In similar vein, incumbents may be reluctant to provide long-term squatters, vendors or immigrants with registration rights, thereby perpetuating a large informal sector (Holland 2016). Combined with low incentives to provide public goods such as law and order, roads, sanitation, functioning schools and health clinics, or reduce public bads such as corruption of appointed officials or pollution, a low-level development trap can result. A similar adverse dynamic could result from elite capture, wherein solidly entrenched local elites block development programmes (as exemplified by above cited work of Kochhar 2008 and Pandey 2010) to perpetuate local inequality. Borguignon and Verdier (2000) and Acemoglu and Robinson (2008) present theoretical models which illustrate this possibility. In Borguignon and Verdier's model, a low-level trap arises if historically inherited inequality exceeds a critical threshold. For other regions that inherit less historical inequality, a self-sustaining development process is set in motion, generating a virtuous cycle which lowers inequality and undermines the power of local elites in the long run. Hence, the gap between regions can grow over time.

1.3 Systemic Reforms Needed

Both elite capture and clientelism result from a deeper weakness of state institutions, wherein the state is forced to allocate discretionary authority to bureaucrats or local government officials to manage delivery systems. This owes in turn to its own inability to identify its citizens and transfer both cash and in-kind benefits to them directly. Safety net programmes in developed countries are based on nationwide identification systems such as social security numbers or citizen registration documents. Most citizens have access to accounts in financial institutions, linked to their identification details. This permits the state to implement formula-bound comprehensive income support and safety net programmes without relying on local intermediaries.

Owing to various reforms in political institutions, the late nineteenth and early twentieth century witnessed the decline of clientelist politics and replacement by universal transfer programmes in the UK, USA, and other countries in Western Europe, culminating in social security and the welfare state. Similar processes have been under way in recent decades in Latin America, especially in the form of conditional cash transfer (CCT) programmes where income support payments are made directly to households based on formulae based on enrollment of their children in school and regular visits to health clinics. Analyses of these federally administered CCT programmes show they have been politically neutral and induced significant reductions in poverty, accompanied by improvements in health, education and increased political competition in local governments wherein long-established political elites have been swept away (Fried [2011], Frey [2015]). In Mexico they have been complemented by land reforms in both rural (de Jainvry et al. 2014) and urban (Larraguy, Marshall, and Trucco 2015) areas with similar effects.

Such a transition is yet to occur in India. The process has begun with *Aadhar* the nationwide biometric identification system, combined with a thrust to widen access to bank accounts and link them to Aadhar. Entitlement to cooking gas subsidies, as well as to other anti-poverty programmes are in the process of being linked to Aadhar registration. The implementation of these programmes have been controversial, with various errors or inclusion and exclusion reported frequently in the media, besides concerns of security, invasion of privacy, and legal authority. While the fraction of adult population with bank accounts has increased rapidly in recent years, rising from less than 60 per cent in 2015 to 80 per cent in 2017 (World Bank 2017), the extent to which these accounts are actually being used or accessed by their owners is not known. Limited financial literacy and proximity to bank branches and ATMs for large segments of the rural population possibly limit effective access to these accounts. Other teething problems include unreliable facilities to link PDS entitlements to Aadhar-linked bank accounts and Aadhar-authentication failures, resulting in unfortunate denial of benefits to some.

One hopes and expects such problems to be overcome in the medium to long term, owing to advancement and diffusion of information technology, literacy, and financial access especially amongst the young. What kind of a welfare system should India aim for in the long run?

1.4 Designing the Future Welfare State: Key Questions

There is a range of relevant issues concerning delivery of private good benefits: (i) *Design:* Should transfers be cash or in kind? Should they be targeted to specific groups, or universally to the entire population? Should they be conditioned on forms of behaviour, such as enrollment of children in school, or health check-ups as in the Mexican or Brazilian conditional cash transfer programmes? Should households or individuals be recipients? (ii) *Scale:* How large would the benefits be, and how will the transfers be financed? (iii) *Delivery mechanism:* How will benefits be delivered to recipients—via bank accounts, mobile phone transfers, local agents such as banking correspondents, or government offices? And finally, how will fiscal resources be allocated between private transfers and provision of *public goods* such as infrastructure, sanitation, health, and education?

Universal Basic Income (UBI) proposals have recently been presented by Bardhan, Joshi and the 2017 Economic Survey (ES) of the Indian government, summarized in IJHD (2017). They propose to replace a number of existing leaky and poorly targeted programmes with a single universal and unconditional cash transfer. NREGA, child support and nutrition are sought to be retained. Both Joshi and ES propose a quasi-universal UBI, covering 70–75% of the population, with selectivity achieved via use of information concerning income tax status, ownership of durables, and self-selection based on administrative requirements and voluntary opt-out opportunities. ES proposes providing each individual a support of Rs 7,620 per year, which would cost 4.9 per cent of GDP. However, it subsequently describes problems with financing a programme of this scale, since eliminating 'middle-class' subsidies (including cooking gas (LPG), railway, urea subsidies and income tax exemptions) would generate 1 per cent of GDP, while eliminating food (PDS), fertilizer and petroleum subsidies would generate another 2 per cent. Besides noting the likely political resistance to eliminating these subsidies, ES admits they would be insufficient to fund the entire UBI programme. Hence, it ends up proposing a gradual phase-in starting with females only and providing them each Rs 3,240 a year, funded by eliminating only the middle-class subsidies. Joshi proposes providing a benefit of Rs 3,500 a year to 70 per cent of the adult population, and estimates that it would cost 3.5 per cent of GDP. The ES estimates suggest this would cost less, around 2.4 per cent of GDP, which seems financially feasible if 'middle-class', PDS and either petroleum or fertilizer subsidies are eliminated.

These transfers would be made directly to Aadhar-linked bank accounts. Given that substantial portions of the population are yet to have access to such accounts, ES proposes supplementing them with transfers via banking correspondents (BCs) appointed by the banks to reach others using Aadhar-based verification methods. It also notes the incidence of authentication failures, at high rates particularly in backward states (49 per cent in Jharkhand, 37 per cent in Rajasthan compared with 6 per cent in Gujarat). Clearly, the scheme cannot currently be installed for the entire country. Rollout would have to be gradual, with full implementation possible only when the country reaches near universal financial access.

A quasi-UBI on this scale would provide support to the tune of Rs 600 per household per month. This is roughly comparable to the benefits received by a participating household in NREGA in its 'star' state Andhra Pradesh of Rs 146 per week per beneficiary, which translates to Rs 560 per month per household (based on estimates reported by Muralidharan, Neihaus, and Sukhtankar [2016]). The coverage of the programme would, of course, be much wider. Instead of only one-third of the poor population that the PDS reaches, the coverage would be near universal, assuming that the financial access and authentication challenges are overcome. Most importantly, being formula bound and direct, this would be achieved without any reliance on local intermediaries, thus removing scope for diversions, elite capture, and clientelism. As Brazil and Mexico's experiences with CCTs suggest, it would markedly reduce dependence of the poor on local elites and on local government officials. It thereby has the potential of altering the character of India's democracy dramatically by attacking the root problems that undermine the effectiveness of current programmes.

Critiques of these proposals have included the following points (see, for example, IIHD 2017):

a. Unconditional cash transfers would promote laziness and welfare dependence among the poor, and could result in lower expenditures on merit goods such as nutrition, child schooling, and health, while raising spending on non-merit goods such as alcohol. Conditioning transfers on investments in child schooling and health, as in CCTs or the Kanyasree programme in West Bengal (and a similar bicycle scheme in Bihar) for girls enrolled in secondary and high school would ameliorate these problems.

b. The near universal nature of the scheme increases inclusion errors (as many non-poor are provided support) while reducing exclusion errors (of the truly poor). The former represents a form of leakage, though in a form that will become legalized and institutionalized. The overall leakage may therefore increase. Conversely, targeted programmes with some self-selection built in (such as NREGA where beneficiaries have to work to receive benefits) could be more cost effective in lowering poverty.

c. Food markets do not function well in many parts of the country, resulting in localized food shortages and periodic spikes in foodgrain prices. PDS insures against these uncertainties. In similar vein, variations in weather cause fluctuations in earning capacity of the poor, which NREGA provides some insurance against owing to its self-selection feature. For instance, NREGA utilization rises during the agricultural pre-monsoon season when agricultural labour markets are slack. It also rose in weeks immediately following demonetization in November 2016.

d. NREGA programmes create local infrastructure besides providing income support to those employed. Targeting performance of existing programmes such as PDS is improving in many states. Efforts should be made to improve its performance further. Comparing an existing programme and an untested hypothetical programme is inherently biased against the former.

Empirical evidence (summarized in ES) does not support contention (a) with regard to effects on labour supply or expenditure composition of the poor. Part of the reason is that many of the in-kind benefits are intra-marginal for the majority of recipients, so are effectively equivalent to cash transfers. CCTs might induce higher schooling enrollment rates of children, but are administratively difficult to enforce owing to problems in verifying school enrolment, and opens the door for corruption. A vast majority of children now go to private schools that are largely unregistered. Requiring regular child health check-ups is similarly difficult with the large number of non-functioning public health clinics and unregistered private clinics.

Regarding (b), Murgai and Ravallion (2005) and Imbert (2018) have assessed the comparative cost-effectiveness of NREGA and untargeted cash transfers for Bihar and all of India, respectively, using different periods, datasets, and methods, and arrive at different conclusions. Imbert's analysis shows how the comparison depends on the specific poverty measure used (headcount rather than poverty gap ratio) and whether general equilibrium effects on wages are incorporated. However, the differences in the estimated impacts are not large: poverty gap ratio under NREGA is estimated to be 8.3 per cent or 8.8 per cent depending on assumptions regarding the opportunity cost of time of participants, while it would be 8.8 per cent with unconditional cash transfers that cost the same as NREGA. In addition, none of the UBI proposals advanced eliminate NREGA, so comparisons of NREGA with untargeted cash transfers are not germane. Comparisons of cost effectiveness of cash transfers with PDS, petroleum or fertilizer subsidies would be more relevant; one would expect cash transfers to better targeted than either of these. Similar counter arguments apply to (d), while granting that the performance of PDS could be improving. But if food benefits are intra-marginal for most, they would be unlikely to ever be better targeted than cash transfers that cost the same.

Point (c) pertaining to insurance against local price and weather shocks is more substantive. Not much is known about the comparative insurance benefits of PDS (or NREGA) and cash transfers in the Indian context. Conceivably, cash transfers could be conditioned on these shocks, enlarging its scope to an insurance cum anti-poverty scheme. There may be a need to supplement it with provisions to monitor and intervene in food distribution in remote areas where local markets are thin and vulnerable to price manipulation by private traders.

The political feasibility of UBI, however, remains in question. Polls even in advanced countries have rejected it. UBI would be politically unpopular, with examples of specific implementation failures highlighted in the media, while gains in coverage receive comparably less publicity. This would be compounded by resistance from those losing subsidies: the middle classes and lobbies representing farmers, fertilizer, and petroleum industries. On the other hand, astute and far-sighted political entrepreneurs may perceive the potential of quasi-UBI to generate substantial support from large numbers of poor and lower-middle-income households once they start receiving a regular and guaranteed stream of benefits without having to toil in public works programmes, bribing government officials or countering resistance from local elites.

References

D. Acemoglu and J. Robinson (2008). 'Persistence of Power, Elites, and Institutions', *American Economic Review*, 98(1) (March): 267–93.

S. Anderson, P. Francois, and A. Kotwal (2015). 'One Kind of Democracy', *American Economic Review*, 105(6).

F. Afridi, V. Iversen, and M. Sharan (2017). 'Women Political Leaders, Corruption and Learning: Evidence from a Large Public Program in India', *Economic Development and Cultural Change*, 66(1).

P. Bardhan and D. Mookherjee, D. (2006). 'Pro-poor Targeting and Accountability of Local Governments in West Bengal', *Journal of Development Economics*, 79(2): 303–27.

P. Bardhan and D. Mookherjee, D. (eds) (2007). *Decentralization and Local Governance in Developing Countries: A Comparative Perspective*, New Delhi: Oxford University Press.

P. Bardhan, D. Mookherjee, D., and M. Parra Torrado (2010a). 'Impact of Political Reservations in West Bengal Local Governments on Anti-poverty Targeting', *Journal of Globalization and Development*, 1(1), available at: http://people.bu.edu/dilipm/publications/jgdrevised.

P. Bardhan and D. Mookherjee (2012). 'Political Clientelism-cum-Capture: Theory and Evidence from West Bengal', Working paper, Institute for Economic Development, Boston University.

——— (2018), 'A Theory of Clientelistic Politics versus Programmatic Politics', Working paper, Department of Economics, Boston University.

P. Bardhan, S. Mitra, D. Mookherjee, and A. Sarkar (2009). 'Local Democracy and Clientelism: Implications for Political Stability in Rural West Bengal', *Economic and Political Weekly*, 44(9): 46–58.

P. Bardhan, S. Mitra, D. Mookherjee, and A. Nath (2014). 'Changing Voting Patterns in Rural West Bengal: Role of Clientelism and Local Public Goods', *Economic and Political Weekly*, (15 March), 54–62.

——— (2018), 'Resource Transfers to Local Governments: Political Manipulation and Voting Patterns in West Bengal', Working paper, Boston University.

T. Besley, R. Pande, and V. Rao (2012), 'Just Rewards? Local Politics and Public Resource Allocation in South India', *World Bank Economic Review*, 26(2).

F. Borguignon, F. and T. Verdier (2000). 'Oligarchy, Democracy, Inequality and Growth', *Journal of Development Economics*, 62(2): 285–313.

R. Chattopadhyay, R. and E. Duflo (2004). 'Women as Policy Makers: Evidence from a Randomized Policy Experiment in India', *Econometrica*, 72(5): 1409–43.

N. Chaudhary, J. Hammer, M. Kremer, K. Muralidharan, and F. Rogers (2006). 'Missing in Action: Teachers and Health Worker Absence in Developing Countries', *Journal of Economic Perspectives*, 20(1): 91–116.

S. Chaudhuri (2007). 'What Difference Does a Constitutional Amendment Make? The 1994 Panchayati Raj Act and the Attempt to Revitalize Rural Local Government in India'. In P. Bardhan and D. Mookherjee (ed.), *Decentralization and Local Governance in Developing Countries: A Comparative Perspective*, New Delhi: Oxford University Press.

S. Dey and K. Sen (2016). 'Is Partisan Alignment Electorally Rewarding? Evidence from Village Council Elections in India', IZA Working Paper No. 9994.

P. C. Dower and T. Pfutze (2015). 'Vote Suppression and Insecure Property Rights', *Journal of Development Economics*, 114(C): 1–19.

B. Fried (2012), 'Distributive Politics and Conditional Cash Transfers', *World Development*, 40(5): 1042–53.

A. Frey (2015), 'Cash Transfers, Clientelism and Political Enfranchisement: Evidence from Brazil', Working paper, University of British Columbia.

K. Gajwani and X. Zhang (2008). 'Gender, Caste and Public Good Provision in Indian Village Governments', IFPRI Discussion Paper No. 807, IFPRI, Washington, DC.

Government of India Expert Committee Report, 'Towards Holistic Panchayati Raj, 20th Anniversary Report of the Expert Committee on Leveraging Panchayats for Efficient Delivery of Public Goods and Services', Vol. 1, Policy Issues, 24 April 2013, New Delhi.

P. Heller, K.N. Harilal, and S. Chaudhuri (2007). 'Building Local Democracy: Evaluating Impact of Decentralization in Kerala, India', *World Development*, 35(4): 626–48.

A. Holland (2016). 'Forbearance', *American Political Science Review*, 110(2): 232–46.

C. Imbert and J. Papp (2015). 'Labor Market Effects of Social Programs: Evidence from India's Employment Guarantee', *American Economic Journal: Applied Economics*, 7(2): 233–63.

C. Imbert and J. Papp (2018). 'Short-term Migration, Rural Public Works and Urban Labor Markets: Evidence from India', Working paper, University of Warwick.

C. Imbert (2018). 'Poverty Alleviation under the NREGA', Working paper, University of Warwick.

Indian Journal of Human Development (IJHD) (2017). 'Symposium on Universal Basic Income', New Delhi: Sage Publications.

A. de Janvry, M. Gonzalez-Navarro, and E. Sadoulet (2014). 'Are Land Reforms Granting Complete Property Rights Politically Risky? Electoral Outcomes of

Mexico's Certification Program', *Journal of Development Economics*, 110(C): 216–25.

S. Jha and B. Ramaswami (2011). 'The Percolation of Public Expenditure: Food Subsidies and the Poor in India and Philippines', India Policy Forum 2011–2012, New Delhi: Sage Publications.

M. Kanz (2012). 'What Does Debt Relief Do for Development?' Policy Research Working Paper 6258, Development Research Group, World Bank.

Kochhar, A. (2008). 'Schooling, Wages and Profit: Negative Pecuniary Externalities from Schooling and Their Consequences for Schooling Investments', *Journal of Development Economics*, 86(1): 76–95.

H. Larraguy, J. Marshall, and L. Trucco (2015). 'Breaking Clientelism or Rewarding Incumbents? Evidence from the Urban Titling Program in Mexico', Working paper, Department of Government, Harvard University.

Ministry of Rural Development (2012), MNREGA Sameeksha: An Anthology of Research Studies, Ministry of Rural Development, Government of India.

K. Muralidharan, P. Niehaus, and S. Sukhtankar (2016), 'Building State Capacity: Evidence from Biometric Smartcards in India', *American Economic Review*, 110(6). 2895–929.

R. Murgai and M Ravallion (2005), 'Is a guaranteed living wage a good anti-poverty policy?', Policy Research Working Paper Series 3640, The World Bank.

P. Niehaus and S. Sukhtankar (2013), 'The Marginal Rate of Corruption in Public Programs: Evidence from India', *Journal of Public Economics*, 104(C): 52–64.

P. Pandey (2010). 'Service Delivery and Corruption in Public Services: How Does History Matter?', *American Economic Journal: Applied Economics*, 2190–204.

I. Rajaraman and Gupta, M. (2010). 'Public Expenditure Choices and Gender Quotas', Working paper, Indian Statistical Institute, New Delhi.

A. Ruud (1999). 'From Untouchable to Communist: Wealth, Power and Status among Supporters of the Communist Party of India (Marxist) in Rural West Bengal (1977-90)'. In B. Rogaly, B. Harriss-White, and S. Bose (eds), *Sonar Bangla? Agricultural Growth and Agrarian Change in West Bengal and Bangladesh*, New Delhi and Thousand Oaks, London: Sage Publications.

S. Sukhtankar (2016). 'India's National Rural Employment Guarantee Scheme: What Do We Really Know About the World's Largest Workfare Program?', India Policy Forum 2016–2017, New Delhi: Sage Publications.

World Bank (2017). 'Measuring Financial Inclusion and the FinTech Revolution', The Global Findex Database 2017, World Bank Group, Washington, DC.

2 Is a Decentralized Right-to-Work Policy Feasible?

MARTIN RAVALLION[*]

T he idea of using workfare to help implement a 'right-to-work' (RTW) policy has surfaced often in the history of social policy. For example, in the last few years of his life, Dr Martin Luther King Jr. turned his attention from civil rights to poverty in America, where he saw high unemployment among poor families. King's response was, 'We need an Economic Bill of Rights. This would guarantee a job to all people who want work and are able to work' (Myers-Lipton 2015: p. xv). This was clearly an instrumental case for RTW, in which ending poverty

* For comments on this paper, the author thanks Ken Kletzer, Rinku Murgai and Dominique van de Walle.

was seen as the overarching goal.[1] The idea of a Federal Jobs Guarantee has resurfaced recently in the US (Paul et al. 2017).

RTW has also been influential in India, where the idea took the form of 'Employment Guarantee Schemes'. An influential early example is the Maharashtra Employment Guarantee Scheme (MEGS), started in 1973 in response to the threat of famine. The idea was scaled up to the national level in 2005 in the form of the Mahatma Gandhi National Rural Employment Guarantee Act (NREGA), which is clearly the largest workfare scheme in the world. It promises 100 days of work per household per year, on demand, to all adults willing to supply unskilled manual labour to labour-intensive public works projects. The projects are mostly for water conservation/harvesting, drought protection, irrigation, roads, and sanitation. The work is to be paid at the statutory minimum wage rate notified for the programme, and workers are to be paid within 15 days of doing the work. If the work demanded cannot be provided, then an unemployment allowance is to be paid by the state government. Compared to MEGS, NREGA gives a more important role to local (including village-level) officials in implementation.

Rights-based ideas about distributive justice have had a long history (Fleischacker 2004; Ravallion 2016, Part 1). It is a superficially attractive idea to create new legal rights for things that matter to poor people, such as work, to help reduce poverty. However, will these rights be respected in practice? The same factors that made some people poor in the first place may well operate to undermine attempts to expand their effective rights. This chapter addresses that question in the context of India's employment guarantee schemes.

---

[1] For example, Myers-Lipton (2015, p.6) writes that Dr King's proposal "…would provide poor people of all races the money necessary to pay for housing, food, transportation and health care." Earlier (pre-King) RTW proposals by Presidents Franklin D. Roosevelt (FDR) and Harry Truman, and later discussions around the Humphrey-Hawkins Full Employment Act (influenced by King's proposals) passed under President Jimmy Carter also made a case for RTW as an anti-poverty policy (Myers-Lipton, 2015, Chapter 1).

The following section discusses the arguments in favour of using workfare to implement RTW. Section 2.2 reviews evidence indicating that the RTW in India is not being realized in general through the country's employment guarantee schemes, especially in poor places. The key issue addressed by the chapter is whether it is feasible in practice to guarantee employment with decentralized implementation in poor places. Sections 2.3 and 2.4 take up that issue and outline two reasons—based on administrative costs and corruption (respectively)—why RTW may not be attainable in such a setting.

2.1 The Potential Benefits of a Right-to-Work

In principle, a workfare scheme can directly serve longer-term development goals by generating assets that could improve the wealth distribution, or shift production functions to permit higher returns to existing assets. The assets could be of direct benefit to poor people, or of indirect benefit, such as through the revenue implications of using the scheme to produce taxable gains to non-poor people.

However, in practice, workfare schemes in India have primarily been seen as short-term palliatives against poverty. Indeed, one often hears anecdotes that NREGA assets are mostly worthless; certainly, 'NREGA roads' have a bad reputation in rural India, often washed away in each monsoon, though this is a questionable stereotype (Verma 2011; Narayanan et al. 2015).[2]

Workfare is a member of a class of policies that apply behavioural conditions for participation. In the case of workfare, that condition is the work requirement.[3] In workfare, the cost of compliance with the

---

[2] There is a trade-off here; durable asset creation in workfare tends to make the program less labor intensive, with lower impact on current poverty. For further discussion of this trade off and its implications see Ravallion (1999). A review of the evidence on asset creation in NREGA can be found in Ravallion (2019).

[3] Another example of this class of policies is the Conditional Cash Transfer (CCT), which requires that the children of recipients attend school and (in some cases) comply with health-care requirements. CCTs have emerged in a number of developing countries, following early examples such as the *Food-for-Education* (FFE) program in Bangladesh and

conditions tends to rise with income from other sources, which yields the classic 'self-targeting' feature (Ravallion 1991; Besley and Coate 1992). As long as the workfare wage rate is not too high, the non-poor will not seek relief and participants will have an incentive to take up other work when it becomes available. Screening is achieved without explicit targeting. This has long been an important reason for imposing work requirements in settings with limited information about who is in need. The self-targeting aspect does not depend crucially on whether RTW is attainable.

However, other arguments made for workfare depend on the ability to implement the RTW goal. A true RTW policy can provide insurance in settings in which risk markets are imperfect or non-existent. A shock induces participation, which falls in the recovery period. The empirical relationship between rainfall and participation in the MEGS is suggestive of this insurance function, at least in the period in which job guarantee appears to have been honoured (Ravallion et al. 1993).

RTW implemented through workfare can also have general equilibrium effects in supporting a floor to the wage rates for labour generally, including in sectors of the economy where work is not in fact guaranteed (Ravallion 1990). Indeed, India's various employment guarantees can be thought of as means of implementing a minimum wage rate in settings in which this is not otherwise enforceable. As long as work is available when wanted, and labour markets are reasonably competitive, the workfare wage provides a floor to all wages. There is some evidence that states of India where NREGA has worked better (such as in providing work on demand) have seen wage gains (Imbert and Papp 2015).

The potential benefits of implementing RTW through workfare must be balanced against the costs, most notably those generated by the work requirement. There are administrative costs, including supervision on worksites and any non-labour inputs. These costs are more visible than other costs that are no less important for a complete evaluation. While workfare participants may well be underemployed otherwise, they will rarely be idle, especially if poor, as their survival may then be in jeopardy. Poor households can be expected to behave in ways that

---

the *PROGRESA* program (renamed *Oportunidades* and most recently *Prospera*) in Mexico. Fiszbein and Schady (2010) review the literature on CCTs.

attenuate forgone income, such as through the intra-household allocation of work, as shown by Datt and Ravallion (1994) for Maharashtra.
However, there will typically be some forgone income for participants
even when there is widespread underemployment. Dutta et al. (2014)
find that workers on NREGA in Bihar had to give up work days equivalent to 40–45 per cent of the total NREGA employment received.[4]
There are also costs of supervising the labour and providing any materi-
als needed. The costs will undoubtedly vary from one setting or time to
another, with implications for the policy choice and programme design
(Ravallion 1999).

In an early assessment, Ravallion and Datt (1995) found that, once
one takes account of all the costs involved, the labour earnings from the
original Maharashtra scheme are unlikely to have had a higher impact
on current poverty than a universal basic income (UBI).[5] The same conclusion was reached by Murgai et al. (2016) who found that NREGA
in Bihar does not have a higher poverty impact than a revenue-neutral
UBI. The potential of NREGA is great; Dutta et al. (2014) estimate that
if the scheme worked as its designers intended then it would reduce the
rural poverty rate in Bihar by at least 14 per cent points (from 50 per
cent to 36per cent). In reality, however, the impact was around a 1 per
cent point drop in the poverty rate—about what a UBI could do with the
same budget. Both these studies for India found that the self-targeting
feature worked well. The poor performance stemmed instead from: (i)
the failure to assure that everyone who wanted work could get it, and be
paid in a timely way; and (ii) the costs incurred by both recipients and the
government in supervision and implementation (including corruption).
The results of Dutta et al. (2014) suggest that (i) is the dominant factor
reducing performance against poverty relative to the scheme's potential.
So, the following discussion focuses on this.

There has been some research on how NREGA performance might be
improved, suggesting the scope for higher benefits to participating workers, at least in states where the scheme already works reasonably well, such

---

[4] Other evidence on forgone incomes in workfare programs can be
found in Datt and Ravallion (1994) (for Maharashtra India) and Jalan
and Ravallion (2003) and Ravallion et al. (2005) (both for Argentina).

[5] For further discussion of this policy option see Ravallion (2019).

as Andhra Pradesh (AP).[6] Muralidharan et al. (2018) found that the use of biometric 'smartcards' to facilitate NREGA payments to workers in AP increased their earnings, and the benefits also spilled over in the form of higher wages for non-NREGA workers. In a state such as Bihar, where the scheme is not thought to be working as well as (say) AP, the evidence is more mixed. Ravallion et al. (2015) found that a randomized information intervention at village level in Bihar led to higher NREGA wages for illiterate participating workers, but not for other workers, and there was little sign of other gains such as in access to NREGA jobs on demand. Similarly, in a large field-experiment in Bihar that improving administrative processes for NREGA, Banerjee et al. (2020) found that corruption was reduced but there was little increase in the wages and employment of workers.

2.2 Rationing of Work on India's Employment Guarantee Schemes

Many of the potential benefits from using workfare to implement RTW (as discussed in the previous section) require that people can get this work when they need it. The guarantee of work at a stipulated wage rate can be interpreted as a means of implementing a 'living wage' as a labour–market equilibrium in settings in which that is not enforceable as a legal mandate. Then the general equilibrium effects could be large. The guarantee also promises much-needed insurance benefits to poor families. But all this begs a key question: Is the guarantee attainable in poor areas?

The administrative records on NREGA indicate virtually no unmet demand for work on the scheme.[7] This is not believable. What is called 'demand for work' in the administrative data is unlikely to reflect the true

---

[6] A good measure of state-level performance of NREGA is the rationing rate—the share of rural households who wanted work on the scheme but did not get it (Dutta et al., 2012). The rationing rate in AP in 2010 was 25% as compared to 44% nationally. By contrast, the rationing rate in Bihar was 79%.

[7] According to the official Government of India website for MGNREGA (http:\\nrega.nic.in), 53 million households in India demanded work in 2009/10, and 99.4% were provided work.

demand since state and local governments have neither the means not the incentive to identify and report unmet demand. (One reason being that any recorded unmet demand implies that the state government should pay unemployment allowances.)

A better measure of demand for work is obtained by asking people directly, in the privacy of their homes and independently of the scheme. Suitable data for this purpose can be found in the 66th Round of India's National Sample Survey (NSS) for 2009–10. This round included questions on participation and demand for work in NREGA that allow one to estimate demand and rationing rates across states.

This data source reveals extensive rationing. In some states, NREGA appears to conform fairly closely to its designers' intentions, and in those states there may well be larger impacts on wages, and larger insurance benefits.[8] But that is not the norm in much of India. Using the NSS, Dutta et al. (2012, 2014) find evidence of extensive rationing, as determined by asking survey respondents if they wanted work on NREGA but did not get it. Nationally, Dutta et al. find that 44 per cent of those who wanted NREGA work did not get it. This was confirmed in a more recent independent survey by the National Council of Applied Economic Research (NCAER), which found even greater rationing than suggested by the NSS data (Desai et al. 2015).

The existence of this rationing was not news to those who had studied these schemes in the past. For the original Maharashtra scheme, Ravallion et al. (1993) provide an econometric model of the relationship between monthly employment on MEGS and rainfall, and find a large reduction in employment after a doubling in the MEGS wage rate. This is suggestive that the wage hike led to rationing, which appears to have been mainly achieved by selective opening and closing of MEGS worksites.

Another salient observation about NREGA is that the incidence of rationing tends to be greater in poorer states of India, where the scheme is presumably needed the most. This pattern can be seen in Figure 2.1, which plots the incidence of rationing (as a proportion of rural households) against the official poverty rate. The share of rural households rationed ranges from an average of about 10 per cent in the least poor

---

[8] As noted, the findings of Imbert and Papp (2015) suggest that the scheme has had more impact on casual wages in states with more effective implementation.

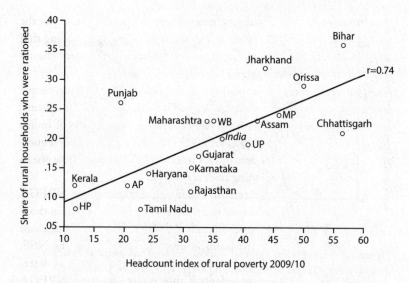

Figure 2.1 Incidence of rationing in India's Employment Guarantee Scheme plotted against the poverty rate across states.
Source: India's National Sample Survey 2010.
AP=Andhra Pradesh; HP=Himachal Pradesh; MP=Madhya Pradesh; UP=Uttar Pradesh; WB=West Bengal

states to around one-in-three in the poorest states.[9] There is a variance at any given poverty rate; for example, with about the same poverty rate, Bihar has more rationing than Chhattisgarh. But the tendency for more rationing in poorer states is evident.

A further point of interest is revealed in Figure 2.2, which plots the NREGA participation rate (share of the state's population of rural households who participate) against demand for NREGA (share of the state-specific population of rural households who want work, some of whom got it while some did not). The scheme only comes into action (in expectation) when demand for work exceeds 17 per cent of rural households (with a standard error of 3 per cent). Thus, while the average participation rate is 0.56, the marginal rate is substantially higher; the regression coefficient is 0.91 (with a robust standard error of 0.09). Rationing appears to be less of a problem at the margin.

[9] Expressing the rationing as a % of those wanting work gives higher numbers of course.

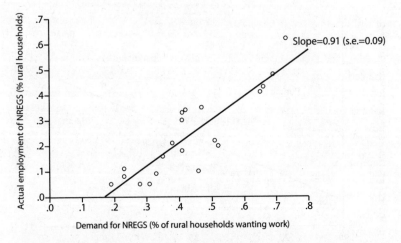

Figure 2.2 There is less sign that workfare jobs are rationed at the margin than on average in India's National Employment Guarantee Scheme
Source: India's National Sample Survey 2010, via Dutta et al. (2014).

The rationing rules found in practice need not work against the interests of poor people. Indeed, there is some evidence that certain groups (such as defined by caste and landlessness) that are associated with above-average poverty rates tend to be favoured in the local rationing process (Drèze and Khera 2011; Dutta et al. 2014). Those with the more typical profile of India's rural poor are less likely to be turned away. Possibly local officials strived for 'pro-poor' targeting so as to help reduce poverty, although that is not the only explanation as we will see soon. The key point for now is that RTW is not being attained in general.

2.3 Administrative Costs with Decentralized Implementation

How might this rationing arise? Inadequate funding by the central government is an obvious reason. If the centre fixes both the wage rate and the overall budget and the latter is inadequate then rationing is likely. This can also take the form of delays to wage payments, which have been reported in the media.[10] This is plainly inconsistent with the objectives

[10] For example, in 2018 civil society groups in India reported substantial delays to the payment of NREGA workers, apparently stemming from inadequate funds made available from the center (The Hindu, 2018).

of the scheme—to provide NREGA work on demand and pay wages in a timely way.

Here the focus will be on explanations for local-level rationing when the center is willing to guarantee RTW. The first explanation relates to local costs of implementation using workfare, while the second relates to local corruption, which is taken up in the next section. Both also suggest how rationing might be reduced.

Implementation of national workfare programmes is often heavily decentralized. This can be hard to avoid in practice and is seen to foster local-level participation in the choices about what work gets done, with the presumption that this will make for better projects. But this mode of delivery also imposes costs on local implementing agents. Some degree of cost-sharing between the central and local governments is considered desirable for incentive reasons. The centre covers a large share of the cost of NREGA, but there are still local costs and these are not always explicit, and are hidden from view in official accounts. Diverting scarce skilled labour in the local-government bureaucracy from other tasks to deal with the center's 'red tape' of reporting and approval requests will entail opportunity costs.

Decentralized implementation should be seen in the relevant institutional context. More systematic assessments have supported the anecdotal observations from field work that there is a chronic underinvestment in local state capacity in India, as evident in under-resourced and overworked local bureaucracies (Dasgupta and Kapur 2017). Also important to the functioning of the scheme at local level is the availability of 'brokers' who can be trusted by local leaders to mediate between them and the various stakeholders, including workers but also local officials and landowners (Witsoe 2012). Local leaders or their close family members often act as money lenders as well as contractors, making advance payments to workers and intervening between the delivery point (often the local post office) and the intended beneficiary.

While it is plausible that the local implementing official incurs a cost per worker employed on the scheme, it is unlikely that the official is indifferent to the amount of unmet demand for work. The local official has the option of not hiring all those who want work, but the official surely does not want to drive employment down to zero. If one is thinking about a local government in a federal system then one can imagine that the local official is either sympathetic with the objectives of the scheme, or that he or she perceives a likely (economic or political) penalty of unmet demand for work. This penalty falls to zero when there is no unmet demand for work but rises with higher unmet demand. It is plausible that the penalty rises more steeply as the excess demand rises; at very high levels of unmet demand the protests may well be vastly greater than at low levels. The local official minimizes the direct cost plus the penalty attached to rationing. Thus, the official sees a trade-off between the cost of employing extra workers under the scheme and the desire to meet the demand for work.

To provide a more formal exposition of this trade-off facing local officials, consider the following model. The central government requests the local government to provide work for all those who want it at the stipulated wage rate. The central government pays the unskilled labour cost (and possibly some other costs). The local official still incurs a cost, and chooses the level of employment E to minimize a generalized cost function subject to the constraint that people cannot be forced to work. (All functions are twice differentiable when required.) The demand for work, D, is taken as given by the official. The average rationing rate is $1 - E/D$ while the marginal rate is $1 - \partial E/\partial D$.

The local official's problem is to choose E to solve:

$$\text{Min } cE + p(D - E) \text{ s.t. } E \leq D \tag{1}$$

where c is the unit cost and the function $p(.)$ penalizes the unmet demand for work (as discussed earlier). It is assumed that the penalty function is strictly increasing and convex with $p(0) = 0$. Let E^* denote the level of employment such that:

$$p'(D - E^*) = c \tag{2}$$

Inverting (2) we have:

$$E^* = D - f(c) \tag{3}$$

where $f(.)$ is the inverse function of $p'(.)$. The value of $f(c)$ gives the minimum level of demand for work before the government will begin to hire any workers. It is readily verified that $f(c) > 0$ and $f'(c) = \dfrac{1}{p''(c)} > 0$. If there is rationing in equilibrium then it will be in the amount $f(c)$. Above this, the marginal rate of rationing is zero (though that will change when corruption is introduced in the next section).

The local government may comply with the center's request to guarantee employment even though the local government incurs a share of the cost. But the share cannot exceed a critical value. One can distinguish two regimes: In Regime 1 we have:

$$c \le c^* \equiv p(f(c))/f(c) \qquad (4)$$

Then the local government official will choose to comply with the central dictate to employ all those who want work, noting that (4) implies that the cost of compliance, cD, is no greater than the minimum cost of rationing, $E^* + p(D - E^*)$.

By contrast, in Regime 2, $c > c^*$. Then the unit cost facing the local official is sufficiently high for rationing to emerge in equilibrium, in that the cost of employing E^* workers is less than the cost of employing all those who want work. Then E^* is the official's optimal level of employment to be provided and there will be unmet demand in equilibrium, in that $E^* < D$ with $f(c)$ workers rationed. A reduction in the unit cost will increase employment and reduce the overall rationing rate.

The upshot of this argument is that local costs of implementation imply that rationing can emerge as an equilibrium outcome in a scheme such as NREGA even when the central government makes an open-ended commitment for funding a large share of the cost. Above some critical level of the local unit cost of employment, rationing emerges. However, and importantly for policy, the rationing rate (as a proportion of demand) is likely to be lower at the margin than on average, so the average rate will tend to fall as demand increases.

Reducing local administrative costs (including enhancing the capacity and productivity of local administrators) will make RTW more feasible in this type of scheme. Alternatively, a similar outcome may be possible through some form of results-based payment to implementing agents, whereby the center rewards (verifiable) success in accommodating the demand for work locally. However, we must also consider the scope for corruption and the role of central efforts to fight corruption.

2.4 Corrupting the Right-to-Work

The administrative challenges in implementing RTW through workfare come with scope for corruption. It is not too surprising that we often hear in the Indian press about (for example) Bihar's 'millionaire Mukhiyas' (Gupta 2013).[11] Less obviously, as we will see, central governmental efforts to fight corruption can have perverse effects—increasing the amount of rationing and so further undermining RTW. Deeper reforms are needed.

At first glance, corruption is probably not an intuitively obvious reason for rationing. If corrupt officials can skim off their 10 per cent (say) from workfare participants then they will still have an incentive to provide work to all who want it. The model of corruption in a programme like NREGA may, however, be more complex than suggested by a fixed-share rule.

One can illustrate this by augmenting the model of decentralized administration in Section 2.3 to allow for corruption. It is still assumed that local official chooses the level of employment she wants to provide, given an exogenous demand for work on the scheme. There is a pecuniary benefit to the official that naturally depends on the level of employment. We can think of this as the official's cut on the wages paid. But there is also a cost facing the local official. This includes the side-payments that the official must make to cooperating agents, and the cost must factor in the risk of getting caught and the penalty then incurred. The total expected cost of corruption rises with the number of workers employed, as this will require opening more work sites and higher payments to 'ghost workers', with further side payments required to cooperating workers and officials, and higher risks of exposure. It is also likely that the expected marginal cost of corruption facing the official will rise as employment rises. The local official may have to expand the set of people he bribes beyond his own 'comfort zone' of those he trusts, and even those he trusts will face greater risk of exposure at larger scale, and so require higher compensation.

The marginal cost of providing extra employment now includes the expected marginal cost of corruption as well as the local administrative cost already discussed. The ideal level of employment from the perspective of the local official equates the total marginal cost (MC) with the marginal benefit (MB), as illustrated in Figure 2.3. If this turns

---

[11] "Mukhiya" is the local name for village leaders.

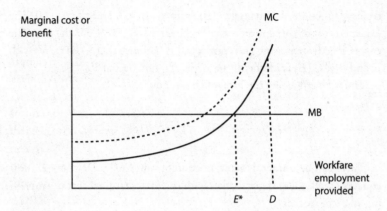

Figure 2.3   Local officials facing a steeply increasing marginal cost of corruption

out to be less than the number who want work then rationing arises in equilibrium.

To provide a more formal exposition, let us assume that the official can extract an illegal 'rent' from NREGA of r per worker employed, but the official faces an expected cost of doing so that depends on the probability of getting caught and the fine incurred (including the cost of jail term in some cases). When the official is 'on the take' in a specific NREGA project this is more-or-less observable to those employed on the project. For example, the workers can see that a digging machine had been brought in overnight (against the rules of NREGA) or the workers agree to be 'ghost workers', who sign up but do not do any work. Thus, there is a risk of being caught due to local informants. We can imagine that the official has greater trust for some people within the relevant village(s) than others. The level of trust varies across people exogenously according to past socio-economic connections (including caste). Workers can be taken to be otherwise identical, so the official hires the most trusted first among those who want work. At low E the official is among a safe group of highly trusted 'friends'. However, the marginal effect of hiring extra workers on the probability of getting caught rises sharply at higher levels of employment when the official gets well outside her trusted circle.

In short, we can assume that trustworthiness of E workers, and (hence) the probability of getting away with the corrupt activity, is a decreasing concave function of E, namely, $\tau(E)$, with $\tau'(E) < 0$ and $\tau''(E) < 0$. The expected cost of corruption is $C(E) = [1 - \tau(E)]F$, where F is the fine. The cost is strictly increasing and convex in E.[12] (Notice that $C(E)$ varies with F, and that $C'(E)$ is implicitly an increasing function of F.)

The problem facing the local official is now:

$$\text{Max } (r-c)E - C(E) - p(D-E) \text{ s.t. } E \leq D \tag{5}$$

There can be unmet demand in equilibrium if $E^* < D$, where E^* now equates the illegal rent per worker with the total marginal cost of employing an extra worker:

$$r = C'(E^*) + c - p'(D - E^*) \tag{6}$$

This is illustrated in Figure 3 where $MB \equiv r$ and $MC \equiv C'(E)$ $c - p'(D - E)$. Notice that, with this addition to the model, there will now be rationing at the margin, since:

$$0 < \frac{\partial E^*}{\partial D} = \frac{1}{1 + C''(.)/p''(.)} < 1 \tag{7}$$

Suppose now that the central or state government tries to clamp down on local corruption by (*inter alia*) imposing higher fines, or with extra auditing/policing and/or more transparent record keeping, implying a higher probability of being caught. This can be interpreted as a shift in the expected marginal cost of corruption facing the local official. In the "trust" example above, we have $C'(E) = -\tau'(E)F$, which is an increasing function of the fine. Then, for this case, it is readily verified that:

$$\frac{\partial E^*}{\partial F} = \frac{\tau'(E^*)}{p''(.) - \tau''(.)F} < 0 \tag{8}$$

[12] A more general model would allow r to be chosen by an official facing a cost of corruption $C(E, r)$. One might assume that $C_r > 0$, $C_{rr} > 0$ and that $0 < C_{rE} < 1$. Then the optimal r is an increasing function of E^*.

The upshot of these observations is that clamping down on local corruption in a neighborhood of the equilibrium will decrease employment and increase rationing—making RTW harder to attain, as can be seen from the shift in the MC curve in Figure 2.3. High levels of rationing in poorer states (as in Figure 2.1) may thus reflect central and state government efforts to clamp down on corruption in poor places.

On combining local administrative costs with corruption we can now understand the ambiguity of partial reform efforts. Note that a reform that simultaneously shifted up $C'(E)$ while reducing the local administrative cost, c, by the same amount would leave E^* unchanged. The benefits to workers of a reform that reduces local administrative costs can evaporate when the reform also increases the expected marginal cost of corruption facing local officials. This offers an interpretation of the Banerjee et al. (2020) finding for Bihar that better administrative processes for NREGA reduced corruption but did little to increase the wages and employment of workers. The reforms in this experiment essentially combined a lower local administrative cost with a higher expected marginal cost of corruption facing local officials. Corruption fell but employment did not change indicating that the rationing largely remained.

There is likely to be heterogeneity in the cost of corruption facing a local official, depending on characteristics of workers. Suppose, for example, that literate and/or higher-caste workers are more likely to complain about an official's corrupt rent-seeking efforts, with implications for the probability of the official getting caught. In particular, suppose that the expected MC of corruption is higher for such workers. Then, of course, the official will tend to favor other, more acquiescent, workers in deciding how to assign employment. Thus, one can also understand why Dutta et al. (2014) find that the implicit rationing rules in Bihar's NREGA tended to favour workers with the more typical profile of the poor, and we can understand this finding without believing that the officials are trying to reduce poverty.

***

A 'right-to-work' policy implemented through public employment can seem an attractive option when poor people face risky environments, high unemployment rates, the reliable information for targeting is limited, and there is much useful work to do in poor areas. Realizing that potential is another matter. The self-targeting feature is plausible and consistent with the evidence. But it is far from obvious that this will be the best way to reduce poverty—taking freedom from poverty to be the overarching right—once one considers all the costs involved. These include implementation costs, pecuniary costs to the participants in the form of forgone earnings (which can exist even for underemployed workers) and the welfare loss from the work requirement relative to unconditional transfers (Murgai et al. 2016; Alik-Lagrange and Ravallion 2018).

The chapter has reviewed evidence for India suggesting that the country's Employment Guarantee Schemes have been less cost effective in reducing current poverty through the earnings gains to workers than one would expect from even untargeted transfers, as in a UBI. This calculation could switch in favour of workfare schemes if they can produce assets of value (directly or indirectly) to poor people, though the evidence is mixed on this aspect of the schemes so far in India. The Indian experience also suggests diverse performance across states of its Employment Guarantee Schemes. It is worrying that the schemes tend to work less well in poorer states, where they are probably needed more. Arguably that is not too surprising, as the same factors that make a place poor impede efforts to change.

The chapter tries to understand how this happens. It is argued that local rationing of the work opportunities provided by these schemes in poor areas can readily arise from the existence of (often latent) local administrative costs in implementation and from the partial means used by the centre to fight local corruption. The main concern with rationing is not that it undermines pro-poor targeting; indeed, that is not implied by the model of local corruption used here, and nor is it consistent with the evidence for India. However, rationing undermines the gains to poor people from the employment guarantee, including its insurance and empowerment benefits. Scaling up may well help; indeed, with local administrative costs, the marginal rationing rate will tend to be lower than the average rate.

With decentralized implementation of the RTW, rationing can emerge in equilibrium given the local costs of employing workers and the scope for corruption. The RTW need not be feasible. Nonetheless, the share of demand that is rationed may well diminish as the scheme expands. The data for India are consistent with the prediction of the theoretical model that the rationing rate at the margin will be less than the average rate. By implication, the insurance and other benefits of the work guarantee will tend to emerge as the scheme expands above some point. Those benefits will also rise if local implementation costs are reduced. However, combining a lower local administrative cost with anti-corruption reforms that increase the expected marginal cost of corruption need not help attain RTW.

The chapter has also shown that anti-corruption efforts and administrative reforms from the centre can have ambiguous effects on the extent to which RTW can be achieved in practice. Raising the expected marginal cost of corruption facing local officials is likely to reduce the extent to which employment is available to those who need it. Cutting local administrative costs can help, but when this is achieved within a reform that also raises the marginal cost of corruption facing local officials (such as by making record-keeping and reporting more transparent as well as easier) there may be little net gain to workers in terms of attaining RTW. Assuring that local agents do not have the power to ration work would appear to require a deeper local institutional reform. 'Social audits'—open village meetings fostering public disclosure of concerns—could help, backed up by credible public procedures for responding to grievances (Dutta et al. 2014).

References

Alik-Lagrange, Arthur, and Martin Ravallion (2018). 'Workfare versus Transfers in Rural India', *World Development*, 112: 244–58.

Banerjee, Abhijit, Esther Duflo, Clement Imbert, Santhosh Mathew, and Rohini Pande (2020). 'E-governance, Accountability, and Leakage in Public Programs: Experimental Evidence from a Financial Management Reform in India', *American Economic Journal: Applied Economics*, forthcoming.

Besley, Timothy and Stephen Coate (1992). 'Workfare vs. Welfare: Incentive Arguments for Work Requirements in Poverty Alleviation Programs', *American Economic Review*, 82(1): 249–61.

Dasgupta, Aditya, and Devesh Kapur (2017). 'The Political Economy of Bureaucratic Effectiveness: Evidence from Local Rural Development Officials in India'.

Datt, Gaurav, and Martin Ravallion (1994). 'Transfer Benefits from Public-Works Employment', *Economic Journal*, 104: 1346–69.

Desai, Sonalde, Prem Vashishtha, and Omkar Joshi (2015). *Mahatma Gandhi National Rural Employment Guarantee Act: A Catalyst for Rural Transformation*, New Delhi: National Council of Applied Economic Research.

Drèze, Jean and Reetika Khera (2011). 'Employment Guarantee and the Right to Work', in Reetika Khera (ed.) *The Battle for Employment Guarantee*, New Delhi: Oxford University Press.

Dutta, Puja, Rinku Murgai, Martin Ravallion, and Dominique van de Walle (2012). 'Does India's Employment Guarantee Scheme Guarantee Employment?', *Economic and Political Weekly*, 48 (April 21): 55–64.

——— (2014), *Right to Work? Assessing India's Employment Guarantee Scheme in Bihar*. Washington DC: World Bank.

Fiszbein, Ariel and Norbert Schady (2010). *Conditional Cash Transfers for Attacking Present and Future Poverty*, World Bank, Washington, DC.

Fleischacker, Samuel (2004). *A Short History of Distributive Justice*. Cambridge MA: Harvard University Press.

Gaiha, Raghav (1997). 'Rural Public Works and the Poor: The Case of the Employment

Guarantee Scheme in India'. In S. Polachek (ed.) *Research in Labour Economics*, Connecticut: JAI Press.

Gupta, Alok (2013). 'Millionaire Mukhiyas', Blog Post, Down to Earth.

The Hindu (2018). '99% of MGREGA Wages Remain Unpaid', April 12.

Imbert, Clement and John Papp (2015), 'Estimating Leakages in India's Employment Guarantee'. In Reetika Khera (ed.) *The Battle for Employment Guarantee*, New Delhi: Oxford University Press.

——— (2015). 'Labor Market Effects of Social Programs: Evidence from India's Employment Guarantee,"' *American Economic Journal: Applied Economics*, 7(2): 233–63.

Jha, Raghbendra, Sambit Bhattacharyya, Raghav Gaiha, and Shylashri Shankar (2009). 'Capture' of Anti-Poverty Programs: An Analysis of the National Rural Employment Guarantee Program in India', *Journal of Asian Economics*, 20(4): 456–64.

Jha, Raghbendra, Raghav Gaiha, Manoj K. Pandey (2012). 'Net Transfer Benefits under India's Rural Employment Guarantee Scheme', *Journal of Policy Modeling*, 34(2): 296–311.

Mansuri, Ghazala and Vijayendra Rao (2012). *Localizing Development: Does Participation Work?* Washington, DC: World Bank.

Muralidharan, Karthik, Paul Niehaus, and Sandip Sukhtankar (2018). 'General Equilibrium Effects of (Improving) Public Employment Programs: Experimental Evidence from India', San Diego: University of California.

Murgai, Rinku, Martin Ravallion, and Dominique van de Walle (2016). 'Is Workfare Cost Effective against Poverty in a Poor Labor-Surplus Economy?', *World Bank Economic Review*, 30(3): 413–45.

Myers-Lipton, Scott (2015). *Ending Extreme Inequality: An Economic Bill of Rights to Eliminate Poverty*. London and New York: Routledge.

Narayanan, Sudha, Krushna Ranaware, Upasak Das, and Ashwini Kulkarni (2015). 'MGNREGA Works and their Impact: A Study of Maharashtra', *Economic and Political Weekly*, 50(13): 53–61.

Paul, Mark, William Darity Jr., and Darrick Hamilton (2017). 'Why we Need a Federal Job Guarantee', Jacobin.

Ravallion, Martin (1990). 'Anti-Hunger Policies in Market Economies: Effects on Wages, Prices and Employment'. In Jean Drèze and Amartya Sen (eds), *The Political Economy of Hunger*, Oxford: Oxford University Press.

——— (1991). 'Reaching the Rural Poor through Public Employment: Arguments, Experience and Lessons from South Asia', *World Bank Research Observer*, 6: 153–75.

——— (1999). 'Appraising Workfare', *World Bank Research Observer*, 14: 31–48.

——— (2016). *The Economics of Poverty: History, Measurement and Policy*, Oxford and New York: Oxford University Press.

——— (2019). 'Guaranteed Employment or Guaranteed Income?' *World Development*, 115: 209–21.

Ravallion, Martin and Gaurav Datt (1995), 'Is Targeting Through a Work Requirement Efficient? Some Evidence for Rural India'. In Dominique de Walle and Kimberly Nead (eds), *Public Spending and the Poor: Theory and Evidence*. Baltimore: Johns Hopkins University Press.

Ravallion, Martin, Gaurav Datt, and Shubham Chaudhuri (1993). 'Does Maharashtra's "Employment Guarantee Scheme" Guarantee Employment? Effects of the 1988 Wage Increase', *Economic Development and Cultural Change* 41: 251–75.

Ravallion, Martin, Emanela Galasso, Teodoro Lazo, and Ernesto Philipp (2005). 'What Can Ex-Participants Reveal about a Program's Impact?', *Journal of Human Resources* 40: 208–30.

Ravallion, Martin, Dominique van de Walle, Puja Dutta, and Rinku Murgai (2015). 'Empowering Poor People through Public Information? Lessons from a Movie in Rural India', *Journal of Public Economics*, 132: 13–22.

Ravi, Shamika, and Monika Engler (2015). 'Workfare as an Effective Way to Fight Poverty: The Case of India's NREGA', *World Development*, 67: 57–71.

United Nations (UN) (2006). *Right to Work: Article 6 of the International Covenant on Economic, Social and Cultural Rights*, Economic and Social Council, United Nations.

Verma, Shilp (2011). *MGNREGA Assets and Rural Water Security: Synthesis of Field Studies in Bihar, Gujarat, Kerala and Rajasthan*, Anand: International Water Management Institute (IWMI).

Witsoe, Jeffrey (2012). 'Everyday Corruption and the Political Mediation of the Indian State', *Economic and Political Weekly*, 47(6): 47–54.

World Bank (2011). *Poverty and Social Exclusion in India*, Washington, DC: World Bank.

3 When Are Cash Transfers Transformative?

BRUCE WYDICK

'In India, apart from its anti-poverty potential, (a basic minimum income) can be a substantial measure to improve autonomy and dignity by giving workers an escape ladder from socially despised occupations.'

—Pranab Bardhan, *Times of India*, 3 May 2017.

Perhaps unknown at the time, the 1997 introduction of Mexico's *Progresa* cash transfer programme became a watershed moment for both economic development and development economics. *Progresa* began cash transfers to low-income Mexican households conditional upon children's enrollment in school, regular check-ups at health clinics, and attending nutritional education meetings. During the early phase-in of *Progresa* in 1998, the government randomly chose 320 treated villages while 185 acted as controls that were phased in two years later, greatly facilitating the early identification of large treatment effects on education (Schultz 2004) and health (Gertler 2004).[1]

The demonstrated impacts of *Progresa* on the well-being of the poor inspired its sweeping replication across Latin America.[2] In 2002 alone, Colombia initiated the conditional cash transfer (CCT) programme *Familias en Acción*, Chile introduced *Chile Solidario*, and Brazilian President Fernando Henrique Cardoso scaled up *Bolsa Escola*, previously introduced only in Brasília by governor Cristovam Buarque, to create the largest CCT programme today, *Bolsa Familia*. Honorati et al. (2015) identify 63 countries with CCT programs, as well as 130 low- and middle-income countries that have now implemented unconditional cash transfer (UCT) programmes, in which cash is transferred to eligible segments of the population without conditions upon behaviours (Bastagli et al. 2016). The rapid spread of cash transfer programmes has helped spur the argument for a basic minimum income (BMI) (sometimes called universal basic income or UBI) that would provide a minimum cash grant to all citizens of a country.

Accompanying the rapid spread of cash transfer programmes has been an extensive empirical literature seeking to ascertain the impacts of CCT and UCT programmes on poverty alleviation more generally, and in specific domains such as education, health, and labour activity. But with the movement of development economics towards empirical research, a theoretical framework for understanding the impacts of cash transfers is not as well developed as its empirical counterpart. While reduced-form causal econometrics excels at identifying net effects of cash transfers, it is less helpful at helping policymakers to understand why cash transfers, varying in type and context, exhibit heterogeneous effects on recipient behaviour.

This has made it more difficult to assess some of the controversies related to cash transfers, such as questions over whether they disincentivize

---

[1] A comprehensive review of the benefits of the programme and its impacts is Parker and Todd (2017).

[2] As a national-level conditional cash transfer program (CCT), *Progresa* was preceded only by the 1994 introduction of the Female Secondary School Assistance Project in Pakistan.

work, foster consumption at the expense of savings, and increase expenditures on 'temptation goods' such as alcohol and cigarettes. For example, while an analysis of formal cash transfer programmes in developing countries fails to uncover any evidence of increases in temptation good expenditures (Evans and Popova 2017) or decreases in work (Banerjee et al. 2015), other evidence indicates that in the US a large percentage of the cash transferred to the poor on the street is spent on temptation goods (Lee and Farrell 2003) and that cash transfers inherent to US welfare programmes decrease work incentives (Hoynes et al. 2012). What might account for these apparent contradictions? Perhaps most importantly, when might we expect cash transfers, rather than disincentiving work, instead to facilitate investments that create permanent increases in future income, and in this sense to be 'transformative' in moving recipients out of poverty?

Here I offer a review of the empirical evidence on the effects of cash transfers, and then a framework to address these questions in the development of a simple neoclassical model that points to the conditions under which cash transfers are likely to be transformative. Subsequently, I propose some extensions to the model from the perspective of behavioural economics to consider how these predictions may change given different assumptions about the behaviour of cash transfer recipients. Specifically, I consider cases in which rates of time preference are endogenous to first-period consumption, when cognitive capabilities and executive control are constrained by poverty, and then where preferences are shaped not by standard neoclassical utility, but by aspirations.

3.1 The Impacts of Cash Transfers: A Review of Empirical Evidence

An enormous research effort over the last decade has documented the impact of cash transfers on different measures of welfare and economic well-being. These include impacts on consumption and other general poverty measures, children's schooling, child and maternal health, and labour market outcomes. They include evaluations of randomized controlled trials in which inference is derived from experimental data as well as quasi-experimental studies which make use of natural experiments and other phenomena to isolate the impact of cash transfers on dependent variables. Fiszbein and Shady (2009) provide a comprehensive summary of early evidence for positive impacts across consumption, schooling, and health. While impacts vary across research designs and across world regions, the volume of this and subsequent research, and several carefully executed meta-studies, has allowed for some identification of distinguishable patterns of impact from CCTs and UCTs across the impact variables mentioned earlier.

Impacts on Poverty, Income, and Consumption

While CCTs are typically designed to incentivize particular economic behaviors related to the health and education of children, the cash transfer itself provides a benefit to households designed to facilitate movement out of poverty. As a result, CCT programmes exhibit substitution effects on economic behaviour in that they increase the opportunity cost of child labour by providing monetary rewards for child schooling. But like UCT programmes, they also create income affects from the cash grants themselves, which will tend to promote the consumption of a wide class of normal goods. In contrast, UCT programmes exhibit only income effects, and they are implemented with poverty reduction goals specifically. What does the evidence say about the impact of cash transfers on basic measures of poverty reduction?

It would seem that consumption should increase with any type of cash transfer, but it is conceivable that potential increases in children's schooling with CCTs may be offset by losses in income from child labour and from additional schooling costs. Hagen-Zanker et al. (2011) present a meta-study of 37 employment guarantee schemes (EGSs), UCT programmes, and CCT programmes, of which 18 measure changes in household income, consumption, and poverty reduction. Of these 18 programmes, 17 indicate reductions in poverty, although most of the studies did not report statistical significance to estimates. CCT programmes in their analysis consistently (although not universally) increase household income and consumption, where they also find that across studies, the cash transfer programmes consistently outperformed EGSs in each of these areas.

In addition, Kabeer et al. (2012) carry out a meta-study of 46 evaluations of 11 CCT programmes in Latin America. Similarly, they find that across Latin America, CCT programmes significantly boost food and non-food consumption, most especially in studies by Gitter and Caldes (2010) in Nicaragua, Attanasio et al. (2006) in Colombia, and by Angelucci and Attanasio (2006), Hoddinot and Skoufias (2004), and Gertler et al. (2012) in Mexico through *Oportunidades/Progresa*. Overall, Kabeer et al. (2012) find that CCTs increased household consumption by about 7 per cent across seven high-quality programme evaluations. Especially in Latin America, the evidence is overwhelming that cash transfer programmes, at least while recipients continue to receive transfers, reduce poverty.

Haushofer and Shapiro (2016) study the impacts of the GiveDirectly UCT intervention on 1,372 households in Kenya. Here the authors analyse treated households in treated communities and untreated households in treated communities relative to a sample of pure control households. They also randomize the magnitude of the UCT (US$404 vs. US$1,525), the timing of the transfer (one-month installments over nine months vs. a one-time transfer), and whether the transfer was given to the wife or husband of a household. The Haushofer and Shapiro study has offered some of the most convincing evidence for big, short-term impacts from cash transfers, finding a US$36 increase in monthly non-durable consumption over a baseline control mean of US$158. Perhaps most importantly, they find asset holdings increased by US$302 from US$495, increasing the income stream from animal husbandry and agriculture by US$16 (over a control group mean of US$49). Notably, the impact on consumption from the large transfer treatment was nearly 50 per cent higher than the impact of small transfers, but the impact for large transfers on asset accumulation was nearly double, making the marginal expenditure on investment greater as transfers increased. The transfers also realized positive psychological effects on the well-being of transfer recipients: a 0.16 s.d. increase in happiness, a 0.17 s.d. increase in life satisfaction, and a 0.26 s.d. reduction in stress.

A concern commonly voiced with cash transfer programmes is that they facilitate increases in spending on 'temptation goods', such as alcohol and tobacco. Studies of the homeless in North America indicate that a substantial fraction of the cash transfers received by panhandlers from altruistic donors on the street is spent on tobacco, alcohol, and narcotics (Lee and Farrell 2003; *San Francisco Chronicle* 2013). Using survey data from a random sample of panhandlers in Toronto, Bose and Hwang (2002) estimate, that from the $638 average monthly income in their sample (about half of which is obtained through panhandling) $200 is spent on food, $112 is spent on tobacco, and $80 on alcohol and narcotics. The New Leaf project in Vancouver provides some preliminary evidence from a randomized trial that larger cash transfers may actually reduce spending on temptation goods. Among 100 homeless adults that took part in the pilot study, those receiving cash transfers of $7,500 decreased expenditures on cigarettes, alcohol, and illegal drugs, by 39 per cent, while increasing expenditures on clothing, rent, and food (*Foundations for Social Change* 2020). But while this stereotype of mis-spent cash appears to have some backing in the data among the North American homeless, it is not borne out empirically from cash transfers that occur in the developing world.

Evans and Popova (2017) note that changes in spending on temptation goods may be affected through several channels: an income effect (more income may lead to increased purchases of all normal goods), a substitution effect (the incentives for schooling investment in a CCT should move consumption away from temptation goods) the labelling effect (where governments overtly discourage the use of cash transfers for temptation goods), and a household bargaining effect (where cash transfers directed towards mothers may reduce temptation good spending by fathers). Evans and Popova conduct a meta-study on 50 estimates from 19 countries, finding virtually no evidence of increased average spending on temptation goods resulting from cash transfers. Indeed, point estimates in the study consistently indicate a *decrease* in expenditures on alcohol and tobacco, where this decrease is statistically significant for the subset of Latin American countries. This result holds true for a number of robustness checks, including limiting the study to seven especially high-quality randomized trials. It seems possible then that in some contexts, small cash transfers may be used to medicate feelings of hopelessness, while larger transfers may be directed towards more fruitful ends.

Impacts on Labour Market Activity

Another common concern related to cash transfer programmes is that they reduce participation in the labour market, that is, they discourage work. Like spending on temptation goods, these concerns stem not just from stereotypes of welfare recipients in the US and other industrialized countries, but from studies which have documented such an effect. Cole and Ohanian (2002) find a negative effect on willingness to work in the post-War years from the generous cash transfer programme contained in the British dole. Hoynes et al. (2012) use county-level difference-in-difference estimation on data from the Panel Study of Income Dynamics

(PSID) from 1968–1978 to examine US food stamp programme (FSP) impacts on labour supply, earnings, and income. Their results indicate modest reductions in both employment and hours worked as a result of food stamp programme introduction, where impacts are larger on female-headed households. The authors find no significant impacts of the FSP on earnings or family income. These results are consistent with a set of earlier studies summarized in a review by Moffit (2002) that show modest but significant reductions in labour market participation in a majority of studies from the impact of US welfare programmes.[3]

Perhaps more noteworthy is evidence showing that negative effects in the labour market from US cash transfers exhibit protracted effects. Price and Song (2018) report on the long-term effects of the 1970s Seattle-Denver Income Maintenance Experiment, which gave thousands of randomly selected families a guaranteed annual income of $26,000 for 3–5 years. In response to the programme, they show that adult work hours dropped by 12 per cent, and the households earned $1,600 less per year than households that didn't receive the free income. More disconcertingly, recipient households continued to earn $1,800 less per year decades after the experiment ended (although there were no discernible impacts on recipients' children). Such results indicate 'transformative' effects from sustained cash transfers, but in a direction in which participation in the economy is discouraged rather than enhanced.

Similar to expenditures on temptation goods, the effect of cash transfers on disincentives to work does not seem to extend to low- and middle-income countries. In a review of seven RCTs on cash transfer programmes in six developing countries,[4] Banerjee et al. (2015) discover no evidence from cash transfer programmes on either the propensity to work outside the household or the overall number of hours worked for either men or women. Why there exist such notable differences in the effects of cash transfer programmes on labour market activity between industrialized countries and developing counties is an unresolved question and a compelling topic for research.

[3] The Jones and Marinescu (2018) study of cash transfers from the Alaska Permanent Fund provides evidence that partially contradicts these results, finding that the general equilibrium effects of cash transfers are neutral on labor supply.

[4] The seven programmes included Honduras' PRAF II, Morocco's Tayssir, Mexico's Progresa and PAL, Philippines' PPPP, Indonesia's PKH, and Nicaragua's RPS.

Impacts on Education

Increasing schooling levels among children is a primary goal of most CCTs. In a meta-analysis Saavedra and Garcia (2012) study the effect of CCT programmes on schooling outcomes across 42 studies from programmes in 19 developing countries, 12 in Latin America, six in Asia and one in Africa, where they find a positive and statistically significant effect of CCT programmes on enrollment and attendance in both primary and secondary education. Increases in enrollment are about 6 percentage points for both, but relative effects are considerably larger for secondary education because baseline levels of enrollment are much higher in primary education (84 per cent) than in secondary education (59 per cent). Results for school attendance also show a significant difference, a 3 per cent increase for primary school and a 12 per cent increase for secondary school. Importantly, Saavedra and Garcia also find that impacts are increasing in the size of the transfer; larger transfers augment increases in school enrollment and attendance.

Baird et al.'s (2013) meta-study on the impacts of both CCT and UCT programmes on schooling enrollment from 75 studies cover 35 cash transfer programmes worldwide, 19 programmes in Latin America and the Caribbean, eight programmes in Asia, and eight programmes in Africa. The studies they incorporate include five UCTs, 26 CCTs, and four that provide comparisons between the two. They find unequivocally positive impacts on schooling enrollment, where household participation in a CCT programme increases the statistical odds of a child being enrolled in school by 41 per cent. The effect of UCT programmes on enrollment is smaller, a 23 per cent increase in the odds of enrollment, but still highly significant. The difference between UCTs and CCTs is statistically insignificant, but they find much larger effects (a 60 per cent increase in the odds of enrollment) for CCT programmes that have strong monitoring systems to ensure compliance with school enrollment of children. Although school enrollments are higher as a result of cash transfer programmes, the authors do not find improvements in school test scores.

There is other evidence that larger transfers are more likely to have bigger impacts on schooling. Using a natural experiment in which the *Oportunidades* CCT programme increased the average grant in middle and high school in 2009 by about 30 per cent in 263 of 630 urban localities in Mexico, Araujo et al. (2018) find that students in the Mexican households with access to the larger grants exhibited lower dropout rates during middle school, and then increased secondary school completion by about 33 per cent. Moreover, they find the expected income from this additional schooling to be more than double the cost of the CCT. Akee et al. (2010) study the impact of cash transfers in the United States among Eastern Cherokee reservation families receiving an average of $4,000 per person every year from casino profit-sharing. Relative to their non-Native American neighbours, they find that the cash transfers (implicitly a UCT) caused the Cherokee children to complete an average of one additional year of education. Both CCTs and UCTs are likely to exhibit bigger impacts on school: Larger CCTs more strongly incentivize schooling relative to child labour, and the augmentation of both types of transfers creates an income effect in the present that permits households to invest in future consumption.

Impacts on Health and Nutrition

There is substantial evidence that both CCTs and UCTs improve health. Gertler (2004) finds positive impacts on a number of health measures on children born during this time to families benefiting from the *Progresa* transfers. The rate of illness from children born in programme villages during this two-year period was 25.3 per cent lower than that of children born in control villages, and children born in the three years before the programme was phased in experienced a 39.5 per cent reduction in reported illness. The programme also appears to have reduced stunting. Remarkably, Gertler reports children born in program villages grew approximately 1 cm more during the first year of the programme alone. For example, Chakrabarti et al., (2020) find insignificant impacts on child height from an evaluation of the Zambia Child Grant Program.

Some of the health benefits from *Progresa* are likely to accrue through the impact of cash transfers on improved diet. Angelucci and de Georgi (2009) estimate that *Progresa* increased food expenditures by 30 pesos over a baseline of 154 pesos for households eligible for the programme in treated villages. The programme also increased consumption among *ineligible* households in treated villages by 19 pesos over a 201-peso baseline, illustrating the importance of spillover effects to the programme. Caloric intake also increased for specific foods including chicken and beef, milk, and an array of vegetables.

Early results on the health effects of *Progresa* cash transfers have been externally validated in work that has studied other CCT programmes. Guanais (2015) finds that increasing coverage of cash transfers under *Bolsa Familia* were key to reducing infant mortality when combined with the Brazilian government's family health programme. Using data from the *PANES* cash transfer programme[5] in Uruguay, Amarante et al. (2016) find that *PANES* led to a significant reduction in instances of low birthweight, results attributed to faster intrauterine growth. In a meta-study covering research on 13 CCTs, Meghna and Lagarde (2012) conclude that CCTs have been highly effective in fostering the use of preventive services, improving immunization coverage, a number of standard health outcomes, and in encouraging healthy behaviours.

Long-term Effects of Cash Transfers

The aggregated results on the effect of cash transfers overwhelmingly indicate significant impacts on schooling and health during the time a household is receiving them. But whether or not these positive impacts have long-term transformative effects—and under what conditions—is a question that is less settled and remains an active subject of research. There is mixed evidence that the short-term positive effects on schooling and health, especially for UCTs, endure when the cash transfers end.

Evidence for longer-term impacts is greater for CCT programmes such as *Progresa*. Behrman et al. (2011) find that impacts on schooling from the programme had lasting effects among children who had stronger exposure to the *Progresa* cash transfers 10 years later. Gertler et al. (2012) studies the programme's long-term impact on consumption and the relationship of this increase in consumption to investment in productive activities. They find that for every peso transferred to a low-income household in Mexico, about 74 centavos are consumed and 26 are invested in income-generating activity. Gertler et al. (2012) demonstrate how this investment in income-generating activity from the transfers appears to yield long-run increases in consumption: Five years after the initial programme rollout, consumption among treated households was 42 pesos per month higher

---

[5] *PANES* was originally conceived as a CCT programme, but because the government at the time of the research did not enforce conditionality, it can be viewed as a *de facto* UCT programme.

than the 160-peso baseline among control households. Nine years later, monthly household consumption among participant households had grown by 54 pesos relative to the control. They connect this long-run increase in consumption to the higher levels of investment that occur through the fraction of the monthly transfer. The end result they find is sustainably higher levels of consumption, believed to be permanent even when households stop receiving the transfers. Parker and Vogl (2018) execute a long-term evaluation of Oportunidades to ascertain the extent to which transfers affected measures of poverty and development in the next generation, who were of school age when transfers began. They find that early beneficiaries of the transfers completed 1.4 years of schooling over the control group, increasing labour market participation by women female beneficiaries by 7–11 percentage points while labour earnings increased by US$30-40 per month—about half of average earnings in the control cohorts. Parker and Vogl (2018) find effects on male labour outcomes to be somewhat lower, but still positive and significant. Thus, especially for females, the evidence obtained from Oportunidades/ Progresa/Prospera indeed weighs in favour of transformative effects from CCTs, at least in a middle-income economy such as Mexico's that offers significant economic opportunities for those able to achieve higher levels of education.

The evidence from other studies on the long-term impacts of cash transfers is more mixed, especially for UCTs. Araujo et al. (2016), examining the 10-year effects of cash transfers in Ecuador, conclude that any effect of cash transfers stemming from the 1–2 percentage point increase in secondary school completion on the inter-generational transmission of poverty in Ecuador is modest. Evans et al. (2019) study long-term effects from a CCT programme in rural Tanzania, finding that while the programme significantly increased clinic visits in the first 1.5 years after transfers, this impact vanished by 2.5 years, although after this point they find increases in preventive health investments and health insurance. Baird et al. (2017) explore whether notable reductions in HIV prevalence, teen pregnancy, and marriage along with increases in school participation and test scores realized during the early phases of UCT and CCT programmes in Malawi exhibited sustained impacts. They find that two years after the programme ended, girls who had received the UCTs were no better-off than a control group, the treated girls having rates of HIV and pregnancy apparently unaffected by having received the earlier transfers. They do find potential evidence of long-lasting effects among a group of girls who had dropped out of school and were offered the CCT as an incentive to return.

The evidence here appears to point to an advantage of CCTs over UCTs in that they force households into investments in schooling and health that are more likely to yield long-term transformative effects, albeit at the expense of the short-term consumption gains with UCTs that would have been realized among those unwilling to comply with the conditionality of a CCT. Brudevold-Newman et al. (2017) find similar results in a randomized evaluation of a programme working among impoverished young women in Nairobi. One treatment arm provided cash grants for business while the other also included mentoring and franchising components. While results after one year showed a 30 per cent increase in weekly income, these income gains disappeared in the second year of the programme.

Haushofer and Shapiro (2018) shows results from a three-year follow-up study of GiveDirectly cash transfers in Kenya. They find asset holdings among the treated households to be US$416 (40 per cent) higher than untreated households in the same village accompanied by increases of 0.20 s.d. in a food security index, 0.15 s.d. an educational index, and a 0.16 s.d. improvement in psychological well-being, but zero impacts on health. But is difficult to ascertain how much of these differences are due to negative spillovers to non-recipients in the treated villages. The authors find similar-sized impacts on household assets when treated households are compared to households in pure control villages yet not in other impact variables, although the lack of baseline controls in control villages make comparisons difficult. As a result, Haushofer and Shapiro reveal fairly convincing evidence of long-term impacts on assets, but inconclusive impacts on food security, health, education, and psychological well-being.

Achieving longer-term effects to cash transfers appears to be more likely if behavioural considerations are incorporated into programming. Barrera-Osorio et al. (2016) study CCT programmes in Colombia when combined with a creative set of structured incentives. In one treatment arm, these force families to save a third of the stipend each month until they make enrollment decisions for the next academic year; in a second treatment arm they provide a stipend for secondary school graduation and tertiary school enrollment. They find that both of these result in significant improvements in long-run schooling outcomes, with the stipend treatment increasing tertiary enrollment by 5.7 percentage points over a baseline of 35 per cent.

A discernable pattern also exists in which both CCTs and UCTs tend to have long-term impacts in countries in which greater employment opportunities exist and where individuals are able to realize a higher level of returns to schooling. These results are consistent with other work such as Wydick et al. (2013) which finds *educational* impacts from an international child sponsorship programme higher in sub-Saharan Africa, but long-term impacts on *employment* to be higher in Asia and Latin America, where economic opportunities for those with higher levels of schooling are arguably greater. Similarly, Filmer and Schady (2014) find a large impact on schooling outcomes from scholarships in Cambodia, but little subsequent impact on long-term economic well-being due to the country's limited economic opportunity. Thus, the gains from CCT programmes are likely to yield transformative effects when economies provide recipients employment opportunities for those who have been induced to realize higher levels of schooling through the transfers. Without such opportunities, the average economic return to these marginally added years of education will be lower.

In conclusion, the empirical evidence is that cash transfers exhibit heterogeneous effects not only across different measures of poverty, but these effects depend on conditionality and the context in which the transfer is executed. In the subsequent section I consider what may be some of the underlying rationale for these heterogeneous effects.

3.2 Basic Model

To understand the qualitatively different effects across cash transfers of different sizes, consider a two-period model in which consumption occurs in 'the present' (C_1) and 'the future' (C_2). Let utility be equal to $U(C_1) + \delta U(C_2) - \overline{\ell}$, wherein our basic neoclassical formulation $U(\cdot)$ is concave and twice differentiable, U_1' and U_2' represent the marginal utilities of consumption in the first and second periods, $\delta \in (0, 1)$ discounts future utility relative to present utility, and $\overline{\ell}$ represents a fixed cost of labour activity across periods. Labour activity can either include the effort expended in seeking charity from others (for example, begging) or labour for earned income such that $\overline{\ell} \in \{\overline{\ell}_b, \overline{\ell}_l\}$ where for simplicity but without loss of generality we assume that $\overline{\ell}_b = \overline{\ell}_l$. Although this is true, we assume that $\overline{\ell}_l$ is more desirable from a social point of view since the activity $\overline{\ell}_b$ represents a transfer from others that is not given in a mutually beneficial exchange of goods or services.

The context for the model is an individual in poverty (whom we will refer to as the agent) who is able to obtain b in each period through charity at a utility cost of $\overline{\ell}_b$, and is able to save from the present period to the future period, but is not able to borrow. Thus, the agent maximizes utility subject to the constraints $C_1 \leq b$ and $C_2 \leq 2b - C_1$. Incorporating the two constraints in an optimization framework with Lagrangian multipliers λ_1 and λ_1, respectively, the maximization problem becomes

$$U(C_1) + \delta U(C_2) - \overline{\ell} + \lambda_1(b - C_1) + \lambda_2(2b - C_2 - C_1) \tag{1}$$

where differentiation with respect to the first and second arguments yields the first-order conditions $U_1' - \lambda_1 - \lambda_2 = 0$ and $\delta U_2' - \lambda_2 = 0$, respectively. Subtracting the second of these from the first yields the relationship at optimum, $U_1' = \delta U_2' + \lambda_1$.

Suppose that along with the possibility of saving some fraction of income from the present to the future period, the agent may make a durable investment that requires a minimum fixed investment d in the present that yields $r = (1 + R)d$ in future period income above b, where $R > 0$. This 'lumpy' durable investment could take a number of forms, each requiring a lump sum outlay of present resources. This could literally represent a durable investment in physical capital such as a shop, a machine, or other types of equipment that increase the agent's future productivity to r. Likewise, it could represent investment in education or other forms of human capital that result in a future wage income of r. Any such investment is thus 'transformative' for a person living in poverty in the sense that it changes the agent's labour activity from $\overline{\ell}_b$ to $\overline{\ell}_l$, from dependence on the charity of others to self-reliance and the socially preferred outcome.

Here we can expect different levels of cash transfer b to exhibit not just quantitatively different, but *qualitatively* different effects on the agent's behaviour. Specifically, I offer the following proposition:

PROPOSITION: *Small cash transfers $b \in (0, b^*]$ will result in increases in the agent's present consumption with no change in future consumption and a continued reliance upon charity. Intermediate levels of cash transfers $b \in (b^*, b^{**}]$ will increase both present consumption and savings for future consumption, but a continued reliance upon charity. Large cash transfers $b \in (b^{**}, \infty]$ will result in investments in future productivity that have 'transformative' effects on income and labor activity.*

Proof: Consider first the case of a small cash transfer. With consumption initially equal to b across periods, $\lambda_1 = U_1'(b) - \delta U_2'(b) > 0$. Let $h^* > 0$ be the transfer that satisfies $U_1'(b+h^*) - \delta U_2'(b) = 0$ and where $\lambda_1 = 0$. Thus, for $\delta > 0$, $\exists\, h \in (0, h^*]$ for which $U_1'(b+h) \geq \delta U_2'(b)$ and therefore a small transfer h is consumed only in the present period. Because $\delta U_2'(b) > U_1'(b+h)$ at $h > h^*$, there exists an optimal savings level s^* such that $U(b+h-s^*) + \delta U(b+s^*) > U(b+h) + \delta U(b)$ that maximizes utility. However, $\exists\, h^{**} > h^*$ above and only above which the agent will prefer the durable investment rather than save. For transfers below h^*, and with a sufficiently large investment d needed for the durable and sufficiently low R and δ, $U(b+h) + \delta U(b) > U(b+h-d) + \delta U(b+r)$ because as $d \to b + h^*$ and R and $\delta \to 0$, utility under the durable investment tends toward zero. For transfers above h^*, the first-order condition from maximization of $U(b+h-s) + \delta U(b+s)$ with respect to s is $-U_1' + \delta U_2' = 0$, where total differentiation yields $\frac{ds}{dh} = \frac{U_{11}}{U_{11} + \delta U_{22}} > 0$, meaning that the optimal s^* is increasing in h. But as h increases and $s^* \to d$, the marginally utility loss in the present period from the durable investment falls sufficiently after h^{**} such that $U(b+h^{**}-d) + \delta U(b+r) > U(b+h^{**}-s^*) + \delta U(b+s^*)$ and the durable investment becomes preferable since its return is $1 + R > s/s = 1$.

Figure 3.1 illustrates the main results of the Proposition. It also serves as a guide into understanding the relative behavioural reactions to

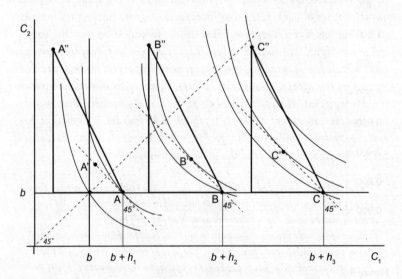

Figure 3.1 Responses to Higher Levels of Cash Transfers

CCTs and UCTs. For example, if a cash transfer of size h_1 is a CCT that is granted conditional upon undertaking the durable investment, it will be rejected although a UCT of any size will be accepted. The terms of a CCT of size h_1 conditional upon undertaking the durable investment will be accepted, although it yields a utility lower than a UCT of the same size. Finally, a CCT of size h_3 conditional upon undertaking the durable investment will be accepted, and the durable investment is actually preferred to merely saving for second-period consumption. Thus, when cash transfers are smaller, a CCT that is conditional on the durable investment may be rejected or at the very least is less preferable to the household than a UCT of the same size. But sequentially larger UCTs both increase the likelihood of durable investment in the first period and begin to mimic the transformative economic choices that would have existed anyway under a CCT of the same size. Figure 3.2 shows a utility simulation with $b = 1$, $R = 0.10$, $d = 5$, and $\delta = 0.70$, showing how optimal behavior increases from

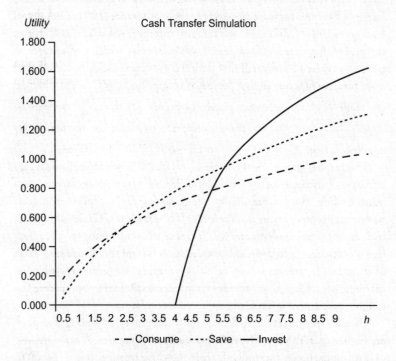

Figure 3.2 Simulation of Optimal Behavioral Responses to Cash Transfers ($b = 1$, $R = 0.10$, $d = 5$, and $\delta = 0.70$)

consumption to savings and then to durable investment as the size of cash transfers increases.

3.3 Behavioural Extensions

In this section I consider how responses by cash-transfer recipients may change as we move from a neoclassical economics to a behavioural economics framework. I consider three possibilities: 1) how cash transfer recipients may behave when the rate of time preference is endogenous to consumption as well as issues of self-control; 2) considerations related to executive control and cognitive ability; and 3) when utility is not neoclassical, but rather is shaped by aspirations.

Endogenous Time Preference and Self-Control

Both theoretical and empirical work has demonstrated that the discount factor is likely to increase in poverty status (Lawance, 1991; Becker and Mulligan, 1997). Moreover, one can also interpret the discount factor as the probability that a second period will even exist, which in dire cases of poverty may be a function of first period consumption. Suppose then that δ is a positive function of first period consumption, or $\delta(C_1)$. This changes the slope of the indifference curves in Figure 3.1 from $\frac{dC_2}{dC_1} = -\frac{U_1'}{\delta U_2'}$ to $\frac{dC_2}{dC_1} = -\frac{U_1' + \delta'(C_1)U(C_2)}{\delta U_2'}$ and the consumption rule based on the first-order conditions from $U_1' = \delta U_2' + \lambda_1$ to $U_1' + \delta'(C_1)U(C_2) = \delta U_2' + \lambda_1$.

This implies that h^*, or the critical level of UCT needed before savings occurs will increase as the marginal utility of first-period consumption must decline more substantially before saving for second-period consumption becomes optimal. Likewise, h^{**}, the critical UCT level required to induce durable investment will increase to compensate for the effect that a reduction in first-period consumption has on the discounted value of its return in the second period. It also implies that under endogenous discounting, a CCT that provides transfers conditional upon making the durable investment is likely to result in lower take-up.

There is considerable evidence that discount rates among the poor are higher than those of the rich, especially in situations of malnutrition or with households and individuals living close to subsistence (Bardhan 1996). Endogenous discount rates have been modelled as a poverty trap

(Chakrabarty 2000; Haaparanta and Puhakka 2004) in which poverty leads to high discounting of the future while simultaneously high discount rates discourage investment in the future. Thus, if poverty causes high discount rates, it is likely to perpetuate poverty. While the effect of high discount rates on poverty is less disputed, experimental work has attempted to establish causality in the opposite relationship--from poverty to high discount rates.

Haushofer et al. (2013) provide just such an experiment among a sample of students at the University of Zürich given varying degrees of endowments. Subjects were given positive and negative 'income shocks' and then led through a series of intertemporal choices. What they find is that positive income shocks reduce discount rates among subjects, while negative income shocks increase them. Their results support the hypothesis that falling into poverty increases causes people to more heavily discount future income flows, creating poverty traps from skewed intertemporal decision-making that inhibits long-term investment.

Issues of endogenous time preference are related to the relationship between self-control and poverty, a subject of increasing research in behavioural development economics. As Bernheim et al. (2015) note, self-control differs from simple time discounting based on the observation that people often employ, and indeed are often willing to pay for, commitment devices to help them make choices consistent with the time preferences of a 'present self'. Psychologist George Ainslie (1975, 1992) describes the mechanisms by which ordinary people exhibit self-control, where they are often through the adoption of 'private rules' that regulate consumption choices in the present, such as 'I never eat dessert'. Deviations from these private rules in the present are often viewed by the present self as having implications for future behaviors, where eating dessert today implies that one is likely to break the private rule in the future as well (Bernheim et al. 2015). Thus, these kinds of private rules, though in some sense non-optimal by imposing arbitrary constraints, are able to create personal habits that keep high rates of time preference in check.

How habits are related to individual identity is a fascinating subject of research and pose challenges in our understanding of the impact of cash transfers once these behavioural nuances are considered. It may be that through episodes of chronic poverty, habits are developed among the poor that make present consumption a focal point. An inertia may develop with respect to intertemporal choices that thwart investments with returns that lie in the relatively distant future. This may include present-focused behaviours such as drug use and impulsive violence, behaviours whose future consequences are (under)valued at high discount rates. The extent to which poverty becomes geographically concentrated, and social behaviours begin to reinforce each other through network effects, may compound the difficulties in transmitting even substantial cash transfers into transformative investments in the future.

One innovative approach has been to combine cash transfers with cognitive behavioural therapy (CBT). Viewed in a time-discounting framework, along with addressing other important issues, CBT helps individuals to reflect on behavioural choices (Hoffman et al. 2012), exhibit greater self-control (Almund et al. 2011), and build a stronger mental connection between present choices and future consequences (Lipsey et al. 2007). Blattman et al. (2017) experiment with a creative randomized trial in which cash transfers (UCTs) amounting to US$200 were crosscut with a CBT intervention involving approximately 1000 men with criminal backgrounds in Liberia. The therapy attempted to develop self-control, a non-criminal self-image, and foster economic behaviours oriented towards positive future goals. Almost immediately after the eight-week sessions, criminal activity dropped precipitously, thefts falling by one-third and drug dealing by one-half. After one year these behaviors had returned to previous levels among those receiving only cash or CBT alone, but effects were much more sustained for those who were given both the CBT and the cash transfers: While in the pure control group, men reported stealing almost once per week on average, the combination of cash transfers and CBT reduce this rate by 40 per cent.

Cognitive Capacity and Executive Control

Other research (Shah et al. 2012; Mani et al. 2013; Mullainathan and Shafir 2013; Schofield 2014; Schilbach et al. 2016) has studied the impact of poverty on other psychological phenomena related to cogni-tive ability. As with high rates of time preference, correlations have been known for some time between poverty and lower levels of cognition (for example, McLoyd 1998; Barr 2012). A primary objective of this area of research has been to disentangle issues of causality, seeking to understand the extent to which poverty affects cognitive ability. These issues may be critical for understanding how cash transfers may be used by households and individuals living at the edges of subsistence.

Mullainathan and Shafir (2013) develop the term 'mental bandwidth' to describe two major psychological components: 1) cognitive capacity, the psychological mechanisms that underlie our ability to solve different kinds of problems, retain information in our brains, and engage in logical reasoning; and 2) executive control, which governs our ability to plan future courses of action, initiate and inhibit actions, and control our impulses. Both of these components become overloaded when mental bandwidth is taxed by preoccupation, especially for basic needs like food and shelter. In this way, poverty taxes mental bandwidth, affecting decision-making, productivity, and even the utility individuals receive from consumption or different types of activities.

Schofield (2014) illustrates how poor nutrition affects poverty through a randomized controlled trial with adult cycle-rickshaw drivers in Chennai having a BMI less than 20. Half of the participants received an additional 700 calories per day, and half formed the control. Those receiving the additional calories showed improvements in both physical and cognitive tasks. By the final week of the five-week experiment, the treated rickshaw drivers had increased both their labour supply and income by approximately 10 per cent. Rickshaw drivers in the treatment group were also less likely to delay postponing difficult tasks until the next day, also indicating that poverty manifest in low caloric intake may also increase future discounting.

Mani et al. (2013) demonstrate how poverty particularly affects cognitive capacity related to decision-making about money. Not only do those in poverty struggle when they are malnourished; people in poverty struggle specifically with decisions related to money and finances. In a set of experiments involving both rich and poor subjects, they find that, relative to the rich, the mental bandwidth of the poor is taxed specifically in reference to sets of questions dealing with finances.

How might the effects of poverty on cognitive capacity and executive control affect behavioral decisions related to cash transfers? Whereas in an economic model, the choice between present consumption and a durable investment involves a rather straightforward calculus, in practice the option of investing a cash transfer in additional schooling or an income generating asset may involve a series of mental financial calculations, an intimidating navigation through the bureaucracy, or stacks of paperwork. In the context of our model we can represent this tax on the mental bandwidth as 1) an increase in d, the cost of investment in the durable; or perhaps 2) uncertainty over R, the return to the durable investment which may make what is in reality a utility-increasing investment appear to be less certain, or a relatively safe investment appear to be riskier. Furthermore, the depression often accompanying poverty may both add to the mental costs associated with d and also cause an individual to become pessimistic about R if he or she believes recent episodes of 'bad luck' are likely to persist in the future (de Quidt and Haushofer 2016). It may thus prove less mentally taxing to simply use UCTs for present consumption when the more complicated set of economic costs and benefits related to an investment in the future are more difficult to rationally process.

This branch of research appears nearly unanimous in recommending the use of 'nudges' and defaults in designing programmes and policies intending to address the needs of people in poverty (Shah et al. 2012; Pace et al., 2019). In some respects, this may speak for the use of CCTs which create a default response as a condition for the transfer. However, UCTs which are given without conditions, but are accompanied by nudges and coaching towards forward-looking behaviours such as investment in microenterprises, schooling, and providing adequate health and nutritional support for children may also constitute valid responses that take into account the taxing effects of poverty on economic decision-making. In an extreme-poverty graduation programme implemented in six countries, Banerjee et al. (2015), for example, packaged two types of cash transfers, temporary cash for consumption and a productive asset grant with vocational training, a life skills coach, support, a formal savings accounts, and health services. Three years after the intervention, eight out of ten poverty indices continued to show significant improvement, highlighting the impact cash transfers may have when thoughtfully combined with other interventions. Subsequent work such as Bedoya et al. (2019) in Afghanistan has also shown marked results, where the fraction of treated households, receiving a holistic transfer package including life coach along with a cash transfer, remaining under the poverty line to fell to 62 percent at endline relative to 82 percent for a control group.

Aspirations-based Utility

A burgeoning literature has suggested that aspirations play a central role in the decision-making of the poor. This is been the subject of recent theoretical work in development economics (Genicot and Ray 2014; Dalton et al. 2016, Lybbert and Wydick 2018) as well as recent experimental and empirical work (Beaman, 2012; Bernard et al., 2015; Glewwe et al. 2018, Wydick and Lybbert 2019). This literature suggests that the aspirations of individuals may create a reference point at which utility either makes a discontinuous jump, or before which marginal utility substantially increases, but then decreases afterwards.

Individuals, of course, may have aspirations over a number of outcome variables, including education, income, savings, or consumption. In Lybbert and Wydick (2018), we suggest the following functional form that is rooted in the Kahneman and Tversky (1979) value function and satisfies four properties[6] that should characterize an aspirations-based utility function:

$$U_A(Y \mid A) = A \left(\frac{C_t}{A} \right)^{\left(\frac{1}{1-\alpha_1} \right)} \cdot 1(C_t < A) + A \left(\frac{C_t}{A} \right)^{(1-\alpha_2)} \cdot 1(C_t \geq A), \quad (2)$$

where A represents an aspiration for consumption in each period and $\alpha_1, \alpha_2 \in [0,1]$ measure the strength of aspirations in shaping utility.

In the special case in which $\alpha_2 = \frac{\alpha_1}{\alpha_1 - 1}$, this aspirations-based utility function simplifies to the standard concave neo-classical utility function in which

$$U_N(Y \mid A) = A \left(\frac{C_t}{A} \right)^{(1-\alpha_2)} = A^{\alpha_2} C_t^{(1-\alpha_2)}, \quad (3)$$

where A^{α_2} is a constant and α_2 indicates relative risk aversion. The aspirations-based utility function U_A in (2) yields the functional form shown in Figure 3.3.

In aspirations-based utility, an aspiration forms a reference point that rewards aspirational attainment increasingly in the value of α, but where diminishing returns set in quickly after the aspiration is realized. This functional form can be easily incorporated into the two-period model in

---

[6] Specifically, these are that (1) Marginal utility is higher immediately below A than it is just above it; (2) Marginal utility increases with the outcome below the aspiration and decreases with outcome at and beyond the aspiration; (3) As aspirations grow in importance to utility, gains in utility become uniquely a function of realized aspirations; and (4) Utility is increasing in higher realized aspirations.

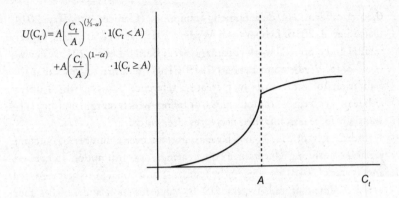

Figure 3.3   Aspirations-Based Utility

(1) so that utility across the two periods remains additive and discounted in the second period by δ.

This aspirations-based utility function generates a set of non-standard-looking indifference curves that reflect the 'kink' in the utility function that represents aspirations attainment. Unlike the standard neo-classical indifference curves portrayed in Figure 3.1, the indifference curves based in Figure 3.3 display a concave shape relative to the origin over the domain in which consumption lies below aspirations for periods 1 and 2. The indifference curves then assume different shapes based on whether consumption lies below or above aspirations in the two periods. (See the appendix for derivation.)

If rather than by standard neo-classical utility, the utility of a cash-transfer recipient is shaped by future aspirations that are below current levels of consumption, cash transfers are more likely to result in the durable investment. This is because (for sufficiently low b) the convexity of the utility function below A implies that the present utility costs d of the durable investment are lower with aspirations-based utility and that the marginal gains from the future return r to the durable in second-period consumption are higher, whether the aspiration is realized or not. More generally, for C_1 less than A and $U'_A(b) = U'_N(b)$ (where U_A is aspirations-based utility and U_N is neo-classical-based utility), $U_A(b+h) - U_A(b+h-d) < U_N(b+h) - U_N(b+h-d)$ and $U_A(b+r) - U_A(b) > U_N(b+r) - U_N(b)$. The latter holds true even in the case that the aspiration is realized in the second period since $U'_A = U'_N$ for $\forall C_t \geq A$. An

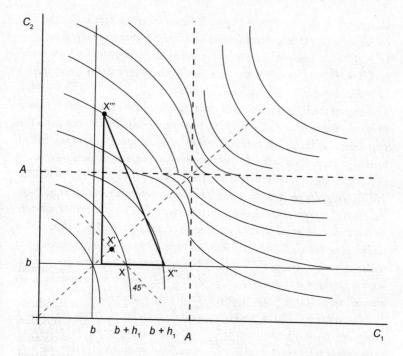

Figure 3.4 Behavioral Responses to Cash Transfers with Aspirations-Based Utility

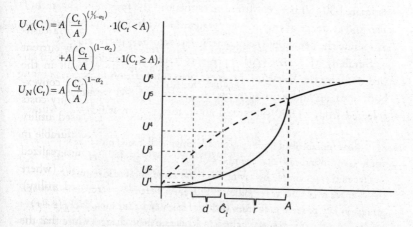

Figure 3.5 Cash Transfers with Neo-classical and Aspirations-based utility.

illustration of this appears in Figure 5. Costs of investment in the durable under aspirations-based utility and neoclassical utility are equal to $U^2 - U^1 < U^4 - U^3$, respectively, while gains in the second period are equal to $U^5 - U^2 > U^5 - U^4$ in the case where the aspiration is (marginally) unrealized and $U^6 - U^2 > U^6 - U^4$ when it is.

Some of the largest impacts of cash transfers have been found in experimental studies where subjects have been randomly chosen, not from the population at large, but from a pool of candidates who have submitted formal grant proposals for durable investment projects, typically for vocational training or small enterprise capital (Blattman et al. 2013, McKenzie 2017). Virtually by definition, such project proposals form an aspiration, creating a focal point for use of a cash transfer. The mere fact that subjects in these experimental studies are able to articulate a goal in a proposal, a pathway to that goal, and confidence in their own agency of navigating the pathway toward the goal (Snyder 1994) suggest the manifestation of an 'aspirational hope' (Lybbert and Wydick 2018) that is likely to serve as an antecedent to transformative effects from cash transfers.

Blattman et al. (2013) carry out a randomized trial among 535 village groups of 10 to 40 members in Uganda submitting formal proposals for cash grants related to vocational training and microenterprises start-up. The researchers find that an array of impacts on the treatment group were large and sustained. Four years after the transfers, assets among those randomly selected for treatment increased 57 per cent relative to control. Earnings were 38 per cent higher, producing annual returns of an estimated 30–50 per cent from investment in the program. The authors also find evidence of employment generation within the microenterprises, extending the benefit of the cash transfers to others in the villages.[7]

Similarly, McKenzie (2017) presents results of a randomized trial carried out with the YouWiN! business plan competition in Nigeria among both start-up and existing firms. A group of 1,841 semifinalists were solicited from 24,000 submitted applications, from which 729 winners

---

[7] New unpublished findings from Blattman et al. based on a 9-year follow-up study seem to indicate that members of the control group were able to achieve similar outcomes simply by saving for these same durable investments. Nor do the changes over nine years indicate differences between treatment and control groups in key poverty indicators such as health and education. Nevertheless, it appears that the cash transfer helped to accelerate these changes within a shorter period of time.

were randomly chosen to receive $50,000 grants given for cash payments conditional on achieving some basic milestones at each stage. McKenzie finds large impacts from the transfers on treatment group businesses after three years: new and existing businesses added 5.2 and 5.6 employees, respectively, a 140 per cent and 80 per cent increase over the endline level of employment in control businesses. Overall, the entrepreneurs receiving the transfers were 37 percentage points more likely to be in business, 23 percentage points more likely to have more than 10 employees, and realized a 0.2–0.3 standard deviation increase in a sales and profitability index. The study represents a clear picture of the transformative effects of cash transfers when properly targeted and carried out in a context of high aspirations.

***

I present here a review of work that assesses the impacts of both conditional and unconditional cash transfers on key areas such as poverty measures, labor market activity, education and, health. I then develop a simple model with neoclassical assumptions to serve as a baseline framework for understanding when UCTs and CCTs are likely to exhibit transformative effects in movement out of poverty through durable investments that yield a permanently higher future income. Extending the model, I consider how responses by cash transfer recipients might be affected by psychological phenomena that are a subject of research in behavioral economics: endogenous discounting, cognitive capability and executive control, and aspirations-based utility. From this exercise I conclude with five factors that indicate conditions under which cash transfers are likely to be transformative:

1) *Both UCTs and CCTs are much more likely to be transformative when they are large.* For the poor to undertake durable investments in the future, UCTs need to satiate present consumption sufficiently in order to induce investments with future returns. The marginal rate of investment in durable assets appears to increase as the size of UCTs grow (Haushofer and Shapiro 2016; Foundations for Social Change 2020). CCTs also need to be sufficiently large to provide for present consumption in order to induce investments with future returns, for example, to outweigh the opportunity cost of child labor in the

present when the marginal utility of first-period consumption is high. The likely presence of endogenous discount rates among the poor magnifies the requirement that cash transfers be large in order to have transformative effects.

2) *There is evidence that CCTs exhibit greater long-term transformative effects than UCTs.* This seems particularly true when CCTs are larger (Saavedra and Garcia 2012; Baird 2013; Araujo et al. 2018). The relative merits of UCTs vs. CCTs can be debated over policy weights placed on short-term consumption versus sustainable long-term impacts. But while UCTs clearly result in short to medium-term increases in consumption, the evidence, especially from Mexico (Parker and Vogl 2018), is that CCTs appear more likely to yield long-term effects among households willing to accept their conditionality.

3) *Cash transfers are more likely to be transformative when their design accounts for psychological and behavioral phenomena that deviate from neoclassical rationality.* Cash transfer designs that force or nudge savings to account for lumpy investments in productive assets or schooling help facilitate investments in durable assets (Barrera-Osorio 2016). Cash transfers packaged with psychological interventions such as cognitive behavioral therapy and life coaching have exhibited significant medium-term impacts (Blattman et al. 2017; Banerjee et al. 2015).

4) *Targeting both UCTs and CCTs at individuals with elevated aspirations is more likely to result in transformative economic effects.* This is clear not only from theoretical results derived from models of aspirations-based utility, but from recent empirical evidence. Experimental interventions suggest transformative effects when cash transfers in the form of business grants have been targeted at those who manifest both general aspirations for economic improvement and concrete proposals for investment in microenterprises and educational/vocational training (Blattman et al. 2013; McKenzie 2017). In the absence of aspirations, permanent UCTs such as a BMI are less likely to yield transformative effects.

5) *To be maximally transformative, cash transfers require complementary policies, programmes, and interventions.* Absent tangible economic opportunities, UCTs are likely to exhibit primarily palliative effects (Baird et al. 2013; Baird et al. 2017; Brudevold-Newman, 2017) that provide significant short-term increases in consumption and

economic well-being, but are unlikely to be transformative. Cash transfers have never been, and should never be, regarded as a silver bullet for poverty alleviation. Evidence for long-term, transformative impacts via investments in education and enterprise is weaker in sub-Saharan Africa than Latin America, where economies tend to be stronger. Macroeconomic policies that create the conditions for widespread economic opportunity and confidence in the returns from investments in the future are strong complements to cash transfers.

Appendix

Derivation of indifference curve mapping. Letting $\alpha_1 = \alpha_2$, that before the aspiration A is reached, the utility function is convex and equal to $(C_t \mid A) = A\left(\frac{C_t}{A}\right)^{\left(\frac{1}{1-\alpha}\right)}$. Setting A equal to 1 for simplicity makes utility equal to $U(C_t \mid A = 1, C_t < A) = C_t^{\left(\frac{1}{1-\alpha}\right)}$ where in the domain after the aspiration is realized we have $U(C_t \mid A = 1, C_t \geq A) = C_t^{(1-\alpha)}$. In the northwest quadrant where the aspiration is reached in the second period, but not the first, the slope of the indifference curves is $\frac{dC_1}{dC_2} - \frac{1}{(1-\alpha)^2} C_1^{\frac{\alpha}{(1-\alpha)}} C_2^{\alpha}$ and hence negative, and where the 2nd derivative $\frac{d^2C_1}{dC_2^2} = -\frac{\alpha}{(1-\alpha)^3} C_1^{\frac{2\alpha-1}{(1-\alpha)}} C_2^{\alpha}$ is negative such that the indifference curves are concave. In the northeast quadrant in which the aspiration is reached in both the first and second period, the slope of the indifference curves is $\frac{dC_1}{dC_2} = -\left(\frac{C_1}{C_2}\right)^{-\alpha}$ and hence negative, and where the 2nd derivative $\frac{d^2C_1}{dC_2} = \alpha\left(\frac{C_1}{C_2}\right)^{-(1+\alpha)}$ is positive such that the indifference curves are convex. In the southwest quadrant in which the aspiration is reached in neither period, the slope of the indifference curves is $\frac{dC_1}{dC_2} = -\left(\frac{C_1}{C_2}\right)^{-\left(\frac{\alpha}{1-\alpha}\right)}$ and hence negative, and where the 2nd derivative $\frac{d^2C_1}{dC_2^2} = -\left(\frac{\alpha}{1-\alpha}\right)\left(\frac{C_1}{C_2}\right)^{2\alpha-1}$ is negative such that the indifference curves are concave. In the southeast quadrant in which the aspiration is reached in the first period, but not the second, the slope of the indifference curves is $\frac{dC_1}{dC_2} = -\left(1-\alpha\right)^2 C_1^{-\alpha} C_2^{\frac{-\alpha}{(1-\alpha)}}$ and hence negative, and where the 2nd derivative $\frac{d^2C_1}{dC_2} = -\alpha\left(1-\alpha\right)^2 C_1^{-(1+\alpha)} C_2^{\frac{-\alpha}{(1-\alpha)}}$ is positive such that the indifference curves are convex.

References

Akee, Randall, William Copeland, Gordon Keeler, Adrian Angold, and Elizabeth J. Costello (2010). 'Parents' Incomes and Children's Outcomes: A Quasi-Experiment', *American Economic Journal: Applied Economics*, 2(1): 86–115.

Ainslie, George (1975). 'Specious Reward: A Behavioral Theory of Impulsiveness and Impulse Control', *Psychological Bulletin*, 82: 463–96.

Ainslie, George (1992). *Picoeconomics*, Cambridge: Cambridge University Press.

Amarante, Verónica, Marco Manacorda, Edward Miguel, and Andrea Vigorito (2016). 'Do cash transfers improve birth outcomes? evidence from matched vital statistics, program, and social security data', *American Economic Journal: Economic Policy*, 8(2): 1– 43.

Almund, M., A.L. Duckworth, J. Heckman, and T. Kautz (2011). 'Personality Psychology and Economics'. In *Handbook of the Economics of Education*, Volume 4, p. 1, Amsterdam: Elsevier.

Amarante, Verónica, Marco Manacorda, Edward Miguel, and Andrea Vigorito (2016). 'Do cash transfers improve birth outcomes? Evidence from matched vital statistics, and program and social security data', *American Economic Journal: Economic Policy* 8(2): 1–43.

Angelucci, Manuela and Giacomo De Giorgi. 2009. 'How do Cash Transfers Affect Ineligibles' Consumption?', *American Economic Review*, 99(1): 486–508.

Angelucci M, Attanasio O. 2006. 'Oportunidades: Programme Effect on Consumption, Low Participation, and Methodological Issues', Economics Working Paper No. WP-06-13. University of Arizona.

Attanasio O, Battistin E, Mesnard A. 2009. 'Food and cash transfers: Evidence from Colombia', Working Paper W09/15. Institute for Fiscal Studies.

Araujo, Caridad, Mariano Bosch, and Norbert Schady (2016). 'Can Cash Transfers Help Households Escape an Intergenerational Poverty Trap?' NBER Working Paper.

Araujo, Caridad, María Adelaida Martínez, Sebastian Martinez, Michelle Pérez, and Mario Sánchez (2018). 'Do Larger School Grants Improve Educational Attainment? Evidence from urban Mexico', Inter-American Development Bank Working Paper Series, IDB-WP-864.

Baird, Sarah, Francisco H. G. Ferreira, Berk Özler, and Michael Woolcock (2013). 'Relative Effectiveness of Conditional and Unconditional Cash Transfers for Schooling Outcomes in Developing Countries: A Systematic Review'. *Campbell Systematic Reviews*.

Baird, Sarah, Craig McIntosh, and Berk Özler (2017). 'When the Money Runs out: Do Cash Transfers Have Sustained Effects on Human Capital Accumulation?', CEGA Working Paper WS-068.

Banerjee, Abhijit, Esther Duflo, Nathanael Goldberg, Dean Karlan, Robert Osei, William Parienté, Jeremy Shapiro, Bram Thuysbaert, and Christopher Udry

(2015). 'A Multifaceted Program Causes Lasting Progress for the Very Poor: Evidence from six countries', *Science*, 348(6236).

Banerjee, Abhijit, Rema Hanna, Gabriel Kreindler, and Benjamin Olken. 2015. 'Debunking the Stereotype of the Lazy Welfare Recipient: Evidence from Cash Transfer Programs Worldwide'. Faculty Research Working Paper Series RWP15-076, Harvard Kennedy School.

Banks, L. M., Mearkle, R., Mactaggart, I., Walsham, M., Kuper, H., and Blanchet, K. (2016). 'Disability and Social Protection Programmes in Low- and Middle-Income Countries: A Systematic Review', *Oxford Development Studies*, 45(3): 223–9.

Bardhan, Pranab (1996). 'Research on Poverty and Development 20 Years after Redistribution with Growth. Proceedings of the Annual World Bank Conference on Development Economics 1995. Supplement to the *World Bank Economic Review* and the *World Bank Research Observer*, pp. 59–72.

Barr, M.S. (2012). *No Slack: The Financial Lives of Low-Income* Americans, Washington, D.C.: Brookings Institution Press.

Barrera-Osorio, Felipe, Leigh L Linden, and Juan E. Saavedra (2016). Medium Term Educational Consequences of Alternative Conditional Cash Transfer Designs: Experimental Evidence from Colombia. CESR-Schaeffer Working Paper no. 2015–026.

Bastagli, Francesca, Jessica Hagen-Zanker, Luke Harman, Valentina Barca, Georgina Sturge, and Tanja Schmidt (2016). 'Cash transfers: What Does the Evidence Say?', United Kingdom: Overseas Development Institute, London (July issue).

Beaman, L., E. Duflo, R. Pande, and P. Topalova (2012). 'Female Leadership Raises Aspirations and Educational Attainment for Girls: A Policy Experiment in India', *Science*, 335(6068): 582–6.

Becker, Gary S. and Casey B. Mulligan (1997). The Endogenous Determination of Time Preference. *Quarterly Journal of Economics*, 112(3): 729–58.

Bedoya, Guadalupe, Aidan Coville, Johannes Haushofer, Mohammad Isaqzadeh, and Jeremy Shapiro. 2019. "No Household Left Behind: Afghanistan Targeting the Ultra Poor Impact Evaluation." World Bank Policy Research Working Paper 8877.

Behrman, Jere R, Susan W Parker, and Petra E Todd (2011). 'Do conditional cash transfers for schooling generate lasting benefits?', *Journal of Human Resources* 46 (1): 93–122.

Bernheim, B. Douglas, Debraj Ray, Şevin Yeltekin (2015). 'Poverty and self-control', *Econometrica*, 83(5): 1877–911.

Blattman, Christopher, Nathan Fiala, and Sebastian Martinez (2013). 'Generating skilled self-employment in developing countries: experimental evidence from Uganda', *Quarterly Journal of Economics*, 129(2): 697–752.

Blattman, Christopher, Julian C. Jamison, Margaret Sheridan (2017). 'Reducing Crime and Violence: Experimental Evidence from Cognitive Behavioral Therapy in Liberia.' *American Economic Review*, 107 (4): 1165–1206.

Bose, Rohit and Stephen Hwang (2002). 'Income and spending patterns among panhandlers', *Canadian Medical Association Journal*, 167(5): 477–9.

Brudevold-Newman, Andrew Maddalena Honorati, Pamela Jakiela, and Owen Ozier (2017). 'A Firm of One's Own: Experimental Evidence on Credit Constraints and Occupational Choice', World Bank Policy Research Working Paper No. 7977.

Chakrabarti, Averi, Sudhanshu Handa, Luisa Natali, David Seidenfeld and Gelson Tembo. 2020. "More Evidence on the Relationship Between Cash Transfers and Child Height." *Journal of Development Effectiveness*. 12(1): 14–37.

Chakrabarty, D. (2000). 'Poverty Traps and Growth in a Model of Endogenous Time Preference', Working Paper. https://www.econstor.eu/bitstream/ 10419/39509/1/362827273.pdf.

Cole, Harold L., and Lee E. Ohanian (2002). 'The Great U.K. Depression: A Puzzle and Possible Resolution', *Review of Economic Dynamics*, 5(1): 19–44.

Dalton, Patricio, Sayantan Ghosal, and Anandi Mani. 2016. 'Poverty and Aspirations Failure', *Economic Journal*, 126:165–88.

de Quidt, Jonathan and Johannes Haushofer (2019). 'Depression through the Lens of Economics: A Research Agenda.' In Christopher Barrett, Michael Carter, and Jean-Paul Chavas (eds.) *The Economics of Poverty Traps*, National Bureau of Economic Research, University of Chicago Press. Chicago, IL.

Evans, David and Anna Popova (2017). 'Cash Transfers and Temptation Goods', *Economic Development and Cultural Change*, 65(2): 189–221.

Evans, David, Brian Holtemeyer, and Katrina Kosec (2017). Cash Transfers and Health: Evidence from Tanzania. *World Bank Economic Review*. Published online 4 June 2017.

Evans, David, Brian Holtemeyer, and Katrina Kosec. 2019. "Cash Transfers and Health: Evidence from Tanzania." *World Bank Economic Review*. 33(2)394– 412.

Filmer, Deon and Norbert Schady (2014). The Medium-Term Effects of Scholarships in a Low-Income Country', *Journal of Human Resources*, 49(3): 663–94.

Fiszbein, Ariel and Norbert Schady (2009). *Conditional Cash Transfers: Reducing Present and Future Poverty*. World Bank Publications.

Foundations for Social Change (2020). 'New Leaf Project: Taking Bold Action on Homelessness' *Foundations for Social Change* 2020 Impact Report. URL: https://static1.squarespace.com/static/5f07a92f21d34b403c788e05/t/5f7 51297fcfe7968a6a957a8/1601507995038/2020_09_30_FSC_Statement_ of_Impact_w_Expansion.pdf

Gantner, Leigh (2007). 'PROGRESA: An Integrated Approach to Poverty Alleviation in Mexico'. In Per Pinstrup-Andersen and Fuzhi Cheng (eds) *Food*

Policy for Developing Countries: Case Studies. URL: http://cip.cornell.edu/dns. gfs/1200428168.

Genicot, Garrence and Debraj Ray (2014). 'Aspirations and inequality', *Econometrica*, 85(2): 489-519.

Gertler, Paul (2004). 'Do Conditional Cash Transfers Improve Child Health? Evidence from PROGRESA's controlled randomized experiment', *American Economic Review Papers and Proceedings*, 94(2): 336–41.

Gertler, Paul J., Sebastian W. Martinez, and Marta Rubio-Codina (2012). 'Investing cash transfers to raise long-term living standards', *American Economic Journal: Applied Economics*, 4(1): 164–92.

Gitter S.R. and Caldés N. (2010). 'Crisis, food security, and conditional cash transfers in Nicaragua', Working Paper No. 2010–07. Towson University, Department of Economics.

Glewwe, Paul, Phillip Ross, and Bruce Wydick. 2018. 'Developing Hope Among Impoverished Children: Using Child Self-Portraits to Measure Poverty Program Impacts', *Journal of Human Resources*, 53: 330–5.

Guanais, Frederico (2015). 'The Combined Effects of the Expansion of Primary Health Care and Conditional Cash Transfers on Infant Mortality in Brazil, 1998–2010', *American Journal of Public Health*, 105(S4): S593–S599.

Haaparanta, Pertti and Mikko Puhakka (2004). 'Endogenous time preference, investment and development traps', BOFIT Discussion Paper No. 4/2004.

Haushofer, Johannes, Daniel Schunk, and Ernst Fehr (2013). 'Negative income shocks increase discount rates', University of Zürich working paper.

Haushofer, Johannes and Ernst Fehr (2014). 'On the psychology of poverty', *Science.* 344(6186): 862.

Hofmann, Stefan G., Anu Asnaani Imke, J. J. Vonk, Alice T. Sawyer, and Angela Fang (2012). 'The efficacy of cognitive behavioral therapy: A review of meta-analyses. cognitive therapy and research cognitive therapy and research', *Cognitive Therapy and Research*, 36(5): 427–440.

Haushofer, Johannes and Jeremy Shapiro (2016). 'The Short-Term Impact of Unconditional Cash Transfers to the Poor: Experimental Evidence from Kenya', *Quarterly Journal of Economics*, 131(4): 1973–2042.

Haushofer, Johannes and Jeremy Shapiro (2018). 'The Long-Term Impact of Unconditional Cash Transfers: Experimental Evidence from Kenya' Working Paper, Princeton University.

Honorati, M., Gentilini, U., and Yemtsov, R.G. (2015). 'The State of Social Safety Nets', World Bank Group. http://documents.worldbank.org/curated/en/2015/07/24741765/state-social-safety-nets-2015.

Hagen-Zanker, J., Mccord, A., Holmes, R., Booker, F., and Molinari, E. (2011). 'Systematic Review of the Impact of Employment Guarantee Schemes and Cash Transfers on the Poor', ODI Systematic Review. London: Overseas Development Institute.

Hoddinott John and Skoufias Emanuel (2004). 'The Impact of Progresa on food consumption', *Economic Development and Cultural Change* 53(1): 37–61.

Hoynes, Hilary Williamson, and Diane Whitmore Schanzenbach (2012). 'Work Incentives and the Food Stamp Program', *Journal of Public Economics*, 96 (1): 151–62.

Jones, Damon and Ioana Marinescu (2018). 'Labor Market Impacts of Universal and Permanent Cash Transfers: Evidence from the Alaska Permanent Fund', Working Paper.

Kabeer, N., Piza, C., and Taylor, L. (2012). 'What are the Economic Impacts of Conditional Cash Transfer Programmes ? A Systematic Review of the Evidence', Technical Report', London: EPPICentre, Social Science Research Unit, Institute of Education, University of London.

Kahneman, Daniel. 2011. *Thinking, Fast and Slow*. New York: Farrar, Strauss, and Giroux.

Kahneman, Daniel, and Shane Frederick (2002). 'Representativeness Revisited: Attribute Substitution in Intuitive Judgment' In Thomas Gilovich, Dale Griffin, and Daniel Kahneman (ed.), *Heuristics and Biases: The Psychology of Intuitive Judgment,*, 49–81. Cambridge University Press.

Lawrance, Emily (1991). 'Poverty and the Rate of Time Preference: Evidence from Panel Data', *Journal of Political Economy* 99(1): 54–77.

Lee, Barrett A. and Chad R. Farrell (2003). 'Buddy, Can you Spare a Dime? Homelessness, Panhandling, and the Public', *Urban Affairs Review*, 38: 299–324.

Lipsey, Mark W., Nana Landenberger, Sandra J. Wilson (2007). 'Effects of Cognitive-Behavioral Programs for Criminal Offenders'. Campbell Systematic Reviews.

Lybbert, Travis and Bruce Wydick (2018). 'Poverty, Aspirations, and the Economics of Hope, *Economic Development and Cultural Change*, 66(4): 709–753.

Mani, Anandi, Sendhil Mullainathan, Eldar Shafir, and Jiaying Zhao (2013). Poverty impedes cognitive function, *Science*. 341, 976.

McKenzie, David (2017). 'Identifying and spurring high-growth entrepreneurship: experimental evidence from a business plan competition', *American Economic Review*. 107(8): 2278–307.

McLoyd, Vonnie (1998). 'Socioeconomic Disadvantage and Child Development', *American Psychologist*, 53: 185–204.

Moffitt, Robert A. (2002). 'Welfare Programs and Labor Supply', In Alan J. Auerbach and Martin Feldstein (ed.), *Handbook of Public Economics*, Vol. 4, Amsterdam: North-Holland.

Mullainathan, Sendhil and Eldar Shafir (2013). *Scarcity: Why Having Too Little Means So Much*. New York: Henry Holt & Company.

Pace, Noemi, Silvio Daidone, Benjamin Davis, Luca Pellerano. 2019. "Shaping Cash Transfer Impacts Through 'Soft-Conditions': Evidence from Lesotho" *Journal of African Economies*, 28(1): 39–69.

Parker, Susan W., and Petra E. Todd. 2017. 'Conditional Cash Transfers: The Case of Progresa/Oportunidades', *Journal of Economic Literature*, 55(3): 866–915.

Parker, Susan W., and Tom Vogl. (2018). 'Do Conditional Cash Transfers Improve Economic Outcomes in the Next Generation? Evidence from Mexico', NBER Working Paper No. 24303.

Price, David and Jae Song (2018). 'The Long-Term Effects of Cash Assistance', Working Paper, Stanford University.

Ranganathan, Meghna and Mylene Lagarde (2012). 'Promoting healthy behaviours and improving health outcomes in low and middle-income countries: A review of the impact of conditional cash transfer programmes', *Preventive Medicine*, 55(1): S95–S105.

Ray, Debraj (2006). 'Aspirations, Poverty, and Economic Change', In Banerjee, Abhijit, Roland Benabou, and Dilip Mookherjee, *Understanding Poverty*, 409–21. New York: Oxford University Press.

Robertson, Laura, Phyllis Mushati, Jeffrey W. Eaton, Lovemore Dumba, Gideon Mavise, Jeremiah Makoni, Christina Schumacher, Tom Crea, Roeland Monasch, Lorraine Sherr, Geoffrey P Garnett, Constance Nyamukapa, Simon Gregson (2013). 'Effects of Unconditional and Conditional Cash Transfers on Child Health and Development in Zimbabwe: A Cluster-Randomised Trial', *The Lancet.* 381(9874): 13–19, 1283–92.

Saavedra, Juan Esteban and Sandra García (2012). 'Impacts of Conditional Cash Transfer Programs on Educational Outcomes in Developing Countries: A Meta-analysis', RAND Population Research Center Working Paper WR-921-1.

San Francisco Chronicle (2013). 'Panhandlers Tell Their Own Story' by Heather Knight. https://www.sfgate.com/bayarea/article/The-city-s-panhandlers-tell-their-own-stories-4929388.php#page-1.

Schilbach, Frank, Heather Schofield, and Sendhil Mullainathan (2016). 'The psychological lives of the poor', *American Economic Review: Papers & Proceedings*, 106(5): 435–40.

Schofield, Heather (2014). 'The Economic Costs of Low Caloric Intake: Evidence from India', Working Paper, Harvard University.

Schultz, Paul (2004). 'School Subsidies for the Poor: Evaluating the Mexican Progresa Poverty Program', *Journal of Development Economics* 74: 199–250.

Shah Anuj, Sendhil Mullainathan, and Eldar Shafir (2012). 'Some Consequences of Having Too Little', *Science* 338, 682.

Wydick and Lybbert (2019). 'Hope as Aspirations, Agency. and Pathways: Poverty Dynamics and Microfinance in Oaxaca, Mexico.' In Christopher Barrett, Michael Carter, and Jean-Paul Chavas (eds.) *The Economics of Poverty Traps*, National Bureau of Economic Research, University of Chicago Press. Chicago, IL.

Wydick, Bruce, Paul Glewwe, and Laine Rutledge (2013). 'Does International Child Sponsorship Work? A Six-Country study of impacts on Adult Life Outcomes', *Journal of Political Economy*, 121(2): 393–426.

4   *Improving Healthcare Delivery in India*[*, **]

ABHIJIT BANERJEE AND ESTHER DUFLO

4.1 The Problem of Healthcare

During the last two decades, significant progress was made in improving poor people's access to healthcare. Under five mortality declined from

    * Pranab Bardhan's contributions to the field of economic development are too numerous to be fully described. This chapter illustrates just one of them that has perhaps had the most influence on our own professional lives: Pranab's insistence that we need to collect data in the field to truly understand how the poor lead their lives.

    ** This chapter builds on several years of work in Udaipur, which started with Angus Deaton, starting in the winter of 2002. This paper also builds on early analysis of this data we performed together with Angus (Banerjee, Deaton and

11 per 1,000 in 1990 to 26 per 1,000 in 2017. Nevertheless, frustrating gaps remain. Vaccination rates have plateaued at 85 per cent. Every year, 19.9 million children do not get the full dose of DTP, an essential vaccine. Around 60 per cent of these children live in 10 countries. Among those 10, India stands out as the one of the richest.

While the delivery of high-quality social services to the poor is never easy, there are several factors that make healthcare especially difficult. First, as has been widely documented, a person's decision about when and where to seek healthcare often has very little to do with his or her medical condition itself: It could just as well reflect how the person is feeling about life in general and health in particular,[1] or his or her theories about the nature of diseases and treatment. These decisions may have little to do with the quality of care, since it is not easy to judge the efficacy of the treatment one is getting, given that one does not know what would have happened without the treatment. For example, it is estimated that 80 per cent of all diseases in a setting like India are self-limiting in the

---

Duflo 2004). This is collaborative work, involving many people. We particularly thank the team at Seva Mandir, especially Neelima Khetan, CEO at the time this project took place, Dr Sanjana Mohan (the head of the health unit when this project was started, who was instrumental in designing the evaluations in this project) and Priyanka Singh (head of the health unit when the project was finished, and then CEO of Seva Mandir). We thank Hardy Dewan (Organisation Secretary, Vidya Bhawan), Tushita Lodha (Project in Charge for the Health Study) and Pramod Tiwari (Field Coordinator), from Vidya Bhawan, for directing and coordinating the data collection. Several research assistants have done spectacular work in the field over the years: Annie Duflo, Callie Scott, Danielle Li, Vanessa Valentino, Cindy Palladines, Andrew Fraker, Anuja Singh, Payal Sinha, Neil Shah, Dhruva Kothari and Michael Eddy. We are grateful to the Center of Health and Well Being at Princeton University, the MacArthur Foundation, and the National Institute of Health for funding this research. A version of the first five sections was initially prepared for the Stanford India conference, and we are grateful for organizing committee for allowing us to use the text here.

[1] Das (2005) discusses a number of case studies of TB patients in India that eloquently illustrate this point.

sense that one would get better without any treatment, but people may not be aware of this and as a result may credit the doctor with the cure. To make matters worse, patients may not be aware of the possibility that he could be actually harming you by giving you powerful medicines for something that was self-limiting. In this setting, the types of care which patients demand may have very little to do with what would be socially efficient to deliver. This problem of demand makes it particularly difficult to deliver heathcare to the poor.

Second, there is no obvious aggregate measure of the performance of the healthcare system that is comparable to the matriculation rate in the case of education or the number of brown-outs in the case of electricity. The problem is that age-specific death rates may reflect the state of the health system where and when the person was a child, rather than the health system he currently lives under. This makes it difficult to assess the performance of a system. Without a correct assessment of the system and an identification of the main problems, designing and evaluating possible solutions is almost impossible.

This chapter starts by bringing together some recent evidence, which highlights some of the difficulties that will have to be faced by any government that is serious about improving healthcare for the poor. Most of this evidence comes from a survey we conducted in 100 villages, over 100 public health facilities, and several hundred private and traditional providers in rural Udaipur district in 2002 and 2003, and we also draw on a survey of seven Delhi neighbourhoods between 2001 and 2003 (reported in Das and Hammer 2004, 2005).

On paper, India s public health care system looks like the model for delivering universal health services in a large, poor country. Its comprehensive three tier design ensures that all households, rural and urban, are close to a free government health facility. The infrastructure for this system is operational: The average household is within 2 kilometres of the nearest public facility; the facilities all fully staffed, by qualified medical personnel; and, while not free, public facilities are still far and away the cheapest option available for qualified medical care (Banerjee, Deaton, and Duflo 2004). Yet, the system quite apparently fails to deliver. Even though government facilities are cheaper and staffed by trained and certified personnel, most households prefer to see private providers, who are not only unregulated, but are often unqualified.

This situation could either reflect a problem of supply, a problem of demand, or both. Public healthcare centres are closed more than half the time, whereas private doctors are available round the clock. On the other hand, private doctors happily deliver shots of antibiotics and steroids that the patients appear to demand, which public doctors are often (rightly) not allowed to prescribe. To investigate the role of supply and demand, and how they may interact, we have conducted two randomized experiments, in collaboration with Seva Mandir, a local NGO, and Vidhya Bhawan, a network of schools and teaching colleges. In the first one, Seva Mandir collaborated with the government to monitor nurses on specific days. The intervention was initially successful in reducing absenteeism, but was eventually undermined from within. This illustrates the difficulty to improve supply reliably without some feedback coming from the demand. In the second intervention, Seva Mandir provided very reliable immunization services in villages. This improved the rate of full immunization significantly (from 5 per cent to 17 per cent), but adding small incentives further increased the rate (from 17 per cent to 38 per cent). Combined, these two studies suggest that increasing demand for preventive care (and for the 'proper' curative care) is essential for any supply-driven intervention to be sustained in the long run. But they also suggest, fortunately, that improving demand may not be so difficult—households may be more indifferent than opposite. Once demand is stimulated, it may be possible to use it as a lever to improve supply.

In the remainder of the chapter, we first describe the Udaipur health survey (Section 4.2). The results are discussed in Sections 4.3 to 4.5. In Section 4.6, we pose the central challenge of healthcare—a combined supply and demand problem. Section 4.7 describes and interprets several experiments on demand and supply of basic healthcare services.

4.2 The Udaipur Rural Health Survey

The data collection took place between January 2002 and August 2003 in 100 hamlets in Udaipur district, Rajasthan. Udaipur is one of the poorest districts of India, with a large tribal population and an unusually high level of female illiteracy (at the time of the 1991 census, only 5 per cent of women were literate in rural Udaipur). The survey was conducted in collaboration with two local institutions: Seva Mandir, an NGO that works on health in rural Udaipur, among other things, and Vidya Bhavan, a consortium of schools, teaching colleges, and agricultural colleges, who supervised the administration of the survey. The sample frame consisted of all the hamlets in the 362 villages where Seva Mandir operates in at least one hamlet.[2] This implies that the sample is representative only of the population served by Seva Mandir, not of rural Udaipur district as a whole; Seva Mandir tends to operate in poorer villages, with a larger tribal population. This sample frame presents several important advantages, however. It represents a population of interest to this chapter—households in India who are among the most likely to be under-served by the healthcare system. Seva Mandir's relation with the villages ensured collaboration with the survey, and allowed us to collect very detailed information at the village and household levels. Seva Mandir's long-standing relationship with the health authorities also gained us their full collaboration, making possible a weekly survey of all public health facilities and subsequently, allowed Seva Mandir to implement a number of health interventions based, in part, on the results from the survey. Finally, the extensive network of Seva Mandir's employees in the district allowed us to hire, when needed, large numbers of reliable employees. The sample was stratified according to access to a road (out of the 100 hamlets, 50 hamlets are at least 500 metres away from a road). Hamlets within each stratum were selected randomly, with a probability of being selected proportional to the hamlet population.

The data collection had four components—a village survey, where we obtained a village census, a description of the village's physical infrastructure, and a list of health facilities commonly used by villagers (100 villages); a facility survey, where we collected detailed information on activities, types and cost of treatment, referrals, availability of medication, and quality of physical infrastructure in all public facilities (143 facilities) serving the sample villages, all 'modern' private facilities mentioned in the village surveys or in the household interviews (we have surveyed a total of 451 facilities) and a sample of the *bhopas* (traditional healers) mentioned in the village surveys (98 traditional healers were surveyed); a weekly

---

[2] A hamlet is a set of houses that are close together, share a community center, and constitutes a separate entity. A village is an administrative boundary. One to 15 hamlets constitute a village (the mean number of hamlets in a village is 5.6). Seva Mandir in general operates in the poorest hamlets within a given village.

visit to all public facilities serving the villages (143 facilities in total, with 49 visits per facility on average); and a household and individual survey, covering 5759 individuals in 1024 households.

The data collected in the household survey include information on economic well-being using an abbreviated consumption questionnaire similar to the one that was used in the National Sample Survey in their 1999–2000 survey (the 55th Round), measures of integration in society, education, fertility history, perception of health and subjective well-being, and experience with the health system (public and private), as well as a small array of direct measures of health (hemoglobin, body temperature, blood pressure, weight and height, and a peak flow meter measurement of lung capacity).

The Continuous Facility Survey (CFS) may be the most original part of the survey. We identified all the public facilities (143) serving the sample villages, and hired one para-worker who lives close to each facility, who was given the responsibility of checking the facility every week. The para-worker pays an unannounced visit to the facility during opening hours, checks whether the facility is open, and counts the number of doctors, nurses, other medical and non-medical personal, as well as of clients present in the facility. If the facility is closed, because the staff is performing a scheduled village visit, the para-worker goes to the village that the staff is supposed to be visiting, and checks whether he or she can be found in that village. To ensure the quality of the data collected in the Continuous Facility Survey (CFS), we have put in place a strictly enforced monitoring system: every four weeks, all the CFS para-workers of a block met, and we collected their data entry forms. They were also given a schedule indicating on which day they must complete their visit in each week of the following month. Two members of the team of investigators used motorcycle transport to visit several facilities everyday, following the schedule given to the CFS para-worker. The para-workers were paid only if their visits have been completed on the planned day, and if there were no unexplained discrepancies between their report and that of the CFS monitor. The CFS monitors also visited the facilities on different days, so that we could check that there was no collusion between the para-worker and the facility staff. This survey took place for 13 to 14 months, including a 'pilot period' of one to two months in each facility, where the system was fine-tuned. We report data for 12 months for each facility. The survey is complemented by a detailed one-time facility survey, which, among other things, will allow us to identify correlates of absenteeism in the centres.

4.3. Health Status

The households in the Udaipur survey are poor, even by the standards of rural Rajasthan at the time. Their average per capita household expenditure (PCE) is 470 rupees, and more than 40 per cent of the people live in households below the official poverty line, compared with only 13 per cent in rural Rajasthan in the latest official counts for 1999–2000. Only 46 per cent of adult (14 and older) males and 11 per cent of adult females report themselves literate. Of the 27 per cent of adults with any education, three-quarters completed standard eight or less. These households have little in the way of household durable goods and only 21 per cent of the households have electricity.

In terms of measures of health, 80 per cent of adult women, and 27 per cent of the adult men have haemoglobin levels below 12 grams per decilitre. 5 per cent of adult women and 1 per cent of adult men have haemoglobin levels below 8 grams per decilitre. Strikingly, using a standard cutoff for anaemia (11 g/dl for women, and 13 g/dl for men), men are almost as likely (51 per cent) to be anaemic as women (56 per cent) and older women are not less anemic than younger ones, suggesting that diet is a key factor. The average body mass index (BMI) is 17.8 among adult men, and 18.1 among adult women. 93 per cent of adult men and 88 per cent of adult women have BMI less than 21, considered to be the cutoff for low nutrition in the US (Fogel 1997). We also used peakflow meter measurement to measure lung capacity in an attempt to detect asthma or other respiratory disorders (for example, chronic bronchitis). Among adults, the average peak flow meter measurement is 316 ml per expiration (anything below 350 for an adult 1.60 metres tall is considered to be an indicator of respiratory difficulties).

Symptoms of disease are widespread, and adults self-report a wide range of symptoms. A third report cold symptoms in the last 30 days, and 12 per cent say that the condition was serious. A third reported fever (14 per cent serious), 42 (20 serious) per cent reported 'body ache', 23 (7 serious) per cent reported fatigue, 14 (3 serious) per cent problems with vision, 42 (15) per cent headaches, 33 (10) per cent back aches, 23 (9) per cent upper abdominal pain, 11 (4) per cent had chest pains, and 11 (2) per cent had experienced weight loss. Few people reported difficulties in taking care of themselves, such as bathing, dressing, or eating, but many reported difficulty with the physical activities that are required to earn a living in agriculture. 30 per cent or more would have difficulty walking 5 kilometres, drawing water from a well, or working unaided in the fields. 18 to 20 per cent have difficulty squatting or standing up from a sitting position.

In Table 4.1, we show the number of symptoms reported in the last 30 days, BMI, fraction of individuals with haemoglobin count below 12, peak flow meter reading, high blood pressure, and low blood pressure, broken down by which third of the distribution of the monthly per capita expenditure they fall into, which we collected using the abbreviated consumption questionnaire. Individuals in the lower third of the per capita income distribution have, on average, a lower body mass index and lower lung capacity and are more likely to have a haemoglobin count below 12 than those in the upper third. Individuals in the upper third report the most symptoms over the last 30 days, perhaps because they are more aware of their own health status; there is a long tradition in the Indian- and developing-country literature of better-off people reporting more sickness (see, for example, Murray and Chen 1992 and Sen 2002).

Despite these poor readings, most respondents grade their own health as rather good. Shown a ladder with 10 rungs, 62 per cent of respondents place themselves on rungs 5 through 8 (more is better), and less than seven per cent place themselves on one of the bottom two rungs. Unsurprisingly, old people report worse health, women at all ages also consistently report worse health than men, which appears to be a world-wide phenomenon (Sadana et al. 2002), and richer people report better health than poorer people. Most people report themselves close to the middle. Nor do our life-satisfaction measures show any great dissatisfaction with life—on a five-point scale, 46 per cent take the middle value, and only 9 per cent say their life makes them generally unhappy. Such results are similar to those for rich countries; for example, in the United States, more than a half of respondents report themselves as a three (quite happy) on a four-point scale, and 8.5 per cent report themselves as unhappy or very unhappy. People in rural Udaipur are presumably adapted to the sickness that they experience, in that they do not see themselves as particularly unhealthy nor, in consequence, unhappy. These optimistic health reports do not imply that people never complain.

Table 4.1 Selected health indicators, by position in the per capita monthly expenditure distribution

Group	Reported Health Status	No. of Symptoms Self Reported in Last 30 Days	BMI	Hemoglobin Below 12 g/dl	Peak Flow Meter Reading	High Blood Pressure	Low Blood Pressure
Bottom third	5.87	3.89	17.85	0.57	314.76	0.17	0.06
Middle third	5.98	3.73	17.83	0.59	317.67	0.15	0.08
Top third	6.03	3.96	18.31	0.51	316.39	0.20	0.09

Note: Means based on data collected by the author from 1024 households. See text for survey and variable description

When asked about their financial status, which was also self-reported on a ten-rung ladder, the modal response was the bottom rung, and more than 70 per cent of people live in households that were self-reported as being on the bottom three rungs.

These health evaluations suggest the possibility that people are not particularly demanding about their own physical well-being and hence may under-use healthcare facilities. A glance at the actual use data, however, disrupts this quick conclusion, as the average adult in the Udaipur survey visits a health facility once in two months. In the next section we consider the kinds of facilities that they visit.

4.4 Healthcare Facilities in Rural Udaipur

Types of Facilities

There are three broad categories of facilities: Public, private, and traditional. The official policy on public facilities requires that there should be one sub-centre, or sometimes an aid-post, staffed by one trained nurse (ANM), for every 3,000 individuals. These sub-centres provide the first point of care, the PHICs or CHCs the next step, and the referral hospitals deal with the most serious health problems. In our data, each subcenter serves 3,600 individuals on average, and is usually staffed by one nurse. Almost none of the sub-centres report vacancies, that is, there are as many nurses posted to the sub-centre as there are posts. A primary health centre serves 48,000 individuals and has on average 5.8 medical personnel appointed, including 1.5 doctors. Once again, very few of the PHCs report vacancies.

What we include as private facilities are all the places that our respondents report as private providers that they have visited. Private facilities include a wide range of options ranging from facilities run by people who have completed their medical training and have additional post-graduate medical degrees, to traditional birth attendants (TBAs/*daimas*) and pharmacists who in most cases have no formal medical training whatsoever.

Within traditional healers there are two main categories. Out of the 98 we have in our sample, 63 are *jhad-fook* practitioners who focus mainly on exorcisms and prayers, five just do *desi ilaaj* (they give traditional, usually herbal, medicines), and the rest do both.

Doctor's Qualifications

The ANM in a sub-centre is someone who has at least a high-school degree and has then undergone training to be an ANM (in Rajasthan the training lasts a year and a half). They are trained to handle a limited set of health conditions and to identify a wider set, which get referred to the PHC/CHC or to the referral hospital. The doctors in the PHC/CHCs are fully qualified to practice as general practitioners and might have some specialized degrees (87 per cent of the CHCs and 13 per cent of the PHCs have one or more specialists).

Table 4.2a in the appendix reports that 27 per cent of the private doctors who are described as the main provider in their facility claim to have some kind of specialist degree over and above the standard medical college degrees. Another 28 per cent self-report a medical college degree, though this includes a sizeable fraction who have degrees in Ayurvedic (traditional Hindu) medicine (BAMS) or Unani (traditional Islamic) medicine. Only 10.7 per cent have an MBBS, the qualification for conventional modern medicine. The rest do not claim a medical college degree. They may, however, be trained as a compounder (that is, a pharmacist) or have attended a course that gives them some medical training. In the local parlance, these doctors are referred to as Bengali doctors.

However, looking only at the main providers in the facility may be misleading. Each facility reports 2.6 staff members, of which only one can be the main provider (by the way a main provider gets defined). However, 87.8 per cent of all the staff members are reported to see patients. This implies that most of these other staff members also see patients. Among them 67.2 per cent have no formal qualifications, and less than 3 per cent are qualified as an MBBS. Whether this is a problem depends on whether they are just helping the main doctor or whether they actually independently deal with patients. The anecdotal evidence suggests that they do act as independent providers. One hears about the doctor's son who now takes care of the practice, because the older doctor who has the qualifications is now retired or the well-known (and well-qualified) doctor who rents out her name to a large number of local clinics. This is an area where we clearly need more data.

The fraction of these doctors who claim to have an MBBS (37.7 per cent) is slightly higher than the corresponding fraction in low-income neighbourhoods in Delhi (34 per cent according to Das and Hammer (2004)). Given how backward this area is in other ways compared even to the poorer parts of Delhi, this might suggest that the self-reports tend to exaggerate the qualifications.

Apart from those described as private doctors, there are also self-described compounders, nurses and pharmacists, who also practise medicine. About 10 per cent of the compounders and nurses claim to have a degree from medical college, always an Ayurvedic college. The rest have no college degrees, though more than half the nurses claim to have been trained to be an ANM.

About 36 per cent of the private doctors do not have a college degree in any subject (Table 4.2b). Among them, the average years of schooling is 11 years, which is a year less than what it takes to graduate from secondary schooling. The education level among the nurses and compounders is very similar.

Table 4.2a also shows that traditional healers do not claim to have any formal medical training. They are also less educated than the private doctors, with an average schooling level of between 4 and 5 years (Table 4.2b).

Competence

Having a degree is not necessarily evidence that the doctor knows what he is doing. In a recent innovative study, Das and Hammer (2004) attempt to quantify the competence of doctors in seven Delhi neighbourhoods using a combination of vignettes and item responses. They started with a sample of 205 public and private providers from seven Delhi neighbourhoods. The original sample frame was the set of providers who were visited by anyone in the Delhi healthcare survey (Das and Sanchez 2004), which was a representative sample of 1641 individuals from these seven neighbourhoods. They then added a certain number of additional providers who were in the same neighbourhoods, but had never been visited by those in the survey.

Each of these providers was presented with five vignettes representing the symptoms of five common health problems and asked what questions they would ask about the patient's history if someone showed up with the symptoms described in the vignette, what steps they would use to examine the patient and what treatment would they recommend. The answers were then compared to the 'ideal' answers to these questions and an item-response methodology was used to extract a single parameter that predicts the ability of the provider to give a correct answer to each of these questions. This is what they call the doctor's competence.

The average competence in the sample was remarkably low. Even in the top quintile of the competence index, doctors asked no more than 48 per cent of the history questions that they were supposed to ask, which went down to 15 per cent at the lowest quintile. For the treatment, doctors had to be between 0.6 to 1.3 standard deviations above the mean in competence before their recommended treatment had a more than 50 per cent chance of not doing harm.

Das and Hammer (2004) go on to correlate competence with doctor characteristics. They find that public doctors in hospitals are 0.4 standard deviations better than public doctors in small clinics, while private MBBS doctors are more than one standard deviation better than private non-MBBS doctors. Both types of public doctors are located between the two types of private doctors in terms of competence. Doctors located in the poorest neighbourhoods are one full standard deviation worse than doctors located in the richest neighbourhoods and this is as true of public providers as it is of the private. This inequality is compounded by the fact that the fraction of MBBS private providers is only half as high in the poorer neighbourhoods as it is in the richer ones.

Distance to Facilities

Returning to Udaipur, the median distance to the closest public facility is 1.53 kilometres while the mean is 2.09 kilometres. The mean distance to the closest PHC/CHC is 6.7 kilometres. The median distance to the closest private provider that anyone in our sample has reported using is 2.83 kilometres and the average is 3.78 kilometres. The median distance to the closest self-described qualified private doctor (once again, that anyone has reported using) is 6.72 kilometres while the mean is 8.01 kilometres. Traditional healers are much closer. The closest traditional healer in our sample is 0.62 kilometres away (median, the mean is 1.53 kilometres), and this probably understates how close they are since we only have a sample of the traditional healers.

Cost of Treatment

The services of the government doctors are supposed to be free, though everyone who is above the poverty line is required to pay for medicines, tests, and so forth. Nevertheless, visits to sub-centres are cheap. Table 4.3

in the appendix reports that the average visit to a sub-centre/aidpost costs only Rs 33, whereas visiting a Bengali doctor costs Rs 105. The average cost of visiting a PHC/CHC is Rs 138 (only Rs 100 if we leave out operations and tests), while visiting a qualified private doctor costs Rs 179 (not including operations and tests).[3] Surprisingly, visiting a traditional healer can be quite expensive—the average visit costs Rs 131 (typically because you have to bring a chicken or a goat).

Equipment and Infrastructure

Every public health facility has syringes and needles, but beyond these, equipment availability is patchy. About 20 per cent of the aidposts and one-third of the sub-centres lack a stethoscope, or a blood pressure instrument, or a thermometer or a weighing scale, and only a quarter of the sub-centres have a sterilizer. Since every facility is supposed to have at least one of each of these, there is some concern that the practitioners might have 'privatized' the equipment that was provided to them.

The quality of the infrastructure is also unimpressive. None of the sub-centres have a water supply, 7 per cent have a toilet for patients and 8 per cent have electricity. It is therefore not surprising that only 3 per cent rooms have fans, despite the 50 degrees centigrade plus weather in the summer. Finally, 45 per cent of the rooms leak when it rains.

Unfortunately, we do not have comparable data on private facilities. Casual observation suggests that the infrastructure is not much better there, but almost all of them seem to have a stethoscope and a thermometer (this is part of what makes them credible as doctors).

4.5 Patterns of Healthcare Use

The evidence in the previous section, while somewhat mixed, suggests that in terms of observable characteristics, public health facilities tend to dominate their private equivalents. The government ANM is significantly

---

[3] In a previous paper we had said that visits to public and private facilities cost more or less the same. The difference comes from a relatively small number of operations/tests in public facilities which were very expensive. Our interpretation is that these procedures are inherently expensive and the government facility may well be the least expensive and perhaps the only place to get them done.

closer than the private unqualified doctor and much cheaper. In terms of 'human capital' they seem comparable: The ANM has at least 12 years of schooling and is sure to have gone through a year and a half of training, while the qualifications of the unqualified private doctor are often either nonexistent (especially given that the non-main providers also see patients) or of questionable worth (many claim to be Registered Medical Practitioners (RMP), which only guarantees six months of training). Moreover, among the private doctors who have no college degree, years of schooling is only 11 years. Among the higher-quality facilities, once again, the PHC is both closer and cheaper than a qualified private doctor and there is no obvious difference in the qualification. Yet, as we will see, most people, including the poorest, visit healthcare providers quite often but do not make much use of the public facilities. The extra cost of the private facility therefore adds up to a significant financial burden.

How Frequent are Healthcare Visits?

In the household survey we asked where people go to get healthcare. Table 4.4 shows these results. We see that adults visit a health facility on average 0.51 times a month. The poor, defined here as people who are in households in the bottom third of the distribution of PCE (average Rs 219) per month, visit a facility 0.43 times in a month, while an adult in the middle third of the distribution (average PCE Rs 361) visits a facility 0.54 times a month and an adult in the highest group (average PCE Rs 770) visits the facility 0.55 times a month. The difference between the top third and the middle third, on the one hand, and the bottom third on the other, is significant, and remains so with village fixed effects.

Das and Sanchez (2004), using data from the Delhi survey, find the opposite relation between visits and income. The Delhi survey followed 1,621 individuals in seven Delhi neighbourhoods over a period of 16 weeks with detailed weekly interviews. In their data, the poor are actually twice as likely as the rich to visit a health provider for what Das and Sanchez call a short-term morbidity, which are non-chronic illnesses that are medically expected to get cured in less than two weeks. This is partly because the poor are sicker but the main difference comes from the fact that the rich are much more likely to self-medicate than the poor.

The difference between our results and those in Das and Sanchez (2004) may reflect the difference between our settings. Urban Delhi

Table 4.4 Frequency of healthcare visits

	Per capita Monthly Expenditure	Total number of visits in the last 30 days			
		ALL	Public	Private	Bhopa
PANEL A: MEANS					
ALL	470	0.51	0.12	0.28	0.11
Poor	219	0.43	0.09	0.22	0.12
Middle	361	0.54	0.11	0.29	0.13
Rich	770	0.55	0.15	0.33	0.07
PANEL B: OLS REGRESSIONS: dependent variable: number of visits					
Middle		0.11	0.02	0.07	0.01
		(.052)	(.023)	(.034)	(.027)
Rich		0.12	0.06	0.11	−0.05
		(.05)	(.024)	(.034)	(.022)
PANEL C: OLS REGRESSIONS, WITH VILLAGE FIXED EFFECTS					
Middle		0.14	0.02	0.09	0.02
		(.047)	(.024)	(.033)	(.023)
Rich		0.13	0.04	0.11	−0.03
		(.05)	(.026)	(.036)	(.025)
Villages Fixed effects		yes	yes	yes	yes

Note: Omitted dummies in panel B and C: poor Standard errors in parentheses below the coefficients

is vastly richer than rural Rajasthan and in particular the rich in Delhi (defined as those with per capita monthly income of about Rs 6,000) are much richer from those we call rich in the Udaipur sample (defined as those with per capita monthly expenditure of Rs 770)—to the extent that this difference in earnings is mirrored in the difference in their sophistication in matters of health, we might expect very different patterns of behaviour. The rich in Delhi are much more likely to have the know-how and the confidence to self-medicate than the rich in rural Udaipur.

In the Udaipur survey each adult interviewee was also asked what symptoms of ill-health he/she had had in the past month and what he/she did about it. Table 4.5 in the appendix reports the results. When respondents report a symptom, they visit some facility 31 per cent of the time. This frequency varies substantially by disease. They will see a provider more than 50 per cent of the time for hot fever and more than 45 per cent for diarrhea, but less than 20 per cent of the time for chest pains, trouble breathing, genital ulcers, blood in sputum, worm in stools, weight loss, night sweats and hearing and eye-sight problems. The pattern seems to be that they are more likely to see someone for relatively short-duration morbidities than for more chronic problems (other conditions which make them go to the doctor include vomiting [40 per cent of the times], cold symptoms, headaches, and productive coughs [about a third of the time each]). This is especially striking given that most of the short-duration morbidities tend to get cured on their own, or in the case of acute diarrhea, with help of some simple home remedies, while many of the chronic conditions are either potentially debilitating (hearing problems, eye-sight problems, and so forth) or possible symptoms of some grave condition (chest pains, breathing problems, blood in sweat and so forth).

Choice of Healthcare Providers

Where do these people get the healthcare they are buying? In the Udaipur survey, of the 0.51 visits to a health facility that the average person in our survey reports in a month, only 0.12 visits (that is, less than quarter) are to a public facility. The fraction of visits to a public facility is highest for the richest group, and lower for the other two groups, but about the same for each. Overall, the rich have significantly more visits to public facilities than the poor. No one uses public facilities very much, and if anything, the poor use them less than the non-poor. The majority of the rest of the visits (0.28 visits per adult per month) are to private facilities. The rest are to bhopas (0.11 visits per adult per month), who are the traditional healers. For the poor, the fraction of visits to a bhopa is well over a quarter of all visits, while for the richest group it is about an eighth of all visits.

Patients also seem to associate specific diseases with specific providers. Table 4.5 lists the conditions in the order of how likely it is that the person will see a doctor for them. When we compare public versus private facilities there is no discernable pattern, except that those who have blood in cough tend to go to the public facility relatively more often. This might reflect the success of the government TB programme. On the other hand, it is clear that the person is somewhat less likely to see a bhopa for the conditions at the top of the Table, which are the conditions which the patient presumably takes most seriously (since he goes to the doctor more for them). People are more likely to see the bhopa for spitting blood, weakness, headache, backache, shortness of breath, abdominal pains, genital ulcers than for cols, dry cough, diarrhea and skin disease. A regression of the share of visits to the bhopa on the probability of seeing anyone for that condition delivers a coefficient which is negative and almost significant. Of course, this would be more reassuring if we were confident that they were seeing the doctor for the right reason.

How Much Do You Spend?

In terms of health expenditure, columns 1 and 2 of Table 4.6 show the monthly expenditure on health in the Udaipur survey, calculated in two ways: from the expenditure survey, and from the expenditures reported in the adult and children survey. The numbers are similar, except for the rich where the expenditure derived from the expenditure survey is much larger than the expenditure calculated from adding up the previous month's visits to the 'doctors'. Column 3 shows the expenditure as a fraction of household total expenditures, and from the expenditures reported in the adult and children survey, as a fraction of personal expenditures. The average household spends 7 per cent of its budget on health. While the poor spend less in absolute amount, they spend the same amount as a share of their budget. Column 4 shows the average health expenditure for adults. It is about Rs 60s, or 13 per cent of the monthly PCE of his family, which tells us, among other things, that most of the spending is on adults. This fraction is highest for the poorest (15 per cent) and lowest for the richest group (11 per cent).

The Delhi survey shows similar but more extreme results. Das and Sanchez (2004) report that the poor and rich spend the same absolute amount on short duration morbidities, which is not surprising given that the poor go to doctor more often. On the other hand, the middle- and high-income groups spend more than 7 times as much as the poor on treating chronic illnesses. Nevertheless, the share of monthly income that is spent on health is significantly smaller for the rich.

In terms of expenditures poor adults in the Udaipur survey spend 13 per cent of their total health expenditures at public facilities, 23 per cent on bhopas, and the rest at private facilities. The rich spend 23 per cent of their total health expenditures at public facilities, and less than 10 per cent on bhopas, while the middle group spends more than 17 per cent of their health expenditures on bhopas and 13 per cent at the public facilities.[4] The rich therefore spend a significantly larger fraction of their health rupees on public facilities than do the poor, and a significantly smaller fraction on bhopas. Part of the difference in the consumption of public healthcare can be attributed to where the rich live, since, once we control for village fixed effects, the difference is smaller (5 per cent) and insignificant.

4.6 The healthcare Knot: Supply, Demand, or Both?

The evidence reviewed earlier is rather damning for India's public health system. Poor patients seem to largely avoid it, despite the fact that private doctors are less qualified, further away, and more expensive. The policy response crucially depends on why this is the case. A first possibility is that the public system is much worse in reality than it appears to be on paper. A second possibility is that the demand for healthcare may be distorted, because people do not understand what is good for them. In this view, the public healthcare system is (rightly) concerned with preventive care, and correct drug regiments. However, because learning about the effectiveness of any health treatment is particularly difficult, patients want something entirely different, and a completely unregulated private system is ready to provide that to them. The two phenomena can easily coexist and reinforce each other. For example, nurses may have very little motivation to go to work if they know that their prospective patients have no interest in what they do.

Our data shed light on both hypotheses. The public health system is indeed worse than it appears. The most obvious problem is that many providers are almost never there. Public sub-centres and primary health centres are supposed to be open 6 days a week, 6 hours a day. In the Udaipur survey, public health facilities were surveyed weekly, and we have on average 49 observations per facility. Table 4.7 summarizes the main results. On average, 44 per cent of the medical personnel are absent in sub-centres and aidposts, and 36 per cent are absent in the (larger) primary health centers and community health centers. These high rates of absence are not due to staff outreach activities since, whenever the nurse was absent from a sub-centre, we made sure to look for her in the

---

[4] The percentage do not necessarily add up to 100, because some people did not know whether some facilities were public or private.

Table 4.7　Continuous facility survey: summary statistics

	Subcenters & Aidposts	PHC & CHC
Doors closed	0.56	0.03
No personnel found	0.45	0.03
Fraction of medical personnel found	0.55	0.64
Doctor is appointed	0	0.89
Fraction of doctors present	–	0.55
At least one medical personnel is missing	0.56	0.78
Observations	5268	1716
Number of facilities	108	35
Number of visits per facility	49	49

community. Since sub-centres are often staffed by only one nurse, this high absenteeism means that these facilities are often closed—we found the subcenters closed 56 per cent of the time during regular opening hours. Only in 12 per cent of the cases was the nurse to be found in the catchment area of her sub-centre. The situation does not seem to be specific to Udaipur. Similar rates of absenteeism are found in nationally representative surveys in India (where absenteeism in PHCs was found to be 43 per cent) and Bangladesh (where it was found to be 35 per cent) (Chaudhury et al. 2003, Chaudhury and Hammer 2003).

Appendix table A4.8 reports results on the kinds of facilities we are most likely to find closed. The 6 per cent of subcenters that are far from the road have only 38 per cent of the personnel present, compared to about 55 per cent for the average. Facilities that are closer to Udaipur or to another town do not have lower absenteeism. The available amenities (water, electricity) do not seem to have a large impact, except for the presence of living quarters, which has a large impact on the fraction of personnel present, particularly in subcenters. Reservations of the position of chairperson (Sarpanch) of the local government (panchayat) for women, sometimes suggested as a lever against absenteeism because women are said to care more about healthcare, have no impact on the observed absence in subcenters, but seem to be associated with increased presence in PHCs.

The weekly survey allows us to assess whether there is any predictability in the fraction of staff present at a center or sub-centre. Table 4.9 shows a regression of the fraction of missing personnel on facility dummies (columns to 1 to 3), day of the visit dummy, and day of the visit interacted with facilities dummies (in column 2) and time of the visit dummy, interacted with facility dummies (column 3). The facility dummies are strongly significant, with F statistics of 6.16 for the sub-centres, and 17.5 for the PHC and CHC. There are clearly better and worse facilities. However, the F-statistics for the interaction between day of the week and the time of the day and the facility dummies are much smaller. For each centre, we ran a regression of the fraction of personnel missing on dummies for each day of the week, time of the day, and seasonal dummies. We find that the day of the week dummies are significant at the 5 per cent level in only 10 per cent of the regressions for the sub-centres, and in none of the regressions for the PHC and CHC; the time of the day dummies are significant only in 17 per cent of the regressions for the PHC, and 9 per cent for the sub-centres. The public facilities are thus open infrequently and unpredictably, leaving people to guess whether it is worth walking for over half-an-hour to cover the 1.4 miles that separate the average village in our sample from the closest public health facility. The probability that a centre is open is correlated with utilization of these facilities. In random visits, we find that, on open days, public facilities where the personnel are present more often have significantly more patients than those where the personnel is present less often. In the household survey, we find that, in villages that are served by a facility that is closed more often, the poor (though not the middle class or the rich) are less likely to visit the public facilities, and more likely to visit the bhopa. Of course, the causality could be running either way; from utilization to presence of the personnel, or from presence of the personnel to utilization.

Compounding the problem of facilities being closed, when you do get to an open public facility, the wait can be quite long. Figure 4.1 shows how long people had to wait, based on the household survey. 35 per cent had to wait more than half an hour. Another 25 per cent had to wait an hour or more.

Surprisingly, neither the fact that the facility is closed nor that there is a wait came up very often when we asked people who had never been to a public facility why they have not. Out of 898 people who responded (roughly 35 per cent of those asked) the most common answer, chosen by over 250 people, was 'no proper treatment at government facilities'. Another 60 people said that 'better treatment (was) available elsewhere'. The other most common answers were 'I did not need to go' (roughly 175 people), followed by 'too far' (roughly 100 people), 'too expensive', 'do not know where it is' (roughly 50 people each), and 'do not know about government hospitals' (roughly 35 people).

The last few answers suggest disinterest, but there is clearly a large group that feels that they are not getting the care they want. Part of this may be due to the fact that public doctors spend less effort with their patients. We have no direct evidence on the quality of care in our data, but for Delhi, Das and Hammer (2005) reports very clear evidence. Approximately one month after the vignettes that we described earlier were administered, one of the interview teams sat with the provider for a whole day, recording details of their interaction with each patient. These included some information about the patient such as age, gender, whether s/he was a repeat patient, the number of days sick before seeking treatment for this episode and the symptoms reported. They also recorded details about the transaction including the number of questions concerning the history of the problem, examinations performed, medicines prescribed, and (for the private sector) prices charged. Finally, they noted down the medication given, including the names and types of medicines dispensed or prescribed along with the dosage. In total, they observed 4,108 doctor/patient interactions for 193 providers.

The overall sense of healthcare in India that we get from their study is nothing short of frightening. In the median (mean) interaction the provider asks 3 (3.2) questions regarding the illness and performs some examinations (which would probably involve using a stethoscope and checking the patient's temperature). The patient is then provided with 3 (2.6) different medicines (providers dispense rather than prescribe medications in 69 per cent of all interactions) and the interaction is over in 3 (3.8) minutes. Patients are seldom referred (less than 7 per cent), given instructions (50 per cent of the time), or offered guidance regarding follow-up (35 per cent of the time). Care appears even worse in the public sector. The median public provider (median in terms of ability, as measured by performance in the vignette) spends 2.19 minutes with the patient (compared to 4.06 for a private provider), asks 2.17 questions (3.55 for private providers) and does any sort of physical exam 42 per cent of the time (against 75 per cent for the private provider). A part of this difference is explained by the fact that public providers have to see more patients, but even after controlling for the case-load they spend more than one-and-a-half minutes less with patients. Moreover, after controlling for the case-load *and the time spent with the patient*, public providers do an examination in 28 per cent less cases. This is also not because the cases are less difficult. If anything, the average case in the public facility is slightly more serious than that in the private facility.

For diarrhea and cough without fever, Das and Hammer collects specific data on what doctors did, which allows them to compare what they know (from what they said they would do in the vignette) to what they actually do. They show that doctors always do less in real exams than what they know to do (as evidenced by what they say in the vignettes) but this gap is much larger for public providers. Finally, they compare how public and private providers examine patients. In the case of diarrhea, public providers ask questions much less often about fever and the nature of the stool. This, they conclude, implies that a public provider would probably be unable to differentially diagnose dysentery from viral diarrhea, with potentially life-threatening consequences.

The private providers ask more questions and also tend to prescribe more medicines, which may not be warranted. After controlling for qualifications and the type of illness, public providers prescribe 0.13 less antibiotics (this amounts to 0.2 standard deviations of the distribution of antibiotics prescribed) and 0.53 less drugs overall (amounting to almost 0.4 standard deviations of the distribution of the number of drugs prescribed). Given that most of the cases they were treating were of the self-limiting kind, this suggests (but does not prove) that private doctors tend to over-medicate. This is consistent to what we observe in Udaipur, where the patient is given a shot in 68 per cent of the visits to a private facility and a drip in 12 per cent of the visits. A test is performed in only 3 per cent of the visits. In public facilities, they are much less likely to get an injection or a drip (32 per cent and 6 per cent, respectively) but no more likely to be tested. Among private doctors, in this sample, it does not appear that more qualified doctors are less likely to administer shots. Given the evidence on the nature of the ailments that people see doctors for it does seem likely that shots and drips are being overused, at least by the private doctors, and perhaps even by the public providers.

Advocates for an expanded public health system point to facts like these to argue that we cannot expect the market to function effectively in this environment. People simply do not have the necessary judgement. For example, a number of public health officials told us that private doctors were popular because people wanted to be given shots and drips even when they were not medically necessary and private doctors were willing to give them what they wanted, while they, the public health providers, were discouraged from doing so. They also claimed that they needed to buy shots and drips from the market and sell them to the patients, in order to compete effectively with the private doctors.

There is thus evidence that people find it difficult to navigate the market for private healthcare. The pattern of doctor visits we described earlier is consistent with the view that people do not demand the services most important for their health. Adults are more likely to see doctors for acute conditions that will go away on their own than for symptoms of chronic conditions that are potentially much more serious. The fact that people spend so much money on bhopas and trust them to deal with what could be serious health problems (28 per cent of the visits for a pain in the upper abdomen, 33 per cent of the visits for a pain in the lower abdomen or a genital ulcer, and 40 per cent of the visits for menstrual problems are to the bhopa) is obviously worrying, as is the fact that many of them (especially the poor) treat short-duration morbidities but not dangerous chronic conditions.

Das and Sanchez (2004) and Das (2000) reach the same conclusion based on the analysis of a data set from Uttar Pradesh and Bihar, as well as the observations in the Delhi survey. They conclude that there are reasons to be concerned about the possibility that the poor are wasting their money on curing diseases that will cure themselves, while the rich know that they are better off self-medicating and letting nature take its course. It is true that this evidence is not entirely water-tight. After all, it is possible that what the poor describe as short-duration morbidities are actually symptoms of some chronic illness. However, as Das and Sanchez point out, the fact that the ratio of expenditures on chronic illnesses relative to short-duration morbidities is much higher for the rich than for the poor remains true when the sample is restricted to those who are under 30 and, therefore, have very few chronic illnesses. And while it is possible that the poor are just much more ill when they have a short-duration morbidity, the rich–poor gap remains when Das and Sanchez control for the type and duration of the illness.

There is also reason to be concerned about the fact that competition does not eliminate the many private practitioners who are both unqualified and incompetent. One reason may be that people actually do not know the qualifications of the people they see. In Udaipur we asked people who they saw and whether he/she was a qualified doctor. Comparing these answers with the provider's sell-description (we can match 440 facilities), we see that when the household say that the provider is not qualified, he/ she has an MBBS or equivalent in 27 per cent of the cases and is semi-qualified (RMP and so forth) in 32 per cent of the cases. When they say he/she is qualified, 24 per cent turn out to be entirely unqualified and another 26 per cent are semi-qualified. Thus, while people do not always know about the qualification of the providers they see, there is no evidence that they are systematically deluded.

There is thus potentially some truth to both the supply and the demand hypotheses. Finally, there is some evidence that they interact. Where public health facilities are available, people are less likely to go to unqualified private doctors. In the Udaipur data we recorded the GPS location of each of the facilities and the households. From this, we computed the distance from each household to all the private and public facilities in the sample. We use this to identify the closest modern private facility (doctor, compounder, RMP, and so forth) from this sample household, the closest qualified doctor (a private facility where at least one provider has an MBBS degree or equivalent) and the number of modern private facilities within 5, 10, and 20 kilometres from the household, respectively. Likewise, we identified the closest public facilities, and the closest PHC or CHC.

We then regressed a dummy for whether the last health visit of the individual was at a bhopa, a private practitioner, or a public facility (qualified or unqualified) on the distance from the closest PHC, the distance from the closest public facility, the number of qualified and unqualified doctors within 5 kilometres, and other control variables. The results show that people are more likely to visit a private unqualified practitioner if the PHC or CHC is further away. We also find that people are more likely to visit bhopas when the public facilities are closed more often, though it is not clear how we should interpret this last piece of evidence. Is it the case that patients are more desperate in places where public facilities are closed more often, and turn to bhopas? Or is it the case that nurses' intrinsic motivation plummets when they find that there is no demand for their services, and that they stop coming to work?

4.7 Identifying Policy Levers: Two Randomized Experiments

The evidence presented earlier suggests that both supply and demand play a role in the low quality of healthcare received by the population in

Udaipur, and that they probably mutually reinforce each other. It leads to two essential research and policy questions. First, what can be achieved by intervening exclusively on the supply side? Is it possible to influence supply without affecting demand? Or would such a policy fall flat on its face without popular pressure to sustain the intervention? Second, what can be achieved by intervening on the demand side? Is it possible to direct demand towards 'right' behaviour, or is pandering to what poor patients want the only way to affect demand for the public healthcare, as the discouraged nurses in Udaipur say? Second, what can be achieved by intervening exclusively on the supply side? Is it possible to influence supply without affecting demand? Or would such a policy fall flat on its face without popular pressure to sustain the intervention?

To answer these questions, we set up two randomized experiments in collaboration with Seva Mandir and with the district administration in Udaipur. We also started dreaming of a third that took some years to be finally implemented.

4.7.1 A Failed Supply-side Intervention: Monitoring the Nurses

The first intervention (Banerjee, Duflo, and Glennerster 2008) was a pure supply-side, top-down, targeted at the problem of absent nurses, which was one of the priorities that emerged from the public discussions of the results from the 2003 Udaipur Health Survey. Seva Mandir had some experience in dealing with absenteeism. Faced with a 40 per cent teacher absence rate in its schools, it introduced a system of strict monitoring and incentives based on presence, which halved teacher absence, increased the number of child-days in the schools by 30 percentage points, and increased test scores by 0.2 of a standard deviation (Duflo, Hanna and Ryan 2008). In 2004, Seva Mandir opened negotiations with the government to implement a similar monitoring and incentives programme for nurses. By this time, a number of sub-centers had two nurses—a 'regular', tenured ANM, and an 'additional ANM', hired on a yearly contract basis). In November 2005, Seva Mandir and the government agreed that Seva Mandir would monitor the additional ANM for three days a week (the days were agreed to with the local administration), in 16 randomly selected centers (12 two-nurse centres were assigned to be controls). In January 2006, the district administration also passed a directive requiring all nurses in all centres to be at their centre every Monday (so no field visit and no meetings were supposed to occur on this day). Seva Mandir was asked to monitor the regular ANMs on Mondays in 33 randomly chosen centres with just one ANM. Thirty-nine single ANM centres were left as controls for this experiment.

To monitor presence, Seva Mandir used date and time stamping machines, locked into a caddy and password protected to prevent tempering. The ANM was supposed to stamp a register secured to the wall of the sub-centre three times a day: once at 9 a.m., once between 11 a.m. and 1 a.m., and once at 3 p.m. She must both sign and stamp following a routine that ensures that only the ANM can sign. If an ANM does not stamp on a particular day but has a legitimate reason, she indicates this on the register. Some absences are 'excused' and count as presences; we refer to those days subsequently as exempt days. In particular, any absence that is the result of a government-mandated meeting, survey, or other health work is authorized. Exempt days are then supposed to be verified by the ANM's supervisor in the PHC. Another reason why an ANM may not be able to stamp is if the machine malfunctions, in which case the ANM was given the responsibility of warning the office to get a replacement.

The sub-centre registers were collected at the beginning of each new month by Seva Mandir, and delivered to the nurses' supervisors, who were supposed to verify them and then send them to the district headquarters. The incentives based on these reports were supposed to have some bite. In February 2006, the Chief Medical Health Officer (CHMO) of Udaipur District announced the following incentives to complement the monitoring in the randomly assigned centres: ANMs absent for more than 50 per cent of the time on monitored days would have their pay reduced by the number of absences recorded by Seva Mandir's monitoring system for that month. Further, ANMs absent for more than 50 per cent of the time on monitored days for a second month would be suspended from government service.

The main results of the evaluation are presented graphically, in Figures 4.1 and 4.2 (updated from Banerjee, Duflo, and Glennerster (2008), with the data set from the full time period of the intervention). These graphs show the rate of presence of nurses, as verified by random checks at unannounced times. As we explained earlier, there were two distinct experiments: the monitoring of the single ANM and the monitoring of the additional ANM in two ANM centres. Figure 4.1 shows the fraction of centres where the regular ANM was present in treatment and control centres. We separate out data for Mondays—the days when these ANMs were monitored and had to stamp the register—and for the other days of the week.[5] Figure 4.2 shows the results for the second ANM in two ANM sub-centres. In this case, the second ANM is monitored three days a week. Again, we show presence for monitored and unmonitored days separately and contrast this with the control. Both graphs tell the same story. Early on, there was a large impact of the experiment. For centres where there was a single ANM, presence was initially 60 per cent in the treatment group, and 30 per cent in the control group; for the additional ANM in centres with two ANM, the rate of presence of the treatment ANM is about 15 percentage points higher than for the control ANM. However, the presence of the monitored ANM plummets over time (whereas some improvement is observed in the control group, for single ANMs on Monday). After 6 months, the treatment effect entirely disappears, and even turns negative in some cases. Furthermore, the rate of presence of both treatment and control ANM by the end of the evaluation period are both staggeringly low, much worse than the 44 per cent documented in 2002–2003.

What accounts for these results? An analysis of the register data given by the nurses sheds some light on this. As presence declined in the registers (consistent with our data), two categories gained in importance over time, 'exempted' days and 'broken machines'. The 'machine problems' are likely to be the result of the ANM's response to the incentive system. When a machine is broken, she does not have to stamp until she gets a new one or gets hers fixed. But she cannot get a new one if she is not at the sub-centre to meet the programme monitor. So, if she deliberately stops coming to the sub-centre after the machine starts malfunctioning, she does not need to stamp (and is therefore not monitored anymore). Over time, we saw a number of machines that had very clearly been deliberately broken.[6] It also took longer and longer to find the ANM after she

[5] In the first few weeks of the evaluation, due to a miscommunication in the field, random checks happened only on Mondays in the treatment centers and only on other days in the comparison centers. In all the analysis below, we control for the day of the week in which the random check happened.

[6] Some of them were in a state suggesting they had been hurled onto a wall. The ANM also explicitly told Seva Mandir that this is what they would do.

reported a problem. The increase in the number of 'exempt days' is very likely to be a systemic response also. The exempt days can only be granted by the PHC (they are intended to make it possible for the ANM to perform other duties or attend meetings) and therefore the PHC officials can always check if there are any fake exempt days. The ANM cannot lie about the number of exempt days without the explicit complicity of the PHC officials that she reports to. In turn, the activities at the PHC are monitored by the CMHO of the district, who also gets data and graphs showing the increase in the number of exempt days over time from Seva Mandir. In short, one of two essentially equivalent things is happening. Either the PHC, knowing fully well that being exempt from monitoring is essentially a license to stay home, is providing those excuses to the ANM; or the ANM is making them up, and the PHC is not sanctioning them. In either case, the health administration has undermined the system it had itself put in place, so that the incentives, which remain on the books, no longer have any bite.

Thus, the monitoring system collapsed from within. Why did the district administration undermine a very successful system of incentives that it had introduced? One possibility is that the idea that the nurses should be given some incentives came from the collector, the head of the district administration, but he was not directly in charge of implementing it. Given that the idea came from the head of the district, the health administrators (the CMHO and the doctors at PHC) probably could not refuse to implement it. However, they (the CMHO and other health officials) were probably the people who faced pressure from the ANMs to get rid of the new policy. Rather than press for cancelling the system, which would have been somewhat embarrassing given that it only required that the ANMs come to work half of the time, it was easier to arrange things so that the incentives were not binding. This was a convenient way to save face while being compliant with the orders, at least on paper, though it meant Seva Mandir was wasting resources by monitoring the nurses. Since the rules were respected, it gave the collector no reason to take disciplinary action against anybody.

But there remains a bigger puzzle. Why was the health administration free to let the nurses off? Why were they not under pressure from the would-be beneficiaries, through the political system, to actually deliver improved services? A part of the answer is that the local governments have little power over the health administration. The only way to put pressure on the health officials is to go all the way up to the areas representative in the state assembly (the 'MLA'). The MLA represents many villages, each with multiple demands. Unless the health system is a top priority for a large number of these villages, it is not clear that it would ever claim enough of the MLA's attention to make a difference. And improving the public health system is probably not at the top of the list of what people are demanding. This is consistent with the evidence that, even when the nurses were coming to work (during the first six months of the programme), and this was announced in the communities, we don't find any increase in the (very low) number of patients in the health centres.

The fact that demand for the nurse system was low does not have to mean that people do not care about healthcare, not even for the type of healthcare provided in the health facilities. It could mean that they have decided the government is unlikely to be particularly effective at providing health care. In this particular case, had they switched from their private provider to the public system just after the programme was introduced, they would have regretted it, because the improvement was extremely short-lived. In other words, the lack of a demand response to the supply improvement may be due to the fact that this supply improvement was rightly perceived as unreliable and temporary.

4.7.2 A Successful Supply-side Intervention: Immunization Camps

To find out whether a significant, credible and durable improvement in the supply of one particular kind of health services would result in a change in the pattern of healthcare demand, we designed another experiment with Seva Mandir (the results are reported in Banerjee, Duflo, Glennerster, and Kothari 2008). Seva Mandir, which enjoys a very strong reputation for reliability, earned through 50 years of dedicated work in the district, set up some regular camps in 60 villages, randomly chosen out of 134. Lack of immunization is a serious issue in Udaipur district. At baseline, less than 3 per cent of the children aged 1 to 5 were fully immunized, although almost half had received at least one of the required shots (and almost all of them had been given the pulse polio drop at least once). These results are much bleaker than what is usually assumed. Official statistics vastly inflate the number of immunized children, because everyone, from the nurses to the government, has incentives to over-report. Nurses are subjected to numerical targets (Coutinho, Bisht, Raje 2000), and state governments like to show off their immunization rates.[7] Even survey data (such as the National Family Health survey) over-estimates immunization because parents are simply asked whether or not the child received certain vaccines. But when parents do not have the card, it is unreasonable to assume that they actually remember exactly what the child has received, or to be able to accurately identify between vaccine doses and shots that were intended as a treatment for a disease, and this tends to inflate the number of doses that are claimed to have been received.

In 30 of these villages, the camps simply tried to replicate what would be a reliable supply of immunization services, organizing an immunization camp once a month, at a fixed date in the village. The nurse in charge of the immunization and his assistant were hired by Seva Mandir, and their pay was tightly tied to attendance (which was monitored using time and dated stamps, as in the teacher project). As a result, over 95 per cent of the scheduled camps took place. Furthermore, a Seva Mandir para-worker was in charged of mobilizing mothers to attend them camp. The para-worker was rewarded as function of children who attended the camp. Given the trust in Seva Mandir as an organization, this intervention probably represented the best possible scenario for a purely supply-driven intervention. Mistrust of immunization, which is sometimes an issue in India (immunization has sometimes been accused by people of causing sterilization, for example, see Nichter 1995), was minimal, and villagers were assured that the camps would indeed be held as announced, and they would not waste their time coming to the village centre to get their child immunized. Furthermore, the para-worker played exactly the role that the new cadre of health worker, introduced under India's National Rural Health Mission (the 'ashas'), are supposed to play, an intermediary between the population and the formal health system.

The results of setting up this infrastructure were positive, but relatively modest. An average of 4.5 children per month attended each camp. After

[7] Although the countries they cover do not cover India, Murray et al (2009) show the extent of overestimation of immunization in the official statistics in countries that receive GAVI payments (about $20 per child immunized above the baseline). In the sample they look at, compared to survey data, the number of additional children receiving DTP was overestimated by a factor of 2 in the official statistics, compared to the survey data.

two years, 17 per cent of the children aged 1–3 were fully immunized in the villages were the camps were held (against 5 per cent in the control group). There was no spillover to neighbouring villages. We surveyed children in villages in a neighbourhood of about 6 kilometres and there was essentially no increase in immunization in villages located near the treatment villages, compared to other villages in the control group. On balance, it does not seem that a pure supply-side intervention would be sufficient to induce large increases in the take-up of the services provided in public health centres. Furthermore, because few children attended each camp, this approach turns out to be rather expensive, on average $55 to fully immunize a child in the camp. This is more than the $20 dollar a month disbursed by GAVI to its partner countries for additional children immunized (and of course significantly more than the budget for immunization in India, something of the order of $2 a child).

4.7.3 Influencing Demand: 'Conditional Lentil Transfers'

If even a fully reliable supply of immunization, doubled with a real effort to inform and motivate parents via the para-workers, does that mean that convincing households to get preventive care is impossible? Does a health system that does not pander to demand lose any chance to attract clients?

The pattern of results in the immunization camps does not suggest that the relatively low rate of immunization is due to fear or mistrust, as 77 per cent of children receive at least one shot, and 72 per cent receive at least two shots, in two separate visits. Thus, it is not the case that, for example, that the first shot did something they did not expect, and this discouraged them from coming back. It is by the third shot that the rate starts to go down (42 per cent of children receive three shots or more— the full course being five shots). Parents were at least willing to give it a try but progressively lost interest. The failure to fully immunize is more likely to be a certain indifference than any real resistance. The reason for this indifference might either be a lack of understanding of how immunization works or some form of procrastination, a certain tendency to delay incurring some small costs. If this is the case, a small incentive might tip the balance in favor of immunization. To test this idea, Seva Mandir selected another 30 villages (they were also randomly selected out of the 134 villages) where the same camps were introduced, but in addition villagers were offered a kilogram of lentils (worth about half a day of the minimum wage) for each immunization and a set of plates for a completing a full round of immunization.

The results of this seemingly small inducement were impressive. The complete immunization rate jumped to 38 per cent, and 46 per cent of children received at least four shots. Moreover, immunization rates also increase in neighbouring villages. The immunization rate in villages located within a radius of 6 kilometers increased to 20 per cent. The number of children immunized in these camps was on average 13 per month. Since the fixed cost was spread over a larger number of children, the cost per child fully immunized turned out to be lower in these camps despite the cost of the lentils (on average around $28 per child).

4.7.4 Can This be Done at Scale?

These results were so impressive that we immediately started finding ways to form partnership with governments to perform a larger trial, perhaps as a prelude to scaling up. We encountered a surprising level of resistance to the idea. In State after State, we were served the same ideological comment that people should not be paid for doing things that they should do anyways (never mind the fact that, in India, there are incentives for any number of behaviour, from sterilization to delivery in hospital). Similarly, large foundations, like the Bill and Melinda Gates foundation, had put on their money on improving the supply of services: Entire health departments were busy with microplans and beautifully crafted maps or where nurses were supposed to be immunizing kids. A first breakthrough came when a UNICEF executive embraced the idea, and it picked the interested of the government in Haryana in 2012. Over the course of several years, we completely changed the programmes to make it workable at scale: nurses registers were replaced by a tablet loaded with a simple e-health application. Lentils gave the way to cell phone recharges, that can be delivered simply and do not face any procurement issues. The programme was implemented at scale, randomized across 140 PHC, covering 2400 villages, and hundreds of thousands of children (298489 children were recorded in the system). The scale also allowed to test whether payment amounts matter, and whether a flat or a 'slopped' schedule were more likely to optimal. The results are clear. Even at that large scale, incentives work. Every month, 14 per cent more children attend the camp in the villages where incentives were progressive. How much was paid does not matter, but the profile mattered: Flat incentives, did nothing (Banerjee et al. 2019).

4.7.5 Improving the Supply Side: Training 'Bengali Doctors'

As already noted unqualified private providers play an important, if potentially ambiguous, role in the healthcare system. Governments have however mostly refused to engage with them, on the grounds that they lack legitimacy. In recent years, however, an NGO in West Bengal called Liver Foundation has started to train them, mostly in being effective intermediaries (for example with respect to triage) rather than doctors. Das. et al. (2016) reports on a RCT of the impact of a 9-month training program that involved classes every weekend. We find that the training program reduced the gap in treatment quality between the unqualified providers and the qualified providers in public healthcare system by half for providers with mean attendance (56%) and reduced the gap almost entirely for providers who completed the full course. This seems to be the result of better adherence to the condition-specific checklists, rather than an increase in the quantum of their knowledge. Consistent with this, there was an economically and statistically significant improvement in the number of patients that visited these providers and their earnings. However there was no change in the prescription of unnecessary medicines, though both treatment and control practitioners in this population are substantially less likely to prescribe unneeded medicines than the trained public sector doctors.

***

At one level what we need to do might seem obviously clear: Get rid of the unqualified doctors, regulate treatments better, and improve incentives to put in effort, especially in the public sector. The question, of course, is 'how'.

There are some relatively easy ways to improve regulation, at least if the political will exists. The fact that any Indian can walk into a pharmacy and buy essentially any drug without a prescription is one of the main reasons why so many unqualified and semi-qualified practitioners survive and flourish. First, the law on who can prescribe what could be tightened and enforced better. One can imagine random checks of what was prescribed or even sting operations to make the law more effective. Second, pharmacies could be penalized for selling scheduled drugs without a valid prescription from somebody who is allowed to prescribe that particular drug (as they are supposed to be). Once again, sting operations could be used to identify violators. Once these two restrictions are in place, unqualified doctors would have a hard time staying in business since their patients would not have access to any drugs. Moreover, the tendency to over-medicate would somewhat be curbed, because a lot of the semi-qualified doctors would be limited in what they are allowed to prescribe.

The government could also create a standardized system for classifying doctors that is simple enough to be intelligible to all patients: say, specialist, qualified, semi-qualified. These classifications should be verified and updated every five or ten years, to avoid the problem of hereditary doctors. The current classification of the doctor would be required to be prominently displayed at the dispensary, using colours or icons that anyone can identify.

None of this really solves the core problems of distorted demand and doctor indifference, at least in the short run. At best, the regulations will improve the average quality of the doctors that people see and put some limits on how easily the patients can be mistreated. But if the patients really want a certain type of treatment, they will probably be able to get it. Over-medication is as much a problem in the case of qualified private doctors as it is for the unqualified (Das and Hammer 2005), and a black-market in drugs may emerge to circumvent the regulations. Nevertheless, the fact that these drugs are now harder to obtain and more expensive, combined with the fact that they now hear that these drugs are illegal, might, in the long run, persuade people to try the alternative of letting self-limiting ailments take their course. And perhaps once they see that it works, they might actually grow to think of it as the norm. More generally, educating patients has to be a priority if the system is to work better.

The harder question is how to get doctors to behave, to use what they know, and put more effort into examining patients. The most basic issue here is how to deal with absence in public facilities. Local control is the one solution that is being widely discussed these days. This was the main approach advocated by the World Bank (2004) Development Report on social services delivery. Shanta Devarajan, who directed the report, summarizes the idea:

Services can work when poor people stand at the center of service provision - when they can avoid poor providers, while rewarding good providers with their clientele, and when their voices are heard by politicians - that is, when service providers have incentives to serve the poor.

In Uganda, Bjorkman and Svensson (2009) found significant improvement in the quality of the healthcare provided in public facility after a successful campaign to strengthen local control over the health facilities. The situation is quite different in Uganda than in India, however. There are few private doctors in Uganda, and the alternative to government facilities are either self-remedy or traditional healers who offer very different services. Local control would be much less likely to work in India where people are largely indifferent to what is happening in the public facilities.

Low and distorted demand unfortunately affects more than community-control. Through the political channel, it also undermines the effectiveness of purely supply-driven intervention. Without demand for these services, the pressure to maintain them cannot be sustained, as the ANM experiment demonstrated.

If the demand for private practitioners is bound to remain high, then perhaps the reasonable objective should not be to get rid of them but to give them an actual role by training them better to manage the simpler conditions, and triage those that cannot be managed. At least, the private doctors are trusted by their patients and have the incentives to treat them well.

One problem that is not solved by the intervention is that the providers continue to over-prescribe unnecessary drugs, perhaps because patient demand for those is too strong to be resisted. It thus seems that finding successful ways to affect demand is essential. Fortunately, it does not seem to be so difficult, as the results of the 'lentils for vaccine' programme suggests. Affecting demand turns out to be much easier than what may have been expected. This is consistent with evidence from a number of settings and countries, suggesting a very large price elasticity of the demand for preventive products.[8] One consistent finding of a number of independent

[8] This is of course also consistent with the evidence that conditional cash transfers increase the take up of preventive health services (see Fiszbein and Schady (2008) for a review), but CCT are typically much larger transfers, which would be expected to have both income and price effects.

randomized studies is the price elasticity of demand around zero is huge. Kremer and Miguel (2007) found that raising the price of de-worming drugs from 0 to 30 cents per child In Kenya, reduces the fraction of children taking the drug from 75 per cent to 19 per cent. Also in Kenya, Cohen and Dupas (2007) find that raising the price of insecticide treated bednets from 0 to 60 cents reduces the fraction of those who buy the nets by 60 percentage points. Raising the price of water disinfectant from 9 cents to 24 cents, Ashraf, Berry, and Shapiro (2007) found, reduces the fraction who take up the offer in Zambia by 30 percentage points. Similar large responses are also found with small subsidies. Most remarkably, a reward of 10 cents got 20 percentage more people in Malawi to pick up the results of their HIV test (Thornton, 2007). Moreover, Dupas (2009) finds encouraging results that, when a household has received one free bednet, they are at least as likely (and even somewhat more likely) to pay for a second one, and that their neighbors are also more likely to acquire one. This suggests that affecting the demand for health services may not be so difficult. Once demand is stimulated somewhat, one may hope that this will provide the necessary feedback to allow improvements in care to be sustained over time.

Appendix

Table A4.2a Medical Training

Facility Type	No Formal Qual	RMP	BAMS	BIMS	BUMS	MBBS	BHMS/ DHMS	MBBS +Spec	ANM	Pharm	Seva Mandir	Other NGO Training	Govt Training	Other Training	Total
Private doctor	13.9%	21.3%	6.6%	0.8%	0.0%	10.7%	10.7%	27.0%	0.0%	0.0%	0.0%	0.0%	0.0%	14.8%	105.7%
Nurse/MPW	0.0%	0.0%	11.1%	0.0%	0.0%	0.0%	0.0%	0.0%	55.6%	0.0%	0.0%	0.0%	0.0%	33.3%	100.0%
Compounder	15.6%	6.3%	12.5%	0.0%	3.1%	0.0%	0.0%	1.6%	6.3%	3.1%	0.0%	0.0%	6.3%	45.3%	100.0%
Pharmacist	75.0%	0.0%	0.0%	0.0%	0.0%	0.0%	0.0%	0.0%	0.0%	6.3%	18.8%	0.0%	0.0%	0.0%	100.0%
TBA/Dai	76.6%	0.0%	0.0%	0.0%	0.0%	0.0%	0.0%	0.0%	0.0%	0.0%	22.5%	0.0%	0.0%	0.0%	99.1%
VHW	4.5%	0.0%	0.0%	0.0%	0.0%	0.0%	0.0%	0.0%	0.0%	0.0%	86.4%	9.1%	4.5%	0.0%	104.5%
Community Health Worker	0.0%	0.0%	0.0%	0.0%	0.0%	0.0%	0.0%	0.0%	0.0%	0.0%	50.0%	0.0%	0.0%	50.0%	100.0%
Home Remedy Worker	0.0%	50.0%	0.0%	0.0%	0.0%	0.0%	0.0%	50.0%	0.0%	0.0%	0.0%	0.0%	0.0%	0.0%	100.0%
Trad healer/ Desi ilaj Practitioner	60.0%	0.0%	0.0%	0.0%	0.0%	0.0%	0.0%	0.0%	0.0%	0.0%	20.0%	20.0%	0.0%	0.0%	100.0%
Jhaad fonk Practitioner	100.0%	0.0%	0.0%	0.0%	0.0%	0.0%	0.0%	0.0%	0.0%	0.0%	0.0%	0.0%	0.0%	0.0%	100.0%
Desi ilaj and jhadd fonk	96.7%	0.0%	0.0%	0.0%	0.0%	0.0%	0.0%	0.0%	0.0%	0.0%	0.0%	3.3%	0.0%	0.0%	100.0%
Private hospital	0.0%	2.4%	0.0%	2.4%	0.0%	9.5%	0.0%	63.1%	2.4%	0.0%	0.0%	0.0%	0.0%	27.4%	107.1%
Ayurvedic	50.0%	0.0%	50.0%	0.0%	0.0%	0.0%	0.0%	0.0%	0.0%	0.0%	0.0%	0.0%	0.0%	0.0%	100.0%
Non medical Profession	75.0%	0.0%	0.0%	0.0%	0.0%	0.0%	0.0%	0.0%	0.0%	0.0%	25.0%	0.0%	0.0%	0.0%	100.0%
Other	28.6%	0.0%	0.0%	0.0%	0.0%	0.0%	0.0%	0.0%	0.0%	0.0%	28.6%	0.0%	0.0%	42.9%	100.0%

Table A4.2b Main Provider Education

Factype	Percentage Educated People	Percentage Educated in NFE	Main Providers			Mean Class Reached By People Who Went To School and Do Not Have Grad Diploma
			Percentage Who Went To School	Percentage Graduate People	Percentage Who Went To School But Not Graduates	
Private doctor	100.0%	0.0%	100.0%	63.1%	36.9%	11.1
Nurse/MPW	100.0%	0.0%	100.0%	22.2%	77.8%	11.4
Compounder	100.0%	3.1%	96.9%	34.4%	62.5%	11.5
Pharmacist	100.0%	0.0%	100.0%	6.3%	93.8%	9.3
TBA/Dai	7.2%	5.4%	1.8%	0.0%	1.8%	2.5
VHW	95.5%	4.5%	90.9%	0.0%	90.9%	6.4
Community Health Worker	100.0%	0.0%	100.0%	0.0%	100.0%	10.0
Home Remedy Worker	100.0%	0.0%	100.0%	50.0%	50.0%	11.0
Trad healer/desiilaj practitioner	60.0%	20.0%	40.0%	0.0%	40.0%	4.5
Jhaad fonk practitioner	23.8%	6.3%	17.5%	0.0%	17.5%	5.0
Desi ilaj and jhaddfonk	40.0%	10.0%	30.0%	0.0%	30.0%	3.7
Private hospital	97.6%	0.0%	97.6%	92.9%	4.8%	12.0
Ayurvedic	100.0%	0.0%	100.0%	0.0%	100.0%	11.0
Non medical profession	75.0%	0.0%	75.0%	0.0%	75.0%	8.0
Other	85.7%	14.3%	71.4%	14.3%	57.1%	8.8

Table A4.3 Health-care costs

Facility type	Total Health Visit Cost (w/o Transportation) Clients: Average cost	Visit Cost (average of all) According To — Private Provider: Total Consultation Fee (Poor)	Total Consultation Fee (Rich)	Public Provider: Percentage of Facilities Who Charge Any Fee	Maximum Fee That Can be Charged	Costs with Test/Ope — Client: Cost of Visits with Tests or Operations	Provider: Amount for Lab Test + Operation+ Inpatient Stay	Cost Without Test/Ope — Client: Cost of Visits Without Tests or Operations
CHC/	138.1			87.50%	17.3	683.0	14	100.2
PHC				0.0%				
Government referral								
Hospital	1217.2					3145.2		555.0
Private hospital	889.5	1364.1	1344.5			3106.4		462.4
Ayurvedic hospital	1981.4			0.0%		29326.7		73.6
TB hospital	401.0					6667.0		·
Dispensary	0.0					0.0		·
Aidpost/ subcenter	32.8			0.0%		300.0		32.5

(*Cont'd*)

Table A4.3 (Cont'd)

Total Health Visit Cost (w/o Transportation)		Visit Cost (average of all) According To				Costs with Test/Ope		Cost Without Test/Ope
	Clients	Private Provider		Public Provider		Client	Provider	Client
Facility type	Average cost	Total Consultation Fee (Poor)	Total Consultation Fee (Rich)	Percentage of Facilities Who Charge Any Fee	Maximum Fee That Can be Charged	Cost of Visits with Tests or Operations	Amount for Lab Test + Operation+ Inpatient Stay	Cost of Visits Without Tests or Operations
Angawadi	0.0					0.0		0.0
Health camp	0.0				.	0.0		0.0
NGO clinic	121.8					774.0		78.5
Private qualified doctor	178.6	107.4	130.0			1788.0		145.3
Private nurse/	157.9	53.3	61.7			4410.0		91.4
Componder		44.0	46.9					
Private pharmacist	16.7	38.5	37.3		.			16.7
Bengali doctor	105.2					394.7		99.5

Government doctor, private practice	179.2					3383.3	132.9
Practitionner, private Practice							
Practice	103.7					540.0	93.5
TBA/Dai	103.3	6.2	10.7		·		103.3
VHW/	0.9	4.0	4.5		·		0.9
CHW		42.5	50.0				
HRW	33.2	767.5	767.5		·		33.2
bhopa	130.8						
(desi ilaj/	11.9	11.9					
jhaad fonk/	8.0	8.0					
both)	7.4	12.0					
OTHER	16.1	18.6	27.1			0.0	17.1
Don't know	144.5					2050	103.8
ayurvedic		30.0	30.0				
non medical profession		2.8	2.8				

Note: we do not have detail on operations/lab test for private providers

Table A4.5 Choice of Facilities

Condition	Mean	Any Visit	Fraction of Private Hosp	Fraction of Private Visit	Pub	Pvt	NGO	Bhopa
MILD AND SERIOUS								
Hot Fever	0.32	0.54	0.03	0.02	0.19	0.59	0.01	0.14
Diarrhea	0.16	0.45	0.05	0.02	0.20	0.62	0.01	0.10
Vomiting	0.09	0.40	0.02	0.01	0.18	0.61	0.00	0.16
Pain in Upper Abdomen	0.23	0.38	0.03	0.01	0.20	0.45	0.00	0.29
Body Ache	0.42	0.37	0.04	0.02	0.21	0.51	0.01	0.20
Cold Symptoms	0.33	0.35	0.03	0.03	0.20	0.61	0.01	0.10
Cough with Blood	0.01	0.34	0.20	0.00	0.30	0.40	0.00	0.10
Dry Cough	0.20	0.34	0.02	0.01	0.23	0.60	0.02	0.10
Headache	0.42	0.34	0.03	0.01	0.20	0.53	0.02	0.19
Productive Cough	0.11	0.33	0.07	0.00	0.22	0.54	0.02	0.13
Pain in Lower Abdomen	0.12	0.31	0.01	0.04	0.14	0.47	0.00	0.33
Back Ache	0.33	0.28	0.03	0.03	0.21	0.49	0.03	0.19
Weakness/ Fatigue	0.23	0.25	0.05	0.02	0.18	0.53	0.02	0.19
Skin Problems	0.03	0.24	0.15	0.00	0.10	0.55	0.05	0.10
Swelling Ankles	0.01	0.24	0.00	0.11	0.22	0.33	0.00	0.33
Menstrual Problems	0.06	0.24	0.05	0.05	0.25	0.20	0.05	0.40
Painful Urination	0.10	0.21	0.04	0.00	0.23	0.52	0.02	0.19
Chest Pain	0.11	0.20	0.02	0.02	0.24	0.51	0.02	0.18

Trouble Breathing	0.07	0.19	0.03	0.06	0.17	0.57	0.03	0.14
Genital Ulcers	0.01	0.18	0.00	0.00	0.17	0.50	0.00	0.33
Blood in Spit	0.01	0.17	0.00	0.00	0.25	0.50	0.00	0.25
Worms in Stool	0.03	0.14	0.00	0.09	0.55	0.18	0.00	0.18
Weight Loss	0.11	0.07	0.05	0.05	0.26	0.42	0.05	0.16
Problems with Vision	0.14	0.06	0.05	0.00	0.30	0.45	0.00	0.20
Night Sweats	0.03	0.04	0.00	0.00	0.33	0.67	0.00	0.00
Hearing Problems	0.04	0.03	0.00	0.00	0.00	0.33	0.00	0.67

Table A4.6 Patterns of Health-care Spending

	Household Monthly Health Expenditure			Average adult monthly expenditure on:				Average Cost Per Visit			
	Level		Share/ monthly exp.								
	Expenditure Survey	Individual Surveys	Individual Surveys	All Visits	Share Public	Share Private	Share Bhopa	All Visits	Public	Private	Bhopa
	(1)	(2)	(3)	(4)	(5)	(6)	(7)	(8)	(9)	(10)	(11)
PANEL A: MEANS											
ALL	286	196	0.07	59	0.18	0.66	0.15	117	113	144	74
Poor	70	99	0.07	32	0.13	0.61	0.24	72	71	84	61
Middle	162	195	0.09	52	0.14	0.68	0.17	95	52	130	76
Rich	571	286	0.08	88	0.23	0.68	0.09	166	173	191	90
PANEL B: OLS REGRESSION											
Middle	92	96	0.02	19	0.01	0.07	-0.07	23	-19	46	16
	(21)	(38)	(.018)	(8)	(.042)	(.051)	(.041)	(12)	(24)	(20)	(31)
Rich	500	187	0.01	55	0.10	0.07	-0.16	94	102	107	29
	(109)	(34)	(.012)	(12)	(.042)	(.053)	(.041)	(24)	(45)	(35)	(34)

PANEL C: OLS REGRESSIONS, WITH VILLAGE FIXED EFFECTS

Middle	92	63	0.02	16	0.01	0.08	-0.07	5.7	-33	0.46	-7.9
	(21)	(39)	(.015)	(12)	(.04)	(.049)	(.039)	(26)	(78)	(42)	(36)
Rich	500	135	0.01	43	0.05	0.07	-0.10	76	-21	73	81
	(109)	(42)	(.016)	(13)	(.042)	(.052)	(.041)	(28)	(86)	(43)	(49)
Village Fixed Effects	yes		yes	yes	yes	yes	yes	yes	yes	yes	yes

Table A4.8   Where is absence higher?

		Fraction of Medical Personnel Present	
	Number of Visits	Subcenters & Aidposts	PHC & CHC
Distance from road			
0 Km from road	5103	0.56	0.65
>0 and <=5 Km from road	1478	0.55	0.63
>5 Km from road	403	0.38	
Distance from Udaipur			
closest to Udaipur	2315	0.53	0.61
Farther	2254	0.58	0.68
Farthest	2415	0.54	0.66
Distance from the nearest town			
closest to town	2350	0.56	0.64
Farther	2396	0.55	0.75
Farthest	2238	0.54	0.59
Reservations for women			
no reservation for women	2583	0.57	0.50
reservation for women	1843	0.56	0.68
Electricity			
no electricity	3123	0.56	0.60
Electricity	1564	0.52	0.65
Water			
in facility	757	0.53	0.61
less than 30 meters from facility	2365	0.57	0.68
30 to 100 meters from facility	794	0.49	0.62
more than 100 meters from facility	771	0.59	0.62
Medical personnel living in facility			
no medical personnel living in facility (with living quarters)	2640	0.56	0.80
at least one medical personnel living in facility	853	0.64	0.69
no living quarters available	3171	0.49	0.64

Note: some data covers only a subset of facilities

Table A4.9 Pattern in center opening

	Dependent variable: Fraction of medical personnel present					
	Subcenters and Aidposts			PHC and CHC		
A. F statistics						
Facility dummies	6.16	6.13	5.62	17.51	16.77	17.12
	(0.00)	(0.00)	(0.00)	(0.00)	(0.00)	(0.00)
Day of visits dummies	no	1.99	no	no	1.49	no
		(0.09)			(0.2)	
Facility dummies* day	no	1.17	no	no	1.06	no
		(0.01)			(0.3)	
Time of visit dummies	no	no	5.35	no	no	9.57
			(0.02)			(0.00)
Facility dummies* time of visit	no	no	1.19	no	no	1.91
			(0.05)			(0.00)
Adjusted R2	0.12	0.13	0.13	0.21	0.22	0.23
Observations	6342	6342	6327	2078	2078	2074
B. Fraction of facility level regressions where the dummies are jointly significant						
Day of visit dummies	0.095			0.000		
Time of the day dummies	0.086			0.171		

Note: 1. Panel A report F statistics and p value for the joint hypothesis that the dummies are significant in a regression where the dependent variable is the fraction of personel present on the day of the visit

2. Panel B reports the results from running a separate regression for each facility, where the dependent variable is the fraction of person present on the day of the visit, and the explanatory variables are days of the visit dummies, time of the visit dummies, and season dummies.

References

Ashraf, Nava, James Berry, and Jesse Shapiro (2007). 'Can Higher Prices Stimulate Product Use? Evidence from a Field Experiment in Zambia', NBER Working Paper 13247.

Banerjee, Abhijit, Angus Deaton, and Esther Duflo (2004).'Health Care Delivery in Rural Rajasthan', *Economic and Political Weekly*, 39(9) (28 February): 944–9.

Banerjee, Abhijit, Esther Duflo, and Rachel Glennerster (2008).'Putting a Band-Aid on a Corpse: Incentives for Nurses in the Indian Public Health Care System', *Journal of the European Economic Association*, 5(2–3): 487–500.

Banerjee, Abhijit, Esther Duflo, Rachel Glennerster, and Dhruva Kothari (2007). 'Effectiveness of Conducting Regular Immunization Camps and Providing Incentives in Improving Immunization Rates in Udaipur', mimeo, MIT.

Bjorkman, Martina and Jakob Svensson (2009).'Power to the People: Evidence from a Randomized Field Experiment on Community-Based Monitoring in Uganda', *Quarterly Journal of Economics*, 124(2): 735–69.

Chaudhury, Nazmul and Jeffrey Hammer (2003).'Ghost Doctors: Absenteeism in Bangladeshi Health Facilities, mimeo, Development Research Group, World Bank.

Cohen, Jessica and Pascaline Dupas (2007).'Free Distribution or Cost-Sharing? Evidence from a Randomized Malaria Prevention Experiment', Global Economy and Development Working Paper 11, The Brookings Institution.

Coutinho, Lester, Suman Bisht and Gauri Raje (2000), 'Numerical Narratives and Documentary Practices: Vaccines, Targets and Reports of Immunisation Programme', *Economic and Political Weekly*, 35(8/9): 656–66.

Das, Jishnu and Jeffrey Hammer (2005). 'Money for Nothing: The Dire Straits of Health Car in Delhi', mimeo, Development Research Group, World Bank.

Das, Jishnu and Jeffrey Hammer (2004).'Which Doctor? Combining Vignettes and Item Response to Measure Doctor Quality', mimeo, Development Research Group, World Bank.

Das, Jishnu and Carolia Sanchez-Paramo (2004). 'Short but not Sweet: New Evidence on Short Duration Morbidities from India', mimeo, Development Research Group, World Bank.

Das, Veena and Bhrigupati Singh (2005), 'TB and Urban Poverty: An Essay Critical and Clinical', mimeo, Johns Hopkins University.

Chaudhury, Nazmul, Jeffrey Hammer, Michael Kremer, Kartik Muralidharan, and Halsey Rogers (2003).'Teachers and Health care providers Absenteeism: A multi-country study', mimeo, Development Research Group, World Bank.

Duflo, Esther, Rema Hanna, and Stephen Ryan (2008). 'Monitoring Works: Getting Teachers to Come to School', mimeo, MIT.

Dupas, Pascaline (2009). 'What Matters (and What Does Not) in Households' Decision to Invest in Malaria Prevention?', *American Economic Review*, 99(2): 224–30.

Fiszbein, Ariel and Norbert Schady (2008). Conditional Cash Transfers: Reducing Present and Future Poverty', mimeo, World Bank.

Fogel, Robert W. and Costa, Dora L. (1997). 'A Theory of Techophysio Evolution, with Some Implications for Forecasting Population, Health Care Costs, and Pension Costs', *Demography*, 34(1): 49–66.

Kremer, Michael and Edward Miguel (1997). 'The Illusion of Sustainability', *Quarterly Journal of Economics*, 122(3): 1007–65.

Murray, Christopher J. L. and Lincoln Chen (1992). 'Understanding Morbidity Change', *Population and Development Review*, 18(3): 481–503.

Nichter, Mark (1995). 'Vaccinations in the third world: A consideration of community demand', *Social Science and Medicine*, 41(5): 617–32.

Sadana, Ritu, Ajay Tandon, Christopher J.L. Murray, Irina Serdobova, Yang Cao, Wan Jun Xie, Somnath Chatterji and Bedirhan L. Ustün. (2002), 'Describing population health in six domains: comparable results from 66 household surveys', Geneva, World Health Organization. Global Programme on Evidence for Health Policy Discussion Paper No. 43.

Sen, Amartya (2002), 'Health: perception versus observation. Self reported morbidity has severe limitations and can be extremely misleading', *British Medical Journal*, Vol. 324, pp. 860–1.

Sen, Gita, Aditi Iyer and Asha George (2002). 'Structural Reforms and Health Equity: A Comparison of NSS Surveys, 1986-87 and 1995-96', *Economic and Political Weekly*, April 6, 37(14): 1342–52.

Thornton, Rebecca (2008). 'The Demand for, and Impact of, Learning HIV Status', *American Economic Review*, 98(5): 1829–63.

Vermeersch, Christel and Michael Kremer (2005). 'School Meals, Educational Achievement and School Competition: Evidence from a Randomized Evaluation', mimeo, Oxford University.

5   A Sovereign Fund for India

PARIKSHIT GHOSH[*] AND DEBRAJ RAY[**]

5.1 The Redistribution Debate

Over the past several decades, a rising tide of inequality within nations
has provoked a new urgency to find effective redistributive mechanisms.
It would be nice to describe this urgency as moral, but 'political' is likely
more apt. In developed countries, redistribution appears key to stemming
the backlash against globalization and immigration that has emerged
from the declining fortunes of the working class (Autor et al. 2013). In
labour-surplus developing countries like India and China, higher GDP

  * Author names are in random order.
  ** Ray acknowledges funding under National Science Foundation grant
SES-1851758.

growth and a generally favourable movement of wage-rental ratios have helped retain a greater degree of support for the global economic order. Yet, all is not well. In India, our topic of discussion in this chapter, there is a real sense that the fruits of new prosperity have gone disproportionately to the elite. The available evidence is sketchy but broadly supportive of this claim (Banerjee and Piketty 2005, Chancel and Piketty 2017).

Politicians are under pressure worldwide to restore some sense of equal opportunity and shared prosperity among their voters. India is no exception. As we write, India has just emerged from a historic General Election, where the question of redistributive transfers—and their mode of deployment—lay at the heart of the main policy platforms. Both incumbent and opposition floated the idea of direct cash transfers. There was—and continues to be—vociferous debate on such transfers: whether or not they should be conditioned on the economic circumstances of the recipient, whether transfers should be in kind instead of in cash, or whether the government should be in the business of actually running the transfer programmes, such as the distribution of foodgrain.

Universal basic income (UBI)—a fixed sum to be unconditionally paid by the government to every citizen—has figured prominently in this discussion. That India—a poor country—would even entertain the notion of UBI appears odd at first glance, but not at second. India has built up a bewildering plethora of redistributive schemes and directed subsidies, the latter over long years of pandering to special interests. These range from subsidies on food, fertilizer, transportation, electricity, and water, to government 'revenues foregone' on account of various exemptions and concessions given to payers of taxes or excise and customs duties. Observers of the Indian political and economic landscape often register an understandable frustration with this spiderweb of subsidies, as well as with the lumbering incompetence and corruption that often hangs over direct government interventions.

All that has led to a call for simple transfers that are easy to verify and hard to game. UBI is an obvious contender. It has found support from a wide range of the political spectrum from libertarians to socialists. UBI frees the State from complex targeting exercises, or direct forays into the business of production and distribution, which appeals to the Right. Unlike egalitarian interventions in limited domains, such as food distribution or subsidized medical care, UBI can be scaled up with relative ease, and also avoids the pernicious air of specific subsidies to special-interest groups, which perhaps enhance its attraction to the Left. Even the Indian government's own *Economic Survey*, which often floats trial balloons for policy reform, got into the act: in the 2017 edition, it devoted a whole chapter to UBI.[1] And quite predictably, this rush to dismantle all targeted subsidies has met with its own set of reactions. The opponents of UBI acknowledge the simplicity of universality and cash, but correctly worry that an entire herd of babies will go out with the bathwater—rights to employment, healthcare, nutrition, social insurance, and a host of other basic services, as well as adequate indexation and protection against inflation.

This is an important debate. The main points in it appear to have been made both forcefully and repeatedly—perhaps repetitively. It sets the context for our somewhat separate focus.

5.2 The Flip Side of UBI

In our brief contribution, we emphasize a different factor that goes hand in hand with the idea of universal basic income, which is common ownership of (part of) the wealth of a country. The historical roots of UBI include the Alaska Dividend, which is a universal annual payout from the Alaska Permanent Fund to every man, woman, and child resident in Alaska. The Fund, built on oil revenues, is based on the notion of a shared, universally held wealth, emanating from a philosophy (surely alarming to some) of common ownership of national wealth. As Jay Hammond wrote in his 1994 memoir, 'The dividend concept is based on Alaska's Constitution, which holds that Alaska's natural resources are owned, not by the state, but by the Alaskan people themselves.' This notion of a common heritage extends to the Norway fund: while a percentage of the fund enters the State budget for social expenditures, the dominant use of the fund is as an investment for common ownership by future generations.

The flip side of UBI is a sovereign fund, and we would like to start the conversation about how such a fund is to be built for India.

---

[1] Small-scale, experimental UBI schemes have been introduced in Canada, [ ]nd, and the Netherlands, as well as in Kenya and India, with preliminary [ ] reporting fairly positive outcomes for work, health, and welfare of the

Beyond this fundamental philosophy, there are other reasons to consider a wealth fund. Many developed countries have strong welfare programmes, in which social insurance—healthcare, unemployment insurance, old-age pensions—is a large component of what one might superficially think of as 'transfers'. But these are decidedly *not* transfers. Up to a first approximation, these are essentially payments that persons make to themselves. You can call them transfers if you like, but they are fundamentally payments from one state of a person (employment, say), to be stochastically redeemed in another possible state of that *same* person (in this case, unemployment). Truly redistributive schemes are conceptually separate from and go beyond such social insurance. For instance, universal basic income is a genuine, structural, distributive transfer. Its proper consideration must appear on top of social insurance programmes, not as a substitute. Therefore, while India is not equally strong on social insurance, it should certainly be the case that whatever social insurance we *do* have, such as NREGA, should not be cannibalized for the purpose of making structural transfers such as a universal basic income.

In any case, to deliver significant benefits to the bottom half of the population, a major break-through in the government's revenue generation capacity will surely be necessary. In the United States, a UBI of $1,000 per month per person will cost the Treasury 10 per cent of GDP. In India, that ratio isn't very different if the goal is to simply pay out the poverty line of around Rs 13,000 per year per person. Surely, this is a pittance, but multiply by India's population of 1.25 billion and you are at around 12 per cent of India's GDP, which quite coincidentally equals about all of Central government revenues. Universal basic income doesn't come cheap. Improving the bang-for-the-buck in anti-poverty schemes does not obviate the need for investing more bucks, especially in India where the tax-to-GDP ratio is extremely low by international standards.

In summary: Throwing one's hands up at the *current* price tag is missing the point. UBI is, above all, a slow preparation for a possibly not-too-distant future whose first signs we are beginning to see all over the world, even in India. It is a future in which fast economic growth will no longer be accompanied by fast *employment* growth. The fact that this is happening even in labour-abundant developing countries shows how insidious that process is. With the rise of ever-encroaching automation, the one assured endowment we have—human labour—is no longer assured as a necessary input in production. It must be therefore left to society to replace this endowment by another that is durable, one that's firmly based on the acknowledgement of every citizen's right to a share of collective wealth. Universal basic income flows from this right as a corollary, exactly as dividends flow from the ownership of stocks. The formation of this collective wealth is a gradual process that will require patience. Above all, we are acutely aware of incentive effects—this is not a call to heavy-handed expropriation.

The challenge, then, is two-fold: To rise to the task of sustained socio-economic equality while containing the distortions, leakages and targeting errors that most redistributive policies are rife with (this constitutes the bulk of the debate in India so far), *and* to find the fiscal space to adequately fund such programmes. Here, we briefly take up the second challenge, inspired by the same spirit that underlies the Alaska Dividend or the Norway Fund: common ownership of the wealth of nations—to a limited degree, we hasten to add! But we do not restrict ourselves to natural resources.

5.3 The India Fund

We propose that India build up a sovereign fund, to be invested in portfolios of equity, bonds, and other financial assets, and managed professionally as any fund would be managed, subject to certain constraints that we describe subsequently. A fraction of the returns from such a fund can be paid out equally as a citizen's dividend. But the payout will be slow, and patience is of the essence. We avoid the debate of whether the payout should be in the form of UBI or something that's means-tested. But even uniform payments will serve to reduce income inequality. More pertinently, by socializing a portion of capital ownership, there will be some diversification of earnings for the poor, liberating them from excessive dependence on labour market outcomes. Moreover, that diversification is also spatial: There is a lower susceptibility to local shocks (Moene and Ray 2016).

Ownership of a sizable sovereign fund is still rare among the world's governments. The notable exceptions arise from countries and provinces that have invested windfalls from resource revenues (generally oil) into government-run asset portfolios. The Norway Fund amounts to around $200,000 per Norwegian citizen. It could pay out a UBI from it but as of now, it does not. It does contribute towards funding a good part of Norway's considerable social expenditure. In contrast, the Alaska Permanent Fund (created in 1976 by channeling a quarter of state income from natural resources into the fund) regularly pays dividends, which vary quite substantially with international resource prices and more recently with legislative action. The fund started with a payout of $1000, growing to a peak of just over $2000 in 2015 before falling back in more recent years.

But most sovereigns are not blessed with an abundance of natural resources the way Norway and Alaska are, thereby, posing a distinct challenge. In the United States, there have been proposals to tap into the considerable volume of charity from the rich (Stout and Gramico Ricci 2017), a financial transactions tax (Baker 2016), or higher taxes on flow capital incomes like corporate profits, dividends, capital gains, gifts, and inheritance (Barnes 2014). Even the sovereign fund is far from a new idea—see Lange (1936) and Meade (1965) for early proposals, and Barnes (2014) and Bruenig (2018), among others, for more recent versions. For instance, Bruenig's proposal involves the creation and growth of a Fund through a mix of voluntary contributions, the transfer and consolidation of existing government-held assets, such as auction proceeds from the electromagnetic spectrum, and various levies on companies. Our specific proposal is a variant of this which emphasizes the deliberate dilution of both existing shares and new share issues, for reasons that we clarify subsequently.

The proposal to access Indian corporate value consists of two parts:

I. A one-time directive that will require every publicly traded Indian company to issue new shares to the government, equal to some fraction (say 10–20 per cent) of their outstanding shares in the market. These shares are to be transferred free of cost, resulting in dilution of shareholder value and effectively transferring some fraction of private capital into social ownership.

II. An ongoing obligation to transfer some given fraction (again 10–20 per cent) of every new share issue—whether in the form of an initial public offering or an expansion of the existing share base—to the India Fund.

It is to be clearly noted that the first part is non-distortionary, while the second part is potentially distortionary. The choice of the levy rate should be carefully considered with this asymmetry in mind. It could well be higher for the one-time directive than for ongoing expansions.

There are several advantages of this proposal. Among them, the most important is:

(a) *The Resource Base*: Figure 5.1 (reproduced from the Economic Policy Institute website) shows an important trend break in US labour markets around 1970. Up to that point in the post-war era, labour productivity and average hourly compensation grew almost in tandem. There is, however a sharp divergence since the 1970s as productivity continued to grow, but real wages stagnated. This marks the turning point in the modern era of inequality in the West. The subsequent rise in income disparities has brought us to a stage when the issue of distributive justice can no longer be ignored by people of *any* political persuasion.

That said, and while it is true that in the United States (and to a varying extent in other countries), increases in inequality were initially driven by inequality in labour incomes (a rising skill premium) it is increasingly driven by shifts in the capital-to-labour share of GDP (Piketty and Saez 2003, OECD 2015). Figure 5.2 (reproduced

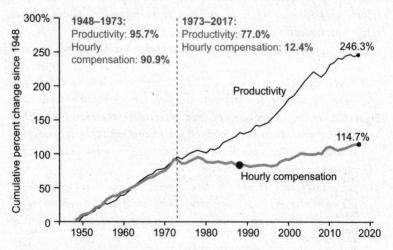

Figure 5.1. Productivity Growth and Hourly Compensation Growth in the United States, 1948–2017.

Source: Economic Policy Institute, 2018.

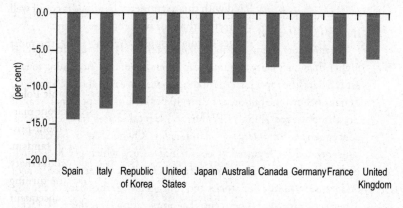

(A) Advanced Countries, 1970–2014

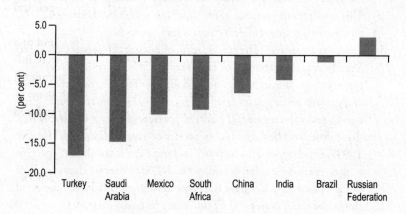

(B) Developing Countries, 1995–2012

Figure 5.2   Change in Labor Share of GDP in Selected Countries.
Source: **OECD (2015).**

from the OECD 2015 report) shows how the share of labour in GDP has declined over the last several decades for most of the major economies. This empirical trend is in agreement with the predictions of both international trade theory (factor-price equalization and Stolper–Samuelson theorems) as well as work on the dynamic and distributive effects of progressive automation (Acemoglu and Restrepo 2018, 2019, Ray* and Mookherjee 2019). Tax rates on flow capital income are low in most countries—and India is no exception—but modern inequality requires targeting precisely the capital share of GDP, which has been growing.

Furthermore, inequality in capital ownership is orders of magnitude higher than inequality in human capital endowments. According to latest US data, the top 1 per cent of the population earns about 20 per cent of national income but owns nearly 40 per cent of net personal wealth. So, the observed shifts in labour and capital shares have enormous consequences for *interpersonal inequality*. Ownership is particularly concentrated for financial assets such as equity, which produce much higher rates of return compared to other asset categories like houses and pension funds. For stocks and mutual funds, the share of the top 1 per cent exceeds 50 per cent. The implications are clear: To tackle inequality head on, one cannot avoid taking it on at its principal source. This is where our proposal of the sovereign wealth fund financed by the dilution of existing and new equity issues comes in.

(b) *Economic Incentives*: The confiscation of outstanding shares is akin to a textbook redistribution of endowments, just as in the second welfare theorem. It avoids the standard disincentive effect on investment and growth arising from taxing flows, such as corporate profits, dividends, and capital gains. If political pressure makes it inevitable that these flows will be taxed highly sooner or later (Alesina and Rodrik 1994), enlightened and forward-looking capitalists should agree to replace them by a suitable equity tax. But we reiterate that part II of our proposal does not have the same advantage, so a large portion of the initial setup plan for the Fund must be based on part I.

(c) *Separation of Ownership and Management*: This feature is what distinguishes this plan from classical socialism, where inefficiencies arise primarily from the State trying to organize and manage production. However, if the State owns large chunks of shares in private firms, to what extent de facto influence over corporate decision-making can be avoided is a debatable point. We propose that under any such plan, the state only be issued 'Class B' shares which confers no control or voting rights on the government.

(d) *Payment via Dilution*: This is conceivably the most compelling point in favour of the plan, especially for India. Stock issues by listed firms are arguably far easier to track down than auditing the portfolio holdings of individuals. There are far fewer incorporated firms than there are individuals, and information about their existing stock as well as increments to such stocks is easily available and verifiable. No payment is required in cash: We seek out a fraction of stock issues so that a sovereign, if it so wants, can hold precisely the national composition of stock wealth—at least initially. Thus, payments are made via dilution of the share base, or of new issues. But dilution also means that *every* investor in the company automatically pays a tax to the government, without having to be tracked or audited. For a country like India where both the tax base and auditing resources are notoriously low, this can be a very effective form of taxation.

(e) *Political Incentives*: Socializing a part of capital ownership effectively narrows the dispersion of capital-labour endowments, and so brings the political incentives of citizens into closer alignment. It blunts the political edge behind policies like protectionism and immigration restrictions that achieve distributive ends at the cost of reducing the size of the pie. The reason behind these conflicts is not personal inequality per se but *functional* inequality in the capital–labour ownership ratios. More generally, one would think of different domains on which a universal income may be conditioned. It could come from a tax on labour, a tax on capital, or a tax that's proportional to national income. The choice of corporate valuations as a domain, as a sovereign fund implicitly does, cannot but bring labour into greater harmony with the interests of capital, though of course it is too much to expect that their incentives would be perfectly aligned. Moene and Ray (2016) discuss this point in more detail.

But there are potential pitfalls and disadvantages:

(a) *Portfolio Management*. It will be necessary to design a credible method to manage these massive portfolios without letting corruption and ineptitude getting in the way. A principal worry is that the government will be coopted by business interests into either buying the shares of a favoured company, or selling the shares of a disfavoured company. Likewise, if the Treasury controls portfolio decisions, other government goals like anti-trust policy or environmental protection may interact with management decisions. It will therefore be absolutely necessary to create an autonomous fund management authority, exactly along the lines of an independent central bank. The India Fund Management Board would be composed of responsible and respectable individuals, who would in no way be accountable to the government. At first sight, this may be a tall order, but India can deliver, as it has with the Supreme Court, the Electoral Commission, and (with a bit more trepidation) the Reserve Bank. The experiences of countries like Norway, China, and Saudi Arabia may be instructive in this regard.

(b) *Constraints on Transactions*. It is to be noted that such a Fund would be very different from sovereign funds held by other nations, which can hold a stock portfolio diversified worldwide. There is a good reason why that cannot happen—or cannot happen immediately—in the case of the India Fund, because the entire fund is based on *contributions in the form of stock* by companies. Each contribution is large, 10 per cent of the base or some close-by number to be decided. An immediate sale of that stock by the government will have large and untoward effects on the stock market. Even a planned divestment, if commonly known in advance, will be tantamount to a large sale upfront.

One might take this constraint to its logical limit. If the India Fund is to really rise and fall on the national fortunes of India, one might even mandate that the Fund hold—to the extent possible— precisely the current composition of Indian corporate wealth. All payouts would be made by selling the Fund but keeping the composition unchanged, and all company dividends paid to the Fund would be plowed back into stock ownership at the current composition of corporate wealth. Such a rule might seem unnecessarily rigid, and perhaps it is, but it would (i) avoid the need for active management, (ii) avoid the corruption and gaming described in item (a) earlier, and (iii) literally mean that the Fund will be held as a proportion of *Indian* wealth, or at least Indian incorporated wealth. We do not necessarily recommend this strategy, but it is worth investigation.

(c) *Commitment Problem*. What guarantees that the initial share dilution of the existing base will be one-time, and not repeated in the future? If it generates such expectations, the incentive advantages are lost. To some extent, there is a built-in disincentive for further dilution because as capital–labour ownership ratios in the population get compressed, the political incentive to use this instrument gets weaker. The exact details of this property require more rigorous theoretical analysis. But in addition, other avenues of commitment can help.

For instance, the India Fund could be set up via a Constitutional Amendment, which specifies the terms for the intervention; specifically, that share dilution of an existing base can only occur *once*. Might that generate the commitment power that the government will need?

(d) *Evasion Incentives*: If only publicly traded shares are diluted, and to the extent this is known in advance, it generates an incentive for changing the corporate capital structure, for example, swapping equity for debt or converting publicly traded companies into proprietorships. To extend the policy and target such proprietorships is difficult. Once a firm leaves the confines of the stock market, it may be hard to track. There is also an incentive to list companies in stock exchanges abroad, though this concern is more easily overcome.

(e) *Domain-Specific Ethics*: Most modern capitalist societies have developed an ethics that legitimizes taxing of income flows but in contrast, renders property rights somehow sacrosanct, though from a purely economic perspective, there should be a one-to-one correspondence between taxing flows and taxing stocks at some corresponding rate. Breaking this psychological barrier is a challenge. But it is an odd barrier, as a one-time taxation of stocks has better incentive properties than the ongoing taxation of flows. Moreover, it is well understood that in a dynamic setting and for incentive purposes, taxation/punishments are best structured if front-loaded rather than stationary (Chamley 1986, Ray 2002) and that is the principle at work here, though as mentioned earlier, it will require commitment at the highest level.

We have emphasized share dilution, because it is the relatively novel part of this proposal, and immensely relevant in the Indian context, given that the tax base is so nebulous. That said, it is to be noted that the Indian stock market is still relatively small (though possibly among the top ten stock markets in the world in terms of market capitalization). It weighs in somewhere north of $ 2 trillion. Currently, the market capitalization for Indian stocks stands at close to 80 per cent of GDP, but this percentage fluctuates quite a bit. A transfer of 15 per cent of its value to the central government will create a fund worth 12 per cent of GDP (which, coincidentally, matches the annual tax revenues of the government, so it is equivalent to a windfall gain of one year's worth of revenues to be treated as an endowment). If the money is invested in a diversified and well managed portfolio of assets, and the returns (capital gains plus dividends) are used for payouts without touching the endowment itself, how much flow income will be available to the government every year to spend on UBI or other welfare programmes? The inflation adjusted annual rate of return on large and mid-cap funds over the last 15 years has been around 10 per cent (Nathan 2018), with dividends adding another 2 per cent or so. The annual disposable income from the fund will come to around 1.5 per cent of GDP.

This is not a bounty at the national scale but neither is it anything to sniff at. Per-capita GDP in India currently stands at around $2,000 at market exchange rates, so a truly universal payout funded this way will only amount to $150 or Rs 1,000 per year for a household of five members. That is not a huge relief, to put it very mildly. If the cash transfer is targeted at the poorest 20 per cent of households (roughly those under the official poverty line), which is what the Indian National Congress proposed to do in its 2019 election campaign, the amount jumps to Rs 5,000 for each household, which begins to look respectable. In the runup to the general elections, the ruling BJP government announced a scheme that pays farmers owning less than 2 acres of land an annual sum of Rs 6,000, only slightly more than the amount generated by a modest share dilution of 15 per cent. More pertinently, some of the big-ticket welfare schemes carry costs which are in the same ball park. For example, the central government's share in public health and public education expenditures are about 0.3 per cent and 1 per cent of GDP, respectively. The massive employment guarantee scheme MNREGA costs about 0.4 per cent of GDP and the food subsidy bill just about crosses 1 per cent of GDP. Some of these schemes could be entirely funded by a modest version of our proposal.

More pertinently, this is just a start with considerable room for growth for a number of reasons. The corporate sector in India accounts for a small fraction of GDP (certainly under 15 per cent) compared to the United States, where it produces 70 per cent or more of GDP.[2] That implies there

---

[2] Oddly enough, the Indian stock market capitalization is still 70 per cent of Indian GDP, despite the incorporated sector accounting for so little of GDP. The United States stock market is currently overheated with corporate valuations at around 150 per cent of GDP, but incorporated firms also account for a much larger share of the economy.

is immense room for the corporate sector to grow, and there is much to be gained for the India Fund to piggyback on that growth. Equity and bonds currently account for less than 20 per cent of funds for even large enlisted firms (Allen et al. 2006), the major share coming from internal funds and alternative funding sources like family and venture capital. As financial deepening continues, the importance of the stock market is likely to grow manifold.

In any case, a mechanistic rule of spending fund returns and holding its real value constant (by reinvesting an amount equal to the rate of inflation) is perhaps a very unimaginative strategy. As Piketty (2013) famously points out, the rate of return on financial assets typically exceeds that of real GDP growth $(r > g)$. Therefore, any owner of a portfolio who has a high reinvestment strategy will outpace income growth in the rest of the economy, and will become disproportionately richer over time. Once the government has some ground to stand on by building a start-up fund, a moratorium on payouts for a period of time will…cause the fund [to] grow…in size relative to the rest of the economy. Eventually it can be much bigger than the initial 12 per cent of GDP we envisaged here. Given a 3 percentage point gap in the real rate of return on stocks and real GDP growth (10 per cent vs 7 per cent), a ten-year moratorium on payouts can make the fund grow from 12 per cent to 16 per cent of GDP in a decade. If the government is able to raise initial capital worth 30 per cent of GDP using sources in addition to share dilution, and postpones payouts by 10 years, the fund will grow to 40 per cent of GDP. The Norwegian sovereign wealth funds own 76 per cent of the country's non-home wealth (Bruenig 2018) which, the oil windfall notwithstanding, is a testimony to good asset management and the economic potential of a portfolio-based approach to public finance. To sum up, if governments are willing to leverage the same forces that shaped the rising inequality in the first place, they could go a long way towards neutralizing those very forces. Fight fire with fire.

Finally, the India Fund can also be built up in more conventional ways, such as taxation of dividends or capital gains. In addition, there are other sources; for example, the selling-off of inefficient public sector units (Air India, BSNL, banks, government lands) and pouring the proceeds into the Fund. These assets do not generate income flows due to poor corporate management. They even put pressure on the Exchequer when run at substantial losses, as they often are. Disinvestment generally allows the government to camouflage fiscal mismanagement by sending the proceeds into the revenue account and artificially lowering the budget deficit. Linking disinvestment explicitly to the India fund solves this problem, and should be used to complement this proposal.

According to the Department of Investment and Public Asset Management of the Government of India, the market capitalization of all public sector enterprises (in which government is the majority stakeholder) is Rs 13.5 lakh crores, a shade under 10 per cent of total corporate wealth in India (which, if you recall, is about 80 per cent of GDP). The value of some of these companies will probably be much higher if their assets and operations are handed over to professional management. There may be a strategic or social mission underpinning some of these ownerships, but there are many that seem like a relic of the past. Air India and BSNL are leading examples—they operate in booming telecom and airline industries which are crowded with private players, and no longer need a helping hand from the State. Judicious disinvestment could add several percentage points of GDP to the India Fund.

There is a general point to be made. Historically, governments have appeared to be excessively wedded to a fiscal strategy primarily consisting of taxing flows rather than building up stocks and endowments. The expropriatory powers of the state and the grand scale of its revenue budget perhaps mask the fact that this is literally a hand-to-mouth existence which, among individuals, is only practised by the poor. The rich build nest eggs and own things. To play that game, one has to entertain the use of their strategies. The portfolio approach advocated here can be applied regardless of what the source of the start-up capital is—oil revenues, share dilution, disinvestment in PSUs or unexploited resources within the revenue budget itself, such as the scrapping of non-merit subsidies and the closing of various tax loopholes (Bardhan 2016, Ghatak 2016). Indeed, these alternative sources for a potential India Fund should be viewed as complements rather than substitutes.

5.4 The Sovereign Fund and the Universal Basic Share

We end by tying the notion of a sovereign fund to the *universal basic share*, a simple modification of UBI discussed in Ray (2016) and Moene and Ray (2016). One valid concern with universal basic income is that it converts commitments in kind—the right to food, to employment, to healthcare— into cash. To be sure, as discussed earlier, some of these rights come under the rubric of social insurance and should not be converted to UBI anyway. But the concern remains: that UBI can be inflated away. And even with indexation, the UBI is a *fixed* real commitment at best. As Ray (2016) writes:

> What happens as national income or profits continue to rise in an automated world? Is no share to be passed on to the population? Must we be reduced to annual debates about how to adjust the UBI? One can imagine that such debates would constitute a continuing sequence of nightmares.

The universal basic share commits not to an income but to a *share* of GDP. Ray (2016) lists several merits of such a proposal, among which are:

A. It is country-neutral, and every country, rich or poor, can commit to it. The actual commitment scales up or down with income. A share can be declared as a common goal that could apply to all countries.
B. One can start small. In the Indian case, the commitment does not have to be high to begin with, but over time, we will get there.
C. The universal basic share allows everyone to share in the prosperity of a country. It is our protection against unbounded inequality as we move into an increasingly automated universe.

A sovereign fund would link the ultimate dividend payout to aggregate company valuations. As the capital share in national income continues to climb (Ray* and Mookherjee 2019), the dividend-to-GDP-ratio would possibly rise over time, so the (ratio-based) commitment implied by a sovereign fund would, if anything, dominate that of the universal basic share. But the *asymptotic* commitment indeed resembles that of a universal basic share. To generate and maintain a sustained lock-step with GDP in the longer-run, a tie-in to capital income is what is required, especially if there is truth to the prediction of ever-increasing automation.

References

Acemoglu, Daron and Pascual Restrepo (2018). 'The Race Between Man and Machine: Implications of Technology for Growth, Factor Shares and Employment', *American Economic Review*, 108(6): 1488–542.

Acemoglu, Daron and Pascual Restrepo (2019). 'Automation and New Tasks: How Technology Displaces and Reinstates Labor', *Journal of Economic Perspectives*, 33(2): 3–30.

Alesina, Alberto and Dani Rodrik (1994). 'Distributive Politics and Economic Growth', *Quarterly Journal of Economics*, 109 (2): 465–90.

Allen, Franklin, Chakaravarti, Rajesh, De, Sankar, and Jun Qian (2006), 'Financing Firms in India', The World Bank.

Autor, David, Dorn, David and Gordon Hanson (2013). 'The China Syndrome: Local Labor Market Effects of Import Competition in the United States', *American Economic Review*, 103 (6): 2121–68.

Baker, Dean (2016): 'Reining in Wall Street to Benefit All Americans: The Case for A Financial Transactions Tax', The Century Foundation.

Banerjee, Abhijit (2016): 'The Best Way to Welfare', *Hindustan Times*, 18 June.

Banerjee, Abhijit and Thomas Piketty (2005): 'Top Indian Incomes, 1922–2000', *World Bank Economic Review*, 19 (1): 1–20.

Bardhan, Pranab (2016). 'Basic Income in a Poor Country', *Ideas for India*, 26 September. https://www.ideasforindia.in/topics/poverty-inequality/basic-income-in-a-poor-country.html.

Bardhan, Pranab (2018). 'Universal Basic Income: Its Special Case for India', *Indian Journal of Human Development*, 11 (2): 141–3.

Barnes, Peter (2014). *With Liberty and Dividends for All: How to Save Our Middle Class When Jobs Don't Pay Enough*, San Francisco: Berrett-Koehler Publishers.

Bruenig, Matt (2018). 'Social Wealth Fund for America', People's Policy Project.

Chamley, Christophe (1986). 'Optimal Taxation of Capital Income in General Equilibrium with Infinite Lives', *Econometrica*, 54(3): 607–22.

Chancel, Lucas and Thomas Piketty (2017). 'Indian Income Inequality, 1922–2014: From British Raj to Billionaire Raj', CEPR Discussion Paper no. DP 12409.

Economic Policy Institute (2018). 'The Productivity-Pay Gap', https://www.epi.org/productivity- pay-gap/.

Ghatak, Maitreesh (2016). 'The Price of Basic Income', *Indian Express*, July 1.

Lange, Oskar (1936). 'On the Economic Theory of Socialism: Part One', *Review of Economic Studies*, 4 (1): 53–71.

Meade, James (1965). *Efficiency, Equality and the Ownership of Property*, Cambridge, MA: Harvard University Press.

Moene, Karl-Ove and Debraj Ray (2016). 'The Universal Basic Share and Social Incentives', *Ideas for India*, 26 September. https://www.ideasforindia.in/topics/poverty-inequality/the-universal-basic-share-and-social-incentives.ht

Nathan, Narendra (2018). 'Returns from Which Investments Have Beaten Inflation? Here's A Comparison', *Economic Times*, 29 November.

OECD (2015). 'The Labor Share in G20 Economies', Report prepared for the G20 Employment Working Group, Antalya, Turkey, 26–27 February.

Piketty, Thomas (2013). *Capital in the Twenty-First Century*, Cambridge, MA: Harvard University Press.

Piketty, Thomas and Emanuel Saez (2003). 'Income Inequality in the United States: 1913–1998', *Quarterly Journal of Economics*, 118(1): 1–41.

Ray, Debraj (2002). 'The Time Structure of Self-Enforcing Agreements', *Econometrica*, 70(2): 547–82.

Ray, Debraj (2016). 'The Universal Basic Share', *Ideas for India*, 26 September. https://www.ideasforindia.in/topics/poverty-inequality/the-universal-basic-share.html.

Ray, Debraj and Dilip Mookherjee (2019). 'Growth, Automation and the Long Run Share of Labor', mimeo, New York University. https://debrajray.com/wp-content/uploads/2018/03/MookherjeeRayAutomation.pdf

Stout, Lynn A. and Gramitto Ricci, Sergio Alberto (2017). 'Corporate Governance as Privately- Ordered Public Policy: A Proposal', Cornell Legal Studies Research Paper No. 17–42. https://ssrn.com/abstract=3042761.

Part B

Labour, Land, and Financial Markets

6   *A Note on Evaluating Growth Processes**

BHASKAR DUTTA

Has the economic performance of China been better than that of India during the last decade? Has West Bengal done better than India as a whole between two points of time? Note that these questions are very different from one which asks whether region A is better-off than region B at a point of time. The latter comparison involves comparing *levels* of welfare while the former set of questions involves comparisons of rates of change. The purpose of this note is to emphasize that this requires a quite different analytical apparatus.

The traditional way of answering such questions has been to compare the rates of growth of China and India (or West Bengal and India)

---

* It is a pleasure to write this chapter in honour of Pranab Bardhan, who has been such an influential contributor to development economics.

during the relevant time period. This simple or naive approach, of course, ignores the fact that the fruits of economic progress are unevenly distributed across different sections of society, and the average rate of growth may simply not reflect social goals. For instance, poorer countries may want to implement policies that are 'pro-poor'. Most countries profess to follow egalitarian policies designed to spread the benefits of growth equally across different income classes. Since growth processes have to be evaluated in relation to the declared aims of government policy, it is clear that the popular practice of using the aggregate rate of growth as a yardstick to evaluate an economy's performance is a nonstarter. The distributional changes, if any, need to be incorporated in any such evaluation exercise.

I distinguish between two, not-necessarily exclusive, types of evaluation exercises that have been carried out recently. The first type is essentially *positive* in the sense that such exercises simply *describe* the distributional implications of growth. The second is *normative* because such exercises attempt to evaluate the growth experience through the lens of social welfare. That is, the comparison is couched in terms of whether the gain in social welfare in China has been higher than that of India.

In what follows, I will first describe the positive approach. I will then discuss the normative approach. Finally, I will illustrate both approaches by evaluating the growth experience of major Indian states between 2004–5 and 2011–12 using National Sample Survey (NSS) data on household consumption data.

6.1 The Positive Approach

The distributional implications of growth can be represented by *Growth incidence curves* (GIC). They simply plot the mean growth rate of real income in a population against income quantiles. A downward-sloping GIC means that rates of income growth are higher for lower-income groups, and so indicates that growth contributes to equalizing the distribution of income. Conversely, an upward-sloping curve implies that richer income groups have experienced higher rates of growth and hence a worsening of the distribution of income. Of course, the shape of GICs may be very diverse. An important issue, therefore, is that of comparing different GICs.

Ravallion and Chen (2003) describe how such comparisons can be made.[1] Let $F_t(y)$ denote the cumulative distribution function (CDF) of income or expenditure, giving the proportion of the population with income less than income level y at any date t. The income of the p quantile can be obtained by inverting the CDF at that quantile.

$$y_t(p) = F^{-1}(p)$$
$$= L_t'(p)\mu_t$$

where $L_t(p)$ is the well-known Lorenz curve and μ_t is the mean of the income distribution. Moreover, $L_t(p)\mu_t$ is the Generalized Lorenz curve originally introduced into the literature by Shorrocks (1983).

The growth rate of income of quintile p between two time periods $t-1$ and t is

$$g_t(p) = \frac{y_t(p)}{y_{t-1}(p)} - 1$$
$$= \frac{L_t'(p)}{L_{t-1}'(p)} \frac{\mu_t}{\mu_{t-1}} - 1$$
$$= \frac{L_t'(p)}{L_{t-1}'(p)}(\gamma_t + 1) - 1$$

where $\gamma_t = \frac{\mu_t}{\mu_{t-1}} - 1$ is the growth rate of aggregate income between periods $t-1$ and t.

Suppose there is no change in the Lorenz curve during the period $(t-1, t)$. This means no change in the distribution of income and so it is not surprising that $g_t(p)$ will coincide with the rate of growth of mean income, γ_t. It is also immediate that the growth rate of the p-th percentile exceeds the growth rate of mean income iff $\frac{y_t(p)}{\mu_t}$ is rising over time. A growth incidence curve also sheds light on distributional changes. A negative slope of g_t indicates that lower income groups have experienced a higher rate of growth of incomes. This must then imply that the level of inequality in period t is lower than that in period $(t-1)$ according to any measure of

---

[1] See also Son(2004). Other related papers include Kakwani (1977, 1984), Cap´eau, B. and E. Ooghe (2007), Mehran (1977), Jenkins and van Kerm (2006).

inequality that is consistent with the Pigou–Dalton transfer principle.[2] In other words, the Lorenz curve corresponding to the t-period income distribution is everywhere above that of the $(t - 1)$-period distribution. Moreover, if g_t is everywhere non-negative, then there is first-order dominance of the t-period distribution over the $t - 1$-period distribution.

First-order dominance may not always hold in empirical distributions. So, it is of some interest to consider second-order dominance. This is easily done by constructing a *cumulative* growth incidence curve. This will show the rate of growth of *cumulative* income of each quantile. So,

$$cg_t(p) = \frac{L_t(p)}{L_{t-1}} \frac{\mu_t}{\mu_{t-1}} - 1$$

$$= \frac{L_t(p)}{L_{t-1}(p)}(\gamma_t + 1) - 1$$

There will be second-order domination of the t-period distribution over that of the $t - 1$-period distribution if $cg_t(p)$ is everywhere non-negative.

How can GICs be used to compare growth performances across countries or states? Suppose the GIC of country 1 is everywhere above that of country 2. This means that the growth rate of income in country 1 has been higher than that of country 2 for every quantile. It is tempting to conclude that the growth performance of country 1 is therefore better than that of country 2. But a word of caution is essential at this stage. Suppose the interest is not in comparing the performance in quantile rates of growth in income, but in that of changes in rates of growth of *social welfare* in the two countries. We show in the next section that dominance of GIC need not necessarily translate into that of social welfare.

We conclude this section with a discussion on a point raised by Bourguignon (2011). Bourguignon points out that the typical experience during any growth process is for at least some change in ranks occupied by individuals in the income distribution, the extent of change depending upon the degree of income mobility. That is, GIC compares the income of individuals who were not necessarily in the same initial position, but that of the possibly different individuals who occupy different quantiles in the initial and terminal income distributions. Similarly, the cumulative GIC shows the difference between the initial income of those individuals who

---

[2] See Pigou(1912), Dalton (1920).

are initially among the p poorest and the income of the p poorest individuals in the terminal distribution, although they are not necessarily the same individuals. Bourguignon goes on to analyse the distributional incidence of growth using the initial distribution as a reference. He defines what he calls non-anonymous Growth Incidence Curves (na-GIC). This change results into taking into account the full joint distribution of individual initial incomes and terminal incomes.

Given any initial distribution of income $F(y)$, let $\phi(z \mid y)$ be the conditional distribution function of terminal income. Here, z is terminal conditional on y being the initial income.

Then, the non-anonymous GIC[3] is given by

$$g(p) = \frac{\int z d(z \mid y) dy(p)}{y(p)} - 1$$

Bourguignon goes on to illustrate the difference between the two versions of the growth incidence curves by constructing the GICs for the global income distribution between 1995 and 2002 using data on GDP drawn from the World Development Indicators. Of course, the two curves are very different constructs. But both serve very useful purposes. Anonymous GIC are illuminating in the description of how growth affects the change in the size and distribution of aggregate income. The na-GIC comes into the picture when the focus is on issues such as income mobility. Notice that the data requirements are more demanding for the na-GIC since the conditional distribution function necessitates the availability of panel data.

6.2 The Normative Approach

At the heart of the normative approach to evaluating income distributional issues is the specification of a social welfare function. For instance, the normative approach to measurement of inequality essentially compares the social welfare corresponding to two income distributions having the same mean income. Inequality is declared to be *higher* in distribution x than in y if social welfare is *lower* according to some social welfare

[3] The non-anonymous cumulative GIC can also be constructed along similar lines.

function. The implicit assumption is that social welfare depends upon the size of the cake as well as its distribution. If two distributions have the same mean income, then any difference in social welfare must come from differences in distribution.

Of course, such comparisons of social welfare and hence inequality depend upon what social welfare function is used. So, the inequality ranking derived from one social welfare function can be different from that derived from another social welfare function. The Atkinson–Sen–Kolm[4] approach to inequality measurement describes a *dominance* approach which rules out such ambiguities. A price has to be paid for this since the dominance approach only generates *partial* rankings over the sets of all income distributions with same mean. Inequality is higher in distribution x than y for all 'sensible' measures of inequality iff the Lorenz curve of x is below that of y.

Bossert and Dutta (2018) modify the AKS framework to compare the *change in social welfare* in country A to that of country B during some period of time. To the extent that two countries may have grown at very different rates of growth, it may, in fact, be more appropriate to focus on comparisons of changes in social welfare rather than inequality. Bossert and Dutta point out that comparisons of changes requires a significant modification of the AKS framework—while welfare *level* comparisons can be made within a purely ordinal framework, comparisons of *changes* in welfare require a cardinal framework. They assume that social welfare functions are cardinal and proceed as follows.

Fix the size of the population at n. Given any two income distributions x^0 and x^1 (say income distributions in a country or region at two different time periods 0 and 1), a measure of welfare change is a function V such that $V(x^1, x^0)$ describes the change in social welfare associated with moving from last period's income distribution x^0 to the current distribution x^1. So,

$$V(x^1, x^0) = W(x^1) - W(x^0)$$

where W is a social welfare function.[5]

---

[4] See Kolm (1969), Atkinson (1970) and Sen (1973).

[5] Bossert and Dutta take the *difference* in welfare as a measure of change. Of course, one could equally well consider the ratio $\frac{W(x^1)}{W(x^0)}$ as a measure of change.

The existence of such a function V allows comparison of growth processes—one simply compares $V(x^1, x^0)$ with $V(y^1, y^0)$ to evaluate whether the change has been higher or lower in growth process x or y. Notice, however, that such verdicts depend crucially on the choice of the social welfare function W. Is there an analogue of the dominance approach in this context? Bossert and Dutta provide a partial answer.

Rearrange all income distributions to be 'bottom ranked' so that $x_1 \le x_2 \le \cdots \le x_n$. That is, in all income distributions, individuals are relabelled so that $x_i \le x_{i+1}$. *This assumption will be maintained throughout the rest of the section.*

Let

$$A = \left\{ \alpha \in \mathbb{R}^n_{++} \mid \alpha_1 > \cdots > \alpha_n \right\}.$$

A welfare function W is a generalized Gini welfare function if there exists a parameter vector $\alpha = (\alpha_1, \ldots, \alpha_n) \in A$ and a number $\delta \in \mathbb{R}$ such that, for all $x \in \mathbb{R}^n_+$,

$$W(x) = \sum_{i=1}^{n} \alpha_i x_i + \delta \tag{1}$$

So, a generalized Gini welfare function defines social welfare as the weighted sum of individual incomes with lower income levels getting a higher weight. Notice that all weight vectors have the property that more weight is placed on the incomes of poorer people. So, social welfare goes up if a unit of income is transferred from a richer person to a poorer person. Hence the inequality measure derived from a Generalized Gini welfare function satisfies the Pigou–Dalton condition, which has come to be considered an essential property of any 'sensible' social welfare function.

The corresponding generalized Gini measure of welfare change for a specific α in A is given by

$$V_\alpha(x^0, x^1) = \sum_{i=1}^{n} \alpha_i x_i^1 - \sum_{i=1}^{n} \alpha_i x_i^0 \tag{2}$$

The class of all generalized Gini measures of welfare change is given by

$$\mathcal{V}_G = \left\{ V_\alpha \mid \alpha \in A \right\}.$$

The objective is to derive a condition on any two pairs of distributions (x^0, x^1) and (y^0, y^1) that will enable one to state that the welfare change between (x^0, x^1) is greater or smaller than the welfare change between (y^0, y^1) for *all* measures of welfare change in the class $\mathcal{V}_G$.

Define

$$\Delta x_i = x_i^1 - x_i^0 \text{ and } \Delta y_i = y_i^1 - y_i^0 \text{ for all } i \in \{1,\ldots,n\}$$

The vector Δ gives the difference in quantile income between x^0 and x^1. Bossert and Dutta prove the following.

Theorem 1. *For all x^0, x^1, y^0, y^1,*

$$V(x^0, x^1) \geq V(y^0, y^1) \text{ for all } V \in \mathcal{V}_G$$

if and only if $\sum_{i=1}^{k}(\Delta x_i - \Delta y_i) \geq 0$ for all $k \in \{1,\ldots,n\}$.

Hence, the (absolute) change in social welfare between x^0 and x^1 is higher than that between y^0 and y^1 iff the Δ-vector for x second order dominates the Δ-vector for y. This provides an easily verifiable condition to evaluate growth processes in terms of absolute changes. In the concluding section, I illustrate its use by applying the measure to NSS data.

I close this section by pointing out that the positive and normative approaches may sometimes yield different conclusions. That is, I construct an example of two pairs of income distributions such that the GIC of one is everywhere above that of the other, but the ranking in terms of rate of change of social welfare.

Example 1. *Let $n = 2$. Consider the following income distributions.*

- $x^0 = (100, 1000), x^1 = (300, 4000)$.
- $y^0 = (1, 4), y^1 = (3, 15.9)$.

Then, the x-GIC curve is the line through $(2, 3)$ while the y-GIC curve is the line through $(2, 2.975)$. Hence, the x-GIC dominates the y-GIC. Suppose now that

$$W(x) = \ln x$$

and consider the corresponding measure of welfare change

$$V(x^1, x^0) = \frac{W(x^1)}{W(x^0)}$$

Notice that this measures welfare change in terms of rate of growth rather than welfare difference. Routine calculations yield

$$V(x^1, x^0) = 1.09, \quad V(y^1, y^0) = 3.57$$

So, the rankings in terms of V and GICs do not coincide. Of course, the specification of W matters. Nevertheless, the example demonstrates that while the growth incidence curves convey a powerful 'visual' image of alternative growth processes, these need to be supplemented by a normative analysis of welfare change.

6.2 Empirical Comparisons

In this section, I illustrate both the positive and normative approaches to evaluate growth using the NSS data on household consumption expenditure in India in the years 2004–5 and 2011–12.

6.2.1 Positive Approach

I start with a discussion on what can be gleaned from the comparison of cumulative growth incidence curves for major Indian states and all India for the urban and rural sectors separately. These are depicted in the next section. In order to restrict the number of figures to manageable numbers, the various states have been clubbed into different regions—South, North, East, and West. The household expenditure data have been divided into ventiles, and the expenditures for both 2004–5 and 2011–12 are represented at 2004–5 prices. The horizontal axis represents the p-poorest ventile groups, while the vertical axis represents the rate of growth in cumulative real consumption expenditure between 2004–5 and 2011–12. As mentioned earlier, we can conclude that the growth process has exhibited pro-poor bias if the cumulative GIC (CGIC) is everywhere positive but has a negative slope. Also, state A has performed better than state B if the CGIC of state A is everywhere higher than that of state B.

Consider, first the urban sector. Aggregating across states, the All-India CGIC shows that the rate of growth at 0.24 is the smallest for the lowest three ventiles. Indeed, the slope of the CGIC is virtually *positive* except for a small dip in the middle-income groups. The CGIC shows that there has been a slight worsening of the urban income distribution. In contrast to the aggregate picture, the state-level CGICs do not exhibit any clear pattern. That is, the slopes of all the state-level CGICs change sign across the different ventiles so that no conclusion can be drawn about whether income distribution has worsened or improved. Another distinction between the All-India CGIC and the state-level ones is that the Indian one exhibits a much smaller range of values, with the lowest being 0.24 and the highest being only 0.31. In contrast, the highest point of the J&K CGIC is 0.96 and the lowest 0.07![6]

The All-India CGIC for the urban sector is everywhere above the horizontal axis, showing that the rate of growth of cumulative income has been positive for all ventiles. This is also true for all states *except for* Assam and Jharkhand. It is also instructive to compare the heights of the All-India CGIC and that of the different states. It turns out that the All-India urban CGIC dominates that of Assam, Bihar, Jharkhand, Chattisgarh, Gujarat, and Punjab. In contrast, the CGICs of Haryana, Kerala, and somewhat surprisingly Rajasthan lie above that of the All-India. CGIC. At first sight, the latter comparison may seem counter-intuitive since Rajasthan is one of the poorer states. However, a state can be poor but still record relatively high rate of change in income or consumption.

Let us now look at the rural sector. At the aggregate level, the All-India CGIC is almost parallel to the horizontal axis with values ranging from 0.17 to 0.24. The higher values are typically at the upper end of the income distribution so that there has been a slight worsening of the income distribution. However, since the CGIC lies everywhere above the horizontal axis, cumulative incomes have improved for all ventiles.[7] As far as the individual states are concerned, the most impressive performance has been in Andhra Pradesh. Not only have the rates of growth of cumulative incomes been consistently high for all ventiles, the CGIC also has a negative slope showing strong pro-poor bias in the growth process. The

---

[6] In fact, J&K is a bit of an outlier.

[7] In fact, even the GIC is everywhere above the horizontal axis showing that *all* ventiles have recorded positive rates of growth.

CGIC for Andhra lies above that of All-India and several other states. The CGICs of Tamil Nadu and Uttarakhand also dominate that of All-India. The worst performance in terms of cumulative growth rates is in Assam with the CGIC hovering close to the horizontal axis—and even crossing it for the middle-income groups. The pattern in Haryana is quite puzzling—cumulative growth rates are satisfactory for all except the last ventile, with the top 5 per cent recording a sharp *absolute* fall in household consumption.

6.2.2 Welfare Dominance

I now illustrate the normative approach using the same set of data. I ask whether the social welfare change in a state is higher or lower than that of All-India according to any Generalized Gini welfare function. Let x^0 denote some state's 2004–5 bottom-ranked consumption distribution, while x^1 is the corresponding distribution for 2011–12. The vectors y^0 and y^1 refer to the 2004–5 and 2011–12 distributions for All-India, while Δx, Δy represent the differences in ventile consumption levels. Using the Bossert–Dutta approach, the social welfare change in the state under consideration is higher than that of All-India according to *any* generalized Gini welfare function if

$$\sum_{i=1}^{k}(\Delta x_i - \Delta y_i) \geq 0 \text{ for all } k \in \{1,\dots 20\}$$

Conversely, the change in welfare at the All-India level is higher than that of the state if the inequality is reversed for all ventiles. We will say that state's *welfare dominates* India if the change in welfare in the former is higher than that of India.

In the urban sector, the welfare changes in Haryana and Kerala have been unambiguously higher than that all over India. Also, the urban All-India welfare change has been higher than that in the states of Assam, Bihar, Chhattisgarh and Jharkhand.[8]

---

[8] Note that welfare dominance is a transitive relation. So, states such as Haryana and Kerala which dominated All-India will in turn dominate states that were dominated by India.

In the rural sector, Andhra Pradesh, Himachal Pradesh, Kerala, Punjab, Tamil Nadu, and Uttarakhand welfare dominate rural All-India. Conversely, All-India welfare dominates Assam, Bihar, and Jharkhand.

We close this section with the observation that the empirical results also demonstrate that the positive and normative approaches can yield different conclusions. For instance, states like Himachal Pradesh and Punjab welfare dominate All-India in the rural sector. However, the CGICs of these states do not lie above that of All-India in the rural sector.

6.3 Cumulative GICs for Major States

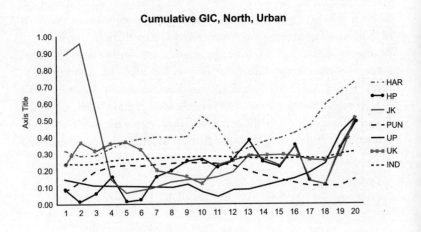

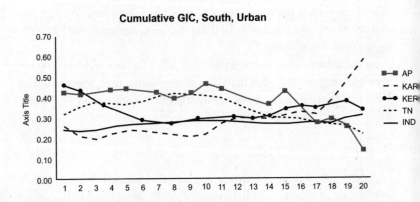

Cumulative GIC, East, Urban

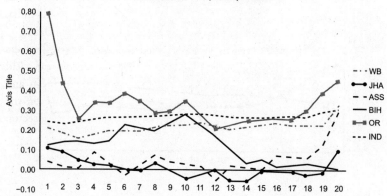

Cumulative GIC, West & Central, Urban

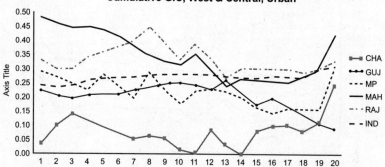

Cumulative GIC, North, Rural

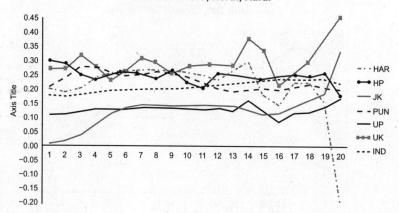

Cumulative GIC, South, Rural

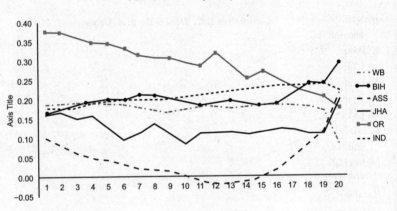

Cumulative GIC, East, Rural

Cumulative GIC, West & Central, Rural

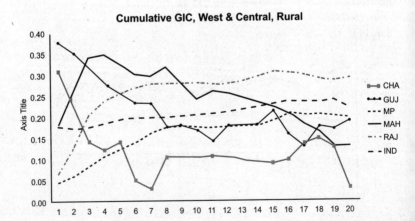

References

Atkinson, A.B. (1970). 'On the measurement of inequality', *Journal of Economic Theory*, 2: 244–63.

Bossert, W. and B. Dutta (2018). *The Measurement of Welfare Change*, mimeo.

Bourguignon, F. (2011). 'Non-anonymous Growth Incidence Curves, Income Mobility and Social Welfare Dominance', *Journal of Economic Inequality*, 9: 605–27.

Cap´eau, B. and E. Ooghe (2007). 'On Comparing Heterogeneous Populations: Is There Really a Conflict between Welfarism and a Concern for Greater Equality in Living Standards?', *Mathematical Social Sciences*, 53: 1–28.

Dalton, H. (1920). 'The Measurement of the Inequality of Incomes', *Economic Journal* 30: 348–61.

Dasgupta, P., A. Sen, and D. Starrett (1973). 'Notes on the Measurement of Inequality, *Journal of Economic Theory*, 6: 180–87.

Jenkins, S.P. and P. Van Kerm (2006). 'Trends in Income Inequality, Pro-poor Income Growth, and Income Mobility', *Oxford Economic Papers*, 58: 531–48.

Kakwani, N.C. (1977). Measurement of Tax Progressivity: An International Comparison, *Economic Journal*, 87: 71–80.

Kakwani, N.C. (1984). 'Welfare Ranking of Income Distributions'. In R.L. Basman and G.F. Rhodes, eds, *Advances in Econometrics, Vol. 3*, Greenwich: JAI Pres, 191–213.

Kolm, S.-Ch. (1969). 'The Optimal Production of Social Justice'. In J. Margolis and S. Guitton (eds), *Public Economics*, London: Macmillan, 145–200.

Mehran, F. (1976). 'Linear measures of income inequality', *Econometrica*, 44: 805–9. Pigou, A.C. (1912). *Wealth and Welfare*, Macmillan, London.

Ravallion, M. and S. Chen (2003). 'Measuring Pro-poor Growth', *Economics Letters*, 78: 93–9.

Shorrocks, A.F. (1983). 'Ranking income distributions', *Economica*, 50: 3–17. Sen, A. (1973). *On Economic Inequality*, Oxford: Clarendon Press.

Son, H.H. (2004). 'A Note on Pro-poor Growth', *Economics Letters*, 82: 307–14.

7 Employer Power, Labour-Saving Technical Change, and Inequality

NANCY H. CHAU AND RAVI KANBUR

Labour-saving technical change is held to be one of the reasons behind rising income inequality. It is argued that technical progress is displacing basic unskilled labour in favour of capital and skilled labour, thereby lowering the share of labour overall and the share of unskilled labour within that (Autor et. al. 2003, Kotlikoff and Sachs 2012, Karabarbounis and Neiman 2014). The theoretical analysis has moved from a conventional capital–labour production framework to a task-based framework (Acemoglu and Autor 2011). Acemoglu and Restrepo (2018) represents further developments in this strand of thinking, where counters to the conventional displacement effect of labour-saving automation are posed in terms of a productivity effect, a capital accumulation effect, and a deepening of automation effect. The impact of labour-saving technical change is thus argued to be nuanced, depending on the relative strengths of these different effects.

However, a striking feature of this literature is how little attention, if any, is paid to market power and specifically to employer power. The labour market is assumed to be competitive. The wage adjusts to clear the labour market in a standard competitive supply and demand framework. Thus, the role of employer power in mediating the impact of labour-saving technical change on employment, wages and inequality is left unexamined. And yet, the issue of degrees monopsony power in labour markets remains central to analysis and policy. The literature launched by Card and Krueger (1994) is still going strong, and the minimum wage remains at the forefront of policy debate (Manning 2003; Ashenfelter, Farber, and Ransom 2010; Bhorat, Kanbur, and Stanwix 2017). And the decline of the bargaining power of labour relative to capital has been a recurring theme in the work of Pranab Bardhan (Bardhan 2017).

Is the impact of technical change on inequality magnified or muted when there is employer power in labour markets? How does the nature of the impact, on employment and on the distribution of wages, vary with the degree of monopsony? This chapter shows that there is indeed a significant interaction effect: While labour-saving technical change and employer power can both increase inequality, the two working together can reinforce each other. Thus, reducing employer power is good for reducing inequality not only on its own terms, but also because it helps to counteract the inequality increasing effects of labour-saving technical change.

The framework we use to develop our analysis is a model of job search frictions whose equilibrium leads to a wage distribution even when skills are homogeneous. Labour-saving technical change is modelled as some tasks now no longer needing to be done by labour. This leads to both a displacement effect and a productivity effect in the terminology of Acemoglu and Restrepo (2018). Employer power is captured by the limited number of firms operating in this labour market and the markup on wages they enjoy as a consequence. Our focus is on equilibrium unemployment and the wage distribution among those employed, and we conduct comparative statics of a higher rate of labour-saving technical change, conditioned by different degrees of monopsony power. We show:

1. Lowering employer power increases expected wages.
2. Lowering employer power generates a Kuznets curve in wage inequality an increase followed by a decrease.
3. Labour-saving technical change polarizes the wage distribution, increasing the unemployment rate but raising the highest wages further.
4. Labour-saving technical change lowers total production efficiency—the sum of wages and profits—when employer power is high, but raises total efficiency when employer power is sufficiently low.
5. Labour-saving technical change lowers the expected wage when employer power is high, but raises the expected wage when employer power is sufficiently low.
6. Labour-saving technical change increases the Gini coefficient of wages when employer power is sufficiently low.
7. With free entry of firms, labour-saving technical change leads to a first-order dominating shift in the distribution of wages, resulting in an increase in the expected wage, and an increase in the Gini coefficient.

The plan of the chapter is as follows. Section 7.1 sets out the basic model of jobs arrival, search and the wage distribution equilibrium with fixed number of firms. Section 7.2 conducts the comparative static analysis of the impact of technical change for varying degrees of employer power. Section 7.3 presents the analysis of long-run equilibrium with free entry of firms. Section 7.4 concludes.

7.1 The Model and Equilibrium

There is a large number N of job seekers, and M number of employers. The lower the ratio of employers (M) to workers (N), $\lambda_o \equiv M/N$, the greater is employer power. Each employer seeks to hire enough workers to complete one unit of labour input. The completion of this unit of labour input requires the completion of a continuum $i \in [0, 1]$ of tasks. The unit labour requirement of each task is assumed constant at a. Let P denote the revenue that an employer receives upon completion of all required tasks, and let p denote the productivity per worker, evaluated as the revenue per worker $p \equiv P/a$.

We treat labour-saving technical change here as an exogenous technological shock, which permits the designation of a fraction $1 - \theta \in [0, 1)$ of tasks to be completed by alternative means, for example, by machines or offshored, at cost r per task performed. θ is thus the fraction of tasks that continues to require traditional labour inputs.

To fill each one of the $a\theta$ number of job vacancies, the employer proposes a wage offer w to a randomly chosen job seeker. Assume that $F_\theta(w)$ is the cumulative distribution function of all wage offers, to be determined endogenously in the sequel. Every job seeker rates any and all offers received, and the best job offer is chosen.

The N job seekers have two employment alternatives: (i) resort to a fall-back option, which earns her a reservation wage c, or (ii) select a job from the (possibly empty) set of job offers that she receives. Specifically, search friction prevents the job seeker from receiving the full set of offers made by every employer in the labour market. The likelihood that a job seeker is met with $z = 0, 1, 2, \ldots$ offers is given by a Poisson distribution with parameter $\lambda_o a\theta \equiv (M/N)a\theta$, or, $\Pr(z; \lambda_o a\theta) = e^{-\lambda_o a\theta}(\lambda_o a\theta)^z / z!$ (Mortensen 2003). The associated cumulative distribution of the maximal offer received is:

$$H_\theta(w) \equiv \sum_{z=0}^{\infty} \frac{e^{-\lambda_o a\theta}(\lambda_o a\theta)^z F_\theta(w)^z}{z!} = e^{-\lambda_o a\theta(1-F_\theta(w))}. \quad (1)$$

$H_\theta(w)$ is the probability that the best offer that a worker receives is less than w.

From an employer's perspective, the likelihood of consummating a match with $a\theta$ workers by offering each w is thus $[H_\theta(w)]^{a\theta}$. The profit maximization problem of each employer is:

$$\pi_\theta(w) = \max_w [H_\theta(w)]^{a\theta}(P - wa\theta - r(1-\theta)) \quad (2)$$

subject to the constraint that wages are no less than the fall-back option c. $r(1 - \theta)$ denotes the cost associated with diverting $1 - \theta$ share of tasks elsewhere. We assume that $r < ac$, so that labour-saving technological change saves cost for all employers that hire positive number of workers.

7.1.1 Two Effects of Labour-Saving Technical Change

The Productivity Effect

In (2), $(P - wa\theta - r(1 - \theta))$ denotes the profits per employer. Henceforth denote

$$p_\theta \equiv \frac{P - r(1 - \theta)}{a\theta}.$$

p_θ reflects the revenue per worker hired net of the cost of alternative inputs $r(1 - \theta)$. Clearly,

$$p_\theta - p_1 = p_\theta - p = \frac{(P - r)(1 - \theta)}{a\theta} > 0. \tag{3}$$

We call this the productivity effect of labour-saving technical change. In essence, by allowing a fraction of tasks to be completed at strictly lower cost through alternative input use, the revenue gains that employers can expect by completing the rest of the tasks workers increases. Since the completion of the rest of the tasks ultimately involves hiring labourers, labour-saving technical change in this setting raises the productivity per worker hired. The size of the productivity increase is given by $p_\theta - p$, a function only of P, r, and the size of the labour-saving technical change $1 - \theta$. Indeed, from this perspective, the larger $1 - \theta$ is, the larger will be the implied productivity gains $p_\theta - p$. The profit maximization problem can thus be simply restated as:

$$\pi_\theta(w) = \max_w [H_\theta(w)]^{a\theta}(p_\theta - w)a\theta. \tag{4}$$

Maximization of (4) by choice of w yields the following:

$$f_\theta(w) = \frac{1}{\lambda_o a\theta} \frac{1}{p_\theta - w}, \quad F_\theta(w) = \frac{1}{\lambda_o a\theta} \ln\left(\frac{p_\theta - c}{p_\theta - w}\right). \tag{5}$$

It follows that:

$$H_\theta(w) = e^{-\lambda_o a\theta} \left(\frac{p_\theta - c}{p_\theta - w} \right). \tag{6}$$

At every point along the distribution $H_\theta(w)$, employers balance the effect of a higher wage offer on profits $p_\theta - w$, and on the likelihood $H_\theta(w)$ of a successful hire.

The Displacement Effect

While $H_\theta(w)$ gives the distribution of the highest wage offer that a worker receives, such a wage offer results eventually in employment if the employer in question is able to attract the required number of additional workers $(\theta a - 1)$ to complete the task at hand. Thus, let $G_\theta(w)$ denote the realized wage distribution facing workers, where $G_\theta(w)$ is the joint probability that (i) the highest wage offer received is at w (with probability $H_\theta(w)$), and (ii) the employer with the highest wage offer is able to amass enough workers to complete the task at wage w (with probability $[H_\theta(w)]^{a\theta-1}$). Thus:

$$G_\theta(w) = [H_\theta(w)]^{a\theta} = e^{-\lambda_o a^2 \theta^2} \left(\frac{p_\theta - c}{p_\theta - w} \right)^{a\theta}. \tag{7}$$

From (7), the likelihood of unemployment is given by the fraction workers paid a wage no greater than c:

$$G_\theta(c) = e^{-\lambda_o a^2 \theta^2}.$$

Clearly, the rate of unemployment is inversely related to the number of employers per worker λ_o, our measure of (the inverse of) employer market power, as well as the number of jobs available per employer $a\theta$. Thus, labour-saving technical change, by decreasing θ, introduces a displacement effect in the labour market:

$$G_\theta(c) - G_1(c) = e^{-\lambda_o a^2 \theta^2} - e^{-\lambda_o a^2} > 0$$

whenever $\theta < 1$.

We summarize these observations in the following proposition:

Proposition 1. *At given λ_o, a labour-saving technical change always gives rise to a productivity effect, raising the revenue per worker hired,*

$$p_\theta - p_1 > 0,$$

in addition to a displacement effect, which increases the overall unemployment rate

$$G_\theta(c) - G_1(c) > 0.$$

To see how these findings, set in a task-based framework with labour-saving technical change, differ from the canonical search friction setting, take the special case where there is no labour-saving technical change ($\theta = 1$), (7) simplifies to

$$G_1(w) = G_1(c)\left(\frac{p-c}{p-w}\right)^a = e^{-\lambda_o a^2}\left(\frac{p-c}{p-w}\right)^a, \qquad (8)$$

as the productivity effect ($p_\theta \neq p$) and the displacement effect $G_\theta(c) \neq G_1(c)$ no longer apply.

Furthermore, (8) can be further simplified by removing task considerations in our model by setting $a = 1$. In this case, the original Mortensen (2003) formulation of a wage distribution applies, where

$$G_1(w) = H_1(w) = e^{-\lambda_o}\left(\frac{p-c}{p-w}\right). \qquad (9)$$

7.1.2　The Role Employer Market Power

Before we turn to the effects of labour-saving technical change as a function of employer power, we review the role of employer market power on aggregate labour market outcomes in a model with search friction such as ours (for example, Mortensen 2003, Chau, Goto, and Kanbur 2016), and derive new results related to wage inequality that will be useful for our analysis to follow. Thus, for now, set $\theta = 1$. Increasing market competitiveness by raising the number of employers per worker, λ_o, gives rise to a first order stochastically dominating shift in the wage distribution $G_1(w)$. At the limit as $\lambda_o \to \infty$, $G_1(w)$ puts unit weight on worker's marginal product

p_1. Along the way, an increase in λ_o unambiguously decreases unemployment since the unemployment rate is given by:

$$G_1(c) = e^{-\lambda_o a^2}.$$

The expected wage in the labor market $\overline{w}_1$ can be expressed as:

$$\overline{w}_1 = cG_1(c) + \int_c^{w_\theta^+} wdG_1(w) \tag{10}$$
$$= \overline{\alpha}_1 p_1 + (1 - \overline{\alpha}_1)c,$$

where $\overline{\alpha}_1 = 1 - (ae^{\lambda_o a} - e^{-\lambda_o a^2})/(a-1)$.

The expected wage in the economy is a weighted sum of the productivity of labour p_1 and the reservation wage c. As should be expected, the expected wage in (10) rises as employer power dissipates through higher values of λ_o. Furthermore, an increase in λ_o improves the pass-through of any change in productivity p_1 to wages. Indeed, for any values of λ_o other than the competitive benchmark where λ_o tends to ∞, there is imperfect pass-through of productivity changes to the expected wage, since

$$\frac{\partial \overline{w}}{\partial p_1} = \overline{\alpha}_1 < 1.$$

Increasing market competitiveness improves this pass-through, as

$$\frac{\partial^2 \overline{w}}{\partial p_1 \partial \lambda_o} = a^2(e^{-\lambda_o a} - e^{\lambda a^2})/(a-1) > 0.$$

Now let Y_1 denote the sum of total profits and income of all workers including the unemployed, and $y_1 \equiv Y_1/N$ the per capita income, it is straightforward to verify that:

$$y_1 = (1 - G_1(c))p_1 + G_1(c)c$$
$$= \alpha_1^y p_1 + \left(1 - \alpha_1^y\right)c,$$

where $\alpha_\theta^y \equiv 1 - e^{-\lambda_o a^2}$.

Thus, national income is also a weighted average of the productivity per worker p_1 and the opt out c. By inspection, since the share α_1^y is strictly increasing in λ_o, competitiveness in the labour market raises per capita output, precisely as it lifts workers out of the unemployment pool.

While the impact of employer market power on aggregate labour market outcomes such as unemployment and the expected relationship would seem to be monotonic, there is an interesting inverted-U Kuznets relationship between wage inequality and employer market power. Specifically, let $L_1(g)$ denote the Lorenz Curve where g denotes percentage of the workforce. $L_1(g)$ gives the share of income of the lowest $g\%$ of the total workforce according to the wage distribution function $G_1(w)$. Using (8)[1]

$$L_1(g) = 1 - \frac{a\left(w_1^+ - p_1 g\right) - p_1(1-g)}{(a-1)\overline{w}_1} + \left(\frac{a}{a-1}\right)\left(\frac{w_1^+ - p_1}{\overline{w}_1}\right)g^{1-\frac{1}{a}}.$$

Let I_1 denote the Gini coefficient of wage inequality associated with the Lorenz curve shown earlier. Figure 7.1 plots the relationship between the Gini coefficient and employer market power.[2] Starting from a perfectly competitive regime with $\lambda_o \to \infty$, there is perfect equality among all workers as they each paid their marginal value product p_1. Starting from this benchmark a small increase in employer power will necessarily increase inequality, as some workers $G_1(c) = e^{-\lambda_o a}$ become unemployed, while almost all others receive a wage less than p_1 based on the wage distribution function $G_1(w)$. Further increases in market power will continue to increase inequality. At some point, additional increases in employer market power *decreases* inequality, as increasingly more workers join the ranks of the unemployed. This process continues until λ_o tends to

[1] To see this, note that for wage rank less than the unemployment rate $G_\theta(c)$, the wage income of the least wealth g percent of the total workforce, $w_1(g)$ is simply c. For $g > G_1(c)$, it follows from (9) that

$$w(g) = p_1 - e^{\lambda_o a}(p_1 - c)g^{-\frac{1}{\theta a}}.$$

The Lorenz curve is

$$L_1(\hat{g}) = \int_0^{\hat{g}} \frac{w(g)}{\overline{w}_1} dg.$$

[2] The parametric assumptions are: $P = 30$, $a = 3$, $\theta = 1$, $c = 1$ and $r = 2.85 (< ca = 3)$.

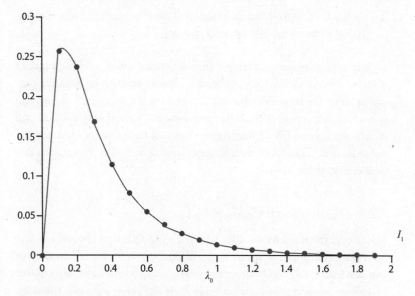

Figure 7.1 Wage Inequality Impact of Employer Market Power

zero, reaching another benchmark of complete equality, with all workers are unemployed, earning the opt out value c.[3]

7.2 The Interactive Effects of Employer Power and Technical Change

We now proceed to show that the productivity and displacement effects of labour-saving technical change in a task-based setting can give rise to a set of very nuanced distributional and overall labour market level consequences. Furthermore, we show that these effects interact in interesting ways with the extent of employer market power. Specifically, we ask

1. What are the distributional and aggregate labour market consequences of labour-saving technical change?

[3] Note the similarity between this pattern and the traditional Kuznets curve arising out of a process of population migration from a low-mean/low-inequality rural sector to a high-mean/ high-inequality urban sector.

2. What are the pre-conditions that will pave the way for a more *labour-friendly* labour-saving technical change?

The first question is a simple 'first difference' effect, which examines whether labour-saving technical change brings positive or negative outcomes along the wage distribution, as well as in the aggregate. The second is a 'cross difference' effect, and questions the pre-conditions that will enable workers to better harness the benefits (or to reduce the adverse consequences) associated with a labour-saving technical change. We discuss each of these in turn.

7.2.1 Distributional Consequences

It is straightforward to see that labour-saving technical change impacts both the equilibrium range of wages offered, as well as the frequency of any particular wage offer along the range. By definition, the wage lower bound is simply the reservation wage c. At the other extreme, the wage upper bound w_θ^+ is defined by $H_\theta(w_\theta^+) \equiv 1$, or equivalently,

$$w_\theta^+ = \alpha_\theta^+ p_\theta + \left(1 - \alpha_\theta^+\right) c, \quad \alpha_\theta^+ \equiv 1 - e^{-\lambda_o a\theta}. \tag{11}$$

The maximal wage in the labour market is a weighted average of worker productivity p_θ and the reservation wage c. The weight α_θ^+ determines the extent to which there is *imperfect pass-through* of the productivity gains $p_\theta - p_1$ to the maximal wage.

From (11), the extent of imperfect pass-through depends on both λ_o and θ. The more competitive the labour market (higher λ_o), the higher α_θ^+ will be and the maximal wage is more responsive to productivity improvements. Note that labour-saving technical change has the effect of reducing the job arrival rate $\lambda_o a\theta$, while reinforcing market power of employers with the remaining vacancies. Thus, labour saving technical change adversely impacts the extent of imperfect pass-through. This tends to decrease w_θ^+. But going in opposite direction, labour-saving technical change directly improves labour productivity p_θ from Proposition 1, which tends to increase w_θ^+. On balance,

$$\frac{\partial w_\theta^+}{\partial(1-\theta)} = \frac{1}{\theta}\left(\left(1 - (1 + \lambda_o a\theta)e^{-\lambda_o a\theta}\right)\frac{p-r}{\theta a} + \left(c - \frac{r}{a}\right)\lambda_o \theta e^{\lambda_o \theta a} \right) > 0.$$

In other words, labour-saving technical change always gives rise to a more dispersed range of wages. Taken together with the displacement effect in Proposition 1, the following result is immediate:

Proposition 2. *For all $\theta \in (0, 1)$, there exists $\overline{w}_\theta \in (c, w_1^+)$ such that for all $w \leq \overline{w}_\theta$,*

$$G_\theta(w) \geq G_1(w).$$

Otherwise, for all $w > \overline{w}_\theta$,

$$G_\theta(w) < G_1(w).$$

Thus, labour-saving technical change produces a single-crossing shift of the wage distribution function $G_\theta(w)$ with crossing from above. This is illustrated in Figure 7.2, in which a pair of wage distributions ($G_1(w)$, $G_\theta(w)$) and the respective ranges ($[c, w_1^+]$ and $[c, w_\theta^+]$) are displayed. The displacement effect raises the fraction of unemployed workers from $G_1(c)$ to $G_\theta(c)$. Meanwhile, the productivity effect widens the range of wages. This results in a more polarized wage structure: A higher fraction of

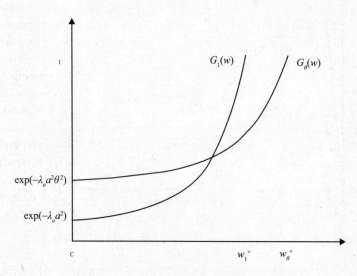

Figure 7.2 The Realized Wage Distribution $G_0(w)$

workers without work, and simultaneously a higher fraction of workers at the highest wage rank.

These suggest two possibly opposing effects that labour-saving technical change may have on overall inequality. In particular, if the displacement effect dominates, and the productivity effect does not translate into significant wage gains, then a labour-saving technical may well improve wage inequality, perhaps paradoxically because it causes more workers join the ranks of the unemployed. By contrast, if the productivity effect gives rise to significant wage gains particularly for workers at relatively higher wage ranks, wage inequality may increase.

As before, define $w_\theta(g)$ as the wage of worker in the g'th percentile along the wage distribution. The Lorenz curve is given by

$$L_\theta(g) = 1 - \frac{\theta a\left(w_\theta^+ - p_\theta g\right) - p_\theta(1-g)}{(\theta a - 1)\overline{w}_\theta} + \left(\frac{\theta a}{a-1}\right)\left(\frac{w_\theta^+ - p_\theta}{\overline{w}_\theta}\right) g^{1-\frac{1}{\theta a}}.$$

Also let I_θ denote the Gini coefficient of wage inequality associated with the Lorenz curve $L_\theta(g)$. Figure 7.3 plots the relationship between the Gini coefficient and labour-saving technical change $1 - \theta$.[4] A family

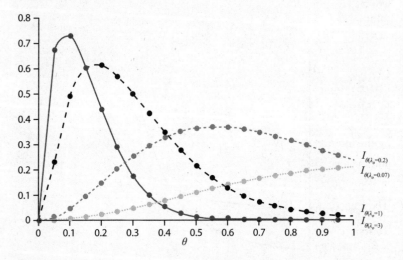

Figure 7.3 Wage Inequality and Labour Saving Technical Change

[4] The parametric assumptions are: $P = 30$, $a = 3$, $\theta = 0.5$, $c = 1$ and $r = 2.85 (< ca = 3)$.

of such relationships are shown with successively higher job arrival rates λ_o, or equivalently, successively more competitive labour markets. Starting from $\theta = 1$, labour-saving technical change (reduction in θ) decreases the Gini coefficient when the employers wield significant market power (for example, $I_\theta(\lambda = 0.7)$ when $\lambda_o = 0.7$). This corresponds to the case where the productivity effect is very small as high levels of employer market power adversely impact the pass-through of productivity gains to workers' wages. Consequently, inequality actually improves upon introduction of labour-saving technical change as more workers enter the unemployment pool.

For higher levels of labour market competition, Figure 7.3 shows that the Gini coefficient first rises then falls with successive increases in labour-saving technical change starting from $\theta = 1$. As employer competitiveness facilitates the pass-through of the productivity effect to raise wages, labour-saving technical change increases both unemployment and the share of workers with the highest wages. The result is an increase in inequality. For any given λ_o, further increases in $1 - \theta$ will continue to reduce the job arrival rate, however. Ultimately, this will have eroded the productivity pass-through to wages so much that any further labour-saving technical change will in fact lower wage inequality, as more and more worker enter the unemployment pool. We thus see once again the possibility of a Kuznets type inverse-U relationship between wage inequality and labour-saving technical change.

7.2.2 Aggregate Labour Market Consequences

In this section, we show that aggregate labour market performance outcomes associated with labour-saving technical change are also impacted by the interplay between the productivity effect, the displacement effect, and the mediating role of the degree of labour market competition.

The Expected Wage

To start, consider the expected wage in the labour market:

$$\bar{w}_\theta = cG_\theta(c) + \int_c^{w_\theta^+} w\,dG_\theta(w) \qquad (12)$$
$$= \bar{\alpha}_\theta p_\theta + (1 - \bar{\alpha}_\theta)c,$$

where $\bar{\alpha}_\theta = 1 - (\theta a e^{-\lambda_o a\theta} - e^{-\lambda_o a^2 \theta^2})/(\theta a - 1)$.

The expected wage in the economy is a weighted sum of the productivity of labour p_θ and the reservation wage c, where the weight placed on productivity, $\overline{\alpha}_\theta$, once again depends on employer market power λ_o, and now also the size of the labour-saving technical change θ. From (11), $\overline{w}_\theta - \overline{w}_1 > (\leq)0$ if and only if the productivity effect is sufficiently large:

$$\frac{p_\theta - p_1}{p_1 - c} > (\leq) \frac{\overline{\alpha}_1}{\overline{\alpha}_0} - 1. \tag{13}$$

Put differently, labour-saving technical change increases the expected wage if and only if the productivity effect $p_\theta - p_1$ is sufficiently large. The minimum required size of the productivity effect depends critically on how quickly productivity increases are passed through to raise wages, as $\overline{\alpha}_1 > \overline{\alpha}_\theta$ from the definition of $\overline{\alpha}_\theta$.[5]

We note that

$$\lim_{\lambda_o \to \infty} \frac{\overline{\alpha}_1}{\overline{\alpha}_\theta} - 1 = 0 \quad \text{and} \quad \lim_{\lambda_o \to 0} \frac{\overline{\alpha}_1}{\overline{\alpha}_\theta} - 1 = \frac{1}{\theta^3} - 1.$$

It follows, therefore, that

Proposition 3. *If the productivity effect is sufficiently large:*

$$\frac{p_\theta - p_1}{p_1 - c} > \frac{1}{\theta^3} - 1, \tag{14}$$

a labour-saving technical change $1 - \theta > 0$ always gives rise to an increase in the expected wage $\overline{w}_\theta - \overline{w}_1$. If, however, the inequality is not satisfied, then there exists a $\overline{\lambda}_o \in (0, \infty)$ such that for all $\lambda_o \geq \overline{\lambda}_o$, the labour-saving technical change increases the expected wage.

It follows that employer market power may indeed prevent the pass-through of the productivity gains from labour-saving technical change from raising the average wage of workers. This occurs particularly when the strength of the productivity effect is not large enough.

---

[5] To see this, recall that $\overline{\alpha}_\theta = (1 - (\theta a e^{\lambda_o a \theta} - e^{-\lambda_o a^2 \theta^2} / (\theta a - 1))$. Routine differentiation shows that $\overline{\alpha}_\theta < \overline{\alpha}_1$.

The Average Labour Share

In our model, there is no explicit bargaining between workers and employers. Any variations in labour share are endogenously determined by how productivity change impacts wages. Importantly, in our context, since the distribution of wages is dispersed, the labour share is dispersed as well. Specifically, define the labour share of any given employer–employee pair as $s \equiv w/p_\theta$.

Using $G_\theta(w)$, the induced distribution of labour shares, henceforth $\Psi_\theta(s)$, is given by

$$\Psi_\theta(s) = G_\theta(sp_\theta) = e^{-\lambda_o a^2 \theta^2} \left(\frac{1 - c/p_\theta}{1-s} \right)^{a\theta}. \tag{15}$$

and s ranges between c/p_θ and $\alpha_\theta^+ + (1 - \alpha_\theta^+)c/p_\theta$.

By inspection of (15), a labour-saving technical change shifts the labour share distribution to the left. This result is intuitive following (12), and directly reflects the adverse impact of technical change on productivity pass-through. Consequently, labour-saving technical change unambiguously reduces labour share as well.

Per Capita Income

Turning now to the aggregate efficiency consequences of a labour-saving technical change, let Y_θ be the sum of total profits and income of all workers including the unemployed, and let $y_\theta \equiv Y_\theta/N$ denote per capita income:

$$y_\theta = (1 - G_\theta(c))p_\theta + G_\theta(c)c$$
$$= \alpha_\theta^y p_\theta + \left(1 - \alpha_\theta^y\right)c,$$

where $\alpha_\theta^y \equiv 1 - e^{\lambda_o a^2 \theta^2}$.

Thus, national income is also a weighted average of the productivity per worker p_θ and the reservation wage c. A labour-saving technical change gives rise to an increase (decrease) in per capita national income, $y_\theta - y_1 > (\leq) 0$ if and only if

$$\frac{p_\theta - p_1}{p_1 - c} > (\leq) \frac{\alpha_1^y}{\alpha_\theta^y} - 1. \tag{16}$$

Thus, labour-saving technical change increases per capita income if and only if the productivity effect $p_\theta - p_1$ is sufficiently large to compensate for the increase in unemployment. With respect to the condition in (16), it is straightforward to show that $\alpha_\theta^y < \alpha_1^y$ is monotonically decrease in λ_o, and furthermore,

$$\lim_{\lambda_o \to \infty} \frac{\alpha_1^y}{\alpha_\theta^y} - 1 = 0 \quad \text{and} \quad \lim_{\lambda_o \to 0} \frac{\alpha_1^y}{\alpha_\theta^y} - 1 = \frac{1}{\theta^2} - 1.$$

Thus, we have

Proposition 4.   *If the productivity effect is sufficiently large such that*

$$\frac{p_\theta - p_1}{p_1 - c} > \frac{1}{\theta^2} - 1,$$

a labour-saving technical change $1 - \theta > 0$ always gives rise to an increase in per capita income $y_\theta > y_1$. If, however, the inequality is not satisfied, then there exists a $\lambda_o^y \in (0, \infty)$ such that for all $\lambda_o \geq \lambda_o^y$, labour-saving technical change increases the per capita income.

The important takeaway here is that a productivity improving labour-saving technical change does not guarantee an improvement in overall efficiency. Quite the contrary, unless the productivity effect itself is sufficiently large, a labour-saving technical change will need to be coupled with a sufficient competitive labour market, in order for the productivity benefits of the technical change to outweigh its adverse unemployment consequences.

Figures 7.4a–7.4c, respectively, plot the aforementioned aggregate labour market outcomes as a function of the degree of market power in the economy. In Figure 7.4a shows the expected wage schedules as a function of λ_o with and without labour-saving technical change, and shows that the expected wage impact is positive only what employer competition for labour sufficiently intense. Figure 7.4b and 7.4c, respectively, display the average labour share and the per capita income as a function of labour market competitiveness. Consistent with the preceding discussion, a labour-saving technical change always lowers the labour share, and does not guarantee an increase in per capita income. Quite the contrary, if the productivity effect is not too large, and if the labour market is sufficiently non-competitive, a reduction in per capita income is perfectly consistent with a productivity improving labour-saving technical change.

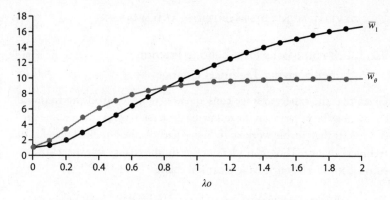

Figure 7.4a Expected Wage Impact of Technical Change and Employer Market Power

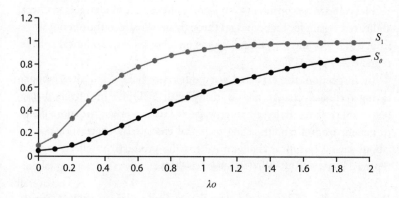

Figure 7.4b Average Labor Share Impact of Technical Change and Employer Market Power

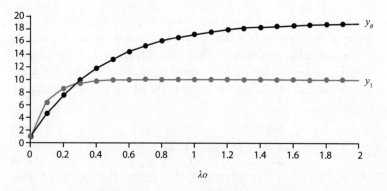

Figure 7.4c Per Capita Income Impact of Technical Change and Employer Market Power

7.2.3 Pre-conditions for a Labour-Friendly Labour-Saving Technical Change

Given that the expected wage consequences of a labour-saving technical change may be negative, in the following discussion we examine some pre-conditions that enable workers to better harness the potential benefits of technical change. Thus, consider once again the change in expected wage subsequent to a labour-saving technical change:

$$\Delta \bar{w}_\theta \equiv \bar{w}_\theta - \bar{w}_1 = \bar{\alpha}_\theta p_\theta + (1 - \bar{\alpha}_\theta)c - [\bar{\alpha}_1 p_1 + (1 - \bar{\alpha}_1)c]$$
$$= (\bar{\alpha}_\theta - \bar{\alpha}_1)(p_1 - c) + \bar{\alpha}_\theta(p_\theta - p_1)$$

Henceforth, we consider two types of policies. The first targets worker's ability to bargain for higher wages through an increase in the opt out wage from c to $c + S$, and the second is a tax on labour-saving technical change to increase r to $r + T$.

By inspection, the expected wage difference before and after labour-saving technical change always rising with S. Quite intuitively, being better able to bargain for a higher wage as c rises, workers are more likely to benefit from a labour-saving technical change. By contrast, a tax on labour-saving technical change weakens the productivity effect as p_θ is replaced by $p_\theta - T(1 - \theta)/(\theta a)$. We have thus:

Proposition 5. *The expected wage change due to a labour-saving technical change, $\Delta \bar{w}_\theta$, is strictly increasing with respect to the subsidy on the reservation wage S, and is strictly decreasing with respect to T.*

This suggests the need to address the root cause for why expected wage is lower in the presence of a labour-saving technical change. In particular, minimizing the productivity effect itself through a tax on employers attempting to save on labour cost cannot bring about an expected wage improvement, but enhancing the ability on the part of workers to bargain for higher wages will.

7.2.4 Long-Run Labour Market Consequences

So far, we have taken the total number of employers as constant. We now examine the consequences of labour-saving technical change in the long run, assuming that in such a longer time horizon, free entry of employers subject to a fixed cost of entry eventually endogenizes the total number of employers λ_o. Since λ_o is our measure of employer market power, we are thus examining circumstances under which in the long run, employer market power can evolve to reflect the profitability of offering new vacancies in the presence of new technologies.

Accordingly, let K be a fixed cost of entry for every employer seeking to hire enough laborers and alternative inputs to complete the unit of task required to generate revenue P. Free entry occurs until expected profits is equal to the cost of entry, or in other words:

$$\pi_\theta(w) = [H_\theta(w)]^{\theta a}(p\theta - w)\theta a = K. \tag{17}$$

It follows that the wage distribution takes the simple form:

$$G_\theta(w) = \frac{1}{\theta a}\left(\frac{K}{p\theta - w}\right).$$

We note that the productivity effect of a labour-saving technical through p_θ alone continues to shift the wage distribution to the right in as before. With respect to the displacement effect, the unemployment rate is now given by:

$$G_\theta(c) = \frac{1}{\theta a}\left(\frac{K}{p\theta - c}\right).$$

Thus, the unemployment rate is monotonically decreasing in p_θ. It follows, therefore, that the job displacement effect changes signs in the long run, as employer entry more than compensates for the reduction in the number of job openings per employer in the presence of labour-saving technical change.

It can now be readily seen that a labour-saving technical change induces a first-order dominating shift in $G_\theta(w)$ to the right. This implies that the range of wages widens, and the expected wage rises with labour-saving technical change. Finally, the Lorenz curve in the long run can be explicitly expressed as:

$$L_\theta(g) = \frac{cg}{\overline{w}_\theta} \quad \text{if } g < G_\theta(c)$$

$$= 1 - \frac{p_\theta}{\overline{w}_\theta} + \frac{p_\theta g - G_\theta(c)\ln(g)}{\overline{w}_\theta} \quad \text{otherwise.}$$

The associated Gini coefficient I_θ can be expressed simply as follows:

$$I_\theta = \frac{G_\theta(c)(p_\theta - c)(G_\theta(c) - 1 - \ln G_\theta(c))}{Ew}.$$

Figures 7.5a and 7.5b, respectively, show the effect of labour-saving technical change as entry cost K increases using the same parametric assumptions as before.[6] In Figure 7.5a, average wage is indeed always increasing with labor saving technical change as shown earlier. Furthermore, wage inequality likewise strictly rises with labour-saving technical change as the range of wages always expands, and unemployment decreases.

7.4 Conclusion

This chapter brings employer power centre stage in the analysis of the consequences of labour-saving technical change for efficiency and in

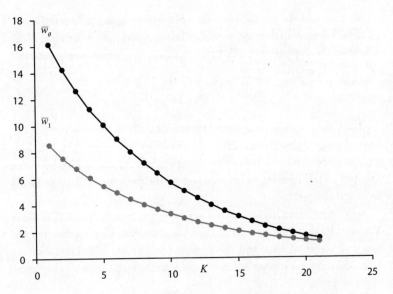

Figure 7.5a   Average Wage Impact of Technical Change and Entry Cost

[6] The addition is the fixed cost of entry and the values are shown in Figures 7.5a and 7.5b.

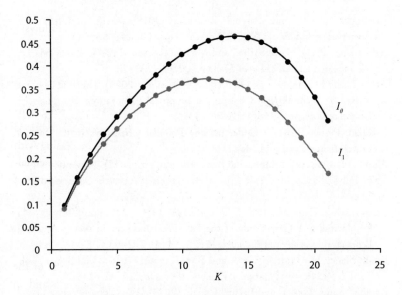

Figure 7.5b Wage Inequality Effects of Technical Change and Entry Cost

particular for equity. In task-based model with labour market frictions, where there is unemployment and wage inequality even with identical workers and identical employers, we show that the number of employers relative to workers plays a critical role in mediating the impact of technical change. In a series of propositions, we show the nuanced interactions between employer power and labour-saving technical change in the determination of wage inequality, including the possibility of a Kuznetsian inverted-u relationship. In general, when employer power is sufficiently low, including the case where there is free entry of firms, labour-saving technical change enhances efficiency but increases wage inequality. Our analysis thus focuses attention on the degree of monopsony power as a key determinant of the efficiency and equity consequences of labour-saving technical change, and raises the issue of regulation of employer power as a major policy issue in the era of automation.

References

Acemoglu, Daron and David Autor. (2011). 'Skills, Tasks and Technologies: Implications for Employment and Earnings', *Handbook of Labor Economics*, 4: 1043–1171.

Acemoglu, Daron and Pascual Restrepo. (2018). 'Artificial Intelligence, Automation and Work', NBER Working Paper No. 24196.

Ashenfelter, Orley, Hank Farber, and Michael Ransom. (2010). 'Labor Market Monopsony', *Journal of Labor Economics*, 28(2): 203–10.

Autor, David H., Frank Levy, and Richard J. Murnane. (2003). 'The Skill Content of Recent Technological Change: An Empirical Exploration', *The Quarterly Journal of Economics*, 118(4): 1279–1333.

Bardhan, Pranab. (2017). 'Understanding Populist Challenges to the Liberal Order', *Boston Review*, 11 May.

Bhorat, Haroon, Ravi Kanbur, and Benjamin Stanwix. (2017). 'Minimum Wages in Sub-Saharan Africa: A Primer', *World Bank Research Observer*, 32(1): 21–74.

Card, David; Krueger, Alan B. (September 1994). 'Minimum Wages and Employment: A Case Study of the Fast-Food Industry in New Jersey and Pennsylvania', *American Economic Review*, 84 (4): 772–93.

Chau, Nancy H., Hideaki Goto, and Ravi Kanbur. (2016). 'Middlemen, Fair Traders and Poverty', *Journal of Economic Inequality*, 14 (1): 81–108.

Karabarbounis, Loukas and Brent Neiman. (2014). 'The Global Decline of the Labor Share', *Quarterly Journal of Economics*, 129: 61–103.

Kotliko, Larry and Jerey D. Sachs. (2012). 'Smart Machines and Long-Term Misery', NBER Working Paper No. 18629.

Manning, Alan. (2003). *Monopsony in Motion: Imperfect Competition in Labor Markets*. United States: Princeton University Press.

Mortensen, Dale T. (2003). *Wage Dispersion. Why Are Similar Workers Paid Differently?* Cambridge MA: MIT Press.

8　Property Rights and Productivity of Resource Allocation in Developing Countries

MAITREESH GHATAK

Even though classical economists from Smith to Marx placed a lot of importance on institutions such as property rights that underpin a market economy, until recently there was relatively less focus on these. Assets such as land or capital were treated as an input in production with little focus on the ownership and contractual structure governing their use. This sometimes creates an impression from outside that 'Economics' as a discipline is too focused on the abstract notion of the invisible hand of the market and its ability to coordinate the decisions of millions of individuals to achieve efficient outcomes, without looking deeper into how markets work. It is as if one is studying electrical lights without thinking about the wiring system that underpin it.

Such an institution-free view of the economy would be justified if institutions were well-developed everywhere and could be taken for granted. But from the Arrow–Debreu complete markets view of the economy or the efficient markets' view of the Chicago school, the discipline has come a long distance to the point that in modern treatment of markets in economic theory, it is customary to specify what is being assumed about institutional imperfections that underpin markets. For example, in the textbook version of the classic model, it is assumed that there is no problem of extortion—one does not have to worry about one's assets or output to be subject to threats of expropriation for private or state actors to be able extract surplus from oneself.

Most economic activity is not instantaneous—there is a lag between investment and production, and production and income generation. Similarly, most economic transactions are not spot transactions, where one does not have to worry about contractual mechanisms to enforce the terms of the agreement. Rather, they are time-separated. For example, in the case of loan or rental contracts, what is traded is money for the use of an asset with a promise to deliver something at a later date. As a result, institutional mechanisms are needed that provide protection from opportunism, extortion, and deliberate defaults on existing agreements. An entire range of formal institutions, such as laws, property rights, contracts, and regulation, as well as informal institutions, such as the role of reputation, repeated relationships, conventions, and social norms are precisely mechanisms that try to minimize the potential frictions that arise in economic activities such as investment and production as well as rental and sales of assets

In the institutional approach to development economics in which Pranab Bardhan played a pioneering role, property rights play a central role. In the earlier era with growth theory focusing on a representative agent as in a Robinson Crusoe economy (where human interactions are a moot point) or standard price theory in the context of competitive market economies with an implicit assumption of perfect institutions, not much attention was paid to the topic of property rights. As an example of an institution that governs one of the most important forms of resource allocation, the topic of property rights is clearly central to the research agenda that seeks to study how institutions affect economic development.

Property rights refer to rules, regulations, and customs governing *non-human* productive assets (for example, land, livestock, natural resources, real estate, machinery, intellectual property like patents, brand name) regarding:[1]

a)   Use rights—their use in productive activity
b)   Contractual rights—claims to current and future streams of income generated from them via their use in economic transactions. This includes compensation for inputs complementary to the asset in production (for example, capital) through pledging, mortgaging, profit-sharing; or, letting others use it via renting out or tenancy.
c)   Transfer rights—transferring them to another party, in the form of sales, gift, or bequest.

Property rights are an example of an economic institution using the classic definition provided by North (1990). Namely, they are a set of rules of the game, or more formally, humanly devised constraints in the contexts defined above that shape economic interactions, and, in consequence, affect economic incentives.

For us to be able to study and evaluate the potentially critical impact of property rights on economic outcomes, there must be a) some imperfections relating to it; and b) a variation in these imperfections across settings that allows us to compare alternative scenarios in terms of economic efficiency. Much of the literature on property rights characterizes imperfections with respect to a 'perfect' system of property rights as a friction, analogous to transport or trade costs, transactions costs, informational asymmetries, externalities, that affects economic activity through a number of mechanisms. Of course, there is the important question what determines these frictions in property rights.

By property rights economists typically refer to *private* property rights, a key feature of which is to be able to legally exclude others from using a good or asset, as well as transfer and exchange rights. Implicitly, economists typically refer to *formal* property rights that are regulated and enforced through a modern legal system. However, other forms of property rights are important in many societies. One example is *collective*

---

[1] Property rights regarding human assets are possible in theory and has been observed in practice via pre-modern coercive institutions such as slavery, and indentured labour. Modern legal systems rule them out, as they also rule out voluntary servitude.

or *communal* property rights which tend to be informal. In the case of common property resources, such as a lake or a forest, individuals have use rights but do not have the right to exclude others from using it. Also, in traditional societies, even when use rights are private, they are governed by community-based mechanisms based on customary law. For example, traditional land rights in Africa often require that the lineage or tribal authority has jurisdiction in this domain. There also tend to be strong restrictions on exchange and transfer rights. Another important theme in the literature on property rights in development is the interaction between formal and informal property rights.

In this chapter, I will focus mainly on exogenous variations in property rights, and their impact on resource allocation via different mechanisms. I will draw on and extend the conceptual framework developed in Besley and Ghatak (2010), and focus on work done over the last decade since that article was published.

While I will not deal with the issue of endogenous property rights, some conceptual points should be noted. An important approach to the question of endogenous property rights is that of optimal or efficient allocation of property rights (for example, Hart 1995). The focus of this literature is to clarify the relationship between contracts and property rights. Both specify a set of decision rights—rights to take some actions and rights to exclude others from taking some actions. In a world with perfect contracting, a rental contract is effectively equivalent to a change in ownership because these rights can be specified for every foreseeable contingency. According to the celebrated Coase theorem (Coase 1960), in a world with complete information and zero contracting costs, resource allocation will be the same independent of the allocation of property rights, even in the presence of externalities. However, in a world with costly contracting, owning and renting are not the same as not all uses of the asset can be specified up front for all eventualities. A corollary of this is the idea that property rights convey residual rights of control over an asset to the owner (Hart 1995). These rights represent a source of freedom to the owner, that is, to decide to do what he or she would like with the object subject to any constraints on the rights. This will also affect his or her incentives to invest in enhancing the value of the asset, as well as those of other individuals who might have contractual rights to use the asset. The property rights theory of the firm assumes absence of borrowing constraints so that optimal assignment of property rights is typically efficient. However, there is literature on tenancy that emphasizes the role of borrowing constraints in the determination of property rights (Mookherjee 1998, Banerjee et al. 2002). In this case, the initial distribution of property rights can have efficiency consequences and therefore reforms in them (for example, land or tenancy reform) can have productivity consequences.

In this chapter I discuss various theories relating property rights to economic outcomes (Section 8.1), review recent empirical evidence in support of various mechanisms that theory highlights (Section 8.2), discuss the emerging research agenda (Section 8.3), and offer some concluding observations.

8.1 Theories of Property Rights and Economic Outcomes

What are the various mechanisms through which property rights affect economic outcomes? In general, property rights affect resource allocation by shaping the incentives of individuals to carry out productive activity involving the asset, undertake investments that maintain or enhance its value, and also, to trade or lease the asset for other uses. The key channels explored are (Besley 1995, and Besley and Ghatak 2010): a) security of property rights reduces the risk of expropriation and consequently, improves the likelihood, that individuals can realize the fruits of their investment and efforts; b) distortion of resource allocation due to private efforts in protecting property rights which, from the economic point of view, is unproductive; c) gains from trade so that assets are put to their most productive use by facilitating separation between ownership and use (for example, by rental markets); and d) supporting transactions by overcoming frictions in other markets, for example, relaxing borrowing constraints by facilitating pledging of assets against default.

This is not an exhaustive list. There are some other potential channels through which property rights may affect resource allocation. For example, more equal property rights may improve certain aspects of resource allocation related to gender—for example, women may have greater say in household matters if they inherited parental property in the same footing as men, and empowerment of women and improvements in some development measures (for example, children's human capital) are well known. They can also interact with various behavioural aspects of how individuals make decisions, for example, by potentially affecting beliefs of individuals about themselves or how the world works. For example, Di Tella et al. (2007) showed that squatters in Buenos Aires who received property titles, reported beliefs that are more favourable to a 'free market' view. However, better property rights also give more options to individuals, and in the presence of behavioural biases, that may also cause them to make unwise impulsive decisions, for example, selling off an asset prematurely. This suggests that the welfare effects of property rights reforms can be quite subtle.

Whether it is affecting people's beliefs or empowering certain groups, to the extent these encourage effort and enterprise or investment in human capital, these could be additional channels through which changes in property rights can affect resource allocation. Other than these specific effects, there are also *general* effects via individual's experiencing an increase in their *effective* wealth and also, a reduction in uncertainty in their economic lives, and both of these effects could affect certain economic decisions and outcomes along standard channels.

These are individual level effects of property rights. At the economy-wide level, improvements in property rights lead to the following systemic effects, beyond the simple aggregation of individual effects listed earlier: a) reduce the deadweight losses and misallocation of resources connected with imperfect property rights; b) by allowing separation of ownership from control it would affect the nature and distribution agency costs (for example, the distribution of production units using the asset such as farms), and the depth and nature of rental and asset markets; c) foster development and functioning of other markets, particularly credit markets, by allowing mortgages; d) facilitating greater competition in all sectors by shifting from a network-based to a rule-based system that is likely to facilitate entry; e) affect the distribution of wealth as well as the inter-generational evolution of the wealth distribution, by having an impact on whether assets can be transferred from parents to children.

8.2 Recent Evidence on the Effect of Property Rights

The key issue whether in micro or macro data is how to identify the causal effect of changes in property rights on investment or productivity. Omitted variables could be driving a simple correlation between the two: For example, better governance could be driving both secure property rights and a more investment-friendly environment. The other issue is that of reverse causality: Investment itself could affect the nature of property rights. In Besley and Ghatak (2010), we review the empirical evidence in detail. Here I briefly discuss some of the more recent papers on this topic that were not covered in this earlier paper.

One interesting development in the recent literature has been the use of randomized control trials to tackle some of the identification-related concerns head on.

For example, Goldstein et al. (2018) presents evidence on a land formalization programme in rural Benin that was rolled on a randomized basis across 300 villages. Specifically, they examine the link between one of the aspects of better property rights, namely, land demarcation on on-farm investment behaviour. They find that households are likely to invest more in long-term crops. They also find that women are more likely than men to switch to a long-term crop, with the reason being their gain in tenure security frees up more labour for long-term crops. They also find that plots, especially those controlled by individuals with lower initial property rights, are more likely to be left fallow as there is less risk associated with leaving land fallow compared to earlier.

Another recent study that uses a randomized field experiment is by Burchardi et al. (2019) revisits the question of whether having a greater crop-share improves the incentives of tenant farmers. For example, Banerjee et al. (2002) showed how Operation Barga, a tenancy reform programme carried out in the Indian state of West Bengal in the late 1970s and early 1980s, changed tenancy arrangements and improved agricultural productivity. However, it was difficult to rule out the possible confounding effects of all other time-varying policies or aspects of the economic environment. The present study was carried out in collaboration with the branch of BRAC (Building Resources Across Communities), the well-known NGO of Bangladesh working in Uganda to induce randomized variation in real-life tenancy contracts. BRAC leased out plots of land to women from low socioeconomic levels who were interested in becoming farmers, effectively acting as a landlord. In the experiment, some tenants received a higher crop share (75 per cent) and some a lower crop share (50 per cent), which are the same as the modal pre-reform and post-reform crop-shares in the Banerjee et al. (2002) study. Burchardi et al. (2019) find that tenants with higher output shares used more inputs, cultivated riskier crops, and produced 60% per cent more output relative to those in the control group, effects that are very similar to those that the earlier study had found.

An interesting paper by de Janvry et al. (2015) revisit the issue of how imperfect property rights can lead to a misallocation of labour. The paper studies the rollout of the Mexican land certification programme from 1993 to 2006, and finds that households obtaining certificates were subsequently 28 percent more likely to have a migrant member. It also shows that even though land certification induced migration, it had little effect on cultivated area due to consolidation of farm units. This provides strong evidence on inter-sectoral misallocation of labour in the agricultural sector of developing countries and the potential gains from improving property rights in releasing labour that stays on in the rural sector to maintain their claims on land through continuous personal use instead of by land titles.

There has also been some recent work on how improved property rights in land facilitate leasing out and a more active rental market.

Chari et al. (2019) analyse the impact of the Rural Land Contracting Law (RLCL) in China which gave farmers legal rights to lease their land while reaffirming the security of ownership rights. Exploiting the staggered timing of implementation of this reform across provinces they find that this led to a significant increase in land rental activity in rural areas, which took the form of reallocation of land towards more productive farmers, who in turn hired more labour. As a result, output and aggregate productivity went up by 8 per cent and 10 per cent, respectively.

Beg (2019) study a reform that led to digitized records and automated transactions accessible to agricultural landowners and cultivators in Pakistan. Using the staggered roll-out of the programme the paper finds that the reform led to landowning families more likely to rent out their land and move to non-agricultural occupations. The paper finds evidence of a reallocation of land used for cultivation towards more productive farmers and an improvement of overall yield and lower dispersion of marginal products of land across farms.

Overall, the evidence in favour of the credit channel of property rights in settings where credit markets are not well-functioning seems weak (see Besley and Ghatak, 2010 and Galiani and Schargrodsky, 2011 for a review) and that picture has not changed much over the last decade. Deininger and Goyal (2012) use administrative data on credit disbursed and registered land transactions from 1995–2007 from the Indian state of Andhra Pradesh where there was shift from manual to digital operation of land registration records. They exploit the staggered implementation of this reform across the land sub registry offices in the state. Their main finding is that this led to a significant but quantitatively modest increase in credit access in urban areas, but not in rural areas.

There are several possible reasons for the evidence in favour of the credit channel to be weak. First of all, it is not easy for banks foreclose in the event of default given the political constraints and the imperfect legal system in developing countries in general. In rural areas, when land is used as collateral taking possession of land in the event of default is rare, given the social norms and values that people attach to land (Narayanan and Chakraborty 2019). Second, most developing countries even the middle-level propertied classes don't find it easy to receive credit. For example, in Peru a minimum of two years of tenure in a formal sector job and a high wage is a pre-requisite for receiving loans from the formal sector. Indeed, Besley et al. (2012) show theoretically that if credit markets are not competitive and borrowers are very poor, then even in standard models of borrowing under moral hazard, improved collateralizability of assets will not result in relaxation of credit constraints.

8.3 The Emerging Research Agenda

There are several ways in which the property rights literature is unique. First, it spans several subfields such as development economics or institutional economics more broadly, law and economics, finance, and contracts and organizations. Second, empirical research in it is active both with macro-level data as well as micro-level data, including the first set of RCTs, as we mentioned in the previous section. Therefore, this allows us to think about ways to combine insights from these different subfields, and also combine different empirical methods (for example, using micro-data to calibrate aggregate models, as in Besley et al. 2012).

Despite the richness and the depth of the literature, there are many conceptual issues that deserve greater scrutiny, empirical questions on which we know little, and topics that are of great importance in current debates in public policy and yet there is relatively little research on (for example, land acquisition for industry or property rights over natural resources). Subsequently, I discuss some of the questions, topics, and approaches that I find most interesting and expect more research to be carried out with regard to.

Use of more quantitative analysis: Given the difficulty of empirical identification of causal effects, we should do more quantitative analysis using a theoretical framework, as macroeconomists routinely do. More broadly, given the possibility of general equilibrium effects and the need to do welfare analysis in second-best environments, for which standard empirical methods are not best-suited, this 'macro-development' approach (see Buera et al. 2015 for a survey of this approach on financial frictions and entrepreneurship) seems to be a promising avenue to pursue. To give an example, consider the papers mentioned earlier that have empirically explored the effect that collateral improvement has on credit contracts. The empirical estimates vary widely and the overall picture is not clear. Besley et al. (2012) show that trying property rights reform in an environment where there is an additional distortion, that is, competition is weak, can be quite a different proposition from doing so when competition is strong. This can explain the rather mixed empirical findings from the regression evidence linking measures of credit market performance to property registration possibilities.

Greater focus on heterogeneous treatment effects in evaluating impact of property rights interventions: Heterogeneity across producers in characteristics such as wealth, access to other inputs and/or markets will tend to affect the marginal effect of an improvement in property rights. Besley et al. (2012) shows that for low- and high-wealth individuals, the effect of improved property rights on improving access to credit will be limited. For the former, since they have very little wealth anyway and for the latter, since they will have other means of accessing credit. Therefore, the effectiveness of a de Soto style property rights reform will depend on the distribution of wealth. Another important dimension of heterogeneity is gender. Goldstein et al. (2018) find that female-managed landholdings in treated villages are more likely to be left fallow which is an important investment in long-term fertility of the soil. Women also respond to the change by moving production away from more secure plots of land to less secure ones, in order to guard those parcels.

Greater emphasis on complementary reforms: As mentioned several times, like any other intervention, in the presence of multiple distortions, reforming just property rights may not be effective at best, and can be counter-productive at worst. Besley et al. 2012 give an illustration of how very poor borrowers may become worse off due to greater threat of dispossession, without a sufficiently compensating increase in credit supply.

In field work regarding land acquisition for industry in West Bengal with my research collaborators (see Ghatak et al. 2013) we found that it is the poorer farmers who are most reluctant to give up their land. It seems that to this group of people with minimal exposure to the world outside agriculture, land is not merely an income-generating asset but among other things, an insurance policy, a pension plan, and a secure way to hold assets. This provides a clue as to why creating property rights that will facilitate a land market will not necessarily result in desired resource allocation away from agriculture to industry. A recent study by Bandiera et al. (2017) show that asset transfer to the very poor is most effective when combined with training. Empirical work that assesses how property rights reforms work in combination of other intervention holds a lot of promise.

Moving beyond individual incentive effects to more economy-wide effects: Recall that in Section 8.1, we listed a number of economy-wide effects of property rights (for example, market development, fostering competition). There is very little work exploring these mechanisms. While this is suggestive, clearly we need cross-country, or within-country regional variation to understand these channels better. The identification problems will be as usual quite difficult and once again quantitative analysis could help.

Better understanding of the interaction between formal and informal property rights: In the context of Africa, the traditional land tenure systems from being looked at as a barrier to modern system of property rights, are now viewed as often flexible, and complex, and compatible with agricultural investment in response to new economic conditions. Yet, there are gains from having greater security, as the work of Goldstein and Udry (2008) and Goldstein et al. (2018) shows. As a result, the focus of policy on land tenure has shifted from a simple emphasis on direct provision of land title to better integration of customary tenure with the formal land system. We need to understand better the interconnection between these different systems of property rights.

Paying greater attention to property rights relating to natural and common property resources: Across the developing world, often conflicts over property rights take place over the attempt of businesses to use natural resources (for example, forests and minerals) that clash with traditional livelihoods of communities. In this setting, from the political point of view, 'property rights' often seems like a technical term for dispossession of poor people. While economic development does require a move way from low-return to high-return activities, one has to consider traditional rights of communities over common property resources and think of designing appropriate compensation mechanisms (see, for example, Ghatak and Mookherjee 2015, in the context of land acquisition using eminent domain).

Studying property rights and various market distortions in an integrated way: Often property rights and other market frictions are treated as independent factors (for example, Johnson et al. 2002). However, often they cannot be studied in isolation. For example, facilitating savings through more secure property rights protection can help overcome frictions in borrowing (see Ghatak 2015). Also, if land-lease markets are subject to frictions due to agency problems, then credit markets may be subject to the similar problems and improving property rights can solve both problems. As noted by Mookherjee (1997), if tenancy involves efficiency losses due to moral hazard, letting the tenant buy out the land using the credit market will not solve the problem, since the problem will simply get transferred from a landlord–tenant agency problem to a lender–borrower agency problem. Also, land in rural areas is an asset whose value may be higher than what might be indicated by its agricultural productivity. Because of imperfect insurance and credit markets, as well as the absence of a formal safety net and old-age support, the implicit value of land to farmers can be quite high and they may not want to sell even if property rights are improved. This suggests the need for more theoretical work to understand when different frictions are substitutes, when are they complements, and when they are two sides of the same coin.

Property rights and gender: Property rights for women is clearly one of the most important factors in economic empowerment of women. Gender discrimination is not just ethically undesirable, it also prevents efficient allocation of resources by depriving half the population from developing and utilizing their productive potential. In this context, understanding the mechanisms through which property rights affects the empowerment of women seems like a very promising area of research. There is some recent work on this, but the focus has been largely on the reform of an Indian inheritance law that stipulated daughters would have equal shares as sons in ancestral property, which turned out not to have increased the actual likelihood of women inheriting property. Roy (2015) shows that this reform seems to have induced parents to compensate their daughters by giving them alternative transfers in the form of either higher dowries or more education following the reform. There is also some recent work (Anderson and Genicot 2015) that shows that these inheritance law reforms have reduced the incidence of domestic violence and the suicide rates of women relative to men.

Political economy of property rights: As mentioned at the beginning, I have largely focused on various mechanisms through which 'exogenous' changes in property rights affect economic outcomes. However, like all institutions, property rights are endogenous to economic, political, and social forces. Political resistance to formalization of property rights in land often comes from the fear that will lead to dispossession. In a second-best environment, it is quite possible that inefficient property rights are chosen endogenously for political economy reasons. The political economy of property rights reform is therefore an important topic for future research.

***

We are at an interesting juncture in terms of research in the effect of property rights on resource allocation, thereby providing important clues about how institutional reforms at the micro level can provide a robust platform for development. The first generation of studies that use randomized control trials are coming out, thereby overcoming some of the identification problems that plagued the earlier empirical literature. In this chapter, we have discussed the potential ways in which theory can be combined with evidence to provide a much richer understanding of mechanisms through which property rights affect economic outcomes.

This in turn would allow us to formulate better policies regarding how to reform property rights. Reforming property rights may help overcome one of the major constraints that has emerged in the context of industrialization in recent times, namely transferring land from agriculture to industry. Theorists of industrialization, such as Arthur Lewis, focused on capital and labour as the key resources, and concentrated on the movement of 'surplus' labour from agriculture to industry as key to capital accumulation and the process of industrialization. As industry offers a much higher expected return than agriculture, the transfer of land to the former from the latter is expected to be smooth. Yet, we have seen, for poor farmers in India and other developing countries with minimal exposure to the world outside agriculture, land is not merely an income-generating asset but an insurance policy-cum-pension plan as well. Only a more secure system of ownership of land with a focus on protecting the most vulnerable small farmers, and enhancing their ability to buy and sell as well as lease in and out would help a more dynamic land market to emerge, which the literature on property rights suggest, is going to be important in facilitating the process of development.

Bibliography

Anderson, S., and Genicot, G. (2015). 'Suicide and property rights in India', *Journal of Development Economics*, 114: 64–78.

Bandiera, Oriana, Robin Burgess, Narayan Das, Selim Gulesci, Imran Rasul and Munshi Sulaiman. (2017). 'Labor Markets and Poverty in Village Economies', *The Quarterly Journal of Economics*, 132(2): 811–70.

Besley, Timothy. (1995). 'Property Rights and Investment Incentives: Theory and Evidence from Ghana', *Journal of Political Economy*. 103(5): 903–37.

Besley, T.J., and Ghatak, M. (2010). 'Property Rights and Economic Development', *Handbook of Development Economics* 5: 389–430.

Besley, T.J., Burchardi, K.B., and Ghatak, M. (2012). 'Incentives and the de Soto Effect', *The Quarterly Journal of Economics*, 127(1): 237–82.

Banerjee, Abhijit V., Paul J. Gertler, and Maitreesh Ghatak. (2002). 'Empowerment and Efficiency: Tenancy Reform in West Bengal', *Journal of Political Economy* 110(2): 239–80.

Konrad Burchardi, Selim Gulesci, Benedetta Lerva, and Munshi Sulaiman. (2019). 'Moral Hazard: Experimental Evidence from Tenancy Contracts', *The Quarterly Journal of Economics*, 134(1): 281–347.

Buera, Francisco, Joseph P. Kaboski, and Yongseok Shin. (2015). 'Entrepreneurship and Financial Frictions: A Macrodevelopment Perspective', *Annual Review of Economics*, 7: 409–36.

de Janvry, Alain, Kyle Emerick, Marco Gonzalez-Navarro and Elisabeth Sadoulet. (2015). 'Delinking Land Rights from Land Use: Certification and Migration in Mexico', *American Economic Review*, 105(10): 3125–49.

Deininger and Aparajita Goyal. (2012). 'Going Digital: Credit Effects of Land Registry Computerization in India', *Journal of Development Economics*, 99(2): 236–43.

Di Tella, Rafael, Sebastian Galiani, and Ernesto Schargrodsky. (2007). 'The Formation of Beliefs: Evidence from the Allocation of Land Titles to Squatters', *The Quarterly Journal of Economics*, 122(1): 209–41.

Galiani, Sebastian and Ernesto Schargrodsky. (2011). 'Land Property Rights and Resource Allocation', *The Journal of Law and Economics*, 54: S4, S329–S345.

Ghatak, M. (2015). 'Theories of Poverty Traps and Anti-Poverty Policies', *World Bank Economic Review*, Papers and Proceedings, 29 (Supplement 1): S77–S105.

Ghatak, M., S. Mitra, A. Nath, and D. Mookherjee. (2013). 'Land Acquisition and Compensation in Singur: What Really Happened?', *Economic and Political Weekly of India*, XLVIII(21): 32–44.

Ghatak, M. and D. Mookherjee. (2015). 'Land Acquisition for Industrialization and Compensation for Displaced Farmers', *Journal of Development Economics*, 110: 239–49.

Glaeser, E., R. La Porta, and F. Lopez-de-Silanes and Andrei Shleifer (2004). 'Do Institutions Cause Growth?', *Journal of Economic Growth*, 9(3): 271–303.

Goldstein, M., and Udry, C. (2008). 'The Profits of Power: Land Rights and Agricultural Investment in Ghana', *Journal of Political Economy*, 116(6): 981–1022.

Markus Goldstein, Kenneth Houngbedji, Florence Kondylis, Michael O'Sullivan, and Harris Selod (2018). 'Formalization without Certification? Experimental Evidence on Property Rights and Investment', *Journal of Development Economics*, 132: 57–74.

Hart, Oliver (1995). *Firms, Contracts, and Financial Structure*. Clarendon Press: Oxford.

Johnson, Simon, John McMillan, and Christopher Woodruff. (2002). 'Property Rights and Finance', *American Economic Review*, 92(5): 1335–56.

Mookherjee, Dilip. (1997). 'Informational rents and property rights in land'. In J. Roemer (ed.) *Property Relations, Incentives and Welfare*. United Kingdom: Palgrave Macmillan, pp.3–42.

Narayanan, Sudha and Judhajit Chakraborty. (2019): 'Land as Collateral in India', *Economic and Political Weekly*, 54(44): 45–52.

North, Douglass C. (1990). *Institutions, Institutional Change and Economic Performance*, Cambridge: Cambridge University Press.

Roy, Sanchari. (2015). 'Empowering Women? Inheritance Rights, Female Education and Dowry Payments in India', *Journal of Development Economics*, 114: 233–51.

9   Financial Inclusion

Concepts, Issues, and Policies for India*

NIRVIKAR SINGH

Financial development, namely, the development of financial markets and institutions, is an obvious component of overall economic development, as

* This is a revised and abbreviated version of an International Growth Centre synthesis paper with the same title, originally written in 2017: the topic seems very relevant for a volume that honors an economist, Pranab Bardhan, who has written extensively on aspects of inclusive development, namely, development which focuses on improving the lives of the poor. I am grateful to Eilin Francis and Arshad Mirza for valuable research assistance, and to Dilip Mookherjee and an anonymous reviewer for incisive comments on earlier versions. Sole responsibility for shortcomings is mine.

well as a driver of growth.[1] Studying the role of financial development in economic growth has gone from measuring it in terms of a single number such as the ratio of bank credit to an overall measure of economic activity (typically GDP) to considering the different dimensions of the concept. A typical decomposition of the concept of financial development considers depth, access, efficiency, and stability (Cihak et al. 2012).[2] Financial depth corresponds to the dimension captured in measures such as credit–GDP ratios. Financial access is essentially the same as financial inclusion, and the latter term has become more common (World Bank 2014).

The 2014 World Bank conceptualization of financial inclusion parallels basic ideas of financial depth: 'the proportion of individuals and firms that use financial services' (p. 1). Subsequently, the Bank has evolved a more elaborate definition:

> Financial inclusion means that individuals and businesses have access to useful and affordable financial products and services that meet their needs—transactions, payments, savings, credit and insurance—delivered in a responsible and sustainable way.
>
> (http://www.worldbank.org/en/topic/financialinclusion/overview#1)

This definition highlights the different aspects of financial services that are ultimately what make finance an important part of the economy. Each product or service may be delivered through different institutional and market arrangements. For example, businesses may access funding for operations or expansion through banks or through stock markets,

---

[1] Recent contributions to the enormous literature on the connection between financial development and growth include Beck et al., (2007), Law and Singh (2014), Aizenman et al., (2015) and Arcand et al. (2015).

[2] Sahay et al. (2015) consider depth, access and efficiency as components of financial development, and consider financial and economic stability separately. These analyses also distinguish between financial markets and financial institutions. Cihak et al. (2012), following earlier work on constructing indices of financial development, discuss various measures of access, including bank accounts per 1,000 individuals and percentage of firms with lines of credit (institutions), as well as percentage of market capitalization outside the 10 largest companies (markets). Sahay et al. (2015) use similar measures.

depending on their own characteristics and those of the relevant financial institutions. Recent analyses of financial inclusion take place in a setting in which technological and regulatory changes are permitting innovations, such as digital payments and peer-to-peer lending.

However, at the most basic level, in developing countries, transaction accounts are the initial gateway to financial inclusion. As the web site notes, 'Access to a transaction account is a first step toward broader financial inclusion since it allows people to store money, and send and receive payments. A transaction account can also serve as a gateway to other financial services …' There are several implicit assumptions in highlighting financial inclusion in this manner, in particular, the notion that the aforementioned financial services are not available to a set of people that is socially optimal, either in an instrumental sense of maximizing aggregate welfare (including social concerns for reducing inequality) and economic growth, or in a broader sense of promoting rights and capabilities for all human beings (Sen 1999). Possible reasons for suboptimality are taken up later in this paper.

The World Bank web site on financial inclusion goes on to list the beneficial ripple effects of financial access, beginning with basic formal transaction accounts. These benefits include lower transaction costs for daily economic activities, the ability to plan for longer-term needs, and the opportunity to create buffers for unexpected emergencies. For the better-off in both advanced and developing countries, both financial access and its benefits are taken relatively for granted, although the limits and challenges of access are much more severe in poorer economies or regions.[3]

Other discussions of financial inclusion have different emphases, but with similar scope. For example, the introduction to a collection (Cull et al. 2012) of empirical analyses of financial inclusion begins by highlighting microcredit as being symbolic of growing financial inclusion, though it goes on to note savings, transfers and insurance as other important services. While many such financial services are missing or barely provided in poorer countries such as India, the challenge of providing microcredit is just one example of pervasive credit market imperfections that hamper

---

[3] The discussion of the benefits of financial inclusion ties in with the detailed micro-level account of the lives of poor people in Banerjee and Duflo (2011). For one example of Pranab Bardhan's many contributions to the topic of improving the lives of the poor, see Bardhan (2007).

development.[4] These imperfections are apparent in the very limited access of most individuals in, say, India to formal credit markets, and the large disparities in borrowing costs between formal and informal credit markets.[5]

Cull et al. (2012) also note the importance of technological and product innovation in improving inclusion. Karmakar et al. (2011) in assessing financial inclusion in India, begin by emphasizing the need to expand the reach of formal financial institutions such as banks, as a channel for access to a range of financial services. They highlight the role of technological innovation in reducing costs of service provision, as well as the need for financial counseling: indeed, behavioural and other demand-side aspects of financial inclusion deserve as much attention as technological and supply-side approaches.

Karlan and Morduch (2010) provided a major survey of 'Access to Finance', which still represents the most comprehensive academic review of the topic. They point out that research in the area had already gone well beyond the initial focus on microcredit for investment by small entrepreneurs. The authors discuss new credit mechanisms and devices that help households manage cash flows, save, and cope with risk. In this context, they consider issues of contract design, product innovation, regulatory policy, and bottom-line economic and social impacts. They also relate the empirical evidence to theoretical concepts rooted in behavioural economics and to the use of randomized evaluation methods. Randomized trials are highlighted as particularly important in the testing of potential innovations in financial products and services, and the institutional and technological contexts in which they are delivered. Karlan and Morduch ultimately emphasize the importance of attention to detail in finding

---

[4] Credit market imperfections are pervasive in all economies, to varying degrees, and are inherent in the informational asymmetries associated with such markets. These ideas are highlighted in the discussion of microcredit, later in the chapter.

[5] Dilip Mookherjee (personal communication, February 2017) has emphasized the benefits of financial inclusion for better targeting of government welfare programs, and also control of corruption by intermediaries. For example, Muralidharan et al. (2016) evaluate the impact of biometric payments infrastructure to make social welfare payments in Andhra Pradesh, and find large reductions in leakage of funds.

workable solutions to lack of financial access, a natural conclusion when trying to reach marginal populations that are not natural sources of profit for sellers of financial products and services.

Aggarwal and Klapper (2013) build on Karlan and Morduch, and organize their discussion around various barriers to financial inclusion, as well as policies to overcome these. Among the barriers they highlight are time and financial costs of opening and maintaining bank accounts, as well as the cost of meeting documentation requirements (which may be effectively infinite if the required documentation is not possible). They discuss ways of reducing these costs, which can include regulatory policy changes, acceleration of adoption of digital technology-based mechanisms, institutional innovations such as the use of bank agents, or, typically, some mix of all three of these approaches.

A still more recent, though relatively brief, survey is that of Karlan et al. (2016). Echoing themes in the two earlier surveys, the authors emphasize the challenges of market imperfections and deviations from fully rational behaviour for efforts to increase financial access. Yet, they draw optimistic conclusions from empirical studies about the potential of digital technologies and of savings products to provide measurable benefits, though noting that areas such as microcredit and insurance present greater difficulties for successful innovation.

This chapter does not substitute for or supersede these surveys, but builds on them. The rest of this chapter is organized in terms of aspects of financial inclusion, or behaviour pertinent to it. These nine sections cover financial inclusion in general, banking, microcredit and microfinance, small firm finance, agricultural credit, farmers' insurance, health insurance, financial literacy, and behavioural factors. Each section discusses research from a variety of developing countries, including India, though it is cannot be exhaustive given the size of the literature. The final section concludes by summarizing what we know and perhaps do not know, with the latter being a guide to possible future research and analysis. A key theme of the paper, in line with previous surveys, is that succeeding in the various goals associated with promoting financial inclusion requires careful attention to detail with respect to institutions, markets and human behaviour, and this in turn requires targeted and well-designed research. The focus on India allows for some potentially more targeted policy recommendations, as well as specific research directions.

Financial Inclusion Overall

Several cross-country analyses of financial inclusion are available. Demirgüç-Kunt and Klapper (2013) summarize a public data set that measures the financial behaviour of adults in 148 countries.[6] They use it to benchmark financial inclusion, and document the most important barriers to bank use, such as the cost of opening account and the need for documentation of identity, residence, and so on. Sarma and Pais (2011) analyse cross section data from several dozen countries, and find that levels of human development and financial inclusion are positively correlated. More specifically, lower income inequality, higher literacy levels, and better physical and communication infrastructure are all associated with greater financial inclusion. Cull et al. (2012) include several overviews of the state of global knowledge of financial inclusion, with data that shows that many of the poor do use formal financial services, suggesting a scope for greater inclusion: poverty by itself need not be an insurmountable barrier.

Karmakar et al. (2011) provide a comprehensive account of the challenges of financial inclusion in India. They identify institutional and resource constraints, and discuss targeting efforts that have focused on rural populations, women's groups, tribal areas, or combinations of these. They consider the different dimensions of financial services, including transactions, savings, credit and insurance, and possible institutional and technological innovations, including digital tools for identification, payments, and storage. The analysis provides a detailed account of many past and current policy initiatives that intersect with various dimensions of financial inclusion, on both the demand and supply sides. It conveys a broad sense of the challenges encountered in policymaking and implementation, but provides no engagement with the empirical academic literature on financial inclusion, so the policy recommendations lack a firm basis.

Also for India, Badarinza et al. (2017) use a large household survey to provide a cross-sectional picture of the asset and liability sides of household balance sheets.[7] They document that, in India, lower proportions

---

[6] Their paper is based on the Global Findex Database: see http://datatopics. worldbank.org/financialinclusion/.

[7] The data is from the 2012 All India Debt and Investment Survey (AIDIS), conducted by the NSSO, with over 100,000 households sampled.

of younger households hold financial assets, even compared to China, let alone developed countries. Other striking features of the financial landscape are that households do not reduce real estate holdings as they cross retirement age, there is no drop-off in mortgage loan participation at these ages, and unsecured debt is more significant in all age groups. Similar differences are reflected in comparisons across the wealth distribution. Savings in retirement accounts are nearly absent. The authors document a high reliance on gold as a form of savings, lack of access to bank branches as a constraint to financial savings, significant regional variations, and the importance of education in supporting higher use of financial savings.

Campbell et al. (2012) analyze India's mortgage market. As indicated from the household survey, Indians' use of mortgages for housing is quite limited. Campbell et al. focus on the impacts of mortgage market regulation, yielding a useful case study of the impacts of national-level policymaking on financial inclusion. They analyse administrative data on over one million loans originated by an Indian mortgage provider, examining loan pricing and default rates. The period was one in which the availability of mortgages was increasing fairly rapidly, but so was regulation of the market. Lending to small borrowers is an important aspect of financial inclusion in the context of the housing market, and the data indicate that regulatory changes designed to promote this goal were successful. However, there was a spike in defaults, suggesting the possible costs of policies that neglect the capacity and incentives of market participants. On the positive side, the data imply that mortgage lenders were able to learn from the experience of surging defaults, and priced risks more accurately in subsequent years. The lessons of this study are potentially generalizable. Policies designed to support goals of financial inclusion require careful attention to market structure and incentives of market participants, as well as learning and adjustment through ongoing analysis of market data. Private profit-making entities have incentives to engage in the latter, but their behaviour ought not to be overly distorted by the regulatory structure: Regulations have to balance risks and efficiency against equity-enhancing goals of financial inclusion.

Banking

Among specific aspects of financial inclusion, we begin with banking, in keeping with the observation that access to a transaction account can serve as a foundation for broader financial access. One can conceptualize banking to include institutional variations such as post-office accounts, and technology-enabled innovations such as 'agent banking', where designated individuals act as agents of banks for some services. Two studies from India provide evidence that targeting bank access can have positive impacts. Burgess and Pande (2005) examine the social banking programme introduced after India's bank nationalization in 1969. Using panel data for 16 states over 1961-2000, with information about the number of bank branches, rural credit and saving shares, and poverty and wage estimates, the authors show that branch expansion was associated with reductions in rural poverty. In a related analysis, Burgess, Wong, and Pande (2005) found that national policy that caused banks to open relatively more branches in less financially developed states and expand into rural unbanked locations reduced poverty across Indian states. They also argued that enforcement of directed bank lending increased bank borrowing among the poor, in particular, for low-caste and tribal groups.

The Burgess–Pande findings were tempered by a subsequent analysis of a similar period: Kochar (2011) used district-level data for India's largest state, Uttar Pradesh, and took account of potentially confounding correlations of two sources of credit expansion at that time. She found evidence of increasing inequality, with the non-poor benefiting more from bank branch expansion than did the poor.[8] Using later data, Young (2015) highlighted several positive impacts of expanding bank access on economic activity, using a well-structured causal analysis, thus providing strong evidence of the benefits of bank expansion in India.

In a more micro-level study, Somville and Vandewalle (2015) conducted a field experiment in rural India to study the effect on savings of identical weekly payments into a bank account (treatment group) or in cash (control group). They found a large and persistent treatment effect, with savings increasing by over 100 percent within three months. Villagers given cash, on the other hand, did not save more in other assets, but increased consumption, suggesting that having a bank account can

---

[8] In contrast, a cross-country study by Anson et al. (2013) suggests that post office savings schemes tend to be of greater benefit to the relatively poor, even though post offices may not have full bank status, as is the case in India. Post office savings accounts in India can also be used to make government welfare payments, as was discussed in the introduction.

have a net positive impact on total savings. However, Prina (2015) found more limited effects of having bank accounts for female household heads in Nepal. They were given access to bank accounts with no fees. Impacts on income, aggregate expenditures, and assets were too imprecisely estimated for definite conclusions, although there was evidence of a higher ability of households to cope with shocks. Finally, Dupas et al. (2016) experimentally tested the impact of expanding access to basic bank accounts in three countries (Uganda, Malawi, and Chile). While the number of deposits increased, survey data showed no clearly discernible effects on savings or any downstream outcomes.

Such studies suggest that policies focused merely on expanding access to basic accounts are not guaranteed to improve outcomes, and that there are other factors that influence success and failure, and which need to be identified. Despite mixed evidence, research suggests that there are mechanisms that can bring down the cost of access to formal banking for poor households, and thereby improve their savings strategies. In India, there has been a massive, nationwide effort to achieve banking access for vast numbers of the country's poorer citizens—the Jan Dhan part of JAM (standing for Jan Dhan (banking), Aadhaar (identity) and Mobile (transactions), discussed subsequently, in the context of digital payments). While technology is an important part of facilitating access and maintenance of bank accounts, making these accounts more useful to small account holders is important for long-run sustainability.[9] Bank operations and everyday practices in India have the potential for improvement (see Singh, 2015 for a brief discussion on credit risk management in Indian banks).

Cole et al. (2015) tackle the issue of bank operations through an experiment with commercial bank loan officers in India. This was a high-stakes field experiment, providing the subjects with tangible incentives, permitting a 'clean' test of how performance compensation affects risk-assessment and lending in a banking environment. The loan officers in the study were paid to review and assess over 14,000 actual (but previously processed)

---

[9] Indeed, in India access to bank accounts is perhaps easier than in many other developing countries, because of the creation or existence of no-frills type accounts and post office accounts. Arguably, therefore, this aspect of financial inclusion in India has moved beyond access to basic accounts to access to useful services and products.

loan applications. They were provided with different kinds of exogenous incentive schemes, and, while the subjects did not know how the loans had performed, this information was available to the researchers. The results indicated that high-powered incentives do lead to greater screening effort, separating 'good' from 'bad' borrowers, and to more profitable lending decisions. However, typical features of loan officer compensation contracts such as deferred compensation and limited liability, toned down the incentive effects. Career concerns and some personality traits also affected loan officer behaviour, but the impact of incentive schemes did not vary with personality traits such as risk-aversion, optimism, or overconfidence. Performance incentives are important across all kinds of organizations, but areas such as bank lending are particularly important in the context of India's financial inclusion goals. Expanding banking without improving the performance of bank employees, particularly those who make lending decisions that can lead to productive investment and job creation, can be a very suboptimal strategy.

A different approach to improving the performance of conventional banks is the creation of alternative kinds of banking institutions. Rural cooperative banks have a long history in India, but have been subject to political capture. Another alternative is the model represented by India's Shri Mahil Self Employment Women Association Sahkari (SEWA) Bank, the oldest women's bank in the world. Targeting women represents a vital aspect of financial inclusion since women at any income level (but especially poorer ones) are less likely to have financial autonomy and access to financial services than their male counterparts. Field et al. (2016) use data on the expansion of the SEWA Bank to examine the impact of access to microfinance on women's labour force participation. These data pertain to urban settings, so the distance or scarcity aspects of constraints to financial access are not salient. Beginning in 1999, SEWA Bank began a major expansion of the number of loan collection officers they employed. This significantly reduced the transaction cost of getting a loan in Ahmedabad, Gujarat's capital and largest city, and thereby increased access for many women to microloans. The results indicate that access to such loans helped integrate women into the labor force over a period of several years. This effect was driven by greater participation of women in household business activity, although not necessarily a sustainable change in female empowerment, since the share of household income produced by women increased but with a diminishing effect over time. An intriguing effect observed in the data was a reduction in fertility associated with increasing participation in the labour force. This analysis hints at the importance of financial inclusion for a range of social and economic outcomes pertaining to the status and welfare of women in India.[10]

Microcredit/ Microfinance

Microfinance and microcredit have received disproportionate attention as vehicles for providing needed access to funds for the poor. Key theoretical ideas behind these efforts include pooling of funds, risk sharing, and joint monitoring and liability. Target populations, even if they have bank accounts, would almost certainly not qualify for traditional bank loans. Many might use 'informal' financial services of moneylenders, with the potential of being trapped in unsustainable debt situations. Of course, it is now recognized that microfinance is not a magic bullet for providing access to credit for the poor, but an enormous body of empirical research provides an understanding of how the institution works in different contexts.

Several meta-analyses are now available. Ahlin et al. (2011) collected data on 373 MFIs and merged it with country-level economic and institutional data to provide evidence for complementarity between MFI performance and that of the broader economy. Van Rooyen et al. (2012) systematically reviewed the evidence of the impacts of micro-credit and micro-savings on poor people in sub-Saharan Africa. They considered impacts on income, savings, expenditure, and the accumulation of assets, as well as a range of non-financial outcomes including health, food security, and education, and concluded that microfinance has mixed impacts on the livelihoods of the poor.

Many recent studies of microfinance have used randomized controlled trials (RCTs). Banerjee, Karlan, and Zinman (2015) provide an introduction and review for six randomized evaluations of microcredit and conclude that there is a 'consistent pattern of modestly positive, but not transformative, effects'. One study in this collection (Banerjee et al. 2015) reports on an RCT conducted in Hyderabad, using random selection of

---

[10] Recently, Jhabvala et al. (2019) have documented the importance of increasing the number of women employed in the financial services sector, for improving access of women to financial services.

areas for opening of a branch of a microfinance institution (Spandana). In the treatment areas, households were more likely to have a microcredit loan, but there were no significant improvements in health, education, or women's empowerment. Households with access to credit were not more likely to start new business, but they did invest more in their existing businesses. Other studies have been able to analyse large-scale government initiatives, such as the Thai Million Baht Village MFI program. Kaboski and Townsend (2011, 2012) used pre- and post-programme panel data and quasi-experimental cross-village variation in credit per household, and found that village MFI funds increased total short-term credit, consumption, agricultural investment, and income, but perhaps decreased overall asset growth.

Two recent studies for India analyse the impacts of certain contractual features in microcredit. Field et al. (2013) conducted an RCT that compared a standard microcredit contract, requiring repayment to begin immediately after the disbursement of the loan, to an alternative contractual setup that included a two-month grace period. The study found that providing a grace period increased short-run business investment as well as long-run profits but doing so also raised default rates. These results suggest that microcredit contracts that require early repayment discourage illiquid risky investment. There are costs to relaxing this constraint because of higher default rates (associated with greater adverse selection as well as moral hazard), but the net welfare impacts of subsidizing microfinance institutions to withstand higher default rates might be positive, because of higher microenterprise growth and greater reductions in household poverty.

Another study (Barboni 2016) also tackles the issue of contractual design in microfinance, focusing as well on repayment flexibility. A model of adverse selection predicts that lenders can achieve higher profits by offering a menu of choices which include rigid and flexible repayment schedules, instead of just the standard rigid contract. A set of in-the-field experimental games conducted with Indian micro-entrepreneurs showed that more entrepreneurial borrowers were more likely than less entrepreneurial ones to take-up the flexible contract. This separation was even more pronounced when the flexible schedule was costlier relative to the rigid contract.

Other studies have checked the robustness of earlier claims. In particular, Roodman and Morduch (2009) replicate and reanalyse an influential study of microcredit impacts on poor households in Bangladesh. That study was celebrated for showing that microcredit reduces poverty, but the re-analysis shows that the original results on poverty reduction disappeared after dropping outliers, or when using an estimation method robust to such outliers. Hence, even in microfinance, an area of financial inclusion where significant research has been carried out, there is much more to be learned about the factors that influence the success of such efforts.

Small Firm Finance

Research on microfinance overlaps with analyses of small firm finance, since the latter can include micro-entrepreneurs. Studies examine information constraints as well as credit constraints. De Mel et al. (2011) examined the role of information through an RCT in Sri Lanka. The intervention was designed to improve access to credit among high-return microenterprises by providing information about the microfinance loan product, along with a reduction in the number of personal guarantors required for these loans, but without subsidizing interest rates or requiring group lending. The outcomes suggest that information alone is unlikely to be enough to efficiently improve access. Dupas and Robinson (2013) used an RCT to identify significant barriers to savings and investment in rural Kenya among the self-employed. Randomly selected individuals were given free access to non-interest-bearing bank accounts among two types of self-employed: female market vendors and men working as bicycle taxi drivers. Despite large withdrawal fees, a substantial share of market women used the accounts, were able to save more, and increased their productive investment and private expenditures. But, for the men, there was no effect.[11] Karlan et al. (2015) experimented with providing consulting and financial capital to microenterprise tailors in Ghana. These infusions changed investment and business practices, but did not lead to significant changes in profit and were not sustained in the long run.[12]

A large literature examines financing constraints for small and medium enterprises (SMEs) more generally, particularly in developing countries.

---

[11]　Hence, this analysis also connects with studies of banking access, discussed earlier.

[12]　See also Cull et al. (2011, 2016).

Beck (2007) surveys empirical research along these lines, showing that SMEs are more constrained by financing and other institutional obstacles than are large firms, with this situation being made worse by weaknesses in the financial systems of many developing countries. For example, Beck and Demirguc-Kunt (2006) use cross-country panel data, and find that financial and institutional development affect SMEs' growth, and that SMEs are credit constrained, so that greater access to external finance can level the playing field between firms of different sizes. Another cross-country study, Love and Pería (2015), finds that greater bank competition improves firms' access to finance.

Country-specific studies of small firm financing constraints find similar types of results. Banerjee and Duflo (2008) use data from a directed lending programme in India to show that firms there are credit constrained. De and Singh (2014) combine panel data of reported financial information for a sample of SMEs in India with data from a survey of the same firms, regarding the role of relationships in supply of inter-firm credit. They find that firms that are unsuccessful in generating internal funds or bank loans have better access to relationship-based credit, but the latter is also rationed. In a similar vein, Ayyagari et al. (2010) find that Chinese private sector firms that have access to formal finance grow faster than firms that rely on informal finance.

To put this issue in context for India, there is considerable evidence that, while liberalization and economic reform beginning in 1991 led to entry of new firms, more recently, industrial dynamism has stalled (Alfaro and Chari 2009, 2014). There are a variety of factors constraining growth of smaller firms, but finance is certainly one of them (Allen et al. 2007; Shukla 2015). These earlier studies did not, however, establish clear causal linkages.

A study by Raj and Sen (2013) fills the gap, analysing very small family firms —the predominant type of firm in the informal sector in India— and the role of finance constraints in preventing them from transitioning to larger firms that employ non-family labour. The authors use unit level data drawn from national surveys of informal manufacturing by the NSSO. They supplement this with panel data analysis of 364 districts, estimating the effects of financial development on firm transition at the district level. They present strong evidence that finance constraints play an important role in firm transition from family-labour-only firms to small firms that use hired labour, but even more so for the growth of the latter beyond six workers. Firm capabilities matter as well: for example, firms that maintain formal accounts are more likely to make the transition than firms that do not. Other factors that affect transition and growth include working as sub-contractors, having access to electricity, being located in an urban area, and being in a district with higher levels of human capital. An important result is that government assistance (such as loans, training, and marketing) does not help firms transition and grow, suggesting that policy may be more effective in focusing on relaxing financing and other constraints for small, informal sector firms.

Agricultural Credit

The importance of food production and the size of the agricultural sector in many developing countries make agricultural credit politically and economically more salient than credit for other kinds of products and services. India is an important illustration of these statements, with loans to farmers and forgiveness of those loans being tied to electoral considerations (for example, Cole 2009). On the other hand, there is also evidence that small and marginal farmers still depend on informal lenders, and this can contribute to agrarian distress in some cases (for example, Singh 2012; Gill 2016).

Micro-studies of loans to farmers suggest that there are inefficiencies in the allocation and use of agricultural credit. A study of 300 farmers in Nigeria (Oboh and Ekpebu 2011) finds delays in disbursing bank loans as well as considerable diversion of loans to non-farm purposes. Rahman (2011) finds that farm credit in Bangladesh may be inefficiently and insufficiently allocated, especially in the context of a positive correlation between the credit and output. Studies for India (for example, Sharma and Kumawat 2014) and Pakistan (for example, Mehmood et al. 2012) also document similar situations: Loans are made and monitored inefficiently, so even though credit is rationed, increasing its supply may not be welfare improving in the absence of institutional improvements such as better targeting and monitoring.

Even when farm loans are subsidized and forgiven, small farmers may still often face substantial financial distress. Maitra et al. (2014) explore an alternative approach to credit for small farmers. Randomly selected villages in West Bengal state in India participated in a field experiment with an innovative variant of microcredit, trader–agent-intermediated lending

(TRAIL): borrowers of individual liability loans in some villages (all small farmers) were selected by local trader-lender agents, who received incentives in the form of repayment-based commissions. In other villages, small farmers had access to a more conventional group-based lending programme (GBL). TRAIL loans did much better than GBL loans in increasing production of the leading cash crop and farm incomes. The underlying mechanism for this result included the fact that borrowers selected by TRAIL agents were more able farmers than those who self-selected into the GBL scheme, although this pattern of selection did not completely explain the observed difference in income impacts. An implication of this work is that it points out a possibility for leveraging existing institutions or expertise, somewhat similar to how ITC used existing commission agents to facilitate its Internet-based e-choupal procurement scheme (Goyal 2010).

A study by Mitra et al. (2012) also has some indirect implications for agricultural credit policy for small farmers. In much of India, small farmers do not sell directly to large buyers, but rely on intermediaries: credit constraints are one factor in this market structure, as are asymmetries of information. This study analyses how potato farmers in West Bengal sell their crop to local traders, including how prices and intermediary margins are determined. Small farmers in randomly chosen villages were provided information about daily wholesale prices, either publicly or privately. The evidence did not support the idea that risk was being shared between farmers and traders, but was consistent with small farmers having limited alternatives for selling their produce, making price information of little value. More specifically, providing farmers with access to market price information to reduce their informational asymmetry vis-à-vis traders did not have a significant average impact on farmgate prices, while raising pass-through of wholesale market prices to farmgate prices, because of the lack of access of these farmers to direct sale in wholesale markets. One possibility is that easing credit constraints for small farmers (so that they have to rely less on trade credit from intermediaries) could improve their bargaining power and increase the value of price information for farmers.

Farmers' Insurance

Insurance for developing country farmers is an important new area of experiments in financial inclusion. Weather insurance and crop or livestock insurance may protect small and marginal farmers from distress.

For example, Nair (2010) used micro data from the Agriculture Insurance Company of India, to argue that weather insurance is more market-based and financially sustainable than yield-based insurance. Cole et al. (2014) examined the market for rainfall insurance purchases by rural farming households in Gujarat. Demand was highly sensitive to payouts being made in a household's village in the most recent year, perhaps suggesting a trust effect. The observations of Gine (2009) complement some of these results, noting the problem of correlation of rainfall and macroeconomic conditions, and the need to make rapid payouts to liquidity-constrained farmers, in order for the insurance to be effective.[13]

Issues of price sensitivity are explored in the context of livestock insurance in Ethiopia by Takahashi et al. (2016). Randomly distributed learning kits improved subjects' knowledge of the products but did not lead to greater insurance uptake. On the other hand, reduced price due to randomly distributed discount coupons had an immediate, positive impact on uptake, without dampening subsequent period demand. The interaction of credit and insurance is analysed in Karlan et al. (2011), trying to address a key question for development: does risk inhibit invest-ment? They conducted an RCT in rural Ghana, and offered the treatment groups loans that forgave 50 per cent of the loan if crop prices dropped below a threshold price. A control group was offered a standard loan product at the same interest rate. Surprisingly, the indemnity component had little impact. Binswanger-Mkhize (2012) also expresses pessimism about agricultural insurance based on weather indices, pointing out that credit and cash constraints for poor farmers make it difficult for them to purchase insurance in advance of the harvest.

However, Karlan et al. (2014) provide more positive evidence of the benefits of access to agricultural insurance. The authors conducted several experiments in which farmers were randomly assigned to receive cash grants, grants of (or opportunities to purchase) rainfall index insurance, or a combination of the two. The observed demand for this insurance was strong, and insurance led to significantly larger agricultural investment as well as riskier production choices. These results indicate that uninsured catastrophic risk can be a binding constraint to farmers' investment. There was also evidence of social network effects and overweighting recent

---

[13] See also Gine, Townsend and Vickery (2008) for earlier evidence of the Indian experience.

events, suggesting that both careful design of policies and financial education are needed in implementing such innovations in financial products.[14]

Agricultural insurance products for small farmers are challenging to implement: Besides being income constrained, farmers lack experience with insurance, financial literacy, and general education. Gaurav et al. (2011) conducted a field experiment (RCT) involving different methods of marketing rainfall insurance to small-scale farmers in Gujarat, India. Financial education had a positive effect on rainfall insurance adoption, but only one marketing intervention, a money-back guarantee, had a consistent and large effect on farmers' purchase decisions. This suggests that farmers do not have the experience to be able to trust the new insurance product, and the guarantee mitigates their risk perceptions. While such guarantees are uncommon or absent for insurance in mature markets, the use of money-back guarantees for various kinds of products is widespread, especially where the product is novel or the seller is not trusted.

An extensive research project (Mobarak and Rosenzweig 2013) examines the interaction between informal risk sharing, index insurance and risk-taking using a large-scale RCT. The authors randomized offerings of rainfall insurance contracts to cultivating and landless households in a set of Indian villages. Census data on caste networks permitted characterization of the nature and extent of informal risk sharing before the contracts were offered. The authors found that: (1) informal group-level risk sharing had the potential to make up for weaknesses in weather index insurance, and increase the demand for such index insurance; (2) index insurance had the potential to do better than informal indemnification in incentivizing farmers to invest in riskier technologies with higher average returns; and (3) offering insurance contracts to cultivators could lead to increased risk-taking, and to increased risk exposure of agricultural labourers, making the latter more likely to purchase weather insurance themselves when aware of this possible effect. Such studies can provide important guidance for the design of weather insurance at a regional scale, and ultimately for policymakers seeking to achieve widespread adoption of such insurance, making it more sustainable.

---

[14] A recent review of the evidence on microinsurance (Platteau et al., 2017) identifies price, quality, limited trust in the insurer, and liquidity constraints as factors limiting demand, along with lack of understanding of the products. See also De Bock and Gelade (2012).

Health Insurance

Health insurance for the poor represents a dimension of financial inclusion that intersects with much larger concerns about access to healthcare. While many industrial countries provide universal publicly funded healthcare, others, most notably the United States, do not, with exclusion disproportionately affecting the less well-off. The centrality of health to people's lives also makes it an exceptionally emotive subject. The financial aspect enters healthcare because of its potentially high costs, and developing countries obviously face more stringent constraints. In such cases, health insurance programmes for the poor are meant to increase access to healthcare when the public delivery system is unable to do so effectively.

One approach to inclusion is through community-based health insurance schemes: essentially a form of mutual insurance. For example, a study for Senegal (Jutting 2003) suggests that these can extend access to healthcare, although the poorest of the poor are still excluded. A study of community-based insurance for China (Wang et al. 2005) found that the benefits of the insurance were skewed towards richer participants, highlighting the difficulties and the importance of proper targeting and design. In general, qualitative case studies across countries suggest that micro-insurance for healthcare is a complex undertaking with significant challenges (McCord 2001).[15]

India has seen significant recent efforts to develop health insurance programmes for the poor, and many studies of these efforts. Palacios et al. (2011) is a collection of such studies with a great deal of institutional detail, including discussing some of the problems of implementation. A study by Nandi et al. (2013) carefully examines the determinants of enrolment in the new health insurance schemes.[16] Selvaraj and Karan (2012) argue that publicly funded health insurance schemes with private provision do not work. They argue against involving the private sector at all, their concerns being that private providers will cherry-pick, and that there are high administrative and other costs associated with private sector involvement. Ravi and Bergkvist (2015) posit a different conclusion: allowing for the length of time of operation of publicly financed health

---

[15] McCord compares schemes for Cambodia, India, Tanzania and Uganda.

[16] Ito and Kono (2010) explain low take up of such schemes in India in terms of behavioral factors such as present bias.

insurance schemes reveals impacts that are more positive than found by Selvraj and Karan. However, two other studies of Indian health insurance schemes (Sood et al. 2013; Karan et al. 2015) also find little or no impact of these schemes on the health expenditure of the poor. Importantly, there are differences between the performance of the national health insurance scheme and various state-level schemes, with some of the latter doing better (for example, Rao et al. 2014).

Implications of health insurance for financial inclusion are brought out in Banerjee et al. (2014). In an RCT, SKS, the largest MFI in India, bundled a health insurance component with micro-finance lending. But no one seemed to demand insurance, even people for whom there was clearly value. A substantial fraction of clients preferred to let go of micro-finance rather than pay a moderately higher interest rate and keep their loan, highlighting that adverse selection was a moot concern in this setting. The study was somewhat confounded by the financial trouble SKS got into by the time that the final survey was done. In a related study, Islam and Maitra (2012) highlighted the health insurance effect of general microcredit. Using a large panel data set from rural Bangladesh, they found that households that had access to microcredit were not forced to sell livestock to insure their consumption, when confronted with health shocks that required unexpected expenditures or led to lost income.

Healthcare is a credence good, relying on trust concerning provider quality. In such cases, referrals through social networks can be very important. These issues are compounded when new health insurance products involve using new or untrusted providers—say a private doctor versus a government doctor. Two recent studies examine aspects of these social network effects in the context of health insurance in India. Berg et al. (2012) study how incentive pay and social distance interact in the process of disseminating information about India's RSBY public health insurance programme, using a large-scale RCT conducted in South India. This involved hiring local agents to disseminate information about the insurance program. These agents were paid either a flat fee or a variable rate that depended on the subsequently measured level of knowledge about the programme in the eligible population. Incentive pay improved knowledge transmission to households that were socially distant from the agent, but not to socially similar households.

Debnath and Jain (2015) examined the role of caste networks, within villages and urban wards, in affecting utilization of Aarogyasri, Andhra

Pradesh's state-level publicly financed health insurance programme. The authors hypothesized that local caste networks could play a vital role in transmitting various kinds of information about the programme and the available healthcare providers, as well as signalling that using formal healthcare through the programme was socially acceptable. Using administrative data on programme claims, the study estimated that a unit increase in Aarogyasri use and associated claim amounts in the same caste and village increased first-time claims in the same group. However, the behaviour of other castes inside or outside the village, or same-caste peers outside the village in the same sub-district, had no significant effect on program utilization.

Payments Technologies

Because the poor face high transaction costs, even when using cash (when trying to save, cash may not be a convenient or safe store of value), reducing such costs through technological innovations can foster inclusion. There is robust evidence that digital payments technologies have positive impacts. Much of this evidence comes from the M-PESA scheme in Kenya (Jack, Ray, and Suri 2013; Jack and Suri 2014): Users are able to make more frequent and longer distance money transfers, and manage income variability better for smoother consumption patterns. In Kenya, the existence of a dominant telecom provider helped, although technological limitations in interoperability reduced access for some and stifled competition (Kendall et al. 2011). In Tanzania (where M-PESA is also available), an interoperability agreement among several providers achieved widespread coverage (Bourreau and Valletti 2015). In other countries, telecom companies have provided specific digital services: for example, Orange Money (Jordan) enables consumers to pay bills and to make point-of-sale purchases; Smart Money (Philippines) and Regalli (Dominican Republic) enable customers to make bill payments. There are complex issues of infrastructure, regulatory policies, and even details of user interface design that can affect the success of digital financial services (Mas and Morawczynski 2009; Medhi et al. 2009).

In India, digital payments have been conceptualized as one component of a three-part strategy for financial inclusion using digital technologies: JAM, introduced earlier. Biometric identity cards in India (Aadhaar) have reduced corruption in welfare programmes, economized on expenditures and even had some positive impacts on outcomes (Banerjee et al. 2016;

Muralidharan et al. 2016; Imbert and Papp 2015). Other examples of positive impacts from using digital technologies include Afghanistan (Callen et al. 2015) and Nigeria (Aker et al. 2014), suggesting that there are replicable opportunities for successful innovations. In India, the JAM framework for policy innovation has the potential to avoid a common problem in policymaking in that country, of broad and shallow interventions, although Ravi and Gakhar (2015) argue for breadth of financial services tied to digital innovation, to take advantage of economies of scope, given the fixed costs of infrastructure and adoption.[17]

Financial Literacy

On the demand side, financial literacy is an important factor in shaping financial inclusion. Consumers have to understand the nature of the products and services they are buying, as well as the implications of these purchases for their welfare. This may be relatively simple in the case of payments and transfers, but even bank accounts can present challenges in terms of weighing consumption and saving tradeoffs. Insurance products are inherently complicated by the difficulties of measuring uncertainty and evaluating risks.

Lusardi and Mitchell (2014) survey issues surrounding financial literacy, although their empirical evidence is from industrial countries, which also face challenges of educating consumers of financial services. In all countries, one basic problem is lack of information (Gine et al. 2014, for Mexico), but how information asymmetries are overcome can be crucial (Alan et al. 2015, for Turkey). Miller et al. (2014) surveyed evaluations of 188 financial education programmes, and found weak evidence for positive impacts on financial knowledge, let alone decision-making. However, it appears that teaching simplified guidelines for behaviour as rules-of-thumb can have a positive impact (Drexler et al. 2014).

---

[17] Digital credit is showing some promise for financial inclusion in countries such as India. Creditworthiness does not have to be dependent on scanty financial history, but can be based on richer mobile phone usage history. Mobile phone usage can predict loan repayment (Björkegren & Grissen, 2015). Furthermore, as in the case of microfinance, dynamic incentives (larger loans at better terms) encourage repayment of digital loans. I am grateful to Eilin Francis for these points.

Financial literacy can have different dimensions and contexts, and several studies focus on specific aspects, such as household saving or managing a business. Cole et al. (2011) used large field surveys in India and Indonesia, and RCTs in Indonesia, to show that prices of financial services have an effect on demand. However, though financial literacy was an important correlate of using financial services, financial training was not effective or cost efficient for promoting the use of bank accounts. In a business context, De Mel et al. (2014) conducted an RCT among low-income women in urban Sri Lanka to measure the impact of a commonly used business training course. They tried two treatments—training only and training plus a cash grant—over two years. Training alone changed business practices but had no impact on business profits, sales, or capital stock. The grant-plus-training combination increased business profitability in the first eight months, but this impact also dissipated in the second year. However, there was some evidence that training might be more effective for new owners. Karlan and Valdivia (2011) conducted an RCT in Peru to measure marginal impacts of adding business training to a Peruvian group lending programme (MFI) for female micro-entrepreneurs. Training had no effect on business revenue, profits, or employment, but there were business knowledge improvements among the entrepreneurs, and increased client retention rates for the MFI.

Halan and Sane (2017) evaluated the effectiveness of information disclosure in the context of the insurance market in India, focusing on a specific life insurance product. They presented product advertisements to customers with four different sets of disclosures: basic information, the actual rate of return on the product in addition to the first set, a benchmark return of a similar product in addition to the second set, and product features of a more cost-effective alternative life insurance product in addition to the third set. Participants in each case were asked to provide assessments of the product and hypothetical purchase decisions. The results suggest that consumers may lose focus with 'too much' information, and that information is more likely to be valuable if understandable in the context of prior financial literacy, highlighting the complexity of making financial innovation work to the benefit of inexperienced consumers.

Behavioural Factors

Because financial services involve complexities with respect to intertemporal tradeoffs and judgements about uncertainty and risk, they are most subject to what economists characterize as behavioural factors, namely, various (mostly systematic) deviations from the ideal of economic rationality. Some of these factors are hard to disentangle from lack of information, and financial literacy considerations overlap with behavioural factors.

An important basic example of a behavioural bias is the difficulty that individuals have in committing to a savings strategy that they realize will be optimal for them over time. Ashraf et al. (2006, 2010) tested commitment savings products in the Philippines, with lock-in periods or penalties for early withdrawal. Women who were offered an individually held commitment savings account reported increased decision-making power, and durable goods purchases shifted towards 'female-oriented' goods, such as kitchen appliances. Those who used the commitment devices had significantly higher savings. In Kenya, Dupas and Robinson (2013) tested a simple 'Safe Box' that allowed users to save for preventive or emergency health, and this significantly increased achievement of health savings goals. In an experiment in Uganda, primary school students were offered a 'softer' commitment device, (funds in the savings account were available for withdrawal but labelled as being 'for education'): Combined with a parental outreach programme, this increased spending on school supplies and improved test scores (Karlan and Linden 2016).

Many other behavioural phenomena have been examined in the context of financial inclusion. For example, Duflo et al. (2011) showed that many farmers in Western Kenya failed to take advantage of apparently profitable fertilizer investments, apparently due to a combination of procrastination and new consumption opportunities, but they did invest in response to small, time-limited discounts on the cost of acquiring fertilizer, such as free delivery. Other studies (Beaman et al. 2014; Dupas and Robinson 2014; and Kremer et al. 2015) show that various types of small business owners in Kenya make profit-reducing decisions with respect to keeping enough change, hours and days worked, and inventory management. A growing number of studies in this vein intersect with studies examining the design and impacts of microcredit schemes. Many of the studies for India discussed in earlier sections have behavioural components to their analysis.

***

Financial inclusion is complex and multidimensional, and this chapter has focused on decomposing financial inclusion into the provision of more specific financial services, and examining the empirical evidence for how well different components of financial inclusion can be accomplished, as well as the methods that might work in specific contexts. While the evidence for different countries and programmes is variable and mixed, this survey suggests that well-designed and implemented research studies can provide clear answers for Indian contexts, for many aspects of financial inclusion. Therefore, careful empirical research can guide policy design in India for financial inclusion. It should be noted that financial markets are inherently subject to difficulties, even in developed economies. Financial transactions typically involve considerations of risk and uncertainty, and intertemporal tradeoffs. These factors make it more likely that asymmetries of information, behavioural biases, and lack of experience will increase transaction costs or even cause market failures. These themes have run through our discussion on specific financial services and inclusion efforts pertaining to each of them.

Turning to more specific conclusions and lessons, we begin with the previous surveys discussed in the introduction. Karlan and Morduch (2010) emphasize the shift from postulating hypothetical improvements in financial access to concrete lessons from experiments, pilots and trials in actual field settings. Aggarwal and Klepper (2013) emphasize how government policy changes can relax existing constraints to financial inclusion, especially with respect to savings, payments, and financial literacy. Karlan et al. (2016) emphasize the positive evidence for the benefits of savings products and digital payments, and generally view digital technology as opening up new possibilities for reducing transaction costs, information asymmetries, and market distortions. They suggest that microcredit and insurance present greater challenges, as do social norms that can disadvantage women, in particular. They also highlight issues of scaling up (including for digital efforts), offering integrated or complementary services, and linking financial inclusion to end goals such as health and education.

In India, much of recent policymaking with respect to financial inclusion is broadly consistent with the direction supported by current research-based knowledge. For example, this includes government-led pushes to increase access to banking, insurance, and digital payments. Cole et al. (2015) and Field et al. (2016) both, in very different contexts, highlight the importance of organizational innovations that improve incentives within the banking sector. This suggests that simply expanding the number of bank accounts may not be an optimal policy. At the same time, organizational changes are delicate matters and need to be context-specific.

In areas such as microcredit and small firm finance, the studies by Field et al. (2013), Raj and Sen (2013), and Barboni (2016) suggest that there is still much to learn in the Indian context about the specifics of relaxing financing constraints for small entrepreneurs, ranging from microenterprises to more substantial small and even medium firms. Issues of contract design, monitoring and enforcement, and training do not seem to be completely understood in the Indian context. In some cases, there is more detailed evidence for other countries, but the transferability of those lessons to India—indeed, even to specific Indian states—needs to be tested. There is also an obvious connection to issues of how the Indian banking sector functions on the side of making loans, in addition to the savings opportunities it offers. This relates back to the point about integration of different aspects of financial inclusion noted by Karlan et al. (2016).

Agricultural credit and farmers' insurance are another example of the need for an integrated approach to financial inclusion initiatives. Gaurav et al. (2011) and Mobarak and Rosenzweig (2013) provide evidence for India on how to design agricultural insurance that is more inclusive and sustainable, including issues of promoting adoption and inclusion (such as extending it to agricultural labourers and not just farmers). However, given variations in agricultural conditions around a large country such as India, as well as differences in income levels, further research can solidify the design of appropriate insurance products, as well as examine their integration with access to agricultural credit, market access (Mitra et al. 2012 and Maitra et al. 2014) and productive investment.

Health insurance is another area where Indian policymaking has been innovative in ways that seek to promote inclusion, and one where further expansion is planned. In this case, the potential link between financial inclusion and outcomes ought to be very direct, but the evidence is still being gathered. Studies by Berg et al. (2012) and Debnath and Jain (2015) represent useful investigations of the processes that drive acceptance and adoption of such innovations as health insurance, which are obvious preconditions for achieving inclusion and positive impacts on health outcomes.

Finally, the size of India's market and the diversity of areas of possible innovations in financial products and services are strongly indicative of the need to conduct further studies of patterns of household financial behaviour. Badarinza et al. (2017) is a good example of preliminary work on documenting these patterns, but much more can be done. Campbell et al. (2012) conducted a useful study of India's mortgage market, and plans to expand low-income housing will increase the need for additional studies that emphasize financial inclusion. Complementing the understanding of specific markets for financial products and services, a much better understanding of financial literacy and effective methods for imparting financial education to consumers and small entrepreneurs is required in the Indian context. The study by Halan and Sane (2017) represents just a small slice of what policymakers and financial sector providers need to know about the potential behavior of individuals as innovations are designed and implemented.

In all of these cases, collaborations and coordination between policymakers, practitioners, and researchers can be vital in achieving financial inclusion in multiple dimensions, making sure that this is done efficiently, and connecting financial inclusion to positive outcomes in health, education, productivity, and employment. Technological innovations certainly open up new possibilities for extending the reach of various financial products and services, but organizational design, regulatory frameworks and financial education have to keep pace. Indeed, that is a valid observation for all economies with respect to the financial sector.

References

Aggarwal, S., and Klapper, L. (2013), 'Designing Government Policies to Expand Financial Inclusion: Evidence from Around the World'. Unpublished working paper, The World Bank, September.

Ahlin, C., Lin, J., and Maio, M. (2011), 'Where does microfinance flourish? Microfinance institution performance in macroeconomic context'. *Journal of Development Economics*, 95(2): 105–20.

Aizenman Joshua, Yothin Jinjarak, and Donghyun Park (2015), 'Financial Development and Output Growth in Developing Asia and Latin America: A Comparative Sectoral Analysis. National Bureau of Economic Research', Working Paper 20917, January.

Aker, Jenny C., Rachid Boumnijel, Amanda McClelland, and Niall Tierney (2014), 'Payment Mechanisms and Anti-Poverty Programs: Evidence from a Mobile Money Cash Transfer Experiment in Niger'. Center for Global Development Working Paper 268.

Alan, Sule, Mehmet Cemalcilar, Dean Karlan, and Jonathan Zinman (2015), 'Unshrouding Effects on Demand for a Costly Add-on: Evidence from Bank Overdrafts in Turkey'. NBER Working Paper 20956.

Alfaro, L., and A. Chari (2009), 'India Transformed: Insights from the Firm Level 1988–2005'. *Brookings India Policy Forum*, 6.

Alfaro, L., and A. Chari (2014), 'Deregulation, Misallocation, and Size: Evidence from India'. Working Paper, Harvard University, February.

Allen, F., R. Chakrabarti, S. De, J. Qian, and M. Qian (2007), 'Financing Firms in India'. Working Paper.

Allen, T. (2016), 'Optimal (Partial) group liability in microfinance lending'. *Journal of Development Economics*, 121(C), 201–16.

Anderson, M., Dobkin, C., and Gross, T. (2012), 'The effect of health insurance coverage on the use of medical services', *American Economic Journal: Economic Policy*, 4(1): 1–27.

Anson, J., Berthaud, A., Klapper, L. F., and Singer, D. (2013), 'Financial inclusion and the role of the post office'. World Bank Policy Research Working Paper 6630, October.

Arcand, Jean Louis, Enrico Berkes, and Ugo Panizza. 2015. 'Too much finance?', *Journal of Economic Growth*, 20(2): 105–48.

Aron-Dine, A., Einav, L., & Finkelstein, A. (2013), 'The RAND health insurance experiment, three decades later', *The Journal of Economic Perspectives*, 27(1): 197–222.

Ashraf, N., Karlan, D., and Yin, W. (2006), 'Tying Odysseus to the mast: Evidence from a commitment savings product in the Philippines', *The Quarterly Journal of Economics*, 635–72.

Ashraf, Nava, Dean Karlan, and Wesley Yin. (2010), 'Female Empowerment: Impact of a Commitment Savings Product in the Philippines', *World Development* 38(3): 3334.

Ayyagari, M., A. Demirgüç-Kunt, V. Maksimovic (2010), 'Formal versus informal finance: Evidence from China', *Review of Financial Studies*, 23 (8), 3048–97.

Badarinza, C., V. Balasubramaniam and T. Ramadorai. (2017), 'The Indian Household Finance Landscape', *India Policy Forum*, forthcoming.

Banerjee, A.V. and Duflo, E. (2008), 'Do firms want to borrow more? Testing credit constraints using a directed lending program', *Review of Economic Studies* [2014] 81, 572–607.

—— (2011) *Poor Economics: A Radical Rethinking of the Way to Fight Global Poverty*, New York: Public Affairs.

Banerjee, A., Duflo, E., and Hornbeck, R. (2014), 'Bundling health insurance and microfinance in India: There cannot be adverse selection if there is no demand', *American Economic Review*, 104(5): 291–7.

Banerjee, A., Duflo, E., Glennerster, R., and Kinnan, C. (2015), 'The miracle of microfinance? Evidence from a randomized evaluation', *American Economic Journal: Applied Economics*, 7(1): 22–53.

Banerjee, A., Karlan, D., and Zinman, J. (2015). 'Six randomized evaluations of microcredit: Introduction and further steps', *American Economic Journal: Applied Economics*, 7(1): 1–21.

Banerjee, A., Duflo, E., Imbert, C., Santosh Mathew, S., and Pande, R. (2016), 'Can E-Governance Reduce Capture of Public Programs? Experimental Evidence from a Financial Reform in India's Employment Guarantee'. Working Paper.

Barboni, G. (2016). 'Repayment Flexibility in Microfinance Contracts: Theory and Experimental Evidence on Take-Up and Selection'. Working Paper, Princeton University.

Bardhan, P. (2007), Globalization and Rural Poverty. In Nissanke, M. and Thorbecke, E. *The Impact of Globalization on the World's Poor: Transmission Mechanisms*. New York: Palgrave Macmillan, 145–62.

Bauer, M., Chytilová, J., and Morduch, J. (2012), 'Behavioral foundations of microcredit: Experimental and survey evidence from rural India', *American Economic Review*, 102(2): 1118–39.

Beaman, L., J. Magruder, and J. Robinson (2014), 'Minding small change among small firms in Kenya', *Journal of Development Economics* 108(C), 69–86.

Bertrand, M., and Morse, A. (2011), 'Information disclosure, cognitive biases, and payday borrowing', *Journal of Finance*, 66(6), 1865–93.

Beck, T. (2006), 'Financing Constraints of SMEs in Developing Countries: Evidence, Determinants and Solutions', World Bank, Development Research Group Working Paper.

Beck, T., and Demirguc-Kunt, A. (2006), 'Small and medium-size enterprises: Access to finance as a growth constraint', *Journal of Banking & Finance*, 30(11): 2931–43.

Beck, T., Demirgüç-Kunt, A., and Levine, R. (2007). 'Finance, inequality and the poor', *Journal of Economic Growth*, 12(1): 27–49.

Berg, E., Ghatak, M., Manjula, R., Rajasekhar, D., and Roy, S. (2013), 'Motivating knowledge agents: Can incentive pay overcome social distance?', IGC Working Paper. F-35010-INC-1.

Binswanger-Mkhize, H. (2012). 'Is There Too Much Hype about Index-based Agricultural Insurance?', *Journal of Development Studies*. 48 (2): 187–200.

Björkegren, D. and Grissen, D. (2015), 'Behavior Revealed in Mobile Phone Usage Predicts Loan Repayment', Working paper, available at SSRN: https://ssrn.com/abstract=2611775.

Bourreau, M. and Valletti, T. (2015), 'Enabling Digital Financial Inclusion through Improvements in Competition and Interoperability: What Works and What Doesn't? Center for Global Development', Policy Paper 065.

Bruhn, M., and Love, I. (2014), 'The real impact of improved access to finance: Evidence from Mexico', *Journal of Finance*, 69(3): 1347–76.

Burgess, R., and Pande, R. (2005), 'Do Rural Banks Matter? Evidence from the Indian Social Banking Experiment', *American Economic Review*, 95(3): 780–95.

Burgess, R., Wong, G., and Pande, R. (2005), 'Banking for the Poor: Evidence from India', *Journal of the European Economic Association*, 3(2/3): 268–78.

Callen, M., De Mel, S., McIntosh, C., and Woodruff, C. (2014), 'What are the headwaters of formal savings? Experimental evidence from Sri Lanka', Working paper 20736, National Bureau of Economic Research.

Callen, Michael, Joshua E Blumenstock, Tarek Ghani, and Lucas Koepk. (2015), 'Promises and Pitfalls of Mobile Money in Afghanistan: Evidence from a Randomized Control Trial', Working Paper.

Campbell, J.Y., Ramadorai, T., and Ranish, B. (2012). 'How Do Regulators Influence Mortgage Risk: Evidence from an Emerging Market', Working paper 18394). United States: National Bureau of Economic Research.

Čihák, Martin, Aslı Demirgüç-Kunt, Erik Feyen, and Ross Levine (2012), 'Benchmarking Financial Systems around the World', World Bank Policy Research Working Paper 6175, Washington DC: World Bank.

Cole, S. (2009). 'Fixing market failures or fixing elections? Agricultural credit in India', *American Economic Journal: Applied Economics*, 1(1): 219–50.

Cole, S., Sampson, T., and Zia, B. (2011). 'Prices or knowledge? What drives demand for financial services in emerging markets?', *Journal of Finance*, 66(6): 1933–67.

Cole, S., Stein, D., and Tobacman, J. (2014). 'Dynamics of Demand for Index Insurance: Evidence from a Long-Run Field Experiment', *American Economic Review*, 104(5): 284–90.

Cole, S., Kanz, M., and Klapper, L. (2015). 'Incentivizing Calculated Risk⊠Taking: Evidence from an Experiment with Commercial Bank Loan Officers', *Journal of Finance*, 70(2): 537–75.

Cull, R., Demirgüç-Kunt, A., and Morduch, J. (2011). 'Does regulatory supervision curtail microfinance profitability and outreach?', *World Development*, 39(6): 949–65.

Cull, R., Demirgüç-Kunt, A., and Morduch, J. (2012). *Banking the World: Empirical Foundations of Financial Inclusion*. Cambridge, MA: MIT Press.

Cull, R., Demirgüç-Kunt, A., and Morduch, J. (2016). 'The Microfinance Business Model: Enduring Subsidy and Modest Profit', Working Paper.

De, S. and M. Singh (2014). Credit Rationing in Informal Markets: The Case of Small Firms in India. Center for Analytical Finance, University of California, Santa Cruz, Working Paper No. 6.

De Bock, O., and Gelade W. (2012). 'The Demand for Microinsurance: A Literature Review', ILO Microinsurance Innovation Facility, Research Paper 26, November.

De Mel, S., McKenzie, D., and Woodruff, C. (2011). 'Getting credit to high return microentrepreneurs: The results of an information intervention', *World Bank Economic Review*, 25(3): 456–85.

De Mel, S., McKenzie, D., and Woodruff, C. (2014). 'Business Training and Female Enterprise Start-up, Growth, and Dynamics: Experimental Evidence from Sri Lanka', *Journal of Development Economics*, 106, 199–210.

Debnath, S., and Jain, T. (2015). 'Social Networks and Health Insurance Utilization. Report to IGC-India', IGC Working Paper. F-35304-INC-1.

Demirgüç-Kunt, A., and Klapper, L. (2013). Measuring financial inclusion: Explaining variation in use of financial services across and within countries. *Brookings Papers on Economic Activity*, 2013(1): 279–340.

Demirgüç-Kunt, A., Klapper, L., Van Oudheusden, P., and Zingales, L. (2013). 'Trust in Banks', Working paper. Washington: Development Research Group, World Bank.

Drexler, Alejandro, Greg Fischer, and Antoinette S. Schoar. 2014. 'Keeping it Simple: Financial Literacy and Rules of Thumb', *American Economic Journal: Applied Economics* 6(2): 131.

Duflo, E., M. Kremer, and J. Robinson. (2011). 'Nudging farmers to use fertilizer: theory and experimental evidence from Kenya', *American Economic Review* 101 (6): 2350–90

Dupas, P., Green, S., Keats, A., and Robinson, J. (2014). 'Challenges in banking the rural poor: Evidence from Kenya's western province'. In Sebastian, E., Johnson, S., and Weil, D.N. (eds) *African Successes: Modernization and Development, Volume 3*. Chicago: University of Chicago Press.

Dupas, P., and Robinson, J. (2013a). 'Savings Constraints and Microenterprise Development: Evidence from a Field Experiment in Kenya', *American Economic Journal: Applied Economics*, 5(1): 163–92.

—— (2013b). 'Why don't the poor save more? Evidence from health savings experiments', *The American Economic Review*, 103(4): 1138–71.

—— (2014). 'The Daily Grind: Cash Needs, Labor Supply and Self-Control', NBER Working Paper 19264.

Dupas, P., Karlan, D., Robinson, J., and Ubfal, D. (2016). 'Banking the Unbanked? Evidence from Three Countries' (No. w22463). National Bureau of Economic Research.

Engelhardt, G. V. and Grubera, J. (2011). Medicare Part D and the Financial Protection of the Elderly', *American Economic Journal: Economic Policy*, 3(4): 77–102.

Field, E., Martinez, J., and Pande, R. (2016). 'Does Women's Banking Matter for Women? Evidence from Urban India', IGC Working Paper, November, S-35306-INC-1.

Field, E., Pande, R., Papp, J., and Rigol, N. (2013).'Does the Classic Microfinance Model Discourage Entrepreneurship among the Poor? Experimental Evidence from India', *American Economic Review*, 103(6): 2196–226.

Finkelstein, A., Taubman S., Wright, B., Bernstein, M., Gruber, J., Newhouse, J. P., Allen, H., and Baicker, K. (2011).'The Oregon Health Insurance Experiment: Evidence from the First Year' (No. w17190), United States: National Bureau of Economic Research.

Gangadharan, L., Jain, T., Maitra, P., and Vecci, J. (2014). 'The Behavioral Response to Women's Empowerment Programs: Experimental Evidence from JEEViKA in Bihar', IGC Working Paper. S-34111-INB-1.

Gaurav, S., Cole, S., and Tobacman, J. (2011). 'Marketing Complex Financial Products in Emerging Markets: Evidence from Rainfall Insurance in India', *Journal of marketing research*, 48(SPL), S150-S162.

Gill, A. (2016). 'Agricultural Credit in Punjab: Have Policy Initiatives Made a Dent in Informal Credit Markets?', In L. Singh and N. Singh (ed.) *Economic Transformation of a Developing Economy*,, pp. 165–82. Singapore: Springer.

Giné, X. (2011).'Access to capital in rural Thailand: an estimated model of formal vs. informal credit', *Journal of Development Economics*, 96(1): 16–29.

Giné, X. (2015). 'Innovations in Insuring the Poor: Experience with Weather Index-based Insurance in India and Malawi', World Bank.

Giné, X., C. Martinez Cuellar, and R. Keenan Mazer. (2014). 'Financial (dis) information: Evidence from an audit study in Mexico', World Bank Policy Research Working Paper 6902.

Giné, X., Townsend, R. and Vickery, J. (2008). 'Patterns of Rainfall Insurance Participation in Rural India', *World Bank Economic Review*, 22 (3): 539–66.

Goyal, A. (2010). 'Information, Direct Access to Farmers, and Rural Market Performance in Central India', *American Economic Journal: Applied Economics*. 2 (3): 22–45.

Halan, M. and R. Sane (2016). 'Misled and Mis-sold: Financial Misbehaviour in retail banks? NSE–IFMR Finance Foundation Financial Deepening and Household Finance Research Initiative', Working Paper, August.

Halan, M. and R. Sane (2017). 'Do Disclosures Matter? The Case of Life Insurance', Working Paper, January.

Imbert, C. and J. Papp. (2015). 'Labor Market Effects of Social Programs: Evidence from India's Employment Guarantee', *American Economic Journal: Applied Economics*, 7 (2): 233–63.

Islam, A., and Maitra, P. (2012). 'Health Shocks and Consumption Smoothing in Rural Households: Does Microcredit Have a Role to Play?', *Journal of Development Economics*, 97(2): 232–43.

Ito, S. and Kono, H. (2010). 'Why Is the Take-Up of Microinsurance So Low? Evidence from a Health Insurance Scheme in India', *The Developing Economies*. 48(1): 74–101.

Jack, W., Ray, A., and Suri, T. (2013). 'Transaction Networks: Evidence from Mobile Money in Kenya', *The American Economic Review*, 103(3): 356–61.

Jack, W., and Suri, T. (2014). 'Risk Sharing and Transactions Costs: Evidence from Kenya's Mobile Money Revolution', *The American Economic Review*, 104(1): 183–223.

Jhabvala, R., Sharma, S., and Mehta, S.K. (2019), 'The Missing women in finance', India Development Review website, https://idronline.org/the-missing-women-in-finance/, August, accessed 14 December 2019.

Jutting, J.P. (2003). 'Do Community-based Health Insurance Schemes Improve Poor People's Access to Health Care? Evidence from Rural Senegal', *World Development*, 32 (2): 273–88.

Kaboski, J.P., and Townsend, R.M. (2011). 'A Structural Evaluation of a Large⊠Scale Quasi⊠Experimental Microfinance Initiative', *Econometrica*, 79(5): 1357–406.

——— (2012). 'The Impact of Credit on Village Economies', *American Economic Journal: Applied Economics*, 4(2): 98–133.

Karan, A.K., Yip, W.C.M., and Mahal, A. (2015). 'Extending Health Insurance to the Poor in India: An Impact Evaluation of Rashtriya Swasthya Bima Yojana on Financial Risk Protection'. Available at SSRN.

Karlan, D., Kendall, J., Mann, R., Pande, R., Suri, T., and Zinman, J. (2016). 'Research and Impacts of Digital Financial Services', National Bureau of Economic Research, Working Paper 22633, September.

Karlan, D., Knight, R., and Udry, C. (2015). 'Consulting and Capital Experiments with Microenterprise Tailors in Ghana', *Journal of Economic Behavior and Organization*, 118(C): 281–302.

Karlan, D., and Morduch, J. (2010). 'Access to Finance', Chapter 71, *Handbook of Development Economics, Volume 5*, Rodrik, D. and Rosenzweig, M. (eds) Amsterdam: North-Holland, 4703-4784.

Karlan, D., Osei, R., Osei-Akoto, I., and Udry, C. (2014). 'Agricultural Decisions after Relaxing Credit and Risk Constraints', *Quarterly Journal of Economics*, 129(2): 597–652.

Karlan, Dean and Leigh Linden. (2014). 'Loose Knots: Strong versus Weak Commitments to Save for Education in Uganda', Working Paper.

Karlan, D., and Valdivia, M. (2011). 'Teaching Entrepreneurship: Impact of Business Training on Microfinance Clients and Institutions', *The Review of Economics and Statistics*, 93(2): 510–27.

Karlan, D., Kutsoati, E., McMillan, M., and Udry, C. (2011). 'Crop Price Indemnified Loans for Farmers: A Pilot Experiment in Rural Ghana', *Journal of Risk and Insurance*, 78(1): 37–55.

Karlan, D., and Zinman, J. (2009). 'Expanding Credit Access: Using Randomized Supply Decisions to Estimate the Impacts', *Review of Financial Studies*, 23(1): 433–64.

Karmakar, K. G., Banerjee, G. D., and Mohapatra, N. P. (2011). *Towards Financial Inclusion in India*. New Delhi: SAGE Publications India.

Kendall, Jake, Maurer, Bill, Machoka, Phillip, and Clara Veniard (2011). 'An Emerging Platform: From Money Transfer System to Mobile Money Ecosystem', *Innovations*, 6(4): 49–64.

Kinnan, C., and Townsend, R. (2012). 'Kinship and financial networks, formal financial access, and risk reduction', *American Economic Review*, 102 (3): 289–93.

Kochar, A. (2011). The Distributive Consequences of Social Banking: 'A Microempirical Analysis of the Indian Experience', *Economic Development and Cultural Change*, 5(2): 251–80.

Kremer, M., J. Lee, J. Robinson, and O. Rostapshova. (2015). 'Rates of Return, Optimization Failures, and Behavioral Biases: Evidence from Kenyan Retail Shops', Working Paper.

Law, Siong Hook, and Nirvikar Singh. (2014). 'Does too much finance harm economic growth?', *Journal of Banking & Finance*, 41: 36–44.

Love, I., and Pería, M.S.M. (2015). 'How Bank Competition Affects Firms' Access to Finance', *World Bank Economic Review*, 29(3), 413–48.

Lusardi, A., and Mitchell, O. S. (2014). 'The economic importance of financial literacy: Theory and evidence', *Journal of Economic Literature*, 52(1): 5–44.

Maitra, P., Mitra, S., Mookherjee, D., Motta, A., and Visaria, S. (2014). Financing Smallholder Agriculture: An Experiment with Agent-Intermediated Microloans in India (No. w20709). United States: National Bureau of Economic Research.

Mas, I. and O. Morawczynski (2009). Designing Mobile Money Services: Lessons from M-PESA. *Innovations*, Spring, 77–91.

McCord, M.J. (2001). 'Health Care Microinsurance—Case Studies from Uganda, Tanzania, India and Cambodia', *Small Enterprise Development*, 12(1): 1–14.

Medhi, I., S.N.N. Gautama and K. Toyama (2009). 'A comparison of mobile money-transfer UIs for non-literate and semi-literate users', *Proceedings of the SIGCHI Conference on Human Factors in Computing Systems*, pp. 1741–50.

Mehmood, Y., Ahmad, M., and Anjum, M.B. (2012). Factors Affecting Delay in Repayments of Agricultural Credit: A Case Study of District Kasur of Punjab Province. *World Applied Sciences Journal* 17 (4): 447-451.

Melzer, B. T. (2011). 'The Real Costs of Credit Access: Evidence from the Payday Lending Market' *Quarterly Journal of Economics*, 126(1): 517–55.

Miller, M., Reichelstein, J., Salas, C., and Zia, B. (2014). 'Can You Help Someone Become Financially Capable? A Meta-Analysis of the Literature', World Bank.

Mitra, S., D. Mookherjee, M. Torero and S. Visaria. (2012). 'Asymmetric Information and Middleman Margins: An Experiment with West Bengal Potato Farmers', IGC Working Paper, F-3010-INC-1.

Mobarak, A.M., and Rosenzweig, M.R. (2013). 'Informal risk sharing, index insurance, and risk taking in developing countries', American Economic Review, 103(3): 375–80

Muralidharan, K., P. Niehaus, and S. Sukhtankar. (2016). 'Building State Capacity: Evidence from Biometric Smartcards in India', American Economic Review, 106(10): 2895–929.

Nair, R. (2010). 'Weather-based Crop Insurance in India: Towards a Sustainable Crop Insurance Regime?', Economic and Political Weekly, 45(34): 73–81.

Nandi, A., A. Ashok, and R. Laxminarayan (2013). 'The Socio-economic and Institutional Determinants of Participation in India's Health Insurance Scheme for the Poor', PLoS ONE 8(6): e66296.

Oboh, V.U. and Ekpebu, I.D. (2011). 'Determinants of formal agricultural credit allocation to the farm sector by arable crop farmers in Benue State, Nigeria, African Journal of Agricultural Research, Vol. 6 (1), pp. 181–5.

Palacios, R., J. Das, and C. Sun (eds) (2011)., India's Health Insurance Scheme for the Poor, Evidence from the Early Experience of the Rashtriya Swasthya Bima Yojana, May, New Delhi: Centre for Policy Research.

Pitt, M.M. and S.R. Khandker (1998). 'The Impact of Group-Based Credit on Poor Households in Bangladesh: Does the Gender of Participants Matter?', Journal of Political Economy, 106(5):958–96.

Platteau, J.-P., De Bock, O., and Gelade W. (2017). 'The Demand for Microinsurance: A Literature Review', World Development, 94: 139–56.

Prina, S. (2015). 'Banking the Poor via Savings Accounts: Evidence from a Field Experiment', Journal of Development Economics, 115: 16–31.

Rahman, M.W. (2011). 'Policies and Performances of Agricultural/Rural Credit in Bangladesh: What is the Influence on Agricultural Production?', African Journal of Agricultural Research, 6(31): 6440–52.

Raj, R.S.N. and Sen, K. (2013). 'How Important are Credit Constraints for Small Firm Growth? Evidence from the Indian Informal Manufacturing Sector', IGC Working Paper. F-35041-INC-1.

Raju, K.V., Naik, G., Ramseshan, R., Pandey, T., Joshi, P., Anantha, K.H., Rao, A.V.R.K., Shyam, D.M., and Charyulu, D.K. (2016). 'Transforming Weather Index-Based Crop Insurance in India: Protecting Small Farmers from Distress. Status and a Way Forward.' Research Report IDC-8.

Rao, M., A. Katyal, P.V. Singh, A. Samarth, S. Bergkvist, M. Kancharla, A. Wagstaff, G. Netuveli, and A. Renton (2014). 'Trends in addressing inequalities in access to hospital care in Andhra Pradesh and Maharashtra states of India: A difference-in-differences study', *BMJ Open*.

Ravi, S. and Bergkvist, S. (2015). 'Are Publicly Financed Health Insurance Schemes Working in India?', *India Policy Forum*, 11 (1): 158–92.

Ravi, S and Gakhar, S. (2015). 'Advancing Financial Inclusion in India beyond the Jan-Dhan Yojana. Brookings India IMPACT Series', New Delhi: Brookings Institution India Center.

Roodman, D., and Morduch, J. (2009). 'The Impact of Microcredit on the Poor in Bangladesh: Revisiting the Evidence. Center for Global Development Working Paper 174.

Sahay, Ratna, Martin Cihak, Papa N'Diaye, Adolfo Barajas, Diana Ayala Pena, Ran Bi, Yuan Gao, Annette Kyobe, Lam Nguyen, Christian Saborowski, Katsiaryna Svirydzenka, and Reza Yousefi (2015). 'Rethinking Financial Deepening: Stability and Growth in Emerging Markets', International Monetary Fund IMF Staff Discussion Notes 15/8.

Sarma, M., and Pais, J. (2011). 'Financial Inclusion and Development', *Journal of International Development*, 23(5): 613–28.

Selvaraj, S., and Karan, A. (2012). 'Why Publicly-Financed Health Insurance Schemes are Ineffective in Providing Financial Risk Protection', *Economic & Political Weekly*, 47(11): 60–8.

Sen, A. (1999). *Development as Freedom*. New York: Oxford University Press.

Shapiro, D.A. (2015). 'Microfinance and dynamic incentives', *Journal of Development Economics*, 115(C): 73–84.

Sharma, B. K. and Kumawat, R. C. (2014). 'Repayment performance of institutional agricultural credit in Jaipur district of Rajasthan', *Economic Affairs*, 59(2): 263–72.

Shukla, R. (2015). 'Corporate Financing in India: Some Stylized Facts of an Emerging Economy', *International Journal of Management Excellence*. 5(2).

Singh, N. (2015). 'Banking on better credit risk management', *Financial Express*, December 11, http://www.financialexpress.com/opinion/banking-on-better-credit-risk-management/177207/.

Singh, N.D. (2012). 'Agricultural Credit Problems of Marginal and Small Farmers in Punjab', *International Research Journal of Agricultural Economics and Statistics*, 3(2): 278–83.

Somville, Vincent and Lore Vandewalle (2015). 'Saving by Default: Evidence from a Field Experiment in India', Working Paper.

Sood, N., Bendavid, E., Mukherji, A., Wagner, Z., Nagpal, S., and Mullen, P. (2013). Government health insurance for people below poverty line in India:

Quasi-experimental Evaluation of Insurance and Health Outcomes. *BMJ (Clinical research ed.)*, 349: g5114.

Takahashi, K., Ikegami, M., Sheahan, M., and Barrett, C.B. (2016). 'Experimental Evidence on the Drivers of Index-Based Livestock Insurance Demand in Southern Ethiopia', *World Development*, 78: 324–40.

Taylor, M. (2012). 'The Antinomies of 'Financial Inclusion': Debt, Distress and the Workings of Indian Microfinance', *Journal of Agrarian Change*, 12(4): 601–10.

Van Rooyen, C., Stewart, R., and De Wet, T. (2012). 'The impact of microfinance in sub-Saharan Africa: a systematic review of the evidence', *World Development*, 40(11): 2249–2262.

Wagner, C. (2012). 'From Boom to Bust: How Different has Microfinance been from Traditional Banking?', *Development Policy Review*, 30(2): 187–210.

Wang, H., Yip, W., Zhang, L., Wang, L., and Hsiao, W. (2005). 'Community-based Health Insurance in Poor Rural China: The Distribution of Net Benefits', *Health Policy and Planning*, 20(6): 366–74.

World Bank (2014). *Global Financial Development Report 2014: Financial Inclusion*. Washington, DC: World Bank.

Young, N. (2015). 'Formal Banking and Economic Growth: Evidence from a Regression Discontinuity Analysis in India', Working Paper, Boston University, April.

Part C

Political Regimes and Economic Development

Political Regimes and Economic
Development

10 Aggregation, Ideology, and the Social Ordering of Caste

ROHINI SOMANATHAN

The discourse on poverty in India defines disadvantage primarily in terms of caste. India has the largest affirmative action programme in the world, with access to politics, public universities, and employment—all governed by caste quotas that are either written into the Indian Constitution or in laws enabled by its clauses. The justification and implementation of caste-preference relies on the existence of a social ordering of castes by privilege. I have two objectives in this essay. First, to show how the process of collecting and aggregating caste data in British India resulted in a distorted picture of the distribution of caste and power on the subcontinent. These distortions have already been documented by others and my purpose is to show how the very enterprise of large-scale data collection on social structure makes them inevitable. Second, to ask why caste became the principal axis of redistributive policy in India. I claim that the linking of caste and disadvantage arose from a particular confluence of ideas and events surrounding the struggle for independence and the years of constitution writing that followed it. These policies are now politically popular and difficult to dislodge even though their effectiveness in bringing about social justice is questionable.

I begin by using a stylized example to illustrate how, in culturally diverse and unequal societies, the process of compiling data on social groups can create orderings that are statistically correct but not locally meaningful. Implicit in these orderings is the assumption that the multitude of local units that comprise the whole are similar in settlement and in the relations between groups. The colonial enterprise of caste enumeration involved aggregation of very heterogeneous communities. Differences in social structure across villages within a district, districts within a province, and across the provinces, were hidden or muted in the caste statistics for British India. Some of the castes at the top of the hierarchy were absent from many areas and present only in small numbers in others. Ironically, many locally powerful groups were, and are, considered disadvantaged at a national level, partly due to these initial rankings.

Comprehensive caste enumeration was abandoned after Independence in 1947. Lists of *Exterior and Depressed Classes* created during the first half of the twentieth century were the basis of *Schedules* of castes and tribes in the Constitution which mandated quotas for their political representation and allowed state policy to direct spending towards them. Over time, new schedules of *Other Backward Classes* were created and more castes received preference. Although the original constitutional clauses for caste preference were in place only for the first decade following Independence, subsequent amendments have made them virtually permanent and the salience of caste in state psychology and functioning today is overwhelming. While courts in many countries, most notably the United States, have systematically eliminated explicit preference based on race and ethnicity, the Indian State continues to expand the ambit of affirmative action and has doubled the fraction of government jobs and university seats reserved for socially disadvantaged castes. Almost all spending on social programmes is earmarked by caste and powerful caste-based movements have emerged in which groups are pushing their claim to backwardness. After years of modernization and rapid economic expansion, one might well ask: Why *caste?*

My answer to this question is more involved, tentative, and particular to the Indian case. In brief, colonialism and western anthropology brought caste to the fore, creating and legitimizing caste orderings. The nationalist movement, desperate to move away from caste discrimination, believed this could only be done by directly addressing the *Untouchability* by which some castes were excluded from participating in society. Since these practices were rooted in notions of ritual purity, these writings pitted the Brahmins, at the top of the ritual order, against the Outcastes at the bottom. In this respect, those aspiring for a new India agreed with those emphasizing her arcane traditions.

The difference between local and western views related to the majority of castes in the middle. Herbert Risley, the census commissioner for British India in 1901, and French anthropologists in the tradition most popularly associated with Louis Dumont, posited a strict status hierarchy based on ritual standing. The nationalists and constitution makers, most famously Gandhi and Ambedkar, were concerned primarily with the stigma attached to groups at the bottom. The constitution, framed under the leadership of Ambedkar, had mandated quotas in parliament for the Outcastes and for Aboriginal Tribes and also allowed for the preferential treatment of *socially and educationally backward classes of citizens* without defining backwardness in any precise terms. Over time, this term has been appropriated by many of the intermediate castes who have found it to be advantageous in competing for access to scarce resources.

Paradoxically, as the Indian State expanded caste-based spending, it knew less and less about the real relationship between caste and deprivation. Comprehensive caste enumeration by the census was abandoned for fear that it would make caste salient, and the goal of a casteless society more difficult to achieve. It was not, however, replaced by data on land, assets, and income which could have provided alternative measures of need. Nationally representative sample surveys have been used to estimate poverty since the 1950s, but they do not have any identifiers for caste. Tax coverage has, to this day, remained hopelessly incomplete and tax records cannot therefore form the basis for transfer programmes as they do in many other countries. Even if coverage expanded, tax returns could not be used to measure caste inequalities since they do not identify caste. The limited data that we do have on castes that were entitled to affirmative action suggests large and growing between-caste inequalities.

10.1 Aggregation and Ordering

I begin with a stylized example to highlight how the aggregation of data on caste by the colonial census could have created a very different impression of social ordering from the one that emerged from local village studies.

Consider a hypothetical region in which a population of 1,000 persons is spread across 10 villages of equal size. There are 3 social groups, label them A, B, and C. Their populations are 70, 630, and 300, respectively. When the groups are in the same location, they are clearly ranked by status, with A at the top and C at the bottom. The source of this status could be education, land, or anything else. If the social composition of all villages were identical, A would be the most influential everywhere and C the least. Suppose, however, that each village has an equal number of group C, but only one of the other two groups. We therefore have one village with A and C, while all others have B and C. Were we to consider the region as a whole we would generate a hierarchy of the three castes as in the identical village case, whereas in most villages, A would be absent and B would be dominant.

This example helps frame the central questions and disagreements in the study of caste in India. First, any attempt to classify caste in India as a whole, or even in a single state or province, has to confront the problem of classifying the thousands of reported caste names into a few manageable categories. Which castes comprise the different categories, A, B, and C or any small number of such categories? Second, at the village level various orderings are possible; ABC, AC, BC, and AB. Which of these comes closest to describing village settlements and their status orderings in India, in the past and in the present day? Finally, how do local orderings relate to global ones and which of these are relevant to egalitarian objectives?

10.2 Caste Rankings and Local Power

In British India, the census broadly used the four-fold *varna* classification of the ancient texts. In 1881, the year of the first caste census, enumerators were instructed: 'In the case of Hindus, enter the caste as Brahman, Rajput, &c.' Before entering the reported caste name, which was termed a *sub-caste*. (O'Donnell 1893: 186) In this ordering, *Brahmins* were followed by the *Rajputs* (the warrior classes), *Vaishyas* (tradesmen), and then *Shudras* that provided labour services to the other three. Outside the caste system were the *Untouchable* castes who performed a variety of degrading tasks and had limited contact with the rest of the village. Dirks (2001) argues that this view of status was formed largely under colonial rule:

> The idea that *varna*—the classification of all castes into four hierarchical orders with the Brahman on top—could conceivably organize the social identities and relations of all Indians across the civilizational expanse of the subcontinent was only developed under the peculiar circumstances of British colonial rule. Hierarchy, in the sense of rank or ordered difference, might have been a pervasive feature of Indian history, but hierarchy in the sense used by Dumont and others became a systematic value only under the sign of the colonial modern. (Chapter 1, p. 14)

His archival research in South India reveals the local nature of caste and power. Castes that had low status in some provinces were local rulers in others:

> The Tondaiman dynasty of Kallar kings wrested control over a significant swath of land in the central Tamil country between Tanjavur and Madurai in the last quarter of the seventeenth century. Whereas "Kallars" had been branded as thieves in much early Tamil literature and as criminals by the British far later under the Criminal Tribes Act, in Pudukottai—a little kingdom that became the only princely state in the Tamil-speaking region of southern India—they became the royal caste. (pp. 65–6)

This skepticism on arriving at a sensible ordering of castes was shared by many of those involved in early census operations. Kitts (1885) published the first compendium of castes in British India based on the Census of 1881 and writes in his Introduction that while the enumeration was designed to set the 'foundation for further research into the little known subject of Caste', it turned out to be

> a subject inquiring into which investigators have been gravelled, not for lack of matter, but from its abundance and complexity, and the lack of all rational arrangement. The subject as a whole has indeed been a mighty maze without a plan. (p. v)

The expense and energy involved in caste enumeration limited the collection of other data that could have been used to create alternative rankings of status or power. Education by caste was recorded carefully in most census years and we do find, on average, that the ritually high castes were also more literate, although literacy ranks did not follow the ritual ones. Of the two dozen castes ranked by literacy in the census report of 1931, Brahman males came in fifth, with 44 per cent able to read and write. This was about forty times higher than rates among the Untouchable castes and Aboriginal Tribes, which were typically around 1 per cent. (Hutton 1933: 330) No data on land or income were collected so we do not have much detail on how these varied by caste.

It is highly unlikely that the overall ranking by ritual purity or literacy reflected power relations in most villages because of the demographic distribution of castes and factors that determined their local influence. The second and third categories in the *varna* system did not exist in many parts of the country and Brahmins formed only 5 per cent of the population between 1891 and 1931, implying their absence or negligible presence in most villages. M. N. Srinivas, a pioneer of social anthropology in India, describes the dominance of the *Okkaliga* caste of peasants in his study of the south Indian village of Rampura in the early fifties:

> The Peasants in Rampura enjoy more than one element of dominance. Numerically they are the biggest caste ... [and] own more land than all the other castes put together ... The ritual rank of Peasants is not very high. While they do rank above the Untouchables and such low castes as the Swineherd, they are well below the Brahmins and Lingayats. In terms of *Varna* they are Shudras ... But this does not mean much in Rampura ... Even on ceremonial occasions, outside pollution contexts, Peasants are shown respect by Lingayats and Brahmins (Srinivas 1959: 2).

Srinivas describes how the spread of democracy through elections to village councils after Independence further increased the influence of the *Okkaligas* who used their power to actively obstruct government efforts to improve the position of the poorest castes in the village and acted as arbiters of justice in village disputes, even when they involved ritually high castes. Rampura seems to typify the *BC* village. High castes, while present in small numbers were not influential. Areas where the *ABC* ordering prevailed were typically those where the upper castes were in larger numbers and owned most of the village land. Even in such cases, their influence seems to have waned with the spread of institutions of local governance that followed the end of colonial rule. André Béteille discusses the changing role of power in one such village:

In the traditional set-up, power within the village was closely linked with landownership and high ritual status. Until a generation ago the Brahmin *mirasdars* [landowners] enjoyed decisive dominance. Today the Non-Brahmins play a much more important part in organising collective activities in the village. The control of the *panchayat* [village council] has been wrested by them from the Brahmins. Nor is caste the only factor today in the control of political organs. Party membership, contacts with officials, and ties of patronage are factors which play an increasingly important part. (Béteille 1965: 183)

We do not know enough about the distribution of castes at the village level to know preponderance of each of the village types described in section 10.1. Village-level data was not tabulated during the colonial period and castes were not comprehensively enumerated after it. The Indian Human Development Survey of 2005 is a nationally representative survey of about 40,000 households and is one of the few that records caste and religion in 8 broad categories.[1] Brahmins form 4 per cent of the rural population in the 1,485 villages surveyed and are only found in a quarter of all villages. In nearly 40 per cent of villages, neither Brahmins nor any of the other ritually high castes are found and in 60 per cent of villages they are less than a tenth of total households. Based on these types of crude approximations, the answer to our second question would be that dominance in village affairs did not closely follow ritual status.

10.3 Bengal in 1891: An Illustration

Bengal was one of the largest administrative units of India during the colonial period. Its area covered that of several modern Indian states and the entire country of Bangladesh. With over 75 million persons in 1891, it comprised 26 per cent of the 287 million-strong population of undivided India. (Baines 1893: 15) The Superintendent of Census Operations for Bengal in 1891 noted in the opening page of his report, 'Amongst countries, whose populations have been scientifically enumerated, the United States of America stand second to the Lower Provinces of Bengal in number of inhabitants.' (O'Donnell 1893: 1)

Table 10.1 provides population statistics for Bengal in 1891. The two-thirds of the population that was *Hindu* or *Animist* was divided into 171

---

[1] See http://www.ihds.umd.edu for details on the survey.

Table 10.1 Population Statistics, Bengal 1891

Characteristic	Statistic
Total population	74,673,824
Hindu (+ Animist)	50,577,075
Muslim	23,658,347
Other	407,944
Average Hindu literacy rate	4.3%
No. of districts	49
No. of Hindu castes	171
Median districts per caste	5
Median castes per district	39

Source: Author's computations based on Census of India, 1891 (Bengal volumes)

distinct castes.[2] These castes were often geographically localized: While the largest castes were found in most districts, half of the castes were found in no more than five of the 49 districts of Bengal.

Table 10.2 lists the twenty most numerous Hindu castes, ordered by literacy levels. Inequalities in education were extreme. Literacy rates for the Kayasths were 200 times those for the Santhals, with just one in a thousand Santhals able to read and write. The Santhals were listed as a *Scheduled Tribe* in 1950 and it was these extreme inequalities that justified early efforts at affirmative action.

Table 10.3 lists the twenty castes of Bengal that reported the highest literacy rates in 1891. In the terminology of Section 10.1, these might be thought of as the *A* in an *ABC* ordering of the castes of Bengal. Most of these castes have relatively small populations and are absent in a majority of the 49 districts of Bengal. For instance, the highest-ranked caste, the Baidyas are present in less than half the districts of Bengal, while the next in rank, the Agarwalas and Joshis are found in just seven and four districts, respectively. Only the Kayasth, Brahmans, and Banias among the top twenty castes are found in nearly all the 49 districts. The second column of the table lists the current classification of each caste for purposes of affirmative action. Despite being among the communities with the best educational outcomes in 1891, as many as eight of the

---

[2] The Census tables ignore castes that contributed less than 1,000 persons to a district's population.

Table 10.2   Top 20 Castes by Population, Bengal 1891

Caste	Category	Literacy	Rank	Population	Districts
Kayasth		22.2%	4	1,534,391	46
Brahman		19.4%	5	2,776,809	49
Bania		12.3%	9	811,428	44
Rajput		6.4%	31	1,500,279	40
Babhan		6.1%	32	1,221,364	14
Kaibartha	OBC/SC	5.9%	33	2,228,823	36
Teli	OBC	4.9%	42	1,511,084	45
Khandait		4.5%	48	668,780	8
Kamar	OBC	4.0%	52	736,201	46
Tanti	OBC	3.6%	58	941,424	45
Koch	OBC	3.2%	61	1,785,416	10
Kumhar	OBC	2.9%	68	744,752	48
Yadav	OBC	2.5%	73	4,990,429	47
Namasudra		2.4%	75	1,765,617	29
Kurmi	OBC	2.2%	79	1,316,678	33
Koiri	OBC	1.9%	87	1,187,642	19
Bagri	SC/OBC	1.3%	104	789,785	19
Chamar	SC	0.6%	140	1,471,705	45
Dusadh	SC	0.4%	149	1,181,440	19
Santhal	ST	0.1%	164	844,326	6

Source: Author's computations based on Census of India, 1891 (Bengal volumes).
The second column is based on the current classification of Backward Classes by the
Government of India.

20 communities listed in our table are considered *backward* enough to
be targeted for affirmative action as Other Backward Classes or OBCs.
Lists of castes eligible for affirmative action vary by state, and some castes
such as the Kaibartha are considered Scheduled Castes in some areas and
OBCs in others. Those with missing entries in this column are not eligible
for affirmative action of any kind.

Table 10.4 illustrates the district-level variation in caste orderings that
is hidden by the province-level aggregation. This table includes one representative caste from each of the ritual ranks of the *varna* system: Brahmans
(a priestly caste, ranked highest), Rajputs (ranked second, as Kshatriya or
warriors), Banias (ritually ranked third, as Vaishya or merchants), Telis
(oil-pressers, ritually ranked fourth as Shudra), and Chamars, traditionally regarded as Outcastes. I restrict attention to the 35 districts of Bengal

Table 10.3   Top 20 Castes by Literacy, Bengal 1891

Caste	Category	Literacy	Population	Districts
Baidya		28.6%	74,679	21
Agarwala		24.6%	12,302	7
Joshi		24.5%	18,119	4
Kayasth		22.2%	1,534,391	46
Brahman		19.4%	2,776,809	49
Sunri	OBC/SC	18.5%	141,450	12
Baishnab		15.1%	17,053	1
Komati		13.5%	2,943	2
Bania		12.3%	811,428	44
Karnam		11.5%	3,834	1
Aguri	OBC	11.3%	83,614	5
Oriya	OBC	11.3%	49,197	7
Darji	OBC	10.9%	1,235	1
Tambuli	OBC	10.8%	99,019	22
Newar		9.9%	4,953	1
Patra	OBC	9.5%	27,314	3
Agrahari	OBC	8.0%	7,933	5
Jaiswar		7.9%	3,353	3
Kansari	OBC	7.8%	30,189	10
Sunawar		7.8%	5,156	1

Source: Author's computations based on Census of India, 1891 (Bengal volumes). The second column is based on the current classification of Backward Classes by the Government of India.

in which all these castes are present. The literacy ordering for this group of five castes at the district level is the same as the province-level orderings in only 10 out of these 35 districts. The last two columns list the number of districts in which there are departures from the province-level ordering. We see that the Telis, who had a province literacy rank of 42 and a literacy rate of less than 5 per cent in 1891, did better than either the Rajputs or the Banias in 10 of the 35 districts, and did better than both of them in another three. They are currently classified as one of the OBCs.

These examples illustrate the difficulties in creating a meaningful ordering of castes over large regions. The problems highlighted here are magnified when considering the country as a whole and looking at changes over long periods of time.

Table 10.4   Variation in Rank Ordering of Major Castes, Bengal 1891

Caste	Literacy Rate	Districts with Rank Changes		Castes (No. of Districts)	
		Improve	Worsen	Supersede	Superseded by
Brahman	19.4%	0	5	None	Bania (3)
					Rajput (2)
Bania	12.3%	3	14	Brahman (3)	Rajput (9)
					Teli (3)
					Rajput and Teli (2)
Rajput	6.4%	11	11	Bania (9)	Teli (7)
				Brahman and Bania (2)	Teli and Chamar (4)
Teli	4.9%	13	1	Rajput (8)	Chamar (1)
				Bania (2)	
				Bania and Rajput (3)	
Chamar	0.6%	5	0	Rajput (4)	None
				Teli (1)	

Source: Author's computations based on Census of India, 1891 (Bengal volumes)
Note: Based on the 35 districts of Bengal where all five castes were present.

10.4 State Policy and Caste

We can now turn to the question of why, in spite of all the evidence on the local dominance of groups with low ritual status, caste orderings developed under colonial rule remained relevant to state policy in India.

There has been a longstanding academic debate on the relevance of ritual versus power rankings and this has had enduring effects on contemporary conceptions of caste and disadvantage. On the one hand were western writers, starting with Herbert Risley and Célestin Bouglé and ending with Louis Dumont, who argued that there was a 'linear order of castes from A to Z' with 'systematically graduated authority'[3] and 'the eminence or baseness of a caste is determined above all by the relations which it has with the Brahman caste.'[4] This was countered by village studies by

[3] Dumont (1970), chapter 2, p. 57 and chapter 3, p. 65.
[4] Bouglé (1971), p. 22.

Indian sociologists such as those by Béteille and Srinivas described earlier. When Srinivas observed that local power relations did not conform to the ritual hierarchy, he coined the term *dominant caste* as distinct from castes with high *ritual status*. Dumont's response to this terminology was to disassociate status and power orderings:

> [T]he solution is obvious: the caste system is characterized in principle by an absolute hierarchical distinction between hierarchy itself and the distribution of power. Let us therefore recognize this real duality by speaking of status on the one hand, of dominance on the other without superfluous and confusing epithets, as status is always religious, dominance always politico-economic. (Dumont, 1966)

This legitimization of the ritual hierarchy rather than one defined by land, income, and power occurred partly because western views were reinforced during the nationalist movement precisely by those who tried their best to eradicate the caste system. B.R. Ambedkar, the draftsman of the Constitution, wrote in the mid-1930s of the caste system as a feature of an uncivilized society:

> [The] caste system is not merely a division of labourers which is quite different from division of labour—it is a hierarchy in which the divisions of labourers are graded one above the other. (Ambedkar, 1968: 37)

His academic writings had earlier argued that the caste system itself was the result of Brahmanical practices of exclusion being imitated by other groups. He believed therefore that the problem of social exclusion had to be tackled head-on, that constitutional provisions for equality would not be enough to allow the stigmatized castes to function as equal citizens. While Ambedkar was pitted against Gandhi on many important questions of nation-building, Gandhi too was committed to ending *Untouchability* which arose from ritual norms. There was therefore widespread agreement on the need for special attention to ostracized castes. This led to the mandated political representation of groups later termed as the *Scheduled Castes* and *Scheduled Tribes*. The former category was based on lists of *Exterior Castes* in the 1931 census and the latter on Aboriginal Tribes that 'remained in their primitive uncivilized state in a land which boasts of a civilization thousands of years old'. (Ambedkar 1968: 46)

These provisions led, over time, to a new type of *ABC* ordering with *B* consisting of a wide range of intermediate castes, including many of those termed *dominant* in village studies, demanding to be classified as *backward* in order to receive preferential treatment in public universities and government hiring. These new contests for backwardness are specifically Indian, yet originate in much earlier attempts to first build and then dismantle a sociological model for India with caste at its center.[5] Inequalities by income and wealth in India are extreme and access to the benefits of the economic expansion of the last decade has been uneven. Over a quarter of the village population is still below the national poverty line.[6] While we do not have any comprehensive studies of the mobility within the system, we do observe a striking divergence within the category of Scheduled Castes which have been monitored closely and over many decades as part of the affirmative action programme. In 1931, only about 1 per cent of the population in most of these groups was literate. Today, the most successful among these groups have school completion rates that are 36 times higher than the least educated. The *Patels*, a dominant caste group in Gujarat and among the most prosperous of the Indian diaspora is now demanding that they either be given affirmative action or that the system of caste-preference be dismantled. These protests turned violent and the capital city of Ahmedabad was under curfew to restore peace. Questions of caste and social justice clearly need rethinking. Creating the political and intellectual space for these debates has acquired new urgency.

[5] Early debates on the inclusion of backward classes in the constitution are found in Galanter (1984), chapter 6. Recent caste-based movements for inclusion in this category are discussed in Somanathan (2010).

[6] Based on estimates released by the Indian Planning Commission in July 2013.

References

Ambedkar, B.R. (1968). *Annihilation of Caste* (India: Bheem Patrika Publications).

Baines, J.A. (1893). *Census of India, 1891: General Report* (London: Government of India).

Beteille, Andre (1965). *Caste, Class, and Power: Changing Patterns of Stratification in a Tanjore Village* (California: University of California Press).

Bougl´e, C´elestin (1971). *Essays on the Caste System* (Cambridge: Cambridge University Press).

Dirks, N.B. (2001). *Castes of Mind: Colonialism and the Making of Modern India* (Princeton: Princeton University Press).

Dumont, L. (1970). *Homo Hierarchicus: An Essay on the Caste System* (Chicago: University of Chicago Press).

Dumont, Louis (1966). 'A fundamental problem in the sociology of caste'. *Contributions to Indian Sociology* 9(1): 3.

Galanter, Marc (1984). *Competing Equalities: Law and the Backward Classes in India* (Delhi: Oxford University Press).

Hutton, J.H. (1933). *Census of India, 1931, Vol. I* (Delhi).

Kitts, E.J. (1885). *A Compendium of the Castes and Tribes Found in India* (Byculla: Education Society's Press).

O'Donnell, Charles James (1893). *Census of India, 1891*, vol. 3 (Calcutta: Bengal Secretariat Press).

Somanathan, Rohini (2010). 'The demand for disadvantage'. In *Culture, Institutions, and Development: New Insights into an Old Debate*, ed. Jean-Philippe Platteau and Robert Peccoud (London: Routledge).

Srinivas, M.N. (1959). 'The dominant caste in Rampura'. *American Anthropologist* 61(1): 1–16.

11 Enlightened Autocrats

Lessons from Bold Experiments in the Lands of Islam

JEAN-PHILIPPE PLATTEAU

Among his many concerns with institutions and their effects on long-term economic development, Pranab Bardhan has always paid great attention to the role of political regimes. He has thus questioned the superiority of Western democracy that was a dominant theme in much of the development literature (see, in particular, Bardhan 1993). Of course, he did not idealize autocracy, since he well understood that authoritarian regimes may be the worst solution if the ruler does not have the qualities of a good leader or a benevolent despot. In the opposite case where he is, autocracy holds important advantages over democracy because of its hierarchical chain of command and its long time horizon: decision-making is quicker, the continuity of state policies is better guaranteed and, hence, drastic reforms with long-term effects are more easily undertaken. On the negative side, autocracy involves a lack of transparency and account-ability and, moreover, it is often fraught with uncertainties surrounding the autocrat's succession (or the undue extension of his rule into old age). Success of a benevolent autocracy hinges upon the degree of legitimacy of the regime and, in the absence of a free election process, this legitimacy must come from another source susceptible of enhancing people's trust that the autocrat acts for the common good.

Clearly, it is obviously impossible to say which system, democracy, or autocracy is more conducive to development as long as the precise char-acteristics of each system have not been spelled out carefully. Historical manifestations of both systems can indeed display important variations that matter for long-term development and capital accumulation. The conclusion reached by Przeworski et al. (2000) should thus not be a cause of surprise:

> There is little difference in favor of dictatorships in the observed rates of growth. And even that difference vanishes once the conditions under which dictatorships and democracies existed are taken into account. Albeit in omniscient retrospect, the entire controversy seems to have been much ado about nothing.
>
> (Przeworski et al. 2000: 178; see also Przeworski and Limongi 1993).

A large body of literature has stressed the virtues of state-led indus-trialization, which often subsumes the presence of an authoritarian state elite at the country's helm. An influential model of developmental autocracy is modern Japan after the Meiji Revolution. Brought about by lower samurai (former warriors) and the intelligentsia, it was a revolution aimed at building a modern state and initiating fast economic growth. Such a drastic move required the removal of the existing feudal system deemed to be an obstacle to the modernization of the country (Morishima 1982: 89). Other experiences of state-led development have received a lot of attention, and they all belong to East Asia, a region where religion is not salient: Taiwan, South Korea, Singapour, Hong Kong, and post-1978 China (Amsden 1989; Rodrik 1997; Seth 2016). In these countries, not unlike what happened in Meiji Japan, a strong and enlightened state prevailed that fostered the emergence of a nucleus of industrial capitalists, transformed traditional institutions, regulated the market, and harnessed the country's resources for the long-term advantages.

This chapter is concerned not with East Asia but with the Middle East and other Muslim countries. I have argued elsewhere that most post-war political regimes in Muslim lands have been autocracies of a non-benevolent kind (Platteau 2017). More precisely, these lands have been ruled by autocrats who were mostly preoccupied with maintaining themselves in power by cozying up to conservative Muslim clerics and defeating the secular opposition from the left. Because they were deeply corrupt, they did not succeed in creating the conditions for political stability and sustainable, long-term prosperity. Notable exceptions to that rule are regimes that enlightened despots established during the last century in order to meet the challenge of modern growth and development, namely, the regimes of Mustapha Kemal (Atatürk) in Turkey, Nabib Bourguiba in Tunisia, king Amanullah and Marxist emulators in Afghanistan, the regime of General Abd al-Karim Qasim (1958–1963), and the first part of the succeeding regime of Saddam Husayn (until the late 1970s) in Iraq. Lack of space forces us to focus on the first two regimes, and refer the reader to Platteau (2017) for a discussion on the cases of Afghanistan and Iraq (see pp. 235–51, 400–2). This choice is justified by the fact that unlike in Turkey and Tunisia, the rule of the enlightened Afghan rulers was of short duration, while in Iraq major international factors (Khomeini's revolution in Iran, the war with Iran, and the invasion of Kuwait) have played a key role in the transformation of the regime.

Although Turkey and Tunisia have evinced a lot of political stability under enlightened autocrats, the hold of the Kemalists on power came to an abrupt end when the first genuinely democratic election was organized in Turkey in 2007, and the political successor of Bourguiba, Zine al-Abidine Ben Ali, was ousted from power on the occasion of the Jasmine Revolution in 2011. It is therefore interesting to examine these experiences in order to gain an understanding of the reasons that led to their demise. Did some adverse circumstances beyond their control prevent the enlightened autocrats from achieving sustainability, or is it the case that they committed serious mistakes that made their regime uselessly vulnerable? In this chapter, it is argued that the second possibility provides the most reasonable answer, leading to the conclusion that not only intentions but also the methods adopted to fulfill them matter critically. In itself, such a conclusion seems to be rather trivial, and it seems to have wide application to many revolutionary experiences attempted during the last centuries. However, elaborating the argument in the context of societies whose culture is largely framed in religious terms and where religious clerics are omnipresent, should make a worthy contribution to the existing literature. This is especially true nowadays since the question of Islam and its potentially negative effects on development is heavily debated.

The outline of the chapter is as follows. In Section 11.1, key relevant features of Islam are highlighted before we sketch a theory that will guide the subsequent analysis and discussion. It belongs to a recent economic literature that pays attention to the specific role of the military in actual or potential dictatorships (Egorov and Sonin 2014; Besley and Robinson 2010; Acemoglu et al. 2009 2010; Leon 2014, 2017; and Aney and Ko 2015). Where our originality lies is in the focus on a three-player relationship—between an autocratic ruler, a centralized army, and a decentralized set of religious clerics. In Section 11.2, the core of this chapter, the experiences of autocratic enlightenment in Kemalist Turkey and Tunisia are presented. Section 11.3 then draws the central lessons from the review and raises a number of important challenges. The conclusion follows.

11.1 A Theory of Political–Religious Relations

Before sketching the theory underlying this chapter, we first need to highlight a number of key characteristics of Islam that must be kept in mind while going through the subsequent theoretical and empirical analysis.

11.1.1 Key Characteristics of Islam

When Islam is seen as both a religious doctrine and an organization, three characteristics emerge: The decentralized nature of Islam's organization, the heterogeneity of the clerical body, and the general principle of estrangement from politics. These characteristics will serve as pillars of the theoretical scaffolding used in this study.

The Absence of a Centralized Organization

In Islam, no ecclesiastical body has ever existed nor any vertical chain of command to direct the believers: Muslim believers directly refer to God and its law on earth, the sharia. There is therefore no need for a class of priests acting as intermediaries between God and the believers, nor for any centralized church to tell the priests what to believe and what to teach. It is revealing that the values of the sharia privilege individual rights and responsibilities (Berkey, 2003: 214). It is because the state was Islamic, and was considered as such by the founder of the faith, that no religious institution separate from the state emerged and was considered necessary: 'The state was the church, the church was the state, and God was head of both, with the Prophet as his representative on earth' (Lewis, 2002: 113, 115).

A direct implication is that the only vital division in Islam is between sectarian and apostate:

> Apostasy was a crime as well as a sin, and the apostate was damned both in this world and the next. His crime was treason —desertion and betrayal of the community to which he belonged, and to which he owed loyalty. His life and property were forfeit. He was a dead limb to be excised (Lewis, 1995: 229).

For the rest,

> The absence of a single, imposed, dogmatic orthodoxy in Islam was due not to an omission but to a rejection—the rejection of something that was felt by Sunni Muslims to be alien to the genius of their faith and dangerous to the interests of their community ... The profession of Islam ... is that God is one and Muhammad is his Prophet. The rest is detail (pp. 229–30).

In other words, tolerance must be extended to all those who 'reach the required minimum of belief', while intolerance is required towards all those who deny the unity or existence of God, the atheists and polytheists (p. 230).

This representation of Islam is confirmed by Abdelwahab El-Affendi (2011) who points out that Islamic teachings cannot be regarded

> as a long catalogue of "off-the-shelf" rules that could be consulted on every occasion ... not only did Islam *not* have a rule for every conceivable situation, but it is moreover *a fundamental rule of Islam not to have such rules*. This leaves the widest possible margin for initiative and fresh thinking on the most appropriate ethical conduct in all areas ... (pp. 19–20).

In Islam, precise legal injunctions, when they exist, tend to be particularly rigid yet they are not necessarily uniform (see earlier), and they are few. These few legal enunciations essentially concern private matters, more particularly family relationships (for example, law of inheritance, polygamy, and divorce by repudiation) and civil transactions (for example, prohibition of usury, and inalienability of landed property constituted as a religious endowment). In fact, many of them are not legal injunctions, but rather consist of moral principles requiring and offering a wide area of discretion and initiative'. The idea that Islamic teachings cover every facet of life and offer ready guidance to the faithful in most circumstances of their life, writes 'is contradicted by unequivocal Quranic verses demanding that believers should not ask too many questions of the Prophet' (p. 19).

In the same vein, Rahman (1982) characterized the Islamic law thus:

> [I]t is not, strictly speaking law, since much of it embodies moral and quasi-moral precepts not enforceable in any court ... Islamic law ... is on closer examination a body of legal opinions or an endless discussion of the duties of a Muslim, rather than a neatly formulated code or codes ... this body ... presents a bewildering richness of legal opinions and hence a great range and flexibility in the interpretation and actual formulation of the sharia (p. 32).

An interesting contrast thus emerges between Muslim and Christian believers. The former appear to be both more and less constrained than the latter. Muslim believers are more constrained in the sense that all aspects of their lives fall under the purview of the sharia, which is 'a composite science of law and morality' and has therefore a much wider scope and purpose than a simple legal system as conceived in the West (Coulson, 1964: 83). But they are less constrained because, in strictly religious matters, they are generally not subject to precise and rigid rules (see earlier).

Since the main role of a centralized church structure typically consists of enforcing a well-defined religious doctrine, it is not surprising that the absence of such an organization in Muslim countries is associated with a large measure of flexibility in the approach to Islamic tenets. This depiction of Islam is not accepted by radical reformers or Islamists, though. For them, indeed, the letter of the scriptures, and not only the spirit, must be strictly followed. No tolerance ought therefore to be displayed towards those who allow themselves to freely interpret the words of God in the way deemed most convenient for them. The intolerance of this scripturalist and puritan brand of Islam results from the fact that, like any fundamentalist movement in other religions, it attempts to reformulate the project of modernity in the presence of a felt threat to their culture and identity. Standing for Islamic orthodoxy, their avowed aim is to re-establish a purified order that rigorously conforms to the injunctions of primeval Islam. In order to rally support, they project the image of a relentless attack against the Muslim community and its religious symbols by a malevolent dominant culture pervaded by corruption and debauchery. In the process, they create a feeling of persecution with all the attendant anxiety (Kakar, 1996: 179–80).

Heterogeneity of the Clerics

Even leaving puritanical Islam aside, a deep heterogeneity exists among the Muslim clerics. An important distinction can be made here between 'high' and 'low' Islams. The 'high' Islam is essentially comprised of the ulama. These are the individuals trained in the Islamic law: The scholars who compiled the sharia, the judges who apply it in the Islamic courts (the qadis), the legal experts who advise the judges (the muftis), and the teachers who educate the Muslim community (the mudarris) (Cleveland, 2004: 27–8; Gleave and Kermeli, 1997). In short, they are the jurists-cum-theologians in charge of interpreting the intent of God's revelations and assessing the legality of the actions of individuals on the basis of their compliance with God's commands (Coulson, 1964: 76–8). Interpretation and judgement were especially needed because many reported hadiths (actions and sayings of the Prophet) appear contradictory and their reliability has not always been well-established (Lee 2014: 57).

Although the ulama do not form a religious establishment that can declare by fiat which is the correct interpretation of the Quran, and their opinions were therefore purely consultative, they were able to provide a measure of unity to law and doctrine by codifying and transmitting religious knowledge. There is no doubt that they have always exercised substantial control and influence over how Muslims interpret Islam, especially in the big (urban) centres of the Muslim lands. Where no consensus was in fact achieved, variant opinions were recognized as equally valid attempts to define God's will, meaning that varying solutions were ratified as equally probable interpretations of God's intent (Coulson, 1964: 78--9). The outcome of this process was not only the appearance of four different schools of Islam but also of different trends inside each school and of a wide range of idiosyncratic ways of combining the sharia with local customs and long-standing practices.[1]

Because the Quran did not in fact enunciate many general principles, and because the solutions and rulings it offers are mostly based on the specific socio-cultural conditions prevailing during the time of the Prophet, Islam (like Judaism) leaves a rather ample margin of freedom for the interpretation of the sacred texts by the ulama. Despite efforts to unify elements of the Islamic doctrine, rules have therefore remained widely scattered throughout the works of many clerics. It follows that ulama act as guides whom believers freely choose for their ability to provide valuable advice based on their personal reputation and charisma.

The above characterization also applies to the clerics of 'low Islam', the mullahs or the heads of Sufi orders, for example. Yet, there is one aspect that distinguishes them from the official ulama: they are charged with the task of combining the Islamic teachings with local realities on the most decentralized level. These local-level representatives of Islam have always lived close to the people and therefore shared their day-to-day problems. This is what makes them especially sensitive to the constraints that ordinary people are confronted with in often harsh circumstances. This awareness makes the mullahs even more inclined than the ulama to temper the injunctions of official Islam with the local social norms, customs, and practices. In large parts of the Islamic world, customs have thus remained strongly resistant to Islamic law when the two stood in clear contradiction. When they did not, they were subtly amalgamated, giving rise to cultural hybridization (Bowen, 2003; Nelson, 2011; Platteau, 2017: 98–112). It is precisely this kind of amalgamation that is deemed totally unacceptable by Islamists, hence their antagonism against Sufi orders and mullahs.

---

[1] Divergences between the four officially recognized schools of Islam -Hanefite, Malekite, Shafeite, and Hanbalite- are often deeper than "mere variations of substantive doctrine", and strike "to the very roots of their juristic method and outlook" (Coulson, 1964: 98; see also Saint-Prot, 2008: 113-24). This is not surprising insofar as their individual characteristics were fashioned by their circumstances and places of origin, which explains why particular regions and populations of the empire tended to adhere to the same school. Yet, competitive hostility between those schools gradually gave way to a mutual tolerance eventually sanctioned by the classical doctrine of ijma.

Political Estrangement: The Rule and the Exceptions

The Quran does not cover genuine constitutional or administrative law (Anderson, 1979: 498). Besides mentioning that it is the duty of the ruler to ratify and enforce the standards of conduct prescribed by the law, it contains only two points about the proper system of government—consultation (meshverret) and obedience to authority (ulu'l emr)—and does not insist on any particular form of government (An-Naim, 2008: 199). Even if the ruler was unjust or impious 'it was generally accepted that he should still be obeyed, for any kind of order was better than anarchy' (Hourani, 1991: 144). The philosopher al-Ghazali (1058–1111) thus wrote that, if 'the jurisconsult serves as master and director of conscience for political authority in administrating and disciplining men so that order and justice may reign in this world', 'the tyranny of a sultan for a hundred years causes less damage than one year's tyranny exercised by the subjects against one another'. Therefore, 'Revolt was justified only against a ruler who clearly went against a command of God or His prophet' (cited from Hourani, 1991: 144). In short, communal strife (*fitna*) or chaos (*fawda*) is the most abhorred state and, to prevent it from emerging, despotism is justified. Religious authorities thus tolerate an oppressive or even an illegitimate political ruler as the lesser of two evils (An-Naim 2008: 52).

Throughout history, the message of social justice and the equality of men conveyed by Muhammad's preaching and preserved in the Quran came up against the realities of tribal and dynastic power (Ruthven 1997: 12). Accommodation with the existing power was seen as desirable by the ulama for whom denouncing a ruler who claimed to be a good Muslim was unjustified. In the words of N.J. Coulson (1964):

> Might, in fact, was right, and this was eventually recognized by the scholars in their denunciation of civil disobedience even when the political authority was in no sense properly constituted. Obviously, the effective enforcement of the whole system of sharia law was entirely dependent upon the whim of the de facto ruler (p. 83).

Gilles Kepel (2005) conveys the same Hobbesian idea when he writes that 'the excommunication of the prince, be he the worst of despots, was pronounced only exceptionally, for it opened the prospect of considerable disorder and created dangerous jurisprudential precedents' (p. 59). Excommunication was deemed an especially dangerous weapon because 'it could all too easily fall into the hands of sects beyond the control of the ulama and the clerics' (p. 56).

Clearly, the tradition is for Muslim clerics to refrain from getting entangled in politics in spite of the professed aim of Islam to establish a righteous world order and to provide guarantees against despotic rule. What is expected from the clerics is that they keep their distance from the rulers of the world while preserving their access to them and their influence upon them. This expectation reflects the primary concern of the jurists of Islam, which is to regulate the relationship of the individual Muslim with his God. The standards of conduct they formulated therefore represented a system of private, and not of public, law (Coulson 1964: 120, 123).[2]

There is now a need to qualify the above approach to politics in two important ways. First, it starkly contrasts with the view of the Islamists for whom no compromise can be struck with any state whose foundations are not thoroughly Islamic (Roy 1993: 495). Their approach rests on a fantasy, the ideal of a complete merger of religion and politics as allegedly observed during the times of the Caliphates. Second, the general principle of estrangement from politics suffers exceptions when circumstances are deemed extraordinarily bad, because the life of ordinary people has been turned into misery, the country has been sold to foreign interests, and/or corruption of the ruler and his clique has reached egregious proportions. Religious clerics, primarily those from the 'low Islam', can then rise into rebellion against the despot in the name of Islam.

11.1.2 Strategic Interactions Between an Autocrat, Decentralized Clerics and an Army

The model that serves as a scaffolding for the conceptual framework used in the following discussion is drawn from Auriol, Platteau, and Verdier (2020), which is itself an extension of the model developed by Auriol and Platteau in two companion papers (2017a, 2017b). Here, we present the basic assumptions and intuitions of this extended model. It is extended in the sense that it analyses the strategic interactions between an autocratic

---

[2] For example, in fiscal law, ulama were primarily concerned with those limited aspects of public finance which were deemed to constitute a man's obligations towards God, such as the payment of the zakat tax (Coulson, 1964: 124).

ruler, the clerics, and the military whereas the role of the latter was ignored in Auriol and Platteau.

The Ruler's Problem

The ruler maximizes his and his clique's income defined as a rent extracted from the national product net of all expenses related to the co-option of the clerics and the military, and to the defense expenditures. He is confronted with the risk of a popular rebellion led by clerics and the risk of a military coup. To mitigate these risks and foster political stability, he may not only seduce the clerics and/or the military, which he does by granting various material privileges, but he also chooses a defense budget that determines the strength of the national army. Moreover, he chooses the intensity of progressive institutional reforms which have a positive impact on economic growth but are susceptible of antagonizing the military and, even more likely, the (conservative) clerics. Think, in particular, of those reforms that challenge erstwhile rules and practices upheld and enforced by traditional authorities (including religious authorities): Reforms aimed at removing land access rules that hamper efficiency or maintain many people under feudal shackles; at emancipating individuals from the sway of communal or collective prescriptions; at replacing rules emphasizing status or loyalty by merit-based selection and promotion criteria; or at combating forms of social discrimination, especially against women and low caste members. By moderating such reforms, the autocrat therefore reduces the temptation of the clerics to instigate and organize a popular rebellion and, to a lesser extent, the temptation of the military to stage a coup. The more he practises reform restraint, the less he needs to resort to paying high perks to the army and the clerics and to equip himself with a strong army.

The Clerics

The clerics are agents whose function consists of, and prestige is derived from, enforcing respect of religious tenets and rituals. At the same time, they are seducible (or corruptible) but to a varying degree since they are heterogeneous. Their preferences, which reflect the trade-off between material benefits and moral uprightness, actually differ: At one extreme we find clerics who are rather easy to buy because they do not require ample material perks to betray their values while at the other extreme are radical clerics whose attachment to religious tenets is so strong that they need very high rewards to violate their principles. The autocrat has to decide the proportion of clerics whom he wants to co-opt, knowing that the higher this proportion the higher the price to pay.

Clerics constitute a potential threat to autocratic power, because they enjoy a lot of prestige among ordinary people and they are able to exert rebellious leadership if they decide to act in defence of these people's interests. As representatives of the supernatural world and as wise men possessing deep knowledge, their influence on the population is strong, especially in societies where most people are uneducated and strongly believe in the role of supernatural forces. However, as hinted at earlier, their willingness to engage in politics and become revolutionary leaders can be countered: There is thus ample evidence that Muslim clerics (not only the ulama but also the Sufi orders) may be quite responsive to material incentives and ready to enter into a cozy relationship with the sovereign. For example, among the privileges typically offered by the sultans of the Ottoman Empire stood out offices involving lucrative functions which included revenue generation and the administration of religious endowments that controlled vast tracts of land. Since the associated incomes were exempt from taxes, religious appointments were highly coveted, and religious families possessing long-standing honourable ancestries competed for the offices as well as for titles and tax farms. When they succeeded, they became a core component of the Ottoman nobility and a linchpin of provincial administration (Hourani 1991: 224–5; 1993; Coulson 1964).[3]

[3] Speaking again about the Ottoman Empire, Ira Lapidus wrote in the same vein:

"The biographies of scholars show that, with the elaboration of a bureaucratic hierarchy, interest in careers outweighed genuine piety and learning. The influence of entrenched families enabled them to promote their children into the higher grades of the educational and judicial hierarchies without having reached the proper preliminary levels, while theological students who could not find patronage were excluded. In the course of the eighteenth century the ulama became a powerful, politically conservative pressure group. As servants of the state the ulama no longer represented the interests of the people, nor protected them from the abuses of political power. No longer did they represent a transcendental Islamic ideal opposed to worldly corruption. Their integration into the Ottoman empire made them simply the spokesmen of Ottoman legitimacy" (Lapidus, 2002: 268).

For those conservative clerics who are rather prone to surrender their ideal of social justice in the name of social order and stability, the price of their submission is low, in contrast to the price demanded by less compromising clerics. If the autocrat chooses to co-opt only a fraction of the clerical body (the so-called 'official clerics'), he creates a divide between them and those who stand outside the ambit of the state. The latter belong to rather independent religious institutions (such as Sufi orders), operate outside of big cities and urban centres (such as rural mullahs), or they are self-appointed clerics and firebrands with no well-established organizational affiliation. As seen in Subsection 11.1.1, the division between official and non-official clerics is possible in the world of Islam because no hierarchy exerts authority over the whole clerical profession. As a consequence, the autocrat must deal with religious clerics individually, implying that he is interested in the marginal rather than the average cleric. This is in contrast to the major part of the world of Christianity where religion is centrally organized and represented by the head of a church with whom he can directly bargain. As shown by Auriol and Platteau (2017a, 2017b), progressive reforms are easier to achieve under the latter form of religious organization.

The Military

The military are important to cajole because they control the means of violent repression that an autocrat may need. They obey a hierarchical structure that resembles a centralized religion. Like the clerics, the men in uniform hold values: Their patriotic values may be more or less progressive depending on the extent to which their concept of the nation is rooted in modernity rather than in tradition. At the same time, they are sensitive to the appeal of material advantages. Specifically, they may care about direct transfers such as wages or defence budgets. They may also care about specific policies that provide them with economic gains, in particular the economic rents derived from productive assets that they are allowed to own and control. By offering them sufficient perks, the ruler can thus expect to buy the allegiance of the army (see, for example, Siddiqa 2017; Sayigh 2019). His problem is nonetheless more complicated because there are now two potential sources of opposition that need to be tamed to the best possible extent. Since resources are limited, the ruler may have hard choices to make. If the religion is decentralized, the option remains open that only a fraction of the clerics are co-opted at equilibrium.

Main Results

From the preceding summary account, it is obvious that the autocrat faces difficult trade-offs: Moderating reforms versus enhancing co-option, cajoling clerics versus cajoling the military, building a strong military to beat back clerics versus limiting the army's strength to avoid a coup. A central result of the equilibrium analysis undertaken by Auriol, Platteau, and Verdier (2020) is that although the autocrat always has an interest in co-opting the military, this is not necessarily true of the clerics. When the army size is fixed exogenously and it is too small (in the precise sense of being smaller than the threshold beyond which the military are able to crush a rebellion supported by the whole clerical body, which we call the exclusive co-option threshold), the autocrat chooses to co-opt the clerics in addition to the military. In the opposite case, he refrains from courting the clerics. In the range where the double co-option regime prevails, the wage bill paid to the military and the intensity of reforms increase with the army size. The impact on religious support is ambiguous because the positive effect caused by a greater deterrent power of the army is counteracted by the negative effect of a bolder reform programme. Under exclusive co-option of the military, reforms are always more important than under double co-option, as they are determined by the military's preferences only. When he chooses the intensity of reforms under the double co-option regime, the autocrat gives more weight to the aversion of the clerics than to the aversion of the military provided that the army is of a sufficiently small size.

When the autocrat can freely choose the size of the army, it is not necessarily the case that only the interests of the military will be taken into account. Consider the case where (i) the exclusive co-option threshold exceeds the threshold beyond which the military are tempted to stage a coup (against whatever type of government, civilian or religious), and (ii) the clerics are rather cheap to buy off not because they have a low aversion to reforms (on average) but because an absence of reforms does not entail significant economic costs (such as is typically true in countries endowed with rich mineral and oil resources). Then, the autocrat will simultaneously choose to seduce clerics and to equip himself with an army of moderate size. If condition (i) is fulfilled but not condition (ii), economic growth requires a progressive institutional environment, he will choose a large army size and ignore the clerics. Finally, when condition (ii) is violated (the threshold for the military coup exceeds the exclusive co-option threshold), the regime in which only the military are co-opted always prevails.

A more precise analysis of the influence of the different parameters of the model reveals that a regime of exclusive co-option of the military with bold reforms is more likely to be established when the initial intrinsic legitimacy of the autocrat is strong, the effectiveness of the army in repressing rebellions is high, religious organizations or groups are weak, and the aversion to reforms of the military and mainly the clerics is rather low. In the two empirical cases examined in Section 11.2, the initial popular legitimacy of the ruler was obviously very strong, and the loyalty of the military, police, and secret services was guaranteed. While Ataturk gained a lot of prestige from his military victory against Greek troops in the battle of the Dardanelles, Bourguiba came out of the anti-colonial struggle with a wide aura and his highly charismatic character helped him win much support in the population.

An Important Refinement

In the earlier presentation, the policy tool available to the autocrat is the intensity of progressive institutional reforms. More radical reforms are good for him (and his clique) to the extent that they generate a larger output from which he appropriates a fixed share. The cost is the antagonism the reforms create among the clerics (and the military), which needs to be compensated through the payment of perks that are subtracted from the output share accruing to the autocrat. Hence a trade-off. But there is another way for him to increase his rent, which is also susceptible of fostering anger among the clerics and the population: appropriating a higher share of a stagnant income through corruption and prebends. He must then choose a policy mix that includes both the extent of progressive reforms and the extent of corruption. This approach is followed in Auriol and Platteau (2017b), where it yields an interesting result: progressive reforms and rent-extracting policies are not necessarily substitutes. It is thus theoretically possible, and far from being an oddity, that the autocrat responds to a parametric change in the model by adopting more progressive reforms and simultaneously intensifying the extraction rate of the ensuing benefits. In so doing, he increases the antagonism of the clerics on a double count.

The image we have of an enlightened despot is one of an autocrat who is able to undertake progressive reforms and keep corruption under control. He can confront conservative forces that oppose reforms for the sake of preserving their traditional prerogatives and maintaining the existing social order. This he tends to do through repression rather than seduction. In our theoretical framework, this description points to two different regimes that are both characterized by a good measure of progressive institutional reforms. In the first regime, the autocrat dispenses with religious co-option altogether and he relies exclusively on his (loyal) army. In the second regime, by contrast, he uses double co-option in which only a small fraction of the clerics (those cheapest to buy off) is seduced, which does not prevent him from undertaking drastic reforms because he enjoys strong legitimacy. The evidence that we provide subsequently seems to suggest that the Kemalist rule in Turkey is closer to the first regime while Bourguiba's rule in Tunisia better fits the definition of the second regime.

11.2 The History of Recent Experiences of Autocratic Enlightenment in Muslim Countries

These two experiences have been sustained during many years yet have ended up badly in the sense that they were discontinued as a result of either a peaceful or a violent political reaction. The important point, however, is that all the achievements of the enlightened autocratic period were not abruptly erased. What is true is that the ruling political regime was shaken and hence the continuity of the reforms undertaken came under threat. In our framework where the autocrat has enough instruments to achieve political stability, such disruption can only result from 'mistakes' of the autocrat, or from an erroneous appreciation by his successor of the new situation created by the demise of a prestigious and charismatic leader (that is, a situation in which the ruler's legitimacy has suddenly fallen).[4] The mistakes can take on several forms, among which the following two seem to have played an important role. First, inequitable social

---

[4] Note that in Auriol and Platteau (2017a, 2017b), political instability is a possible equilibrium outcome if the autocrat chooses to seduce only a fraction of the clerics. This is not possible in the presence of an army, as in Auriol, Platteau, and Verdier (2010): there, a well-informed rational autocrat can always prevent a regime change by choosing the appropriate values for his instruments.

and economic policies and undue appropriation of national wealth by the ruling elite may have gone beyond tolerable limits. Added to progressive institutional reforms, they give rise to tensions and frustrations that the regime is not able to manage. Second, reforms may be implemented in a manner that make them particularly unacceptable for the conservative masses and/or some portions of the clerical body (the clerics most strongly identified with these masses), and hence particularly costly in terms of lost legitimacy for the regime.

While the first mistake may arise from an underestimation of the clerics' aversion to reforms (or from an underestimation of their rebellious strength relative to the army), the second mistake may well be the result of a misjudgment regarding the sensitivity of the clerics to procedures and not only outcomes. Whatever it is, the question as to which factors bear a significant influence on the acceptability or legitimacy of the reforms is one on which only detailed case studies can throw light. We are interested in learning whether the first or the second explanation is more pertinent and, in case of the latter, what aspects of implementation caused reforms to be unpopular. To elucidate this question, we now look at our case material.[5]

11.2.1 Case study 1: Mustapha Kemal Atatürk

A Cultural Revolution Based on Civilizational Change

After independence (October 1923), in their quest for a national identity that would replace the Ottoman one, Kemalist leaders of the new Republic of Turkey opted for far-reaching secularization. Mustapha Kemal and his circle belonged to the radical wing of the Young Turks who believed implicitly in a popularized version of nineteenth-century European positivism. In their eyes, only scientific rationalism could form the basis for the modernization leap Turkey would have to make. What they wanted to achieve was a genuine social and cultural revolution: It was to be founded on principles entirely different from those espoused by the Ottomans who failed to successfully compete with the advanced West. This necessitated that a medieval social system, based for centuries on Islam, be swept away and replaced by a new system based on modern

---

[5] The following account is largely inspired from Platteau, 2017 : Chap. 9.

Western civilization (Zürcher 2010: 232; Kinross 2001: 377). The revolution was meant not only to erase the 'high' Islamic civilization but also to transform the culture of 'low Islam' dominant among the masses. Indeed, European civilization was seen as indivisible and therefore impossible to adopt in any piecemeal manner. Hence, there was no need to attempt any harmonization of European with Turkish culture (Kandiyoti 1991: 40; Zürcher 2010: 149; Kaya 2013: 12–13). In the words of Abdullah Cevdet, 'civilization means European civilization, and it must be imported with both its roses and its horns' (cited from Lewis, 1968: 236).

It is therefore not surprising that secularism became interpreted not only as a separation of state and religion but also as the removal of religion from public life and the establishment of complete state control over religious institutions (White 2013: 28). In order to achieve the ambitious objective of suppressing religious collective identity, an extreme, even racist, form of nationalism was diffused. It was anchored in historical myths extolling the grandeur of a pristine Turkish nation originated from Anatolia, considered as 'the heartland of Islam'. The apparent contradiction inherent in this mythological representation is overcome once it is realized that Islam was used as an identity marker largely deprived of its religious meaning. Indeed, the nation was defined primarily through ethnicity (in terms of race and language), on the basis of a 'Holy Trinity' consisting of being simultaneously 'Sunni-Muslim-Turk'. In contrast to the more tolerant Ottoman policies, under the Kemalist regime Turks converting to Christianity would automatically lose their Turkish identity while Christians (Armenians, Greeks, Circassians, Georgians, and so forth) and Jews would not become Turkish by converting to Islam (Kaya 2013: 13; White 2013: 31, 107). It is in the name of the doctrine of the 'Holy Trinity' that racial purges, including the Armenian genocide and the slaughter of Kurdish-speaking Alawites (in 1938), were condoned and encouraged.

Personalized Authoritarianism Backed by a Strong Army

The Kemalist regime rapidly became authoritarian and even totalitarian. On 12 August 1930, the Free Republican Party (FRP) was created by Ali Fethi Okyar, a friend of Atatürk, with the latter's total support. This was with a view to establishing a democratic system with an opposition party allowed to contest the People's Party (PP) inside which Mustafa Kemal had almost unlimited power. But this experience proved to be short-lived. The reason why it was abruptly terminated, as early as on 17 November 1930, is that it had revealed in a short time the widespread discontent in the country and the unpopularity of the PP. Enormous support for the FRP, which gathered socialist and liberal opponents to top-down rule and religious opponents to secularization, showed that the PP's project of social and cultural modernization had not been accepted by the mass of the population (Zürcher, 2010: 255–6). Interestingly, it is Okyar himself who decided to dissolve the FRP on the ground that more time was needed for Kemalist reforms to be fully consolidated and for the reforming regime to be in a position to withstand the voice of opposition. His move marked the return to the pre-1930 situation in which any voice of dissent would be subject to severe disciplinary measures and all forms of (independent) civil society organizations were eliminated to be replaced with new organizations under the control of the single ruling party (pp. 214, 252–3). In short, the government, the bureaucracy, and the army were forming a single body with Mustafa Kemal as the indisputable head, and in the revolutionary process the army was granted the leading role as the paramount protector of Kemalist values.

State Control Over Religion

Modernization of Turkey was perceived as implying a total eradication of the country's Ottoman and Arab legacy. A first type of reforms were guided by the idea that, unlike the Tanzimat reforms of the late Ottoman empire which resulted in the coexistence of secular and Islamic schools, courts, and laws, institutional change under Kemalism was about outright elimination of autonomous Islamic institutions. The reform movement was actually started in the 1820s and 1830s under sultan Mahmut II, continued during the succeeding decades (the French commercial code was adopted in 1850, and a new civil code based mainly on the Hanafi Law in 1867), and almost completed between 1913 and 1918 under the rule of the Young Turks and their Committee of Union and Progress (CUP). Thus, even before the proclamation of the Republic of Turkey and the abolition of the Caliphate, major institutional reforms had been undertaken. Most noticeably, in spite of the strong resistance of the ulama, the role of Islam had been limited almost exclusively to the realm of family law. When the Swiss civil code and the Italian penal code were eventually adopted in 1926, that is, three years after the foundation of the Turkish Republic, even this restricted domain of the law was taken away from the jurisdiction of the ulama, and religious associations were banned.

As for the educational system, the state decided to unify it throughout the whole country in 1924, opting for a complete secularization that involved the abolition of the madrasas, or religious colleges. Also abolished was the Ministry of Religious Affairs and Pious Foundations which was replaced by two directorates, one for religious affairs (the Diyanet) and the other for pious foundations (the Evkaf), both attached directly to the prime minister's office. All imams and muftis became civil servants while the Diyanet was given sole responsibility for religious guidance. As a result, the contents of Friday sermons (preaches before Friday prayer and sermons during the prayer) became centrally determined and the muftis received precise instructions about how to advise believers. Moreover, the state would define the contents of mandatory religious instruction in public schools and in the Imam-Hatip schools created for the purpose of training imams. These changes, and others (for example, the prohibition of organized prayer in public or private schools) amounted to the greatest transformation of the state bureaucracy brought under the Kemalist republic. As intended, they resulted in much more than a simple separation of state and religion: they established absolute control of religion by the state (Zürcher 2004: 187; 2012: 145, 279–80; Kuru 2009: 165–7, 205–11, 220; Inalcik 1964).

Women's emancipation was also part of the Kemalist reformist drive. Thus, in 1930, Turkisk women were granted the right to vote and to be eligible at local elections. These rights were extended to legislative elections in 1934 and to general elections in 1935.

The Attack on Popular Culture

For Atatürk and the Kemalists, religion and tradition confounded were seen as an obstacle to progress: that the traditional attire was not prescribed by religion did not really matter for them. Islam as a total culture was seen by Atatürk as a 'putrefied corpse' (Sayyid 1997: 57). Until the accession of an Islamic party to power in 2007, the Constitutional Court whose links with the Kemalists have always been strong (Belge 2006), was able to uphold the strict position that 'regardless of whether it [the dress code] is religious or not, anti-modern dresses that contradict the

Laws of Revolution cannot be seen as appropriate'. But 'religious dresses, in particular, constitute a deeper incongruity since they contradict the principle of secularism'. The reason why the dress code is so important is that it reflects the person's mentality and character, 'sentiments and thoughts', while secularism precisely consists of 'a transformation of mentality' (Order N° 1989/12 of The Turkish Constitutional Court, 7 March 1989, cited from Kuru 1989: 189).[6]

Another radical step taken by the Kemalists in the name of secularism and modernism was directly aimed at the 'low', popular Islam of the ordinary people. Complementing the institutional reforms destined to remove the ulama of the 'high' Islam from their erstwhile privileged position, it consisted of the outright suppression of the dervish (Sufi) orders, or mystical fraternities (the tarikats), and of the widespread network of convents and shrines associated with them (as early as in 1925). It constituted a far-reaching form of interference in the daily and personal lives of the people since the Sufi orders played a significant role in articulating the worldview of the popular masses, providing an emotional comfort that lacked in the 'high' religion, offering social protection and cohesion, and supplying an authority structure around the sheikhs (Zürcher 2004: 191–2; 2010: 136). Two of their characteristics made them unacceptable to the regime. First, as religious brotherhoods based on closed and secretive networks, they were perceived as the hallmark of a traditional and obscurantist culture. Second, they appeared as loci of local power lying beyond the reach of a centralized government. The latter held especially true for the Nakshibendi order which played a major role in the anti-constitutionalist uprising in 1909 and in the Kurdish rebellion of 1925 (Kinross, 2001: 397–404).

The drastic long-term consequences of the government's decision have been well captured by Zürcher (2004):

> By extending their secularization drive beyond the formal, institutionalized Islam, the Kemalists now touched such vital elements of popular religion

[6] Note that these measures and the posture supporting them are very similar to those adopted by Peter the Great in Russia: his policy of coercive Europeanization included compulsory cutting off of beards and the imposition of "Germanic" clothes. When an open rebellion erupted in Astrakhan (1705), it was harshly put down by Sheremetev whose police force committed many atrocities against the people (Obolonsky, 2003: 51).

as dress, amulets, soothsayers, holy sheikhs, saints' shrines, pilgrimages and festivals. The resentment these measures caused and the resistance put up against them was far greater than, for instance, in the case of the abolition of the caliphate, the position of seyhülislam, or the madrasas, which was only important to official 'high' religion. While the government succeeded in suppressing most expressions of popular religion, at least in the towns, these did not, of course, disappear. To a large extent, the tarikats simply went underground. But through the simultaneous imposition of an authoritarian and—especially during the 1940s—increasingly unpopular regime and suppression of popular Islam, the Kemalists politicized Islam and turned it into a vehicle for opposition. One could say that, in turning against popular religion, they cut the ties that bound them to the mass of the population (p. 192).

The attack on popular Islam was not only brutal but also indiscriminate and misguided. Thus, even when Islamic leaders displayed a good deal of wisdom and opening up towards modernity, they could ended up being persecuted by the regime. A striking example is the case of Sait Nursi who wisely enjoined Muslims to take God's unity as the basis of their lives, but also to study modern science and technology which he saw as necessary to preserve Islam, the only true basis of social cohesion. He was nevertheless arrested and tried several times for alleged political use of religion, although he did not indulge in direct political activity until the late 1950s. His writings were banned on the pretext that he was preaching against secularism and nationalism (Zürcher 2004: 193).

As witnessed by the above policies and reforms, the movement of the Young Turks and the Kemalist Republic that embodied their ideals betrayed a deep-rooted mistrust of the masses. Because the latter were seen as backward, the Kemalist elite felt they had the right to impose (Western) modernity upon them through any means deemed appropriate. Recruited from the higher ranks of the administration, they saw themselves as an enlightened and self-confident elite charged with the mission of educating the people, removing the hold of religion on their minds, and totally transforming the Turkish legal system, even though a large part of the population was still immersed in a traditional Muslim culture (Kuru 2009: 214–5; Zürcher 2010: 136, 214). This authoritarian–elitist approach to modernization produced a deep-rooted fault-line inside the Turkish society, a division that runs through the economic, social, and political spheres (Kaya 2013: 15; Gellner 1994), and still persists to this date.

How did the Kemalists justify the intolerance of their opposition to Islam, and the particularly assertive form of secularism that they adopted? The answer can be found in statements of Turkey's Constitutional Court and ideologues of the Kemalist regime for whom solid ground existed to apply a stricter secularism in Turkey than in Western Europe. Being the legal foundations of two different civilizations, medieval and modern, the bases of the Islamic and Western legal systems are irreconcilable: Unlike Christianity, Islam is essentially a political project and, therefore, a real separation of state and religion is not possible in a Muslim society (see Berkes 1964: 480–1). It is thus because Islam is not only a religion but also a political ideology, that Muslims will always resist secularism. Based on a 'centuries-old desert law', the sharia is an impediment to progress, and only strict, interventionist state policies will be able to rid Turkey of Islam and 'become part of the universal civilization –the modern West' (Özek 1962: 520). In short, Islam is a structural obstacle to development and only its forceful eradication can free the forces of modernity and progress. Interestingly, in the ongoing debate about Islam in Western countries, this radical diagnosis has been taken up by many scholars, as attested by the writings of Samuel Huntington (1993, 1996), Bernard Lewis (1996, 2002), and many others (for further references, see Platteau 2017: 89–90).

Post-scriptum

Kemalist dictatorship ended in 1945 under the pressure of both internal and external forces (the defeat of the Axis powers in World War II). Although restrictions on expressions of religious feelings were relaxed and autonomous religious organizations, such as the Sufi brotherhoods, were authorized again, what Kuru calls assertive secularism remained the hallmark of the country and its values continued to be strictly upheld and guarded by the Turkish army. In the name of this guardianship role, the army felt entitled to interfere with the democratic process whenever the Kemalist achievements were deemed to be under threat. In a context of rising inequality, this did not prevent the Islamist currents from getting stronger and politicized Islam from taking over the role of the left as the voice of the have-nots (Zürcher 2004: 289; White 2013: 47). It is only in 2007 that a truly democratic election was organized that revealed the wide support enjoyed by an Islamist party, the Justice and Development

Party (AKP) of Recep Tayyip Erdoğan. In no time did the AKP shed its Islamic identity and styled itself as a conservative democratic party. As it became increasingly evident over the years, the new regime retained important characteristics of its predecessor.

First, its authoritarian nature soon became evident: Military forces were simply replaced by a 'civilian' army (consisting mainly of police forces) as the base of support for the regime, the judicial system was purged and duly stuffed with partisan judges, and a climate of mutual defamation and suspicion amongst people was systematically nurtured. Second, it continued to rely on a strongly nationalistic ideology based on the Sunni–Muslim–Turk Holy Trinity. Third, although it reversed measures of assertive secularism (for example, the ban on the veil), it did not end the domination of the state over religion. Contrary to the view of a pious, modest, and ascetic class of professionals and business people, its new elite increasingly behaved as an assertive new bourgeoisie eager to demonstrate its economic success. Fourth, liberal economic policies continued to be pursued.

Despite the change of elites at the top, the line of continuity between successive political regimes in Turkey is more important than what may appear at first sight. This is so not only because of the aforementioned similarities between Erdoğan's regime and Kemalism, but also because Kemalism itself was not the sort of radical rupture with the Ottoman society that it pretended to be. The Ottoman empire was far from being the religion-dominated system represented in Kemalist ideology—the ulama were civil servants paid by the Ottoman state and under direct control of the sultan—and the Turkish Republic actually inherited the secular institutions of the Ottoman empire, such as the schools, courts, and laws, and it followed the political tradition of central statism that prevailed during the late Ottoman era (Kuru 2009: 202–3, 214). Under both systems, temporal authority clearly superseded the religious authority (Inalcik 1964: 53–63; Frey 1964: 211–17; Chambers 1964: 312–22). In praising Turkey's Ottoman roots, the AKP regime has therefore mended the breach with the Ottoman past that Kemalists artificially created. There is a similarity worth noting between the AKP's approach to modernity and that of the Young Ottomans who, unlike the Young Turks (who embraced the Western civilization in toto) and the Tanzimat bureaucrats (who wanted to pragmatically imitate European institutions and schooling system), were convinced that modernizing Turkey could be done while preserving the Islamic identity. Seen in this light, the reappearance of alleged religious symbols, such as the women's headscarf, on the forefront of Turkey's public life should be seen as 'reflecting a process of acculturation and entry into the experience of global modernity by participating in the elaboration of an Islamic social image repertory', rather than as manifesting a deep attachment to tradition and religious orthodoxy (Göle 2011: 49).

In this regard, it is revealing that, especially in the aftermath of the AKP rule, secularist/Kemalist rituals became very common in everyday life, including regular visits to Atatürk's mausoleum, excessive use of the Turkish flag and images of Atatürk, and the use of the slogan 'Turkey is secular and will remain secular' (Kaya 2013: 161). All these acts and slogans, images, and symbols reflected a cult of the hero conceived as the warrior, statesman, and educator whose role is to mould the course of modern Turkish history (Ward and Rustow 1964: 450). Their religious connotation is also evident in the sense that they produce a sacralization of the principles of laicism and secularism (Yeğenoğlu 2012: 296). In the same manner as the strict secularism of the Kemalist state and the barriers to freedom of religion that it erected led to the emergence of Islamist symbols and identity markers, such as the headscarf, the rise of an Islamist party, however moderate, caused the laicists to reinforce their display of Kemalist fervour. Because the symbols used thus serve the function of manifesting political identities in the public sphere, they carry a political and not only a religious or quasi-religious meaning (Kaya 2013: 162, 166–09).

11.2.2 Case study 2: Habib Bourguiba

Because the fate of the regime initiated by Bourguiba cannot be properly understood without looking at subsequent events under the rule of his presidential successor, the space devoted to the case of Tunisia is larger than the space used for Turkey.

The Profile of a Despot

Using his Neo-Dustur party as a powerful political machine and cleverly manoeuvring to wrest power from the monarch Amin Bey, Bourguiba, a lawyer trained in France, succeeded in proclaiming the Republic of Tunisia in July 1957. The next step consisted of eliminating (and eventually assassinating) his arch-rival inside the party, Salah Ben Yusuf, the scion of a prosperous merchant family with close ties to Tunisia's traditional commercial and religious elite. Bourguiba's authoritarian proclivities soon transformed the new Republic into a 'presidential monarchy' in full control of a toothless assembly and a subordinated judiciary. At the root of its power lay a huge patronage system that showered favours on loyal followers. In particular, access to government jobs was conditioned on party membership, and the key qualification for the more important posts was typically the militant record rather than skills or competence-based merit.

Bourguiba was a self-confident and even arrogant person who did not tolerate opposition. He wanted to be surrounded by a loyal coterie of sycophant followers, and it is therefore not surprising that none of the first-generation leaders of Neo-Dustur found their way into positions of responsibility in state bodies. At some point and on some issue, all of them had actually fallen out with Bourguiba and been considered guilty of betrayal or abandonment in moments of crisis (Cohen 1986; Toumi 1989: 21; Perkins 2004: 133).

Bourguiba had always had a particular view of the rule of the law which he saw as essentially resting on a legitimacy of which he was the unique source. Citing Ben Achour (1987):

> His decisions are above the law. The rule of law exists only below the stage where he himself is standing ... He is an order, above all orders. Even the state cannot claim the legitimacy that he has. On the contrary, state legitimacy is derived from his own person. His leadership transcends the state' (p. 157, my translation).

His numerous public declarations to the effect that he was acting 'for and through the people' were mystifying insofar as he never took any step towards establishing popular participation in political decision-making.[7] The truth is that he had a quite paternalistic approach to the people's

---

[7] Thus, when confronted with opposition against his agrarian reform, Bourguiba declared that: "When rebellious elements refuse to be persuaded and prove immune to the appeal to reason, punishment must be meted out on them so as to prevent evil and discourage those who, following their example, might be tempted to threaten *the achievements of the people*" (cited from Toumi, 1989, p. 59 -my translation and my emphasis).

role and a *dirigiste* sense of management of the state (Cohen 1986). He was actually a distant leader ensconced in the idea that the people of his country owed him a great debt of gratitude. All his references to 'popular legitimacy' were therefore fictional and destined to conceal an adept instrumentalization of people's will (Camau 1987: 30).

The indisputability of Bourguiba's power became most manifest when in 1974 he was 'offered' a lifetime appointment to the position of party president by the political bureau whose members were chosen by no one else than himself (Toumi 1989: 88–9; see also Alexander 2010: 45). Therefore:

> Although the monarchy had been abolished soon after independence, in all but title Bourguiba became the bey, exercising his authority, working and residing in his palaces, and reveling in the pageantry and rituals once reserved for the Husainid rulers. The elections that confirmed him in office resembled nothing so much as the bai'a, the oath of fealty sworn to the bey by his retainers.
>
> (Perkins 2004: 208)

Radical Social Reforms

Because of his deep self-assurance and his strong sense that he had an important mission to fulfil for his country, Bourguiba felt he could ride on a wave of popular support to embark upon drastic social reforms. He chose to direct his first efforts to establish state control over religion. He thus decided to confiscate the land property of the Habus Council, a waqf in charge of administering land earmarked for mosques, Quranic schools, and charitable Islamic institutions. Another drastic step consisted in 1956 of absorbing the two sharia courts (for adherents of the Maliki and the Hanafi schools, respectively) into the state judicial system, and integrating the Zatuna mosque-university into the state education system. State control over the Islamic courts facilitated the move to a third and even more impressive policy: the promulgation, in August 1956, of a Personal Status Code considered as the most progressive family code adopted in an Arab country in the twentieth century. Designed to strengthen the nuclear family and reduce existing inequalities between men and women, it prohibited polygamy, granted the women the right of divorce and to approve arranged marriages, expanded women's existing rights in matters of inheritance and child custody, set minimum age limits for marriage, and ended the male right of repudiation. What this reform did stop short of, however, is establishing strict equality in inheritance rights between the two genders. Moreover, the husband continued to be considered as the household head implying that only his place of residence could serve as conjugal residence.

Given Bourguiba's authoritarian and paternalistic approach to reforms, it does not come as a surprise that the Personal Status Code was enacted outside any pressure from women's organizations, and in the absence of any consultation with the population. In particular, the Union Nationale des Femmes Tunisiennes (National Union of Tunisian Women, or UNFT), born within the ambit of the Neo-Dustur party, was more concerned with obtaining civil and political equality with men, meaning enfranchisement, the right to stand for elected office, and greater attention to female education. Regarding the rural masses, priority was put on literacy, health and family planning even though, after the promulgation of the Code, the UNFT did agree to make special efforts to promote it in areas where women and men alike had reservations about the reforms (Perkins 2004: 138).

There is another aspect of Bourguiba's reform of the family code that deserves even more attention. Unlike Atatürk and the Kemalists in Turkey, Bourguiba did not justify the new code on rationalist grounds but in the name of a rejuvenated Islamic law. He thus talked about a new ijtihad, seen as a renewed effort of legitimate free reasoning aimed at elaborating legal solutions to present-day problems in the light of the general principles of Islam. This was an amazing step involving a daring break with the centuries-old tradition of 'classical Islam' that got established after the 'closure of the ijtihad' in the eleventh century. By 're-opening the ijtihad', Bourguiba wanted to bring Tunisia into the modern world without having recourse to an opposition between Western-inspired legislation and religion, or between modernity and tradition. Three essential ideas actually guided Bourguiba in his reform efforts. First, the resolution of present-day problems requires that concrete action is given predominance over abstract rules. Second, the sacred place of Reason in Islam must be asserted: If contemporary Muslim societies are backward and decadent, it is because of their refusal to grant Reason its due place and their consequent ensnaring in tradition and imitation. Finally, study and new interpretations of sacred texts are a precondition of the renaissance of the Muslim community (Camau and Geisser 2004).

In view of these considerations, the claim that Bourguiba's reforms were secular appears somewhat exaggerated: Instead of a separation between state and religion, what he initiated was a system in which the state head becomes a sort of pre-eminent imam vested with the role of a spiritual guide of the country while the official ulama and imams are transformed into cadres and agents of the public administration' (Toumi 1989: 116, my translation).

The issue of dressing habits is different from personal status matters in the sense that Islam does not offer prescriptions for dress except in general and vague terms (the need for women to show modesty, for example). Therefore, ijtihad is not required. Bourguiba's views on the subject were rather similar to those of Atatürk, yet he did not put them into practice with the heavy-handed determination of his Turkish predecessor. He launched a campaign intended to disparage all forms of traditional attire, veiling in particular. He indeed believed, and expressed the belief, that wearing traditional dress was an old-fashioned habit encouraging retrograde modes of thinking and behaviours, and, consciously or not, expressing blank rejection of modernity. In repeated speeches, he went as far as condemning the veil as an 'odious rag' that 'demeaned women, had no practical value, and was not obligatory in order to conform to Islamic standards of modesty' (p. 137). He made equally contemptuous remarks about male traditional garments and always appeared himself in public in a coat and tie. Understanding how deep-rooted these dressing codes were in Tunisian culture, he nevertheless did not enforce any ban except the one prohibiting veiling in classrooms (p. 138).

Religious Reactions to Reforms

Perhaps surprisingly, and although Bourguiba failed to obtain a fatwa approving his new policies, there was little opposition to the Code from the religious establishment. Several factors help explain this situation. First, Bourguiba had appointed a moderately progressive person as rector of the Zaituna mosque-university and, in reorganizing the sharia courts, he was clever enough to reassign and retire some judges whom he did not trust. Second, in order to buy their support, he offered various perks and material advantages to other prominent members of the religious establishment. Bourguiba's co-option tactic was facilitated by the earlier collaboration of the official ulama with the colonial regime, which had considerably weakened their position and eroded their influence. Not only had they failed to play a significant role in the struggle for independence but they had also inherited a privileged economic and social status (Zeghal 2002). Regarding the first aspect, the ulama vigorously opposed the Neo-Dusturians before independence when the party used a religious argument and language to prevent Tunisians from adopting the French nationality. The Neo-Dusturians proclaimed that abandoning the Tunisian nationality in favour of the French one was an act of apostasy. The ulama of Tunis retaliated by issuing a fatwa allowing adoption of the colonial power's nationality (Toumi 1989: 115). Turning to the second aspect, the ulama's privileged status, it is useful to cite Mohsen Toumi (1989) at some length:

> The ulama, in fact, constituted an oligarchy regrouping a small number of family dynasties at the heart of the Tunisian bourgeoisie. Through hereditary links and through co-optation, this oligarchic group had monopolised the best positions in the sectors of education, justice, jurisprudence, and mosque management. During a long period of time, too, it expressed support for the colonial order ... On the one hand, thanks to family relationships, its members were allied to the feudal class of big landowners in the interior of the country and, on the other hand, they hunted down and eliminated all upholders of modernity, especially if they did not belong to their social group or threatened their cultural existence ... The targets of the Zaituna people were not so much selected on the grounds that they did not serve Islam well, or violated its law, but rather because they were guilty of denouncing the decadence caused by those who had arrogated to themselves the monopoly of Islam ... The ulama were thus projecting a negative image of their religion, and they continuously re-invented justifications for the continuation of the colonial order, which was precisely the political service that the colonial authorities required from them.... The stake behind such a compromising support was nothing else than the rewards received by the ulama in terms of social power, immovable assets, and substantial incomes since the Zaituna possessed considerable *Habus* (indivisible) assets the usufruct of which accrued, since centuries, to the same families of qadis (judges) and mourids (teachers) (pp. 114–15, my translation).

Finally, the ulama who did not occupy socially enviable positions and the students from the Zaituna mosque-university who were usually recruited from the interior provinces or from the provincial petite bourgeoisie (in contrast to their teachers who typically belonged to the grande bourgeoisie of Tunis) did not wield sufficient power to stop reforms that they disliked (Salem 1984: 176; Perkins 2004: 137).

Oddly enough, the action of Bourguiba that aroused the most determined opposition turned out to be his disparaging remarks about the fasting ritual of Ramadan. He went so far as appearing on television eating a full plate at mid-day during the Ramadan period, which caused outrage among believers. In a 1960 speech, he announced the beginning of a jîhad against underdevelopment, and he judged that involvement in this jîhad absolved Tunisians from the religious obligation of fasting. To sanction this personal interpretation as a product of ijtihad, he demanded a fatwa of endorsement from the mufti of Tunis. Since the latter did not oblige in a manner deemed fully satisfactory by Bourguiba, he was fired. Tensions did not abate and, during the next year, when Bourguiba prepared to renew his campaign, riots occurred in Kairouan, a venerable religious centre and a Yusufist stronghold since well before independence. Its influential ulama openly denigrated the president's views of Islam, and they contested his claim to act as a religious authority entitled to engage in ijtihad. As for Islamists, in order to ensure proper respect of the Ramadan, they went so far as forcing the closure, and causing the destruction, of cafés and restaurants in Sfax in September 1977 (Toumi 1989: 116–17).

Repression ensued, and Bourguiba alleged that the dissenting religious leaders were actually motivated by their resentment caused by the loss of their economic power through the confiscation of habus lands. But this was eventually a lost battle for the president who had to put up with the reality that 'the vast majority of Tunisians had no intention of breaking with the fundamental religious practices that defined them as Muslims' (Perkins 2004: 141).

The Context-Dependence of Bourguiba's Approach to Reforms

The contemptuous attitude of president Bourguiba vis-à-vis erstwhile customs and religious habits, and the antagonisms that it aroused, offer a striking contrast to the more flexible and tolerant attitude that he displayed during the pre-Independence period. Then, indeed, he professed an understanding that the popular masses in Tunisia would accept change only when it is justified in terms of Islam. Being the perceived source of cultural representations and behavioural norms, Islam had to be mobilized to make the popular masses aware of the injustices inherent in the colonial situation, and act accordingly (Salem 1984: 100). For example, in the struggle for independence, the idea of self-sacrifice was diffused with the support of martyrdom images. Toward that end, Quranic verses eulogizing those who perish for their faith were read aloud in public meetings (p. 110). Also, in those times, Neo-Dustur leaders did not hesitate, 'to use the mosques as their means for spreading their ideas under the guise of lessons in Islamic history' (p. 101). In some sense, these facts are consistent with Bourguiba's later proclivity to use ijtihad to vindicate modernizing reforms, using Islam in support of particular actions. The concept of jîhad was thus invoked to justify both the struggle for independence and the struggle against underdevelopment, and it is in the name of a modern jîhad that the obligation of fasting was allowed to be suspended.

The contrast between pre- and post-Independence becomes more remarkable, however, when one considers what Bourguiba wrote about the women's veil in 1929. In an article entitled 'Le voile', he sees the veil as belonging to the body of Islamic social customs and as a component of the Tunisian personality. In Bourguiba's words:

> I have raised in neat and precise terms the great social problem that has always pervaded our discussions: do we want to hasten, without any transition, the disappearance of our habits and mores, whether good or bad, and of all those small things that together form our personality? My answer, given the special circumstances in which we live, has always been categorically no! (cited from Salem 1984: 133, my translation).

Elsewhere, Bourguiba reasserted the same position by proclaiming:

> Evolution must take place, lest we should die. It will happen, but without break, without rupture, so that we can maintain a unity of our personality that can be perceived as such by our consciences at any point of time in the continuous changes that we are experimenting' (cited from Salem 1984: 135, or Toumi 1989: 113, my translation).

In other words, the issue of women, like other questions arising from tradition, must be linked to the national question. When the central problem was to create unity and social cohesion in order to attain political independence, respect for traditional habits and customs had to prevail since they provided a system of collective representations keeping the mass of people together in harsh circumstances demanding a lot of sacrifices. In other words, in the context of a war against external enemies, religion was an invaluable asset supplying the justification and social cohesion necessary for momentous change. After independence, however, the situation had changed: Tunisia had to be modernized and Westernized, and this new objective justified a change in the attitude towards tradition and religion.

The context-dependence of Bourguiba's approach to reforms could also be determined by considerations of political opportunism. An interesting illustration is the following: As the moment of independence got closer, Bourguiba increasingly toned down his appeals to Islam, avoiding Islamic themes in his speeches and instead stressing the values of 'national unity'. The decisive factor behind that gradual change was his growing conflict with Ben Yusuf from whom he wanted to demarcate himself: Since Ben Yusuf tended to accentuate his references to Islam, Bourguiba chose to reduce them (Salem 1984: 155).

Rising Economic Inequality and the Fall of Bourguiba

A few years after social reforms were enacted, and under the strong impulse of the then prime minister, Ahmed Ben Salah, Bourguiba embarked upon a bold experiment with planning and socialism (in 1962). This proved to be an ill-advised step especially because among the key policies considered were (1) the breaking of all informal trading circuits and their replacement by a centralized network of state organizations and cooperatives, and (2) the integration of all agricultural lands into a cooperative system (for details, see Toumi 1989: 57–70). Stalwarts of the Dustur Party (which had been renamed Parti Socialiste Doustourien, or PSD), particularly big landowners and traders, strongly protested and Bourguiba was compelled to dismiss Ben Salah and change tactic by shifting to the opposite option of economic liberalization. That option worked much better in the sense that significant economic growth was resumed, but the problem of wealth inequalities, and inter-regional disparities especially, was not resolved. Thus, economic prosperity was concentrated along the coast and in Tunis area in particular, while the south, centre and west, the regions in which the most severe levels of unemployment were traditionally observed, remained seriously underdeveloped. Moreover, urban unemployment of young people reached intolerably high levels, almost 50 per cent for young men aged between 15 and 25 in the mid-1970s

(Radwan et al. 1990: 25–6). Social tensions grew up over the years, and anger against the regime was increased by the lack of any political liberalization to accompany economic liberalization.

On the political front, indeed, the highly centralized, authoritarian power structure of the PSD continued to stifle any internal criticism and the freedom of expressing opposing political viewpoints remained severely curbed at all levels. Bourguiba crushed any nascent tendency towards the democratization of the inner workings of both the PSD and the state apparatus. And when he would return from lengthy health treatment abroad, he would immediately reassert his unquestionable authority and silence his critics. Given the economic hardship suffered by ordinary people, the regime's ossifying authoritarianism created a gulf between state and society. It is in these circumstances that strikes, street demonstrations, and other expressions of public outrage took place, especially when the government attempted to remove subsidies on essential goods such as main staples (typically under the pressure of the IMF and the World Bank).

An Islamist Party, the Mouvement de la Tendance Islamique (MTI), also grew in strength, drawing a lot of support from the disadvantaged sections of the population and many middle-class men and women 'who turned to their Islamic heritage when both socialism and capitalism failed to fulfil the expectations of prosperity and security they had raised' (Perkins 2004: 166). This party, founded in 1981, was prevented from presenting candidates to the multi-party (national) elections that Bourguiba was pressed to organize during the same year. Nonetheless, candidates linked to the MTI fared as well as, and often better than, their secular counterparts. A few years later, the movement called for a national referendum on the Personal Status Code, contending that its promulgation had led to a massive entry of women into the labour force causing a significant rise in male unemployment. In this way, the Code allegedly undermined orderly social and family life based on the principle of a neat differentiation between gender roles, and it eroded the traditional role and status of men as breadwinners. In addition to these typically patriarchal concerns, the MTI promoted the limitation of contacts between the sexes and the revival of traditional attire as a symbol of rejection of foreign influence (Perkins 2004: 168–72).

The conflict was unavoidably escalating between the regime and the MTI, reflecting two diametrically opposed views of Tunisia's future, one

Western-oriented and secular, and the other inspired by Islamic values as opposed to imported ideologies. It bears emphasis that determined religious opposition against the regime and its social reforms emerged only after frustrations about its economic policies became widespread in the population. Also, political opposition was not confined to religious circles and this became manifest when all the officially recognized parties, except for the PSD, decided to boycott the municipal elections in 1985 and, later, the national elections in 1986. Clearly, the experiment with multiparty democracy ended up in failure and only an extremely poor health condition succeeded in forcing Bourguiba, in November 1987, to eventually relinquish power in conditions of state disintegration (Alexander 2010: 49–50).

State Racketeering and Regime Collapse Under an Unenlightened Despot

Zine El-Abidine Ben Ali, minister of the interior under the previous government, replaced Bourguiba in the highest position of political power. He immediately tried to calm things down by striking a compromise with the religious opposition. Known as the National Pact (1988), this agreement involved mutual concessions. Ben Ali publicly affirmed Islam as the state religion and proclaimed the centrality of the Arab and Islamic heritages of Tunisia, he authorized radio and television stations to broadcast the call for prayer, made a highly publicized pilgrimage to Mecca, and legalized an MTI student organization. In return, however, he made it clear that he considered the Personal Status Code as an unassailable achievement of his predecessor. The National Pact thus followed a well-established tradition of autocrat rulers of past Muslim empires: while making symbolic concessions, the state ensured its control over religion in the more substantial matters (Platteau 2017: Chapters 4–5). In the present instance, such matters included secular reforms that implied a considerable erosion of the power and prestige of religious authorities. Peace did not last long, however, as the tactical motive behind the Pact soon became manifest: The MTI failed to obtain an eligibility status for the 1989 elections despite the transformation of its name (from MTI to Hizb al-Nahda, or Renaissance Party) to conform to the electoral law prohibiting religious terminology (Owen 2012; Perkins 2004: Chapter 7).

Far from indulging in any political liberalization, Ben Ali's regime was even more totalitarian and repressive than Bourguiba's. Being carefully managed by the ministry of interior, elections were just theatrical plays putting out a false appearance of competition to please foreign donor countries. All the sectors of the administration and the president's party were actually placed under the tight control of the ministry of interior, justifying the definition of the regime as a police state. In particular, this ministry made all the hiring and firing decisions in the public sector, implying that an applicant had no chance of being selected if he was not affiliated with the president's party (the newly named Rassemblement Constitutionnel Democratique, or RCD). Check of the applicant's identity also included querying about whether the applicant, or any close relative, could be suspected of Islamism, or of belonging to any form of opposition to the regime. Likewise, any permanently employed public servant could be fired on a simple instruction, even non-written, emanating from the same ministry. A vast array of departments and services, including customs services, fiscal authorities, external trade and hygiene departments, and so forth, were all mobilized to fulfil police missions or execute politically motivated instructions. The tools used were surveillance, control, intimidation, dissuasion, and even punishment. As a consequence of this all-pervasive network of surveillance (which even used taxi drivers as police informants), the information contained in the police-held file of an applicant could either open the door, or block access, to an employment, to administrative services, to registration with a university, to the permission to start an independent activity, and so forth (Hibou 2006a: 96–7).[8]

In short, the shift from Bourguiba's to Ben Ali's regime can be characterized as a shift 'from a system of control over society to a system of control over the individuals'. The latter was achieved through deep intrusion into the people's private life, engineered by innumerable police interventions and all-pervasive networks of tight surveillance (p. 98). There is another sense in which Ben Ali's regime can be said to have been worse than that

---

[8] According to some calculations, the ratio of police to citizens in Tunisia was about one percent in the first decade of the twentieth century, an estimate that does not include the army of informants working for the security services. Counting the latter, direct and indirect employment in these services sustained about one-tenth of the population (Hibou, 2006b). To these staggering figures, one must add that the RCD itself, with its thousands local branches covering the whole country, acted more like a security apparatus than a political party (Beau and Tuqoi, 1999; Hibou, 2006a).

of his predecessor: Besides adopting unequalizing economic policies, Ben Ali and his inner circle (including his own wife) arrogated to themselves exorbitant economic privileges and illicit advantages obtained through corruption, cronyism, extortion, and racketeering. These methods of illicit enrichment typically included

> the privatization of state assets such as hotels and manufacturing; the transfer of public land to private ownership; the granting of licenses to operate major public services, such as cell phones, airlines, international sea transport, Tunisian cruise ships, and TV and radio stations; and, on some occasions, the forced sale of private assets such as banks and newspapers (Owen, 2012: 78).

They allowed the top regime elite to amass considerable amounts of wealth since economic liberalization reforms, above all the privatization of state companies, made their intensification possible. A system of crony capitalism in which huge rents are secured by an elite tightly interconnected to a totalitarian political regime thus came into existence in marked contrast to the situation prevailing under Bourguiba. The latter's family, indeed, was only peripherally involved in business activities.

At the top of this new system lay a genuine mafia of oligarchs who quickly enriched themselves by building businesses behind protective walls set up by security services, and by preying upon successful existing undertakings and firms either through the imposition of substantial and illicit commissions or through brutal takeovers backed up by criminal acts and threats. Not surprisingly, these manoeuvres and extortions were shrouded in the greatest secrecy, and any public mention of them could result in imprisonment or exile (Owen 2012: 78–9). Hibou (2006a) has described in detail some common predatory practices supported by protection racket politics:

> Rigged attributions of public bids, privatizations conceded to figureheads in obscure conditions that frequently involve pressures from ruling 'clans' aimed at orienting the decision, or at compelling the new owner to associate himself with a particular entrepreneur or importing agent, or to accept a particular intermediary or business partner … such practices are considered as a normal part of the everyday life of Tunisians. The business person who is coerced into an association with a member of a "clan" to import the product that he has traditionally commercialized, is in the worst case just

annoyed by this situation. He can accept it under duress for fear of fiscal reprisals or expropriation of assets but, most often, he will accept it readily, knowing quite well that the commodities will then move quickly and easily through the customs and other administrative controls ... As for the administration, it will comply with the request to deal promptly with the matter insofar as the members of the 'clans' are personal representatives of the president. If the importer were irresponsible enough to refuse the "offer" made to him by people from up there, his working conditions could rapidly deteriorate, his stocks could rot in the customs facilities, the fiscal authorities could start an investigation into his books, the national social security fund could require the immediate payment of his arrears, and the bank could deny him a last credit. Likewise, the research and development group which does not give in to a request from a clan member must expect a lot of administrative troubles that will eventually prevent it from submitting a bid within the prescribed time; and an entrepreneur who refuses to sell a portion of his shares to connections of the president incurs the risk that his business environment becomes abruptly hostile, say because the police exerts strong pressures on his suppliers or service providers to the effect that they stop working with him (p. 337, my translation).

State resources were used by the president as a source of selective patronage both for members of the crony business community and individual members of the security services. A particularly useful instrument consisted of credit which was 'freely provided for many privileged members of the new middle class, allowing them to buy houses and cars but leaving them deeply in debt and so enmeshed in a system of relations that it prevented them from criticizing or opposing the regime' (Owen 2012: 78–9). The continuous threat posed by the vindictive punishment strategy pursued by Ben Ali had the effect of keeping crony capitalists quiet and submissive, entangled as they were in a sort of feudal tie to the president. At lower levels, an army of lesser people were tied together and to the regime through their participation in numerous acts of boycott, extortion, reprisals, racketeering, and police operations.

Ben Ali's kleptocratic regime was so much hated by the population and it alienated such a large portion of the professional and secular elite of the cities that it needed only a small spark to raise the whole country against it. When this opportunity arose in the form of the public suicide of a young man in a remote town of the country, the authorities faced a mass revolt that linked almost everyone in opposition to their rule. Their fate was sealed when the army decided to side with the demonstrators against the security services loyal to the president and ultimately moved against him (Springborg 2014: 145). The regime and all its protection rackets then collapsed without offering any resistance (Brumberg 2014: 50). The way was opened for the rise to power of the Islamist movement of al-Nahda which was then the only force possessing a solid internal organization and a more or less clear vision of the type of society that should replace the abhorred Ben Ali's system.

11.3 Lessons and Challenges

The aforementionedcase study material holds several important lessons, some encouraging and some others uncomfortable. To begin with, it is striking that all the reviewed experiences of autocratic enlightenment in the lands of Islam ended up in a political crisis severe enough to trigger a regime change. In Turkey, as soon as genuinely fair elections were allowed by the republican regime and the army (in 2007), an Islamist party won repeated electoral victories that caused the shift to a conservative, moderate Islamist, regime. In Tunisia, the successor of Bourguiba, president Ben Ali, was ejected from power in the course of the Arab Spring (in 2011), which saw the rise of an Islamist party to power. Yet, for two main reasons, the abrupt termination of enlightened political regimes in Muslim countries should not necessarily worry us too much.

First, in both Turkey and Tunisia, important reforms have not been rescinded by the successor regimes. The societies of Turkey and Tunisia have thus gone through a deep transformation. In particular, the status of women and the education system have been considerably improved, the public role of religion has been significantly reduced, modern laws have been enacted, and mechanisms of effective centralized enforcement have been put into place. These reforms can be expected to form lasting achievements insofar as they have become gradually accepted by large segments of the population and strongly supported by the institutions in charge of their implementation and enforcement (bureaucracy, courts, and so forth).

Second, even though there is unfortunately no counterfactual available to support our claim, evidence seems to suggest that the political crisis could have been avoided if some blatant mistakes had not been committed. While some of these mistakes resulted in an inappropriate policy mix, others were manifested on the implementation level. Implementation errors were the consequence of overweening self-confidence on the part of the enlightened autocrats, or of their lack of wisdom and judgement. The fact that wrong choices of policy mix were observed in some cases and not in others indicates that they are not inherent in enlightened autocratic regimes. In contrast, to the extent that over-confidence is a characteristic of all enlightened autocrats, implementation errors seem to be harder to avoid, thus mitigating our optimism regarding the possibility of successful autocratic enlightenment. Such risk is compounded by the fact that excessive self-confidence often prompts enlightened autocrats to remain too long in power. These considerations are now substantiated in the light of the findings of Section 11.2 from which we draw five different lessons.

1.   The reform-minded autocrat makes his task unusually difficult if he not only chooses to enact radical legal and institutional reforms but also proves unable to prevent blatant economic and social inequality from rising. He becomes particularly vulnerable if he proves unable to tame corruption in the circle of power that supports him or, even worse, if he himself indulges in predatory practices. Thus, in Tunisia, the reforms initiated by Bourguiba had become widely accepted. If, towards the end of his rule, religious clerics succeeded in arousing significant opposition against him, and in questioning his secular reforms in particular, it is because his economic and social policies had been widely resented and his authoritarianism became increasingly unjustifiable. The situation clearly worsened under Ben Ali's regime the demise of which was essentially caused by the neglect of the poor and the unemployed (particularly in the economically deprived regions of the country), the shockingly high level of corruption, cronyism, and favouritism among the political elite, and the entrenchment of a police state perceived to be in their exclusive service.

It is the combination of radical reforms and corruption of the political elite that revived the legitimacy and credibility of religious leaders who protested against an iniquitous regime. In other words, when these clerics fight, or appear to fight, only for the purpose of defending their own privileges, they are not able to draw much popular support. But if they appear to understand the hardship of the ordinary people and are ready to engage politically in order to end it, they gain widespread prestige and influence. This has been repeatedly observed in the history of Islam as epitomized, for example, by the rising influence of Iranian ayatollahs when they took the leadership in the struggle against the iniquitous policies of deeply corrupt Qajar shahs in the course of the nineteenth century (Platteau 2017: 165–75). A truly enlightened autocrat therefore understands that sufficient political stability cannot be obtained if progressive reforms are not accompanied by repression of rapacious elites and the adoption of inclusive economic and social policies that expand economic opportunities in the direction of popular masses. In the case of Tunisia, it did not help that inter-regional inequality grew over time and that the relatively backward and neglected south was also the stronghold of Yusufism, a moderate Islamic movement that was particularly vocal in the protests against the regime (not only under Ben Ali but also under Bourguiba).

2. The policy mix understood in the above sense is not the only major determinant of the success of progressive institutional reforms. The content of these reforms and the manner in which they are implemented also matter. Here, the distinction between 'high'and 'ow' Islam becomes very useful. Measures aimed at modernizing the state apparatus (such as centralization of the state administration, the imposition of taxes, and army conscription) do not generally meet with significant or systematic resistance from religious circles: On the one hand, the official ulama of 'high Islam' tend to accept the pre-eminence of political rulers in such matters and, on the other hand, the mullahs, sheikhs and other representatives of 'low Islam' are too distant from changes occurring in the higher spheres of the society and the polity to feel very much concerned. As for encroachments upon the traditional position and privileges of the ulama, they do not seem to cause long-lasting furor if they can be properly seduced or bought off by the secular autocrat. Thus, their absorption into a modern state administration (in the departments of justice, education, and religious affairs), provided that they are paid handsome and stable salaries and are awarded a honourable status, is often enough to calm them down. Moreover, because they tend to belong to a privileged social class composed of family dynasties enjoying a monopoly over lucrative religious functions, they are estranged from the common people and their religious representatives who are there-

fore unlikely to enter into open conflict with the state to defend the position of what they perceive as elite clerics.

3. How to tame the representatives of the 'low Islam' is an entirely different issue. These clerics live close to the people, understand their day-to-day problems, and share their local culture where religious beliefs and rituals are blended with erstwhile indigenous customs. As a result, their mutual interests tend to be close and their communality of feelings is typically strong. This is true not only for rural areas but also for poor urban quarters which are often inhabited by rural migrants. Directly confronting popular habits and beliefs to impose Western values and mores on ordinary people unaccustomed to them is an unwise and counter-productive strategy: It is certain to cause distress and arouse the ire of these people and the representatives of 'low Islam' who may act as the organizers of (violent) protests. This was most evident in Turkey: There, even though a strong army-backed regime was effective in silencing critics, frustrations were lingering, awaiting the first opportunity to flare up or express themselves in defiant votes if permitted. In Tunisia, this was true above all in the South where the Yusufists (moderate Islamists) never really accepted the centralized rule from Tunis.

Strong-hand tactics have two major disadvantages when they are used to impose drastic changes in personal status matters, in particular on issues of marriage, divorce, and inheritance: They carry a high risk of making the reforms ineffective in the long run, and they create in the minds of the people a nasty association between secularism and coercion, between individualistic values and totalitarianism. When decreed in a top-down manner, progressive, secular reforms are perceived by the traditional masses as a frontal assault on their lives and culture by the urban elite and the ruling circles. This is typically done in the name of modernity, so that ordinary people perceive modern values as antagonistic to their worldview and their habits while modern elites are seen as privileged people willing to deny and destroy erstwhile modes of behaviour with the support of state officialdom. By thus exacerbating the tensions between the old and the new universes, the state stirs a cultural backlash that will sooner or later threaten to undermine the country's social fabric and reinforce the path of authoritarianism.

In personal matters especially, reforms are better targeted on the educated and relatively sophisticated members of the urban elites since they have already been exposed to Western standards, values, and manner of living, and are engaged in activities that require social and institutional change. Being more able to understand the need for such changes, they may actually call for them and, if not, they are unlikely to offer resistance. It is actually revealing that other changes, such as the introduction of Western-inspired codes of commercial, administrative, and criminal law, aroused no serious opposition among the masses, largely because these changes mainly concerned elite groups that actually demanded them or were at least ready for them.

For the traditional sections of the population, on sensitive matters that include civil status but also land-related issues in rural areas, only the optional approach that lies behind legal pluralism is acceptable. This means that people should remain free to choose among different legal systems, traditional and modern. In the case of Turkey, for example, inspiration should be sought in the culture of tolerance instituted by the Ottomans, yet ignored by the Kemalists. Under Ottoman institutions, indeed, not only did the millet system respect the boundaries between religious communities, but also people could choose among different systems of law and associated courts to run their life and business and to settle their conflicts. The correct approach consists in avoiding big public announcements of drastic reforms uniformly applied to the entire population.

4. The situation is made worse when enlightened autocrats add arrogance to coercion, thus aggravating the tensions generated by the reforms. Atatürk and Bourguiba have all displayed a contemptuous attitude towards traditional values and customs, conveying the idea that those are hallmarks of backwardness that slow down the country's development and tarnish its image vis-à-vis the Western world. Feeling aggressed, people react by resorting to political or symbolic methods. Thus, in Turkey, because traditional attire has been disparaged and prohibited, it has become a political symbol used by members of traditional groups to assert their cultural identity and manifest their ascendancy. Wearing customary dresses signals a refusal to be colonized by the Westernized elite.

Bourguiba's modernization strategy contrasted with the assertive and intolerant secularism chosen by Turkey's Kemalists. In a first stage, indeed, he followed a non-confrontational approach that presented the legal reforms as compatible with the Muslim faith. Rather than purporting to rid Tunisia of the influence of religion in the name of Western modernity, Bourguiba chose to cast his reforms in the garb of Islamic principles reinterpreted with the authority of a new ijtihad. He thus acted as the guardian of the faith, a strong claim deemed extravagant by many ulama, yet not by most common believers who respected the president's authority. Later on, however, he made a strange U-turn when he expressed contempt for some customary religious rituals, such as fasting, and thereby aroused angry reactions among wide Islamic circles and the pious masses. Since he had earlier made strong-worded derogatory remarks about traditional clothing, both female and male, his statements about fasting probably reflected his true personal opinion while his moderate statements during the independence struggle were a tactical move dictated by the circumstances of the day.

Context matters, and contingent factors must be considered when devising modernizing reforms. A good example is Tunisia where the influence of the ulama had been dented by their collaboration with the French colonial authorities. Because of their weaker position and prestige, they were easier to co-opt by the ruler. Bourguiba grasped the opportunity: Aware that opposition to reforms from the official ulama would not be as strong as it could have in other circumstances, he did not hesitate to make a bold move. In Turkey, the situation was different: Atatürk was able to rely on a (strong) army whose loyalty and devotion to Kemalist values could be taken for granted. Having been commander-in-chief of the army during the Turkish war for independence (1919–1922), he became a national hero enjoying the unflinching support of the nationalist military officers at its core.

To sum up, Bourguiba's overall approach to institutional reforms appears to have been wiser and less brutal than that followed by Atatürk. Determined and widespread opposition against Bourguiba's rule was not triggered by these reforms but by misguided economic and social policies and by his own estrangement from the everyday livelihood problems of the popular masses. The situation got worse under Ben Ali who compounded the economic predicament inherited from his predecessor by massive and blatant corruption of the clique around him. In Turkey, the situation was roughly the opposite: A top-down and arrogant approach to the modernization of institutions was combined with a good control of corruption and more inclusive economic policies that paved the way for the gradual emergence of a provincial, mainly Anatolian, conservative bourgeoisie. Unlike in Tunisia, the demise of the Kemalist regime was essentially caused by the radical and aggressive Westernization of the whole society imposed by the political elite.

***

Enlightened autocrats seem to be well positioned to carry out important reforms aimed at modernizing the institutions of countries confronted with the need of a quick catch-up with more advanced neighbours. Yet, two major pitfalls are best avoided: (1) corruption of the surrounding elite, which creates a vicious association between modernism or secularism and self-interested behaviour, materialistic values, and callous indifference to the predicament of ordinary people; (2) an overweening confidence of the autocrat, which creates a vicious association between modernism or secularism and authoritarianism or despotism. These two pitfalls create a fertile ground for religious opposition to the extent that clerics can conceal their antagonism to secular reforms behind the veil of arguments framed in terms of social justice, anti-corruption struggle, cultural dignity, and national independence (against Western imperialism).

Unfortunately, while Atatürk's and Bourguiba's lives attest to the possibility of keeping corruption under control, enlightened autocrats easily turn into despotic rulers: A strong sense of their revolutionary mission predisposes them to resort to excessively authoritarian methods. These methods are likely to prove counter-productive in the medium or long term. In Muslim countries, unfortunately, democracy is typically not available to offer an alternative to enlightened autocracy as a way to modernize institutions and policies. It is probably not coincidental that many old democracies of Western Europe started as absolute monarchies, suggesting that modern states tend to be non-democratic during the crucial phase of their formation and consolidation. It is therefore critical that enlightened autocrats prove able to moderate their natural instincts for overreaching themselves.

Regardless of the political system, legal pluralism appears as a promising approach to reforms of institutions and laws dealing with civil matters. In Indonesia, which offers inspiring lessons here, legal pluralism is understood in a double sense: The existence of multiple law and court systems and judicial discretion in reconciling and combining different laws or practices (see Bowen 2003 : 146–99; Platteau, 2017: 418–22). The former feature means that Islamic courts and informal mechanisms of dispute resolution are not dismantled or ignored, but instead are given official or quasi-official recognition. Together with official status comes the possibility of setting constraints on their mode of operation and area of competence. As for the second feature of legal pluralism, it continues a long tradition of acculturing Islamic tenets to local customary practices, thus proving Islam's ability to adapt to people's mores in ordinary circumstances.

To work, the approach of legal pluralism requires that, even in sensitive matters touching on personal status, the political and judiciary authorities enact a modern code that contains progressive provisions to which judges can refer if they so wish. Modern principles of justice and equality are most effectively implemented when the practices already followed in the most developed and sophisticated sectors or regions of the country are turned into statutory or quasi-statutory laws. The hope is that the national code will serve as a magnet able to pull verdicts issued by conservative judges in the desired direction of more equality (gender equality in particular), while simultaneously allowing progressive judges to strictly apply modern principles of law (for a formal argument, see Aldashev et al. 2012; Platteau and Wahhaj 2013). In addition, the national code may establish fundamental rules which apply to everybody and whose violation will not be tolerated. A pertinent example is honour crimes that fall under the purview of criminal courts, lying strictly outside the jurisdiction of traditional courts.

Finally, the Indonesian experience indicates that sufficient attention needs to be paid to the culture of Islamic jurisprudence for legal pluralism to be fully effective. Islamic jurists should continue to present a fiqh-type justification for the radical reshaping of law in the modern code. Judges inspired by Islam will be more willing to pronounce gender-equitable judgments or judgments adapted to modern life if they can rationalize or vindicate them in terms compatible with the faith.

How, in the above perspective, can we conceive of the role of Enlightenment understood as an intellectual movement that privileges the use of reason and science to address issues of social order and economic development? Essentially, Enlightenment is expected to inspire and buttress efforts at restructuring and reorienting the schooling system in a way that promotes critical learning and evidence-based knowledge. This implies the rejection of rote learning and speculative thinking entirely inspired by moral principles and religious dogma. In the absence of such reorientation of education and a determined policy of putting emphasis on its critical place in the development strategy, attempts by reformist leaders to modernize the country's institutions and to effectively enforce progressive laws and policies will prove unsustainable. Moreover, the creation and diffusion of new technologies will be seriously slowed down.

Does that mean that Enlightenment as it has been experienced in Western Europe is a precondition of modernization of Muslim societies as many scholars suggest? The answer is negative in the sense that, alone, Enlightenment cannot succeed in moving a society along the path of modernization. To be receptive to new educational messages, and to choose to put their children in modern schools, people must simultaneously undergo significant changes in their daily lives. Typically, their economic and physical mobility must increase dramatically so that they can be exposed to new life conditions and to urban environments. As a result, their perception of new economic opportunities and the associated skill prerequisites will be enhanced, and their level of aspiration will be raised. To sum up, Enlightenment is best seen as a time-consuming process that accompanies, rather than precedes, economic growth, institutional transformation, and public investment in both physical and human capital (with special attention to the expansion of communication infrastructure for the former, and to the spreading of public schools for the latter).

References

Acemoglu, D., G. Egorov, and K. Sonin (2009), 'Do Juntas Lead to Personal Rule?', *American Economic Review (Papers and Proceedings)*, 99(2): 298–303.

Acemoglu, D., Ticchi, D., and Vindigni, A (2010) 'A Theory of Military Dictatorships, *American Economic Journal. Macroeconomics*, 2(1): 1–42.

Aldashev, G., I. Chaara, J.P. Platteau, and Z. Wahhaj (2012), 'Using the Law to Change the Custom', *Journal of Development Economics*, 97(1): 182–200.

Alexander, C. (2010), *Tunisia—Stability and Reform in the Modern Maghreb*, London and New York: Routledge.

Amsden, Alice H (1989), *Asia's Next Giant: South Korea and Late Industrialization*, New York: Oxford University Press.

Aney, M.S. and G. Ko (2015), 'Expropriation Risk and Competition Within the Military', *European Journal of Political Economy*, 39: 125–49.

An-Naim, A.A. (2008), *Islam and the Secular State. Negotiating the Future of Shari'a*, Cambridge Massachusetts & London: Harvard University Press.

Auriol, E. and J.P. Platteau (2017a), 'Religious Co-option Under Autocracy: A Theory Inspired by History', *Journal of Development Economics*, 127(July): 395–412.

Auriol, E. and J.P. Platteau (2017b), 'The Explosive Combination of Religious Decentralisation and Autocracy: The Case of Islam', *Economics of Transition*, forthcoming.

Auriol, E., J.P. Platteau, and T. Verdier (2020), 'The Quran and the Sword: The Strategic Game Between Autocratic Power, the Military, and the Clerics', mimeo.

Bardhan, P.K., 1993. 'Symposium on Democracy and Development', *Journal of Economic Perspectives*, 7(3): 45–9.

Beau, N. and J.P. Tuqoi (1999) *Notre ami ben Ali: l'envers du 'miracle' tunisien*, Paris: La Découverte.

Belge, C. (2006), 'Friends of the Court: The Republican Alliance and Selective Activism on the Constitutional Court of Turkey', *Law and Society Review*, 40(3): 653–92.

Ben Achour, Y. (1987), 'La réforme des mentalités, Bourguiba et le redressement moral', In Camau, M. (ed.), *La Tunisie au présent*, Paris: Editions du CNRS.

Berkes, F. (1964), *The Development of Secularism in Turkey*, Montreal: McGill University Press.

Berkey, J.P. (2003), *The Formation of Islam—Religion and Society in the Near East, 600-1800*. Cambridge: Cambridge University Press.

Besley, T. and J. Robinson (2010), 'Quis Custodiet Ipsos Custodes? Civilian Control over the Military', *Journal of the European Economic Association*, 8(2–3): 655–63.

Bowen, J.R., 2003, *Islam, Law and Equality in Indonesia: An Anthropology of Public Reasoning*, Cambridge: Cambridge University Press.

Brumberg, D., 2014. 'Theories of Transition', In Lynch, M. (ed.), *The Arab Uprisings Explained—New Contentious Politics in the Middle East*, New York: Columbia University Press, Chapter 2, pp. 29–54.

Camau, M. (ed.) (1987), *La Tunisie au présent*, Paris: Editions du CNRS.

Camau, M. and Geisser, V. (2004), *Habib Bourguiba: la trace et l'héritage*, Paris: Karthala.

Chambers, R.L. (1964), 'Turkey: The Civil Bureaucracy', In Ward, R.E., and D.A. Rustow (eds), *Political Modernization in Japan and Turkey*, Princeton, New Jersey: Princeton University Press,, pp. 301-327.

Cleveland, W.L. (2004), *A History of the Modern Middle East*, Oxford: Westview Press.

Cohen, B. (1986), *Bourguiba, le pouvoir d'un seul*. Paris: Flammarion.

Coulson, N.J. (1964), *A History of Islamic Law*, Edinburgh: Edinburgh University Press.

Egorov, Y. and Sonin (2014), 'Incumbency Advantages in Non-Democracies', Princeton and Oxford: NBER Working Paper No. 20519.

El-Affendi, A. (2011), 'Political Culture and the Crisis of Democracy in the Arab World', In Elbadawi, I., and S. Makdisi (eds), 2011. *Democracy in the Arab World—Explaining the Deficit*, London and New York: Routledge, pp. 11–40.

Frey, F.W. (1964), 'Education: Turkey', In Ward, R.E. and D.A. Rustow (eds), *Political Modernization in Japan and Turkey*, Princeton, New Jersey: Princeton University Press, pp. 205–35.

Gellner, E., 1994. 'Kemalism'. In Gellner, E. (ed.), *Encounters with Nationalism*, Oxford: Blackwell, pp. 81–91.

Gleave, R. and E. Kermeli (eds) (1997), *Islamic Law: Theory and Practice*, London and New York: I.B. Tauris Publishers.

Göle, N. (2011), *Islam in Europe—The Lure of Fundamentalism and the Allure of Cosmopolitanism*, Princeton: Markus Wiener Publishers.

Hibou, B. (2006a), *La force de l'obéissance: économie politique de la répression en Tunisie*, Paris: Editions La Découverte.

Hibou, B. (2006b), 'Domination and control in Tunisia: economic levers for the exercise of authoritarian power', *Review of African Political Economy*, 108: 185–206.

Hourani, A. (1991), *A History of the Arab Peoples*, Cambridge, Mass: The Belknap Press of the Harvard University Press.

Hourani, A. (1993), 'Ottoman Reform and the Politics of Notables', In Hourani, A., Khoury, and M. Wilson (eds), *The Modern Middle East: A Reader*, Berkeley: University of California Press.

Huntington, S. (1993), 'The Clash of Civilizations?' *Foreign Affairs*, (Summer): 22–49.

Huntington, S. (1996), *The Clash of Civilizations and the Remaking of World Order*, London: Simon and Schuster.

Inalcik, H. (1964), 'The Nature of Traditional Society: Turkey', In Ward, R.E. and D.A. Rustow (eds), *Political Modernization in Japan and Turkey*, Princeton, New Jersey: Princeton University Press, pp. 42–63.

Jones, Leroy P. and Il Sakong (1980), *Government, Business, and Entrepreneurship in Economic Development: The Korean Case*, Cambridge, Massachusetts: Harvard University Press

Kakar, S. (1996), *The Colors of Violence: Cultural Identities, Religion, and Conflict*. The Chicago and London: University of Chicago Press.

Kandiyoti, D. (1991), 'End of Empire: Islam, Nationalism, and Women in Turkey', In Kandiyoti, D. (ed.), *Women, Islam and the State*, London: Macmillan.

Kaya, A. (2013), *Europeanization and Tolerance in Turkey: The Myth of Toleration*, Basingstoke: Palgrave Macmillan.

Kepel, G. (2005), *The Roots of Radical Islam*. Saqi Books, London (Originally published as Le prophète et le pharaon, Paris: Editions La Découverte, 1984).

Kinross, P.(1964), *Atatürk—The Rebirth of a Nation*, London: Phoenix.

Kuru, A. (2009), *Secularism and State Policies Toward Religion: The United States, France, and Turkey*. Cambridge: Cambridge University Press.

Lapidus, I. (2002), *A History of Islamic Societies*, Cambridge: Cambridge University Press (second edition).

Lee, R.D. (2014), *Religion and Politics in the Middle East: Identity, Ideology, Institutions, and Attitudes*. Boulder, Col.: Westview Press (second edition).

Leon, G. (2014) 'Loyalty for Sale? Military Spending and Coups d'Etat', *Public Choice*, 159(3-4): 363–83.

Leon, G. (2017), 'The Coup: Competition for Office in Authoritarian Regimes', *Oxford Handbook of Public Choice*, Oxford: Oxford University Press.

Lewis, B. (1968), *The Emergence of Modern Turkey*, Oxford: Oxford University Press.

Lewis, B. (1995), *The Middle East: 2000 Years of History from the Rise of Christianity to the Present Day*, London: Phoenix.

Lewis, B. (1996), 'Islam and Liberal Democracy: A Historical Overview', *Journal of Democracy*, 7(2): 52–63.

Lewis, B. (2002), *What Went Wrong? Western Impact and Middle Eastern Response*, London: Phoenix.

Morishima, M., 1982. *Why Has Japan Succeeded? Western Technology and the Japanese Ethos*, Cambridge: Cambridge University Press.

Morris, C. (2005), *The New Turkey—The Quiet Revolution on the Edge of Europe*, London: Granta Books.

Nelson, Matthew J. (2011), *In the Shadow of Shari'ah: Islam, Islamic Law, and Democracy in Pakistan*. London: Hurst and Company.

Obolonsky, A.V. (2003), *The Drama of Russian Political History—System Against Individuality*. Austin: Texas A & M University Press.

Owen, R. (2012), *The Rise and Fall of Arab Presidents for Life*. Cambridge, Massachusetts and London: Harvard University Press.

Özek, C. (1962), *Türkiye'de Laiklik: Gelisim ve Koruyucu Ceza Hükümleri*, I.Ü. Istanbul: Hukuk Fakültesi.

Perkins, K.J. (2004), *A History of Modern Tunisia*, Cambridge: Cambridge University Press.

Platteau, J.P., 2017. *Islam Instrumentalized: Religion and Politics in Historical Perspective*, Cambridge: Cambridge University Press.

Platteau, J.P. and Z. Wahhaj (2013), 'Interactions Between Modern Law and Custom', In V. Ginsburgh and D. Throsby (eds), *Handbook of the Economics of Art and Culture*, Vol. 2, Elsevier and North-Holland, Chapter 22, pp. 633–78.

Przeworski Adam and Fernando Limongi (1993), 'Political Regimes and Economic Growth', *The Journal of Economic Perspectives*, 7(3): 51–69.

Przeworski, A., M.E. Alvarez, J.A. Cheibub, and F. Limongi (2000), *Democracy and Development—Political Institutions and Well-Being in the World, 1950-1990*, Cambridge: Cambridge University Press.

Radwan, S., V. Jamil, and A. Ghose (1990), *Tunisia: Rural Labor and Structural Transformation*, London: Routledge.

Rahman, F. (1982), *Islam and Modernity: Transformation of an Intellectual Tradition*, Chicago and London: The University of Chicago Press.

Rodrik, D. (1997), 'The 'Paradoxes' of the Successful State', *European Economic Review*, 41(3–5,):411–42.

Roy, O. (1990), De l'Islam révolutionnaire au néo-fondamentalisme. Esprit juillet-août.

Ruthven, M. (1997), *Islam -A Very Short Introduction*. Oxford: Oxford University Press.

Salem, N. (1984), *Habib Bourguiba, Islam and the Creation of Tunisia*, London: Croom Helm.

Sayigh, Y. (2019), *Owners of the Republic: An Anatomy of Egypt's Military Economy*. Beirut: Carnegie Middle East Center, and Washington DC: Carnegie Endowment for International Peace.

Sayyid, B. (1997), *A Fundamental Fear: Ethnocentrism and the Emergence of Islamism*, London: Zed Books.

Seth, Michael J. (2016), *A Concise History of Modern Korea: From the Late Nineteenth Century to the Present*. Lanham: Rowman & Littlefield.

Siddiqa, A. (2017), *Military Inc. Inside Pakistan's Military Economy*. London: Pluto Press (second edition).

Springborg, R. (2014) 'Arab Militaries', In Lynch, M. (ed.), *The Arab Uprisings Explained: New Contentious Politics in the Middle East*. New York: Columbia University Press, Chapter 8, pp. 142–59.

Toumi, M. (1989), *La Tunisie de Bourguiba à Ben Ali*, Paris: Presses Universitaires de France.

Ward, R.E. and D.A. Rustow (1964), *Political Modernization in Japan and Turkey*, Princeton, New Jersey: Princeton University Press.

White, J. (2013), *Muslim Nationalism and the New Turks*. Princeton and Oxford: Princeton University Press.

Yeğenoğlu, M. (2012), *Islam, Migrancy and Hospitality in Europe*, London: Palgrave.

Zeghal, M. (2002), 'S'éloigner, se rapprocher : la gestion et le contrôle de l'Islam dans la république de Bourguiba et la monarchie de Hassan II', In Leveau, R. and A. Hammoudi (eds), *Monarchies arabes : Transitions et dérives dynastiques*, Institut des Etudes Transrégionales, Paris: Université de Princeton, et Institut Français des Relations Internationales (IFRI), Chapter 4, pp. 59–80.

Zürcher, E. (2004), *Turkey: A Modern History*, I.B. London: Tauris (first edition 1993).

Zürcher, E. (2012), *The Young Turk Legacy and Nation Building: From the Ottoman Empire to Atatürk's Turkey*, London: I.B. Tauris.

12 China's Belt and Road Initiative

Hopes and Bumps along the Road*

GERARD ROLAND

P ranab Bardhan has been studying closely the evolution of China's
economic system in an international comparative perspective. His
2010 book *Awakening Giants, Feet of Clay: Assessing the Economic
Rise of China and India* raised a number of important issues related to the
specificities of China's growth success.

Recently, many questions have been raised about the Belt and Road
Initiative (BRI),[1] its strategic significance for Chinese leaders and its
geopolitical implications. Are these just economic development initiatives
that other countries are invited to join, as is often stated in the Chinese

* Previously, it has been called the One Belt one Road" initiative (OBOR) or
the "new silk road".

media? Are these instead first steps towards China attempting to wrestle world hegemony away from the US as its economic power becomes stronger? Five years after it started, reports have started to appear about the results of some of the investments made under the BRI. What do we know? How are those investments to be evaluated?

To answer these questions, one needs to understand the long-term strategy of the Chinese Communist Party (CCP). This strategy is quite original. After Mao's death, under Deng Xiaoping's leadership, the CCP engaged in reforms transforming China from a socialist centrally planned economy to a modern thriving market economy. The goal of these reforms was to generate economic growth in order to keep the CCP in power. Given the success of the Asian tigers in the 1960s and 1970s (mostly Japan, South Korea, Hong, Kong, Singapore), Deng thought that continental China could not afford to stay poor. Otherwise, people would revolt against the CCP, and the latter could lose power. Deng thus embarked on a historically completely new innovation: The introduction of a capitalist economy under a politically communist regime. The Chinese economy has had spectacular growth rates for 40 years since these reforms were introduced, and one can say that Deng's objective (the survival of the CCP) was well achieved. Nevertheless, Chinese leaders are very much afraid that this will not last. They know that growth eventually slowed down in successful East Asian economies. Japan has even had over two decades of quasi-stagnation. Even though the slowing down of Chinese growth is a certainty, Chinese leaders want to make sure that the growth of the Chinese economy does not fall behind that of the rest of the world. It is in that context that we must see the Belt and Road Initiative. This initiative aims at further integrating the Chinese economy in the world economy. This will be done by creating trade routes with the rest of the world that will secure imports of natural resources needed in China, given its relative scarcity of natural resources. These trade routes should also be used to export Chinese goods abroad and broaden China's export performance. Chinese leaders want to protect these trade routes from blockade by establishing a military (mostly naval) presence at various critical spots. This is an interpretation of BRI that is based on the nature of the Chinese regime and the fundamental strategic goals of its leaders. It could be mistaken for geographical expansionism, but we think that would be a mistaken interpretation that could lead to aggressive moves that could fatally endanger world peace.

We develop our argument in several steps. In section 12.1, we explain the nature of the economic system in China: A capitalist regime under the leadership of the Communist Party. On that basis, we explain in section 12.2 the international strategy of Chinese communist leaders. In Section 12.3, we discuss how to evaluate the BRI in that light. The conclusion follows thereafter.

12.1 The Nature of the Chinese Economic Regime

In the light of stagnation of the USSR in the seventies and the chaotic (and lunatic) Maoist management of the economy since 1958, Deng Xiaoping thought that the best strategy to consolidate the power of the Chinese Communist Party (CCP) was to introduce the market economy in continental China, following the examples of Taiwan, Hong Kong, and Singapore, all places where a large Chinese population or diaspora had enjoyed prosperity and economic growth. Deng was pragmatic. He had observed the economic success of Taiwan, Hong Kong, and Singapore (called the Asian tigers at the time), and argued that if the Communist Party was not able to deliver growth rates as robust as those countries, it would inevitably lose power. This vision proved to be quite prophetic. In the late seventies, it was not yet clear that the Soviet system would collapse and that communist regimes in Central and Eastern Europe would disappear. Many of Deng's colleagues wished a return to the central planning system of the fifties. This seemed to be a safer bet, advocated by Party elders like Chen Yun, Deng's main opponent when it came to market reforms. The compromise they agreed on was to experiment with decollectivization in the countryside and to incentivize peasants via the 'Household responsibility system': Maoist communes (large socialist cooperatives regrouping several villages) were disbanded and households received land with a 15-year lease. They were obliged to deliver a fixed quota of grain to the state at a fixed price, but were allowed to freely produce and sell at free prices on markets any additional output they produced. The implementation of the household responsibility system proved to be phenomenally successful and created momentum for further reform leading to China's growth miracle (on the political economy of reform momentum in China, see Dewatripont and Roland 1995, Xie and Xie 2017).

Deng eventually used the power of the CCP to unleash market forces in China relying mainly on two elements: Government decentralization and yardstick competition (meritocracy).[2] Contrary to superficial reports, China's economic success was not due to the State withdrawing from the economy, but to the CCP using all possible instruments at its disposal to achieve high rates of economic growth. Not surprisingly, this process eventually reinforced the power of the CCP in all spheres (military, education, press, and so forth) instead of decreasing it, which had been Deng's avowed goal all along. Private entrepreneurs can since 2001 become CCP members, a move that can be seen as a way for the CCP to keep control over the private sector.

The initial thinking on Chinese reforms was that political reform would sooner or later follow economic reform. After all, the Soviet Union did have a political transition shortly before economic transition. The sequencing of reforms seemed to be different in China, but most observers thought that economic reforms would lead to gradual political liberalization. In hindsight, that view was deeply mistaken. If anything, the opposite happened. The transition to the market economy in China was decided with the goal of preserving and consolidating the power of the CCP. This is no surprise, as Chinese communist leaders always asserted that objective. So far, this has been an unmitigated success! China's economy has been transformed in 40 years beyond recognition, and this has changed the world economy, and will influence the world's political arena in the twenty-first century.

China's current system is one of CCP's power over a market economy.[3] Growth objectives were pursued using existing CCP institutions. CCP's power has not faded with progress of market economy. On the contrary! Thanks to China's economic miracle of the last decades, the CCP has probably become the most powerful organization in all of world history.

---

[2] See the classical paper by Xu, 2011 for the consensus view among researchers on the reasons behind China's success.

[3] Because of the specificities of Chinese capitalism, some people tend to call it state capitalism (due to the still large role of the state sector) or crony capitalism (due to personal relationships between entrepreneurs and party cadres being used to give favors to the former, often in exchange for bribes). I do not object to those denominations. My emphasis is on the fact that China has become a truly capitalist economy, competing successfully on the global market. I would strongly dispute claims that China is *not* a market economy.

The reinforcement of Communist State power has led to a state structure that is very different from that in Eastern Europe, even in the post-communist autocratic states that emerged from post-communist transition. This state structure is unique, and combines China's imperial state structure of the past and a very modern version of Leninism. The Communist Party stays very united and controls all the power levels. The Leninist principle of democratic centralism keeps the party united, as it forbids the formation of political fractions within the CCP. Fractionism is a major sin for Leninists. CCP members are officially allowed to express their opinion only in their own party unit. They are certainly not allowed to organize meetings outside the CCP's organizational structure. The CCP is present everywhere in Chinese society, not only inside the state apparatus, but also in private enterprises, sports clubs, schools, and universities, apartment buildings, and so forth. The CCP is very much present, albeit in a more secret form, in Hong Kong and Taiwan that it plans to take over in due time. The power of the CCP thus exceeds any governmental structure that we can think of, both in history and in modern times. Because the CCP exercises power by being everywhere in society, it is also in my view of a less expansionist nature, since it would be a very costly form of expansionism, requiring the CCP to span its fine grid network over a whole territory. China is already a continent. Communist leaders have openly stated that they want to take over Taiwan after Hong Kong, but for the foreseeable future that is as far as their expansionism goes. There is, for example, no mention of taking over Mongolia or parts of Russia. I will dwell on this important point subsequently.

If the CCP has never been more powerful than it is now, why is there more and more censorship and restriction of freedoms under Xi Jinping? One may think that China's communist leaders are powerful enough that they could afford to somewhat relax censorship and repression. Autocracies, however, function very differently from democracies, and have their own logic. In a democracy, freedom of speech, and freedom in general, do not threaten elected leaders. They can be insulted, jeered, and mocked, but this does not threaten their power, as they acquired it through legitimate contested elections. The mere fact that they were elected implies that they have a power base. Taking away freedoms from citizens would be a sure way to lose votes and political power. In an autocracy, leaders are not elected by universal suffrage, and they cannot count on such visible and official signs of public support as an election. Power inside an autocracy is usually lost to rivals inside the power structure. Autocratic leaders who are perceived as weak are more likely to be challenged by rivals. Therefore, they need to signal strength in order to deter potential challengers. An autocratic leader cannot thus leave any criticism of his rule unchallenged, even if that criticism does not directly represent a threat to his power. This is why absence of democratic selection of leaders under autocracy always goes hand in hand with repression, censorship, and restriction of freedoms.

Having market economies under dictatorial regimes is nothing new. There have been dozens of dictatorial regimes in capitalist countries. What is historically new is that the Chinese system is one of the market economies under a communist dictatorship. This is indeed a paradox as the communist doctrine calls for the abolition of capitalism and its replacement with a socialist system. In China, the socialist system that existed under Mao Zedong has been replaced with a capitalist system. Communist ideology thus appears quite hollow given the Chinese experience. If anything, the historical experience has shown the superiority of the market economy over socialist central planning. The hollowness of the communist ideology, especially in the Chinese context, creates a challenge for Chinese leaders as that ideology appears to be non-credible. The only reason it is used is as a signal of loyalty among cadres and leaders. Ambitious cadres who want to get promotion need to show good economic performance in the region under their supervision, but they also have to show that they can reproduce the slogans of the political campaigns organized by the Chinese leaders. The lack of a legitimate ideology to justify the power of the CCP is nevertheless a clear weakness. This means that CCP leaders must make more use of repression, terror, and intimidation to stay in power. Once people are not afraid of the power of the CCP, the latter risks being overthrown. This will especially be the case if corruption that became widespread with the introduction of market reforms is not kept under control.[4] Note, however, that even if communist ideology appears to be completely obsolete, the propaganda of the CCP can be very effective, especially since it is not challenged by any opposition parties that are not allowed to exist legally. As advanced western countries have shown weakness in recent years, especially since the 2008 crisis, and with the continuous decline of American influence in the world, the CCP has

---

[4] On that, see Roland (2018) or Li et al. (2017).

been successfully making claims that China's existing communist regime works 'better' than Western democracies. Interestingly, that propaganda is mostly for domestic consumption. Chinese leaders have not aggressively been making propaganda outside China, in contrast to Putin's trolls who have been extremely active in Western democracies, undermining elections and the institutions of the European Union. This brings us to try to understand the international strategy of the CCP leaders, given their choice of introducing the market economy to preserve and consolidate their power.

12.2 China's International Strategy

Given the miraculous growth China has experienced over the last 40 years, it has become impossible to ignore China's role in the world and in Asia. China will in the foreseeable future become the country with the largest GDP in the world, overtaking the US. China's population of nearly 1.4 billion people by far outstrips the population of any other country except India. In order to understand directions the international order is taking, one cannot ignore China. The difficulty in this endeavour is, as stated in the previous section, that China has a Communist regime and a thriving market economy, a combination that has never been observed so far.

The existence of democracies is obviously a challenge to CCP power, since democracies have a record of human rights and freedom that does not exist in China, but communist China also represents a challenge to the outside world. Many people fear that China's political regime may spread to other countries.

Other communist regimes collapsed because their socialist central planning system proved to be economically inferior to capitalism. Capitalism under CCP power continues to face a similar challenge. As long as catching up with the West takes place, CCP power should, in my view, be stable with very high probability. If China starts lagging behind the growth of the world economy, the CCP will face a big legitimacy problem. This is the foundation of the fear of low growth among Chinese leaders. Chinese integration in the world economy is necessary to maintain growth and prevent economic 'falling behind'. This may or may not succeed.

Recall that the main objective of Chinese leaders is to keep the CCP in power. Deng Xiaoping thought that without major market reforms bringing growth, the CCP was doomed. He was right because this became indeed the fate of communist regimes in Eastern Europe. Maintaining the CCP in power is also the reason for China's rapid and successful integration in the world economy and for recent initiatives like the Belt and Road Initiative (BRI) that we will discuss subsequently. China's leaders feel that if the Chinese economy does not grow as fast as the world economy, they will be blamed for it, possibly leading to an implosion of the Communist regime, like in Eastern Europe. Integration in the world economy therefore has this objective in mind. Access to world markets is thus crucial for Chinese leaders.

China, as a market economy, has become very dependent on the world economy for its growth. The legitimation of the regime is based on its high growth record relative to the rest of the world, but this growth record itself is based on export-led growth, as was the case with all Asian tigers. China's regime survival thus depends strongly on successful integration in the world economy. Without competition from the world economy, Chinese economic dynamism would likely fade away and the state sector might take again the dominant role in the economy.

In contrast to 20th century communism, China needs strong integration in the world economy. Differences in cultures and political regime with the rest of the world, and especially with advanced Western democracies, will nevertheless undoubtedly lead to frictions that must be managed peacefully. This is what we discuss in this section.

What are China's hegemonic objectives in the current world? It is very important to have an accurate answer to that question.

First of all, in terms of ambitions of territorial expansion, Chinese leaders have expressed the open goal of bringing Hong Kong and Taiwan into the mold of communist rule. It is happening in Hong Kong already. It is not clear how it will happen with Taiwan, but the Chinese leaders are patient. Apart from Hong Kong and Taiwan, China does not have ambitions of territorial expansion. It is important to repeat that a Communist regime has a higher cost of territorial expansion compared to other political regimes. This is because for Chinese Communists, as stated earlier, taking control of a territory implies the need to establish comprehensive CCP control over that territory, which takes time and is relatively costly. British colonialists, for example never tried to have comprehensive control over their colonial territories.

It is also important to know that China is not interested in the spread of communist regimes wordwide, which was a clear objective of various

Communist Internationals in the twentieth century and also an objective of Mao Zedong. As stated in the previous section, China is not doing any propaganda in favour of communism in foreign countries, in contrast to the Maoist years when it was very active in that domain. As explained earlier, this is because communist ideology is dead, following the failure of socialist economies. Inside China, communist ideology is only used formally, but mainly in order to justify existing policies, not at all as a future-oriented eschatology, as was done in the past by true believers of communism. Chinese leaders do not really believe in communist ideology, but they firmly believe in the goal of maintaining the CCP in power in China.

The absence of large territorial ambitions does not mean that China's growth will not lead to some forms of international instability. As it becomes more powerful economically and militarily, China will undoubtedly prove more aggressive in Asia, whether it is about borders in the South China Sea, territorial disputes with Japan, India, Vietnam, and other neighbouring countries.

If we believe current trends, China will also in the future be more aggressive in other domains: Censorship beyond its borders (the Cambridge University Press episode being a good example), retaliation against what the Chinese leaders perceive as 'anti-Chinese' actions. Lacking the soft power of democracies and not even trying hard to do propaganda for their own system outside China, Chinese leaders will resort more and more to threats and blackmail in order to silence criticism abroad of China's denial of Human Rights to its citizens.

Because of their China-centred view of the world, Chinese leaders will not try to take leadership of the international order, but instead claim stronger influence in international organizations proportional to China's economic and demographic power. Chinese leaders accept the existing multilateral international order because it brings more stability, which is to China's advantage. Given its size and the importance of international integration for regime survival (China's openness ratio is above 40 per cent, whereas that of the US is below 30 per cent), China cares a lot about the stability of the international order.

It would be, however, wrong to see China as one of the main defenders of the world order. China will tend to only pay lip service to international rules and is not likely to respect international decisions that go against its interest, but it is not the only country in that case. In the case of China, since CCP leaders view the right to self-determination as the highest principle in international relations, one should not expect them to invest too much in the international order or even try to shape the world in the direction of more multilateralism.

The long-run coexistence of the Chinese communist regime and advanced democracies will be an important challenge in the future because of few shared values between these different regimes. Nevertheless, peaceful coexistence is in my view clearly possible, albeit with frictions, but it is also necessary. There is no realistic alternative. Therefore, peaceful coexistence with China should be an important goal for the international community.

The main challenge for the West is to better understand the nature of CCP power, understand its stability as well as its objectives. Mistakes can unnecessarily increase international tension. This would be the case for example if one thinks that CCP power can be overthrown through outside political pressure. Misreading China's international economic initiatives for political expansionism would also be tragically misguided.

The Trump administration has expressed the misguided will to sabotage the 'China 2025' programme and the drive towards high-tech innovation. This is pure bullying. While China's moves to reduce the income and innovation gap with the West are beneficial for the world economy, there is little chance that China will overtake the US in terms of fundamental innovation[5].

Before the Trump administration, the Obama administration had made moves to try to isolate China from other Asian countries. The Trans-Pacific Partnership TPP could clearly be understood that way, The US government has always blocked moves to increase China's role in international organizations, be it China's representation inside the IMF or the refusal of the US government to participate in the Asian Infrastructure Investment Bank.

The biggest obstacle to coexistence with China is not so much related to trade, which has been beneficial to the whole world, but to foreign direct investment, in particular acquisition of foreign firms. On the Chinese side, there has been the fear that further economic opening will lead to loss of control of CCP over large sectors of the economy such as in banking, internet and social media. On the other side, there

---

[5] See in particular Roland (2018) on that point.

has been the fear that acquisitions of US firms by Chinese investors could be used for political control by the CCP. This argument is used to justify the view that one should block takeovers by Chinese firms. This fear is also widely shared in Europe, as was observed for example in Germany with the takeovers by Chinese firms of Kuka and Cotesa, that were heavily scrutinized before receiving the green light. This is likely to be a bone of contention for quite a while, independently of Trump's trade war against China. Even if relations between China and the rest of the world improve, it is unlikely that trust building will be sufficiently strong so as to remove concerns about the possibility of using takeovers as a form of political leverage. There are, however, many other ways China can invest outside its borders without raising the specter of the danger of political leverage. This is the case for greenfield investment and also for infrastructure investment. Both types of investment may increase China's influence, but do not contribute to diminish national sovereignty over existing firms, and therefore should raise less concern. As for infrastructure, once it is in place, it cannot be used for political blackmail, because it falls under the control of national governments wherever it is situated. Even when it comes to acquisitions, a country can use it for political leverage only if its control over foreign firms is sufficiently large. This means that, on both sides, there is clearly room for takeover activity as long as foreign control remains sufficiently limited. The Chinese leaders seem to have understood that they can tolerate more presence of foreign capital, for example in the banking sector, without feeling that their national sovereignty is threatened.

A major source of misunderstandings is due to the differences in political regime between democracy and communism. On the Chinese side, protests about human rights violation should not be interpreted as signs of US expansionism. In a democracy, the press is free and cannot be censored. Criticism of government is not perceived as weakness. Declarations by politicians on human rights violations serve as signal to domestic voters. Chinese government pressure cannot make such declarations go away. They will always be there and should not be misinterpreted. Disapproval of the Chinese communist regime by the US does not mean that the US and China cannot coexist peacefully. The US has lost taste for international adventures and foreign 'state-building'. The failure of the Iraq war showed then clearly the weakness of the US superpower whose decline has been accelerating with the Trump presidency.

12.3 Understanding the Belt and Road Initiative

In light of the two preceding sections, we can understand better the goals of the BRI. As stated, its goal is to enhance China's integration in the world economy so as to make sure China's growth does not lag behind that of the world economy. How can one understand the main elements of the BRI in that context?

The BRI aims at financing infrastructure projects along the 'silk road economic belt' linking China to Central Asia, South Asia and ultimately Europe. It also aims at securing a 'maritime silk road' linking China to South East Asia, South Asia, Gulf countries, North Africa, and Europe.

12.3.1 China's Motivations and Interests in the BRI Context

It is important to understand first and foremost China's economic and geopolitical interests in launching this initiative. As stated earlier, China's further integration in the world economy is a key economic objective. As China's growth rate will inevitably fall, as was the case with all Asian tigers, this will create a legitimacy problem for the CCP that delivered very high growth rates for 40 years since it started its market reforms. China's best bet to continue delivering relatively high growth rates is to 1) have better access to natural resources, 2) to maintain high export growth. Also, as long as China's growth rates are not below those of the world economy, CCP leaders can hope to minimize the risks of social disruption related to falling growth rates if these objectives are fulfilled. It appears that the BRI is designed precisely to fulfill those objectives.

First, China's continued growth relies more and more on natural resource imports. Contrary to Russia for example, China depends heavily on natural resource imports. China is well endowed with a number of natural resources, such as rare earth for example, but it needs to import oil and gas, cobalt, lithium, copper, iron, gold, and chrome. This is a direct consequence of China's phenomenal growth rates. The BRI will directly help to facilitate imports to China by creating infrastructure to transport these imports. We explain this in a bit more detail below. Moreover, since infrastructure projects in BRI countries will be paid by debt, one way to repay debt is via exports to China. In that sense, BRI will help to stabilize imports to China.

Second, The BRI will also help increase Chinese exports. It will do so through various channels. First, the infrastructure investment will help reduce transport costs. Second, to the extent that BRI investment improves trade relations with BRI countries, it will also help boost Chinese exports, both directly and indirectly. Closer international economic relations between China and other countries will generate business deals leading to direct increases in Chinese exports. Exports to China (the import motive for the Chinese) will be compensated to a certain extent by business deals to import Chinese products. Indirectly, to the extent that infrastructure investment helps the local economy, it will boost local growth rates, which should increase imports, and in particular imports from China. This effect is sure to be present to a certain extent because, from the local country's perspective, the BRI investment should lead automatically to an increase in exports to China, which should increase aggregate demand within the country, eventually leading to an increase in import demand.

Third, as a result of the last two points, the BRI will lead to increased imports to China, but also increased exports to the rest of the world, thereby anchoring China's growth in world economic growth, but also helping to boost the latter.

Without going into too much detail, the role of BRI in Central Asia is quite illustrative of China's motives. Central Asia has tremendous natural resources. Kazakhstan only, with a population of only 18 million, the largest landlocked country in the world, is endowed with a wide variety of large volumes of natural resources: oil, gas, coal, copper, iron, zinc, lead, gold, manganese, uranium, and so on. When Kazakhstan was a Soviet republic, its natural resources were exported to the rest of the Soviet Union, mainly Russia, and it got little benefit from its natural resource endowment. Since its independence in 1991, Kazakhstan was able to diversify its exports and generate large revenues from natural resource exports. Russia is itself well-endowed with natural resources so economic complementarities between Kazakhstan and Russia are not that large, even though, for obvious political reasons, Kazakhstan has signed on to Russia's Eurasian Economic Union. On the other hand, there is a huge trade potential between China and Kazakhstan. The latter has relative abundance of natural resources and relative scarcity of labour. China has relative abundance of labour and relative scarcity of resources. China can thus benefit enormously from increasing natural resource imports from Kazakhstan, while the latter can gain from importing Chinese manufacturing goods. Transport costs have been an important impediment to growth of international trade between Kazakhstan and China. Roads and railway networks between the two countries have been insufficient, and BRI projects aim at substantially improving transport routes between the two countries. BRI projects should also help create better transport connections between Kazakhstan and Turkey, and Europe more generally. Kazakhstan would thus be at the centre of much Eurasian trade transport. Given the numerous mountain ranges along the new silk road, infrastructure investment is key to create these Eurasian trade routes.

Note also that the new silk road route via Kazakhstan would have to cross Xinjiang province, the most Western Chinese province. It is probably no coincidence that the Chinese authorities have been cracking down in recent years not only on Islamic extremists but also on Ouigur separatists in sparsely populated, but geographically very large, Xinjiang province. They want to secure the BRI trade routes both internally and externally.

There is no doubt that BRI also benefits the world.[6] Infrastructure investment that promotes trade is a win-win situation and should be welcomed as such. At the same time, one should not deny that there are geopolitical issues involved. At a time where the US under president Trump is engaging in a trade war with China and is taking initiatives to destroy the multilateral world order, it is no surprise that the BRI, that should have positive effects for globalization, will be under attack from the Trump administration. The most sensitive aspect relates to the maritime silk road. Chinese leaders want to prevent military blockades that would close existential trade routes for China. The US has the capacity to block the Malaga strait, an important route for world maritime trade. The Chinese government aims thus to establish a number of naval bases to protect its maritime trade. A first base has been established in Djibouti, at the horn of Africa, a critical place for maritime traffic not only from the Mediterranean but also from the Gulf states. This will probably be seen as a military threat by the US that has many more naval and military bases around the world. It is nevertheless logical for China to deploy naval bases

[6] See e.g. Garcia-Herrero and Xu (2017).

along the maritime silk road.[7] The geopolitical tensions that may arise from China's economic and military deployment in Asia and along the Indian Ocean could prove to be very dangerous for world peace. Indeed, any Blockade of China's trade routes could lead to a military response from China. This had been the case before WWII when the embargo of exports of oil to Japan led the latter to invade the East Indies and to attack the US in Pearl Harbor. We hope the lessons from history will be learned and that peaceful international trade will be preserved.

12.3.2 Misgivings and Problems with BRI

The BRI is starting to generate more and more buzz in the media world-wide. Given the motives of Chinese leaders in setting up the BRI, it is important to get rid of misgivings about BRI while understanding its real weaknesses.

The most important misgiving is the fear that BRI is an instrument of Chinese leaders to take over the world. As explained earlier, the objectives of BRI are domestic in nature, and the Chinese political regime makes it very difficult and costly to take over a foreign territory. BRI is thus not intended as some neo-colonial initiative. A theme that has nevertheless come up repeatedly in the press in support of the 'neo-colonial' interpretation of BRI is that developing countries that are having difficulties reimbursing BRI-related foreign debt will be 'taken over' by China. The example that is usually given is the case of Sri Lanka. In the context of BRI, Sri Lanka borrowed money to build the Hambantota port and the Mattala International Airport. Both projects are examples of white elephants. Both have failed to generate traffic (the Mattala International Airport has only four flights scheduled weekly and the Hambantota airport has barely generated any cargo traffic). The Sri Lankan government has been unable to reimburse its debts related to those projects and thus sold both the port and the airport to China. What to make of it? It would be exaggerated to conclude that China is taking over control of Sri Lanka. If these are white elephant projects, they will not be of much use to China.

---

[7] China's aggressive behavior in the South China sea is another issue. There are large reserves of oil below the sea floor and China wants to exploit them given its high need for fossil fuels

In the best case, Chinese companies will be forced to use them, but it will not necessarily make them profitable. One cannot, however, exclude that they will be used as military bases. The contracts with Sri Lanka prohibit this, but that does not mean it may not happen. As explained earlier, China will need military bases to secure the safe transport of Chinese imports as well as exports. Whatever scenario one can think of, in no case does it mean that China is 'taking over' Sri Lanka.

I would argue that the vulnerability related to excessive debt accumulated by BRI countries (Pakistan is also talked about, but it is not the only one) lies not with developing countries, but with China. Most BRI projects are infrastructure-related. Once they are built, the Chinese government cannot fundamentally take them away. Precisely for that reason, countries have an incentive to default on their debt once the BRI projects are built. They thus have an incentive to take up excessive debt that they will later default on. Of course, the Chinese government can take over the assets or part of them in case of a default, like in the case of Sri Lanka, but how do you take over ownership of a bridge, a road or a railroad? Governments can easily pass laws to de facto expropriate Chinese ownership over infrastructure. The Chinese government may find various ways of retaliating against governments who default on their debt, but it does not take away the fact that BRI infrastructure debts are forms of sovereign debt. We know from the sovereign debt literature that creditors over sovereign debt cannot use standard bankruptcy laws to recover their loans. We also know from that literature that, even if default has short-term costs in terms of inability to borrow on the international market, this usually does not last long, and countries that default on sovereign debt are able to secure loans in the long run. The Chinese government may thus find itself in a position in the long run where a large proportion of BRI loans cannot be recovered, thus creating a financial problem for China. The optimal solution in case of sovereign default is to agree on debt renegotiation. The Chinese government may, however, face substantial haircuts as a consequence of such renegotiations.

Whatever the outcome, infrastructure investments in developing countries that make economic sense and are not white elephants are beneficial to the world economy. It is precisely for the latter reason that it would be wrong to refuse to participate in BRI initiatives. The recent deal with Italy to revive the port of Trieste (near Venice on the Adriatic Sea) should benefit badly needed job creation in Italy and revive the region around Trieste.

While it is important to debunk wrong interpretations of BRI, one should also grasp the major weaknesses of the Chinese initiative.

First, it exemplifies the phenomenon of rent-seeking by Chinese firms, which is generally ignored by observers of the Chines economy. Many Chinese firms have been eager to join the BRI bandwagon because of opportunities to produce and export new goods. This is probably one of the reasons, though certainly not the only one, Many BRI projects are really white elephants. Chinese firms involved do not suffer the consequences of participating in inefficient projects as long as they get paid and can boast about generating foreign export revenues. By design, BRI projects should be built by Chinese firms. This has led to various forms of rent-seeking behavior by Chinese firms to be 'included' in BRI projects even though these projects are either inefficient or not really related to infrastructure-building.[8] This rent-seeking is in essence similar to the process leading to the selection of investment projects within China.

Second, a related phenomenon is that the expansion of BRI, and of Chinese international presence in general, has brought forth an expansion of corruption. Officials in developing countries have been showered with bribes in order to accept BRI projects. This has led to cost inflation making the projects more expensive to pay for, while kickbacks to local politicians have secured their approval. This corruption not only paves the way for inefficiencies and diversion of funds in the implementation of BRI projects, but also creates political links between China and local politicians. Chinese officials have no second thoughts in bribing officials and politicians in developing countries, even though such corruption is strongly punished at home. There is an element of 'Chinese exceptionalism' at play here that is related to a strong Chinese-centric attitude in international affairs. To the extent that corruption of foreign dignitaries is in the interests of China, then it is seen as somewhat morally right. The fact that norms are different inside China is irrelevant here. It is only if corruption scandals abroad damage Chinese interests that Chinese leaders may decide to change their policy. I hesitate in making comparisons and parallels with 'American exceptionalism' though there are certainly differences.

Third, China has no experience in dealing with sovereign debt issues, and is likely to make mistakes as countries start defaulting on BRI-related

---

[8] For a good description, see Yu (2018).

debts. A too tough attitude risks China being perceived as a neo-colonialist power infringing on national sovereignty of other countries. It also risks China being perceived as weak and encouraging more loan defaults. The former seems more dangerous for world peace as it could lead to military conflicts that could internationalize very fast.

Fourth, and this is also directly related, China is becoming too strong too fast. Its economic power is becoming on par with that of the US. China's foreign policy experts are by far not as competent as the economic experts who have guided economic reforms in the last 40 years. China is very likely to make mistakes in handling any foreign tension related to BRI. Chinese leaders have shown great patience and control in dealing with Trump's trade war. At the same time, the US's bullying attitude in the whole process is generating a lot of pent-up frustration. Chinese leaders will be tempted to show strength in a more minor issue, thereby leading to risks of escalation that could degenerate easily.

Despite these caveats and clear weaknesses, BRI is not bad for the world. It is not fruitful to try to oppose it or to try to sabotage China's increasing role in the world economy. The international community gains in cooperating with China in its BRI initiative. China's global expansion is inevitable. One cannot oppose it, but one can only learn how to live with it. On the other hand, China has recently been presented as more threatening than it really is. As we hope to have demonstrated, it will have enough on its arms in dealing with the inherent weaknesses of the BRI project itself.

***

There has been a lot of confusion in understanding the motives behind China's BRI initiative. We have argued that it is best understood in terms of the long-term strategy of Chinese communist leaders to hang on to power. That was the motivation behind market reforms that spurred 40 years of very high growth. Given the importance that China has gained in the world economy, and its need for natural resources and export markets to continue to sustain its growth, BRI is the answer the Chinese leaders came up with. It is a survival strategy of Chinese leaders, but it will deeply affect the future of world trade, and possibly that of world peace.

References

Bardhan, P. (2012), *Awakening Giants, Feet of Clay: Assessing the Economic Rise of China and India*, Princeton N.J.: Princeton University Press.

Dewatripont., M and G. Roland (1995), 'The Design of Reform Packages under Uncertainty' *American Economic Review* 85(5): 1207–23.

Garcia-Herrero and J. Xu (2017), 'Chinas Belt and Road Initiative: Can Europe Expect Trade Gains' *China and World Economy* 25(6): 84–99.

Li, W., G. Roland, and Y. Xie (2017), 'Crony Capitalism, the Party State and Political Boundaries of Corruption', Working Paper UC Berkeley.

Roland, G. (2018), 'Coexisting with China in the twenty first century', *Acta Oeconomica* 69(1): 49–70.

Xie, Y. and Y. Xie, (2017) 'Machiavellian Experimentation', *Journal of Comparative Economics*, 45(4): 685–94.

Xu, C. (2011) 'The Fundamental Institutions of China's Reforms and Development', *Journal of Economic Literature* 49(4): 1076–151.

Yu, J. (2018) 'The Belt and Road Initiative: Domestic Interests, Bureaucratic Politics and the EU-China relations', *Asia-Europe Journal*, 16(3): 223–36.

Editors and Authors

Editor Bios

Kaushik Basu is Professor of Economics and the Carl Marks Professor at Cornell University. From 2012 to 2016 he was formerly Chief Economist of the World Bank. Educated at St. Stephen's College, Delhi, and the London School of Economics, Basu has published extensively in development economics, game theory, welfare economics and industrial organization. His most recent book *The Republic of Beliefs: A New Approach to Law and Economics* was published by Princeton University Press in 2018.

Maitreesh Ghatak is Professor of Economics at the London School of Economics and previously taught at the Department of Economics at the University of Chicago. He is an elected Fellow of the British Academy. His main areas of research interest are development economics, public economics, and the economics of organizations. He has been the Director of the Development Economics Group at the research centre STICERD at the LSE since 2005. He is a co-editor of the journal Economica since 2016, having previously served as Editor-in-Chief of the Journal of Development Economics from 2009-2015, the Managing Editor of the Review of Economic Studies from 2003-2006, and a co-editor of The Economics of Transition from 2003-2005. He is a Board Member of the Bureau for Research in the Economic Analysis of Development (BREAD); Research Fellow of the Centre for Economic Policy Research (CEPR) in the research areas of Development Economics, Macroeconomics and Growth, and Public Economics.

Kenneth Kletzer is Professor of Economics at the University of California at Santa Cruz. His primary areas of research are international economics and macroeconomics. Many of his publications concern international finance addressing a variety of topics including economic interdependence, international financial integration, financial crises in emerging market economies, and sovereign debt. He has also published research in international trade, development, economic growth, and fiscal policy. His interests in the Indian economy focus on monetary policy and financial liberalization. He has served on several editorial boards including the Journal of International Economics, Journal of Development Economics, and the European Economic Review. He began his career on the faculty of Yale University and holds a bachelor's degree from Stanford University and a PhD from the University of California at Berkeley.

Sudipto Mundle is a Distinguished Fellow at the National Council of Applied Economic Research, New Delhi, and serves on the boards of several organisations. He was a member of India's 14th Finance Commission, the erstwhile Reserve Bank of India Monetary Policy Advisory Committee, and the National Statistical Commission, where he acted as Chairman. He was earlier an Emeritus Professor at the National Institute of Public Finance and Policy (NIPFP) in New Delhi. Mundle spent much of his career until 2008 at the Asian Development Bank, where he was last Director in the Strategy and Policy Department. He graduated from St. Stephen's College, New Delhi, and has a master's degree and PhD from the Delhi School of Economics. His main research interests include development economics, macroeconomic policy, and public finance. He has published several books and papers in professional journals in these fields.

Eric Verhoogen is Professor of Economics and of International and Public Affairs at Columbia University. His primary research area is industrial development, at the intersection of development economics, trade, labor economics, and industrial organization. His work has been published in the Quarterly Journal of Economics, the American Economic Review, the Review of Economic Studies, and other journals. He is Co-Director of the Center for Development Economics and Policy at Columbia University. He is a former co-editor of the Journal of Development Economics and is currently serving as a Research Program Director of the International Growth Centre and as a member of the Board of Directors of the Bureau for Research in the Economic Analysis of Development (BREAD). He holds a bachelor's degree from Harvard, a master's degree from the University of Massachusetts, Amherst, and a PhD in Economics from the University of California at Berkeley.

Author Bios

Abhijit Vinayak Banerjee was educated at the University of Calcutta, Jawaharlal Nehru University and Harvard University, where he received his PhD in 1988. He is currently the Ford Foundation International Professor of Economics at the Massachusetts Institute of Technology. In 2003 he founded the Abdul Latif Jameel Poverty Action Lab (J-PAL), along with Esther Duflo and Sendhil Mullainathan, and remains one of the directors of the lab. Professor Banerjee is the recipient of the 2019 Sveriges Riksbank Prize in Economic Sciences in Memory of Alfred Nobel, awarded jointly with Esther Duflo and Michael Kremer "for their experimental approach to alleviating global poverty." Banerjee is a past president of the Bureau for the Research in the Economic Analysis of Development, a Research Associate of the NBER, a CEPR research fellow, International Research Fellow of the Kiel Institute, a fellow of the American Academy of Arts and Sciences and the Econometric Society and has been a Guggenheim Fellow and an Alfred P. Sloan Fellow. Professor Banerjee received the Infosys Prize 2009 in Social Sciences and Economics. In 2011, he was named one of Foreign Policy magazine's top 100 global thinkers. His areas of research are development economics and economic theory. Banerjee is a member of J-PAL's Executive Committee and previously served as co-chair of J-PAL's Education Sector.

Nancy H. Chau is Professor of Economics in the Charles H. Dyson School of Applied Economics and Management. Her research interests fall under three main areas: international trade, regional economics, and economic development. Professor Chau was recently awarded the Alexander von Humboldt Research Fellowship, and the first T. W. Schultz Award of the International Agricultural Economics Association. She is a senior fellow at the Center for Development Research, a research fellow at the Institute for the Study of Labor (IZA Bonn), and member of an expert panel for the Office of the UN High Commissioner for Human Rights. Professor Chau has published widely, in journals such as Economic Journal, International Economic Review, Journal of Development Economics, Journal of Economic Growth, Journal of Economic Theory, Journal of Labor Economics, Journal of Public Economics, Journal of Public Economic Theory and the World Bank Economic Review.

Esther Duflo is the Abdul Latif Jameel Professor of Poverty Alleviation and Development Economics in the Department of with Abhijit Banerjee and Michael Kremer "for their experimental approach to alleviating global Economics at the Massachusetts Institute of Technology and a co-founder and co-director of the Abdul Latif Jameel Poverty Action Lab (J-PAL). In her research, she seeks to understand the economic lives of the poor, with the aim to help design and evaluate social policies. She has worked on health, education, financial inclusion, environment, and governance. Professor Duflo is the recipient of the 2019 Sveriges Riksbank Prize in Economic Sciences in Memory of Alfred Nobel, awarded jointly poverty." Her first degrees were in history and economics from Ecole Normale Superieure, Paris. She subsequently received a PhD in Economics from MIT in 1999. Duflo has received numerous academic honors and prizes including the Princess of Asturias Award for Social Sciences (2015), the A.SK Social Science Award (2015), Infosys Prize (2014), the David N. Kershaw Award (2011), a John Bates Clark Medal (2010), and a MacArthur "Genius Grant" Fellowship (2009). With Abhijit Banerjee, she wrote Poor Economics: A Radical Rethinking of the Way to Fight Global Poverty, which won the Financial Times and Goldman Sachs Business Book of the Year Award in 2011 and has been translated into 17 languages.

Duflo is the Editor of the American Economic Review, a member of the National Academy of Sciences and a Corresponding Fellow of the British Academy.

Bhaskar Dutta is Professor of Economics at Ashoka University and University of Warwick. His research interests include cooperative game theory, mechanism design, formation of groups and networks, social choice theory and development economics. He has been Professor of Economics at the University of Warwick since 2000. He has had a long association with the Indian Statistical Institute, where he has taught during 1979 -2002. He was winner of the Mahalanobis Memorial Award of the Indian Econometric Society in 1990. He was President of the Society for Social Choice and Welfare (2014-16). He is also a Fellow of the Econometric Society, and the Society for Advancement of Economic Theory. He has been Chair, Standing Committee for India and South Asia as well as a member of the Council of the Econometric Society. He is currently a member of the Council of the Game Theory Society. He was a Managing Editor of Social Choice and Welfare (2011-2019) and continues to serve as Advisory Editor of Games and Economic Behaviour.

Parikshit Ghosh is Associate Professor of Economics at the Delhi School of Economics. He was educated at Presidency College, Calcutta, the Delhi School of Economics and Boston University. He has also held faculty positions at Texas A&M University and the University of British Columbia. His research interests include microeconomic theory, political economy, and development economics. Ghosh is an occasional contributor of op-ed articles on economic policy to Indian newspapers. He is also on the editorial board of Ideas for India, an online portal that makes policy relevant economic research accessible to the general reader. In his spare time, Ghosh's interests are wildlife and photography.

Ravi Kanbur is T. H. Lee Professor of World Affairs, International Professor of Applied Economics and Management, and Professor of Economics at Cornell University. He researches and teaches in development economics, public economics, and economic theory. He has served on the senior staff of the World Bank including as Chief Economist for

Africa. He has also published in the leading economics journals, including Journal of Political Economy, American Economic Review, Review of Economic Studies, Journal of Economic Theory and Economic Journal. He is Co-Chair of the Food Economics Commission and Co-Chair of the Scientific Council of the International Panel on Social Progress. The positions he has held include: Chair of the Board of United Nations University-World Institute for Development Economics Research, member of the OECD High Level Expert Group on the Measurement of Economic Performance, President of the Human Development and Capability Association, President of the Society for the Study of Economic Inequality, member of the High Level Advisory Council of the Climate Justice Dialogue, and member of the Core Group of the Commission on Global Poverty

Dilip Mookherjee is Professor of Economics at Boston University. He received his PhD from the London School of Economics in 1982 and has previously taught at Stanford University and the Indian Statistical Institute. His research interests include development economics, contract, and organization theory. Most of his work on development economics focuses on Bangladesh, India, Nepal, and China, on topics such as agricultural development, financial inclusion, entrepreneurship, and governance.

Jean-Philippe Platteau is Professor Emeritus at the University of Namur (Belgium), and an active member of the Centre for Research in Economic Development (CRED), which he founded at the same university. He is the author of numerous journal articles as well as several books, including Halting Degradation of Natural Resources – Is There a Role for Rural Communities? (Clarendon Press, 1995) with J.M. Baland, Institutions, Social Norms, and Economic Development (Routledge, 2000), and, more recently, Islam Instrumentalized: Religion and Politics in Historical Perspective (Cambridge University Press, 2017). Most of his work has been concerned with the understanding of the role of institutions in economic development and the processes of institutional change. The influence of non-economic factors and other frontier issues at the interface between economics and sociology are a central focus of his work.

Martin Ravallion holds the Edmond D. Villani Chair of Economics at Georgetown University. He is a past Director of the World Bank's research department, past President of the Society for the Study of Economic Inequality and has been affiliated with a number of other scholarly institutions. He has written extensively on economic development and antipoverty policy, including five books and over 250 papers in scholarly journals and edited volumes. He has advised numerous governments and international agencies. His various prizes and awards include the John Kenneth Galbraith Prize, and a Frontiers of Knowledge Award from Spain's BBVA Foundation. He holds a PhD in economics from the London School of Economics and an Honorary Doctorate from the University of Fribourg.

Debraj Ray is Julius Silver Professor in the Faculty of Arts and Science and Professor of Economics at New York University. He received a BA from the University of Calcutta and a PhD from Cornell University. He is a Fellow of the American Academy of Arts and Sciences, a Fellow of the Econometric Society, a Fellow of the Society for Advancement of Economic Theory, and a Guggenheim Fellow. He holds an honorary degree from the University of Oslo. He is Co-Editor of the American Economic Review. Among Ray's teaching awards are the Dean's Award for Distinguished Teaching at Stanford and the Golden Dozen teaching award from New York University.

Gérard Roland is the E. Morris Cox professor of economics and professor of political science at the University of California Berkeley where he has been since 2001. He has received many honors including an honorary professorship from the Renmin University of China in Beijing in 2002. In 2020, the Association for Comparative Economic Studies funded a pre-doctoral fellowship in his name to recognize his research achievements. He is the author of over 150 journal articles and book chapters and has been published in leading economics journals. He wrote the leading graduate textbook Transition and Economics published in 2000 at MIT Press. He co-organized with Olivier Blanchard a Nobel symposium on transition economics in 1999. In recent years, his research has broadened to developing economies in general with special emphasis on the role of institutions and culture. He wrote an undergraduate textbook on Economics of development (2013, Pearson Addison-Wesley).

Nirvikar Singh is Distinguished Professor of Economics and Sarbjit Singh Aurora Chair of Sikh and Punjabi Studies at the University of

California, Santa Cruz, where he also directs the Center for Analytical Finance. He has been a member of the Advisory Group to the Finance Minister of India on G-20 matters and has served as Consultant to the Chief Economic Adviser, Ministry of Finance, Government of India. He currently serves on the Punjab State Advisory Council of the Government of Punjab. His current research topics include Sikh and Punjabi Studies, entrepreneurship, information technology and development, Indian Americans (including Sikhs), and the Indian economy. He has authored over 100 research papers and co-authored or co-edited six books.

Rohini Somanathan is Professor of Economics at the Delhi School of Economics. Her research focuses on how social institutions interact with public policies to shape patterns of economic and social inequality. She is particularly interested in exploring the intellectual and ideological environment within which state policy is created and justified. Within the broad area of development economics, she has worked on group identity and public goods, access to microfinance, child nutrition programs and environmental health. She serves on the governing body of the Institute of Economic Growth and is the chair of the board of Trustees of the NGO SRIJAN.

Bruce Wydick is Professor of Economics at the University of San Francisco and Westmont College and Distinguished Research Affiliate at the University of Notre Dame. His research applies econometric, experimental, and game-theoretic tools to analyze development programs. Recent work has examined the effectiveness of child sponsorship, microfinance, children's shoe donation, wheelchairs for the disabled, and cleft-palate surgery on teenage life outcomes. Other recent work studies the role of hope and aspirations in escaping poverty traps. His academic publications have appeared in the Journal of Political Economy, Economic Journal, the Journal of Development Economics, and other journals. Media coverage of his recent research has appeared in the BBC World Service, USA Today, and The Guardian. He writes regularly on global poverty issues for Christianity Today and helps lead the non-profit organization Mayan Partners that works in the western highlands of Guatemala.